Inverting the Pyramid

By the same author

Behind the Curtain: Travels in Eastern European Football
Sunderland: A Club Transformed

Inverting the Pyramid

A HISTORY OF FOOTBALL TACTICS

Jonathan Wilson

First published in hardback in Great Britain in 2008 by
Orion Books
an imprint of the Orion Publishing Group Ltd
Orion House, 5 Upper St Martin's Lane,
London WC2H 9EA
An Hachette Livre UK Company

1 3 5 7 9 10 8 6 4 2

A CIP catalogue record for this book is available
from the British Library.

ISBN: 978 0 7528 8995 5

Printed in Great Britain by Clays Ltd, St Ives plc

The Orion Publishing Group's policy is to use papers that are natural, renewable
and recyclable and made from wood grown in sustainable forests. The logging
and manufacturing processes are expected to conform to the environmental
regulations of the country of origin.

Every effort has been made to fulfil requirements with regard to reproducing
copyright material. The author and publisher will be glad to rectify any omissions
at the earliest opportunity.

www.orionbooks.co.uk

△▽△▽△▽△▽

Contents

△▽△▽△▽△▽

Acknowledgements

△▽In writing this, I have been humbled by just how generous so many people have been with their time and thoughts. This is a long list, but that should not diminish how vital a role each of the people included in it played.

In Ukraine, Hungary and Russia, my thanks to Taras Hordiyenko, Sándor Laczkó and Vladimir Soldatkin, who were as enlightening and thorough as ever. Thanks also to Aliaksiy Zyl and his coterie of Dinamo fans in Minsk for their advice (and thanks to Chris Fraser for introducing us. Dima: the polonium night at the Emirates will never be forgotten).

In Argentina, my thanks to Marcela Mora y Araujo for introducing me to her vast circle of friends, to Rodrigo Orihuela, Féderico Mayol, Neil Clack and Klaus Gallo for their help in setting up interviews, translating, research and ferrying me around, and to Araceli Alemán for opening up her vast library of material, the regular disquisitions on the superiority of Juan Román Riquelme to, well, everything, and, of course, the extended walking tour.

In Brazil, my thanks to Ivan Soter, Roberto Assaf, Paulo Émilio and Alberto Helena Junior for sharing their time and learning so freely, to Cassiano Gobbet, Robert Shaw and Jordana Alvarez dos Santos for their efforts in research, translation and logistics, and also to Aidan Hamilton and Alex Bellos, for sketching out the background and putting me in touch with experts on the ground.

Thanks to Gabriele Marcotti for all his assistance with the Italian sections, for being such an informed and robust sounding-board, but most particularly for allowing me finally to participate in one of those restaurant debates in which bowls of hummus, tabouleh and tzatziki become the Udinese defence. I'd still like my time-share on the quiz trophy, though.

Thanks to Philippe Auclair for his help in France, to Christoph Biermann, Raphael Honigstein and Uli Hesse-Lichtenberger for their assistance with all matters German, to Simon Kuper and Auke Kok for their words of wisdom on Dutch football, and to Sid Lowe and Guillem Balagué for their advice on Spain. Thanks also to Brian Glanville for his unfailing generosity of spirit and for putting me right on a number of historical matters.

Thanks to Richard McBrearty of the Scottish Football Museum at Hampden and Peter Horne at the National Football Museum in Preston for sharing their expertise in the origins of football, and to the staff of the British Library at St Pancras, the Mitchell Library in Glasgow and the British Newspaper Library at Colindale.

Thanks also, for their various help in reading over sections of the manuscript, translation, and suggesting avenues of research to: Jon Adams, David Barber, Maurício Ribeiro Barros, Hanspeter Born, Duncan Castles, Marcus Christenson, James Copnall, Graham Curry, Sorin Dumitrescu, Dave Farrar, Igor Goldes, Luke Gosset, Gavin Hamilton, Georg Heitz, Paul Howarth, Emil Ianchev, Maciej Iwanski, Richard Jolly, John Keith, Thomas Knellwolf, Jim Lawton, Andy Lyons, Ben Lyttleton, Dan Magnowski, Emma McAllister, Kevin McCarra, Rachel Nicholson, Vladimir Novak, Gunnar Persson, Andy Rose, Paul Rowan, Ljiljana Ruzić, Milena Ruzić, Dominic Sandbrook, John Schumacher, Hugh Sleight, Rob Smyth, Graham Spiers, György Szepesi, Eric Weil, Duncan White, Axel Vartanyan, Shinobu Yamanaka and Bruno Ziauddin.

Thanks to my agent, David Luxton, and my editor at Orion, Ian Preece, for their unflagging support and helpful interventions, and to the copy-editor, Chris Hawkes, for his diligence.

And thanks, finally, to Ian Hawkey for spending so much of the Cup of Nations sharing his expertise in matters of punctuation, and to Network Rail for the points failure that led to the long wait just north of Durham during which the flaw in Reep's theory became apparent to me.

felix qui potuit rerum cognoscere causas*
Virgil, *Georgics,* no 2, l 490

(*Fortunate is he who can understand the causes of things.)

△▽△▽△▽△▽△▽

Prologue

△▽ A tapas bar in the Bairro Alto in Lisbon, the evening after England beat Switzerland 3-0 in Euro 2004. The rioja had been flowing, and a multi-national group of journalists was discussing whether Sven-Göran Eriksson had been right to stick with an orthodox 4-4-2, or if, as it had been suggested he would, he should have switched to a midfield diamond. Had player-power, a late-night delegation of midfielders, forced the unexpected reversion to the flat four in midfield?

'Oh, what's the difference?' an English colleague protested. 'They're the same players. The formation isn't important. It's not worth writing about.'

There was a splutter of indignation. As I raised a drunken finger to jab home my belief that people like him shouldn't be allowed to watch football, let alone talk about it, an Argentinian, probably wisely, pulled my arm down. 'The formation is the only thing that's important,' she said. 'It's not worth writing about anything else.'

And there, in a moment, was laid bare the prime deficiency of the English game. Football is not about players, or at least not just about players; it is about shape and about space, about the intelligent deployment of players, and their movement within that deployment. (I should, perhaps, make clear that by 'tactics' I mean a combination of formation and style: one 4-4-2 can be as different from another as Steve Stone from Ronaldinho). The Argentinian was, I hope, exaggerating for effect, for heart, soul, effort, desire, strength, power, speed, passion and skill all play their parts, but, for all that, there is also a theoretical dimension, and, as in other disciplines, the English have, on the whole, proved themselves unwilling to grapple with the abstract.

That is a failing, and it is something that frustrates me, but this is not a polemic about the failure of English football. Apart from anything else, unless we are making comparisons with the inter-war era, I'm not convinced that English football *is* failing. Sven-Göran Eriksson was derided by the end, but only Alf Ramsey had previously guided England to the quarter-finals of three successive international tournaments. Whether Steve McClaren's failure to get England through a Euro 2008 qualifying group that was far tougher than the xenophobes imagined represents a blip or the beginning of a prolonged slide only history will tell, but it seems perverse to start arranging the wake when England would have qualified had Steven Gerrard converted a simple chance four minutes after half-time in Moscow.

Look at Uruguay, look at Austria: that is decline. Look at Scotland, still punching heroically above their weight despite the restrictions imposed by a population of only five million. Look, most of all, at Hungary, the team who, in November 1953, rang the death knell for English dreams of superiority. By the time Ferenc Puskás, the greatest player of that most glorious of teams, died in November 2006, Hungary had slumped so far that they were struggling to remain in the top 100 of the Fifa world rankings. *That* is decline.

Nonetheless, for English football, the 6-3 defeat to Hungary at Wembley stands as the watershed. It was England's first defeat at home to continental opposition, and, more than that, the manner in which they were outplayed annihilated the idea that England still ruled the world. 'The story of British football and the foreign challenge,' wrote Brian Glanville in *Soccer Nemesis*, his reaction to that defeat, 'is the story of a vast superiority, sacrificed through stupidity, short-sightedness, and wanton insularity. It is a story of shamefully wasted talent, extraordinary complacency and infinite self-deception.' And so it was.

And yet, thirteen years later, England became world champions. The vast superiority may have been squandered, but England were evidently still among the elite. In the past half century, I'm not sure that much has changed. Yes, perhaps we do have a tendency to get carried away before major tournaments, which makes a quarter-final exit sting rather more than it probably ought, but England remain one of the eight or ten sides who have a realistic chance of winning a World Cup or European Championship (freakish champions like Denmark or Greece notwithstanding). The question then is why that opportunity has not been taken. Perhaps a more coherent structure of youth coaching, an increased focus on technique and tactical discipline, limits on the number of foreign players in the Premiership, snapping players out of their complacent bubbles, or any of the other hundred panaceas that have been suggested, would improve England's chances, but success is a nebulous quarry. Luck retains its place in football, and success can never be guaranteed, particularly not over the six- or seven-game span of an international tournament.

A theory has grown up that winning the World Cup in 1966 was the worst thing that could have happened to English football. Rob Steen, in *The Mavericks*, and David Downing in his books on England's rivalries with Argentina and Germany have argued that that success set England back because it established deep in the English footballing consciousness the notion that the functionality of Alf Ramsey's side was the only way to achieve success. I don't fundamentally disagree with either – although the trait predates Ramsey – but it seems to me that the real problem is not so much the way Ramsey's England played as the fact that, in the minds of generations of fans and coaches in England, it laid out a 'right' way of playing. Just because something was correct in a particular circumstance, with particular players and at a particular stage of football's development, does not mean it will always be effective. If England in 1966 had tried to play like Brazilians, they would have ended up like Brazil: kicked out of the tournament in the group stage by physically more aggressive opponents – in fact they would have been worse off, for they had few, if any, players with the technical attributes of the Brazilians. If there is one thing that distinguishes the coaches who have had success over a prolonged period – Sir Alex Ferguson, Valeriy Lobanovskyi, Bill Shankly, Boris Arkadiev – it is that they have always been able to evolve. Their teams played the game in very different ways, but what they all shared was the clarity of vision to successfully recognise when the time was right to abandon a winning formula and the courage to implement a new one.

What I want to make clear is that I don't believe there is a 'correct' way to play. Yes, from an emotional and aesthetic point of view, I warm more to the passing of Arsène Wenger's Arsenal than to the pragmatism of José Mourinho's Chelsea, but that is a personal preference; it is not to say one is right and one is wrong. I am well aware, equally, that compromises have to be made between theory and practice. On a theoretical level, I respond to Lobanovskyi's Dynamo Kyiv or the AC Milan of Fabio Capello. Yet on the pitch, when at university I had for two years the chance to influence the style of my college side (well, the seconds and thirds at least), we played highly functional football. Admittedly, we weren't very good and we probably got the best out of the players available, but I suspect we could have played more aesthetically pleasing football than we did. Amid the beer-soaked celebrations that followed a title each year, I'm not sure anybody was too bothered.

It is not even so simple, though, as to say that the 'correct' way of playing is the one that wins most often, for only the dourest of Gradgrinds would claim that success is measured merely in points and trophies; there must also be room for romance. That tension – between beauty and cynicism, between what Brazilians call *futebol d'arte* and *futebol de resultados* – is a constant, perhaps because it is so fundamental, not merely to sport, but also to life: to win, or to play the game well? It is hard to think of any significant actions that are not in some way a negotiation between the two extremes of pragmatism and idealism.

The difficulty, then, is in isolating of what that extra quality comprises. Glory is not measured in absolutes, and what constitutes it changes with circumstance and time. British crowds soon grow tired of patient build-up, but in, for instance, Capello's first spell at Real Madrid, crowds booed when Fernando Hierro hit long accurate passes for Roberto Carlos to run onto. To the modern sensibility, it is baffling that the early amateur footballers thought passing unmanly, and yet it may be in time to come – as indeed it already is in certain cultures – that the present-day British distaste for diving seems just as naively irrelevant.

Even acknowledging that football is about more than simply winning, though, it would be ludicrous to deny the importance of victory. Wenger can be frustratingly quixotic at times but, as his negative tactics in the 2005 FA Cup final showed, even he at times acknowledges the need to win. To condemn Ramsey, when he brought the only international success England has known is a luxury English fans cannot afford; to accuse him of ruining

English football rather than saluting his tactical acuity seems wilfully perverse.

I'm not saying we should discount them entirely, but it is dangerous, anyway, to read too much into performances at the major international tournaments. It is rare that there is one outstanding side in the world, rarer still that they actually win the World Cup. The example of Brazil in 2002, casually brushing aside the opposition, is almost unique, and even then, particularly given their lethargic qualifying campaign, it seemed almost supremacy by default as the other contenders, weakened by various combinations of injury, fatigue and ill-discipline, capitulated in the heat. France probably were the best side in the 1998 tournament, but they only really showed that in the final. Two years later, they were significantly the best side at Euro 2000, and yet were within a minute of losing the final to Italy.

In fact, two of the greatest sides of all time, the Hungarians of 1954 and the Dutch of 1974, lost in the final – both to West Germany, which may or may not be coincidence. A third, the Brazil of 1982, didn't even get that far. 1966 aside, England's best performance in a World Cup came in 1990, a tournament so beloved for Gazza's tears and an England penalty shoot-out defeat – a trope that would become tediously familiar, but which, back then, carried the resonance of tragic failure – that it helped kickstart the 1990s boom. Yet England's preparation for that tournament was awful: they scraped through qualifying; their manager Bobby Robson was pilloried in the press on an almost daily basis, the media was expelled from the training camp after revelations about the relationship between various players and a local PR rep, and the whole thing was played out in the shadow of hooliganism. Against the Republic of Ireland and Egypt, England were dire, and against Belgium and Cameroon they were lucky; only against Holland and West Germany, neither of which games they won, did they play well. In fact, the only team England beat in ninety minutes was Egypt. And this, somehow, led to football's middle-class revolution.

Over the course of a league season, luck, momentum, injuries, errors by players and errors by referees even themselves out – if not absolutely, then certainly far, far more than they do over seven games in a summer. That England have gone over forty years without winning a trophy is annoying, and for that various

managers, players, officials and opponents bear a degree of responsibility, but it does not equate to a fundamental decline. It is
possible that there is a fundamental flaw in the way England play
the game, and an almost self-conscious Luddism hasn't helped, but
it would be hard to make a serious case for a root-and-branch
overhaul of the English game on the basis of results in major
tournaments alone.

Globalisation is blurring national styles, but tradition, perpet-
uated by coaches, players, pundits and fans, is strong enough that
they remain distinguishable. What became apparent in the
writing of this book is that every nation came fairly quickly to
recognise its strengths, and that no nation seems quite to trust
them. Brazilian football is all about flair and improvisation, but it
looks yearningly at the defensive organisation of the Italians.
Italian football is about cynicism and tactical intelligence, but it
admires and fears the physical courage of the English. English
football is about tenacity and energy, but it feels it ought to ape the
technique of the Brazilians.

The history of tactics, it seems, is the history of two interlinked
tensions: aesthetics versus results on the one side and technique
versus physique on the other. What confuses the issue is that those
who grow up in a technical culture tend to see a more robust
approach as a way of getting results, while those from a physical
culture see pragmatism in technique; and beauty – or at least what
fans prefer to watch – remains very much in the eye of the
beholder. British fans may admire (although most seemed not to)
the cerebral jousting of, say, the 2003 Champions League final
between AC Milan and Juventus, but what they actually want to see
is the crash-bang-wallop of the Premiership. That is not entirely
fair, for Premiership football is far more skilful now than it was
even ten years ago, but it remains quicker and less possession-
driven than any other major league. Judging by the figure paid for
overseas television rights – a three-year deal worth £650million
was agreed in 2007 – the rest of the world thinks it has found a
happy balance.

The mid-fifties saw the publication of a rash of books that tried
to come to terms with England's declining status. Glanville's was
probably the angriest, but just as revealing is *Soccer Revolution* by
Willy Meisl, the younger brother of the great Austrian coach Hugo
Meisl. As staunchly Anglophile as only an immigrant can be, his

work is more of a lament. For them, blaming the unapologetic conservatism of the English game made sense and, with the benefit of hindsight, it can be seen as part of a more general cultural attack on an establishment that had overseen the end of Empire but was yet to find an appropriate role. England's blink-eredness *was* at fault for the loss of footballing superiority. Yes, the rest of the world would have caught up at some stage, for, as Glanville wearily notes, pupils have a habit of overcoming their masters, but these masters, through their arrogance and insularity, were complicit in their own downfall.

That, though, was then. England's fall from her pedestal is no longer news. In that, by tracing the tactical evolution of the game, it attempts to explain how we got to where we are now, this book belongs to the same family as *Soccer Nemesis* and *Soccer Revolution*, but it sets out from a very different present, with England failing to rise rather than falling. It is, anyway, a history, not a polemic.

A NOTE ON TERMINOLOGY

In Britain, the term 'centre-half' is regularly used to describe a central defender. There are historical reasons for this, which are explained at the beginning of Chapter Four, but, for the sake of clarity, I have used 'centre-half' specifically to describe the central midfielder in the 2-3-5 formation. Hopefully all other terms to designate positions are self-explanatory.

△▽△▽△▽△▽△▽

Chapter One

From Genesis to the Pyramid

△▽ In the beginning there was chaos, and football was without form. Then came the Victorians, who codified it, and after them the theorists, who analysed it. It wasn't until the late 1920s that tactics in anything resembling a modern sense came to be recognised or discussed, but as early as the 1870s there was an acknowledgement that the arrangement of players on the pitch made a significant difference to the way the game was played. In its earliest form, though, football knew nothing of such sophistication.

Various cultures can point to games that involved kicking a ball, but, for all the claims of Rome, Greece, Egypt, the Caribbean, Mexico, China or Japan to be the home of football, the modern sport has its roots in the mob game of medieval Britain. Rules – in as much as they existed at all – varied from place to place, but the game essentially involved two teams each trying to force a roughly spherical object to a target at opposite ends of a notional pitch. It was violent, unruly and anarchic, and it was repeatedly outlawed. Only in the early nineteenth century, when the public schools, their thinking shaped by advocates of muscular Christianity, decided that sport could be harnessed for the moral edification of their pupils, did anything approaching what we would today recognise as football emerge. Before there could be tactics, though, there had, first of all, to be a coherent set of rules.

Even by the end of the nineteenth century, when the earliest formations began to emerge, it was rare to subject them to too much thought. In football's earliest days, the notion of abstract consideration of tactics, of charts with crosses and arrows, would have been all but inconceivable, and yet the development of the game is instructive in what it reveals of the mindset of football, the unseen, often unacknowledged hard-wiring from which stemmed British conceptions of how it should be played (and, for forty years after the rules were first drawn up, there was nothing but a British conception).

The boom came in the early Victorian era and, as David Winner demonstrates in *Those Feet*, was rooted in the idea – bizarre as it may seem in hindsight – that the Empire was in decline and that moral turpitude was somehow to blame. Team sports, it was thought, were to be promoted, because they discouraged solipsism, and solipsism allowed masturbation to flourish, and there could be nothing more debilitating than that. The Reverend Edward Thring, headmaster of Uppingham School, for instance, insisted in a sermon that it would lead to 'early and dishonoured graves'. Football was seen as the perfect antidote, because, as E.A.C. Thompson would write in *The Boys' Champion Story Paper* in 1901, 'There is no more manly sport than football. It is so peculiarly and typically British, demanding pluck, coolness and endurance.' There are very good politico-economic reasons for the coincidence, but there is also a neat symbolism in the fact that, after football had been used to shore up the Empire, Britain's ultimate decline as an imperial power coincided with the erosion of the footballing superiority of the home nations.

Football soared in popularity throughout the first half of the nineteenth century, but in those early days rules varied from school to school, largely according to conditions. At Cheltenham and Rugby, for instance, with their wide, open fields, the game differed little from the mob game. A player could fall on the ground, be fallen upon by a great many of his fellows and emerge from the mud relatively unscathed. On the cloisters of Charterhouse and Westminster, though, such rough-and-tumble would have led to broken bones, and so it was there that the dribbling game developed. That outlawed – or at least restricted – handling of the ball, but the game still differed radically from modern football. Formations were unheard of, while the length of the game and even the numbers of players on each side were still to be established. Essentially prefects or older pupils would run with the ball at their feet, their team-mates lined up behind them ('backing up') in case the ball bounced loose in a tackle, while the opposition players – or, at certain schools, fags (that is, younger pupils who were effectively their servants) – would try to stop them.

Interplay among forwards, if it happened at all, was rudimentary; and from that sprouted certain fundamentals that would shape the course of early English football: the game was all about dribbling; passing, cooperation and defending were perceived as somehow inferior. Head-down charging, certainly, was to be preferred to thinking, a manifestation, some would say, of the English attitude to life in general. In the public schools, thinking tended to be frowned upon as a matter of course (as late as 1946, the Hungarian comic writer George Mikes could write of how, when he had first arrived in Britain, he had been proud when a woman called him 'clever', only to realise later the loadedness of the term and the connotations of untrustworthiness it carried).

The differing sets of rules frustrated efforts to establish football at universities until, in 1848, H.C. Malden of Godalming, Surrey, convened a meeting in his rooms at Cambridge with representatives of Harrow, Eton, Rugby, Winchester and Shrewsbury – and, remarkably, two non-public schoolboys – at which were collated what might be considered the first unified Laws of the Game. 'The new rules were printed as the "Cambridge Rules",' Malden wrote. 'Copies were distributed and pasted up on Parker's Piece [an area of open grassland in the centre of the city], and very satisfactorily they worked, for it is right to add that they were loyally kept and I never heard of any public school man who gave up playing for not liking the rules.'

Fourteen years later the southern version of the game took another step towards uniformity as J.C. Thring – the younger brother of Edward, the Uppingham headmaster – having been thwarted in an earlier attempt to draw up a set of unified rules at Cambridge, brought out a set of ten laws entitled 'The Simplest Game'. The following October, another variant, the 'Cambridge University Football Rules', was published. Crucially, a month later, the Football Association was formed, and immediately set about trying to determine a definitive set of Laws of the Game, intending still to combine the best elements of both the dribbling and the handling game.

It failed. The debate was long and furious but, after a fifth meeting at the Freemason's Tavern in Lincoln's Inn Fields in London, at 7pm on 8 December 1863, carrying the ball by hand was outlawed, and football and rugby went their separate ways. The dispute, strangely, was not over the use of the hand, but over hacking – that is, whether kicking opponents in the shins should be allowed. F.W. Campbell of Blackheath was very much in favour. 'If you do away with [hacking],' he said, 'you will do away with all the courage and pluck of the game, and I will be bound to bring over a lot of Frenchmen who would beat you with a week's practice.' Sport, he appears to have felt, was about pain, brutality and manliness; without that, if it actually came down to *skill*, any old foreigner might be able to win. A joke it may have been, but that his words were part of a serious debate is indicative of the general ethos, even if Blackheath did end up resigning from the association when hacking was eventually outlawed.

The dribbling game prevailed, largely because of Law Six, the forerunner of the offside law: 'When a player has kicked the ball, anyone of the same side who is nearer to the opponent's goal-line is out of play, and may not touch the ball himself, nor in any way whatever prevent any other player from doing so, until he is in play...' In other words, passes had to be either lateral or backwards; for Englishmen convinced that anything other than charging directly at a target was suspiciously subtle and unmanly, that would clearly never do.

Dribbling itself, it should be said, was rather different to modern conceptions of the art. In his history of the FA Cup, Geoffrey Green, the late football correspondent of *The Times*, quotes an unnamed writer of the 1870s: 'A really first-class player ... will never lose sight of the ball, at the same time keeping his attention employed in the spying out of any gaps in the enemy's ranks, or any weak points in the defence, which may give him a favourable chance of arriving at the coveted goal. To see some players guide and steer a ball through a circle of opposing legs, turning and twisting as the occasion requires, is a sight not to be forgotten... Skill in dribbling ... necessitates something more than a go-ahead, fearless, headlong onslaught of the enemy's citadel; it requires an eye quick at discovering a weak point, and *nous* to calculate and decide the chances of a successful passage.' In terms of shape, it sounds rather like an elementary form of modern rugby union, only without any handling.

Tactics – if that is not too grand a word in the circumstances – were similarly basic, even after the number of players had been fixed at eleven. Teams simply chased the ball. It wasn't even until the 1870s that the goalkeeper became a recognised and universally accepted position; not until 1909 that he began to wear a different coloured shirt to the rest of his team; and not until 1912 that he was restricted to handling the ball only in his own box – a rule change implemented to thwart the Sunderland goalkeeper Leigh Richmond Roose's habit of carrying the ball to the halfway line. If there were a formation at all in those earliest days, it would probably have been classified as two or three backs, with nine or eight forwards.

Even when Law Six was changed in 1866, following Eton's convention and permitting a forward pass provided there were at least three members of the defensive team between the player and the opponent's goal when the ball was played (that is, one more than the modern offside law), it seems to have made little difference to those brought up on the dribbling game. As late as the 1870s, Charles W. Alcock, a leading early player and administrator, was writing evangelically of 'the grand and essential principle of backing up. By "backing up", of course, I shall be understood to mean the following closely on a fellow-player to assist him, if required, or to take on the ball in the case of his being attacked, or otherwise prevented from continuing his onward course.' In other words, even a decade after the establishment of the FA, one of the founding fathers of the game felt it necessary to explain to others that if one of their team-mates were charging head-down at goal, it might be an idea to go and help him – although expecting to receive the ball from him volitionally seems to have been a step too far.

That, at least, is how it was in the south. The north was making its own advances, particularly in south Yorkshire, where a combination of Old Harrovian teachers at Sheffield College and the traditional folk games of Holmfirth and Penistone led to the establishment of the Sheffield Club on 24 October 1857, initially as a way for cricketers to stay fit during the winter. On Boxing Day that year, the world's first inter-club match was played as they beat Hallam FC 2-0. The sport grew rapidly: within five years crowds of several hundred were common, and fifteen clubs had been established in the area. The Sheffield Club drew up their own set of rules, published in 1862, which, significantly, while showing the influence of Harrow, Rugby and Winchester, made no mention of offside.

There appears, though, to have been some regulation, for when Sheffield's secretary William Chesterman wrote to the newly-founded Football Association on 30 November 1863, submitting the club's subscription and his contribution to the debate over laws, he noted: 'We have no printed rule at all like your *No. 6*, but I have written in the book a rule, which is always played by us.' Exactly what that was remains unclear. Sheffield's formal acceptance of offside came only in 1865, as part of horse-trading over rules ahead of a game against Notts County, and even then required only one defensive player to be goal-side of the forward when the ball was played for him to be onside. That, clearly, made passing far more viable, although it is debatable to what extent the opportunities it provided were taken up.

The FA failed to respond to Sheffield's overtures, and so for several years two codes – or rather, two basic codes, for there were also variations in Nottingham and other cities – existed. They met for the first time in 1866, with a match between London and Sheffield in Battersea Park on 31 March 1866. London won 2-0, with contemporary reports suggesting they had been the more skilful side, but had been unsettled by Sheffield's physicality.

After much to-ing and fro-ing over whose regulations to play by, Alcock brought a London team to Sheffield in December 1871. Playing under Sheffield rules, the home team won 3-1, their victory generally being put down to the fact that they had an organised formation. That, taken in conjunction with their more liberal offside law, might suggest a passing game, but it seems Sheffield were rather more rooted in dribbling even than London. According to Percy M. Young in *Football in Sheffield*, the Sheffield players found 'the dribbling skill of Alcock quite outside their range of experience. Moreover, Alcock was alive to the virtues of the well-placed pass (the local players adopted the simpler and more direct method of ignoring their own colleagues and making straight for goal on every possible occasion) and the delicate combination between himself and Chenery was a revelation to 2,000 delighted spectators'. There would be eighteen further meetings before Sheffield finally came into the FA fold in 1878.

There may not have been a culture of passing in Sheffield, but it does seem they would punt the ball long to clear their lines. In *The World Game*, Geoffrey Green notes that when Sheffield players arrived in London for an exhibition match in 1875 and began 'butting the ball with their heads', the crowd regarded it as 'something for amusement rather than admiration'. In a pure dribbling game, of course, there would have been no need for the ball ever to leave the ground, other – perhaps – than to lift it over a challenging foot. Only if the ball were played a significant distance in the air would heading have been necessary.

The Scottish Football Association annual's report of an 1877 match between Glasgow and Sheffield makes the point clearly: 'That the game was a very well contested one, and victory has rested with the best side, no one will deny; but that it was a pretty game, abounding in fine displays of combined dribbling, which has frequently distinguished a Scottish team above all others, few will admit... The fact cannot be hidden ... that the tactics pursued by the Sheffield team on Saturday were partially responsible for this inasmuch as they play a different set of rules from those of the English and Scottish Associations, and to them our "off-side" rule is next to a dead letter. In this manner, long kicking was largely indulged in on Saturday on their side; and in order to meet the same style of play, the Glasgow men actually lost that united action which had led them on to victory in many a harder fought field.'

The spread of passing itself – that 'united action' – can be traced back to one game, football's first international, played between England and Scotland at Hampden Park, Glasgow, in 1872. England's line-up comprised a 'goal', a 'three-quarter back', a 'half-back', a 'fly-kick', four players listed simply as 'middle', two as 'left side' and one as 'right side', which, to try to apply modern notation, sounds like something approximating to a lop-sided 1-2-7. 'The formation of a team as a rule...' Alcock noted, 'was to provide for seven forwards, and only four players to constitute the three lines of defence. The last line was, of course, the goalkeeper, and in front of him was only one full-back, who had again before him but two forwards, to check the rushes of the opposing forwards.'

Scotland were represented by the Queen's Park club, which, until the foundation of the Scottish FA in 1873, governed the Scottish game – functioning much like the MCC in cricket or the Royal and Ancient in golf. Crucially, they were over a stone per man lighter than England. It is indicative of the physicality of early football that most pundits seemed to have expected that weight advantage would give England a comfortable victory, but what it

First International: Scotland 0 England 0, 30 November 1872, Partick

actually did was to stimulate the imagination. Although direct evidence is sketchy, it seems probable that, as Richard McBrearty of the Scottish Football Museum argues, Queen's Park decided they had to try to pass the ball around England rather than engage in a more direct man-to-man contest in which they were likely to be out-muscled, and their formation was very definitely a 2-2-6. The ploy paid off. England, with a more established tradition and a far larger pool of players from which to select, were firm favourites, but were held to a goalless draw. 'The Englishmen,' the report in the *Glasgow Herald* said, 'had all the advantage in respect of weight, their average being about two stones heavier than the Scotchmen [a slight exaggeration], and they also had the advantage in pace. The strong point with the home club was that they played excellently well together.'

That success may have confirmed the notion of passing as superior to dribbling – north of the border at least – but it could never have worked had passing not been part of the game in Scotland almost from the start. When the Queen's Park club was established in 1867, the version of the offside law they adopted held that a player was infringing only if he were both beyond the penultimate man and in the final 15 yards of the pitch. That, clearly, was legislation far more conducive to passing than either the FA's first offside law or its 1866 revision. Queen's Park accepted the three-man variant when they joined the FA on 9 November 1870, but by then the idea of passing was already implanted. In Scotland the ball was there to be kicked, not merely dribbled, as H.N. Smith's poem celebrating Queen's Park's victory over Hamilton Gymnasium in 1869 suggests:

> The men are picked – the ball is kicked,
> High in the air it bounds;
> O'er many a head the ball is sped...

Equally, it was the prevalence of dribbling upon which Robert Smith, a Queen's Park member and Scotland's right-winger in that first international, remarked after playing in the first of the four matches Alcock arranged between England and a team of London-based Scots that were the forerunners to proper internationals. 'While the ball was in play,' he wrote in a letter back to his club, 'the practice was to run or dribble the ball with the feet, instead of indulging in high or long balls.'

One of Queen's Park's motivations in joining the English association was to try to alleviate the difficulties they were having finding opponents who would agree to play by a standard set of rules. In the months leading up to their acceptance into the FA, they played games of ten-, fourteen-, fifteen- and sixteen-a-side, and in 1871–72, they managed just three games. 'The club, however,' Richard Robinson wrote in his 1920 history of Queen's Park, 'never neglected practice.' Their isolation and regular matches among themselves meant that idiosyncrasies became more pronounced – as they would for Argentina in the thirties – and so the passing game was effectively hot-housed, free from the irksome obstacle of *bone fide* opponents.

'In these [practice] games', Robinson went on, 'the dribbling and passing,' 'which raised the Scottish game to the level of fine art, were developed. Dribbling was a characteristic of English play, and it was not until very much later that the Southerners came to see that the principles laid down in the Queen's Park method of transference of the ball, accompanied by strong backing up, were those that got the most out of the team. Combination was the chief characteristic of the Queen's Park's play. These essentials struck Mr C.W. Alcock and in one of his earlier Football Annuals formed the keynote for a eulogium on Scottish players, accompanied by earnest dissertations advocating the immediate adoption by English players of the methods which had brought the game to such a high state of proficiency north of the Tweed.'

Alcock, in fact, was nowhere near as convinced as that. Although he professed himself intrigued by the 'combination game' – and for all the prowess he had shown at Sheffield – he expressed doubt in that annual of 1879 as to whether 'a wholesale system of passing pays'. Passing, he evidently felt, was all very well as an option, but should never be allowed to supplant the dribbling game.

Nonetheless, it quickly spread, particularly in Scotland, where the influence of Queen's Park was all-encompassing, leading ultimately to the highly romanticised 'pattern-weaving' approach, characterised by strings of short passes zigzagging between the forward- and half-lines. Queen's Park organised the Scotland side for the first two internationals, and even after the foundation of the Scottish Football Association remained a powerful voice in shaping the sport. They acted as evangelists, travelling across the country to play exhibition games. Records of a match against Vale of Leven, who became one of the early powerhouses of Scottish football, describe the game being stopped at regular intervals so the rules and playing methods could be described, while a game in Edinburgh in 1873 kick-started football in the capital. It is perhaps indicative of the impact of those matches that the Borders remain a rugby stronghold: a missionary game Queen's Park were scheduled to play there had to be cancelled because of FA Cup commitments, so football's seeds were never sown. As McBrearty points out, Scotland's demographics, with the majority of the population living in the central belt between the Glasgow and Edinburgh conurbations, made it far easier for one particular style to take hold than it was in England, where each region had its own idea of how the game should be played.

Queen's Park's tactics in the first international raised eyebrows in England, but the southward spread of the passing game can be attributed largely to two men: Henry Renny-Tailyour and John Blackburn, who played for Scotland in their victory over England in the second international. Both were lieutenants in the army, and both played their club football for the Royal Engineers, carrying the Scottish style with them to Kent. 'The Royal Engineers were the first football team to introduce the "combination" style of play,' W.E. Clegg, a former Sheffield player, wrote in the *Sheffield Independent* in 1930. 'Formerly the matches Sheffield played with them were won by us, but we were very much surprised that between one season and another they had considered "military football tactics" with the result that Sheffield was badly beaten by the new conditions of play.'

The passing approach was implanted in schools football by the Reverend Spencer Walker, as he returned as a master to Lancing College, where he had been a pupil, and set about turning 'a mere bally-rag into a well-ordered team'. 'The first thing I fell upon,' he wrote, 'was the crowding of all the forwards on the leading forward. They crowded round him wherever they went. So I made Rule 1: Fixed places for all the forwards, with passing the ball from one to the other. You should have seen the faces of our first opponents, a sort of "Where do we come in?" look.'

For all Alcock's scepticism, it gradually became apparent that passing was the future. The Old Carthusians side that beat the Old Etonians 3-0 in the 1881 FA Cup final was noted for its combinations, particularly those between E.M.F. Prinsep and E.H. Parry, while the following year the Old Etonian goal that saw off Blackburn Rovers, the first northern side to reach the final, stemmed, Green wrote in his history of the FA Cup, from 'a long dribble and cross-pass' from A.T.B. Dunn that laid in W.H. Anderson. Still, the Etonians were essentially a dribbling side.

The final flourish of the dribbling game came in 1883. For the first time the Cup received more entries from outside London than within, and for the first time the Cup went north as Blackburn Olympic beat Old Etonians in the final. The amateur era – at least in terms of mindset – was over; something acknowledged two years later when the FA legalised professionalism.

All the Olympic side had full-time jobs, and it caused something of a stir when their half-back and *de facto* manager, Jack Hunter, took them to Blackpool for a training camp before the final. This was very evidently not the effortless superiority to which the amateurs aspired. Early in the game, injury reduced the Etonians to ten men, but it is doubtful anyway whether they would have been able to cope with Olympic's unfamiliar tactic of hitting long sweeping passes from wing to wing. The winning goal, scored deep in extra-time, was characteristic of the game as a whole: a cross-field ball from Tommy Dewhurst (a weaver) on the right found Jimmy Costley (a spinner) advancing in space on the left, and he had the composure to beat J.F.P. Rawlinson in the Etonian goal.

In Scotland, the superiority of passing was old news. 'Take any club that has come to the front,' the columnist 'Silas Marner' wrote in the *Scottish Umpire* in August 1884, 'and the onward strides will be found to date from the hour when the rough and tumble gave place to swift accurate passing and attending to the leather rather than the degraded desire merely to coup an opponent.' Not that everybody was convinced. Two months later, after Jamestown Athletics had been beaten 4-1 in the Scottish Cup by Vale of Leven, 'Olympian' was scathing of their combination game in his 'On the Wing' column in the *Umpire*. '"Divide and Conquer" was a favourite dictum of the great Machiavelli when teaching princes how to govern.... What shall I say of the Jamestown's attempt to, I suppose, verify the truth of the aphorism. Their premises were right, but then they went sadly wrong with the conclusion. They made the grave mistake of dividing *themselves* instead of their opponents and so paid the penalty. And what a penalty! Tell it not in Gath. Publish

Wrexham 1 Druids 0, Welsh Cup final, Acton, 30 March 1878

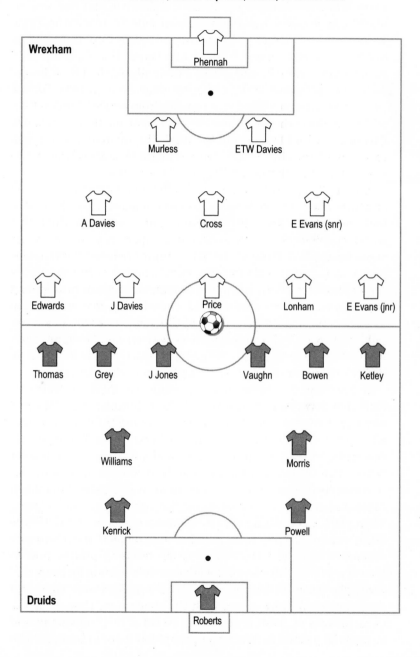

it not in Askelon. Strategy can never take the place of eleven good pairs of nimble legs.'

Well, it can, and it did and, to the consternation of tradition-alists in both England and Scotland, it meant one of the two centre-forwards – who, it was found, tended to replicate each other's role in a passing game – slipping back into a deeper position, eventually becoming, over the course of the 1880s, a centre-half in a 2-3-5 formation: the Pyramid. There is a widespread belief as expressed by, for instance, the Hungarian coach Árpád Csanádi in his immense and influential coaching manual *Soccer*, that the 2-3-5 was first played by Cambridge University in 1883, but there is evidence to suggest they may have been using the system as much as six years before that. Nottingham Forest, equally, were enthusiastic advocates of the system by the late 1870s, inspired in their experiments by their captain Sam Widdowson, who also invented the shinpad.

Certainly Wrexham were employing a centre-half when they faced Druids in the Welsh Cup final in 1878; their captain and full-back Charles Murless, a local estate agent, deciding to withdraw E.A. Cross from the forward line, seemingly because he felt that the pace of the centre-forward who remained, John Price, was sufficient to cover for any resulting shortfall in attack. He was vindicated as James Davies settled a tight game with the only goal two minutes from time.

The gradual spread of the 2-3-5 meant that the centre-half soon became the fulcrum of the team, a figure far removed from the dour stopper he would become. He was a multi-skilled all-rounder, defender and attacker, leader and instigator, goal-scorer and destroyer. He was, as the great Austrian football writer Willy Meisl put it, 'the most important man on the field'.

Intriguingly, the *Sheffield Independent*, in its report on the first floodlit game – an exhibition between the 'Reds' and the 'Blues' played in October 1878 – listed each team with four backs, a half, and five forwards. There is, though, no other evidence of any side playing with any more than two defenders for another three decades, so it seems probable that what is actually being described is a 2-3-5, with the wing-halves, whose job it would become to pick up the opposing inside-forwards, listed not as halves but as backs.

A sense of the outrage prompted by even the idea of defending is given by a piece in the *Scottish Athletic Journal* of November 1882 condemning the habit of 'certain country clubs' of keeping two men back 20 yards from their own goal, there merely, the writer tartly suggests, 'to keep the goalkeeper in chat'. Similarly, Lugar Boswell Thistle, a club from Ayrshire, were deplored for attacking with a mere nine men. The reactionaries, though, were fighting a losing battle, and it was with a 2-3-5 that Dumbarton beat Vale of Leven in the Scottish Cup final in 1883.

It was the success of Preston North End in the 1880s that confirmed the pre-eminence of the 2-3-5. Initially a cricket and rugby club, they played a 'one-off' game under association rules against Eagley in 1878. No positions were recorded for that game, but in November the following year, they met Halliwell, with a team listed in the classic 2-2-6: that is, with two full-backs, two half-backs, two right-wingers, two left-wingers and two centre-forwards. Preston joined the Lancashire Football Association for the 1880–81 season and, although they initially struggled, the arrival of a host of Scottish players – professionals in all but name – transformed the club. By 1883 the team-sheets were for the first time showing Preston lining up in a 2-3-5 system. Exactly whose idea that was is unclear, but it is known that James Gledhill, a teacher and doctor from Glasgow, gave a series of lectures 'showing by blackboard what might be done by a team of selected experts', as David Hunt put it in his history of the club. It was with that system that Preston went on to win the first two Football League titles, the first of them, in 1887–88, without losing a game.

England played a 2-3-5 for the first time against Scotland in 1884 and, by October that year, the system was common enough that when Notts County went north for a friendly against Renfrewshire, the *Umpire* listed their team in 2-3-5 formation without comment. The Scotland national side first used a pyramid in 1887, prompting much grumbling about their aping of what was initially an English tactic. The tone of a profile of Celtic's James Kelly, published in the *Scottish Referee* in 1889, though, makes clear that by the end of the decade the debate was over. 'There are many people who believe that when Scotland adopted the centre half-back position she sacrificed much of her power in the game,' it read. 'We do not share altogether this opinion, and if the players who fill this space in our clubs were men of Mr Kelly's calibre there would be no difference of opinion on the matter, nor would we have any cause to regret having followed England in this matter.'

The pyramid would remain the global default until the change in the offside law in 1925 led to the development, in England, of the W-M. Just as the dribbling game and all-out attack had once been the 'right' – the only – way to play, so 2-3-5 became the touchstone.

△▽△▽△▽△▽△▽

Chapter Two

The Waltz and the Tango

△▽ It wasn't only Britain that found football irresistible; almost everywhere the British went in search of trade and commerce they left the game, and that didn't just include parts of the Empire. There was money to be made from exporting copper from Chile, guano from Peru, meat, wool and hide from Argentina and Uruguay and coffee from Brazil and Colombia, and there was banking to be done everywhere. By the 1880s, 20 percent of Britain's foreign investment was in South America, and by 1890 there were 45,000 Britons living in the Buenos Aires area, along with smaller, but still significant, communities in São Paulo, Rio de Janeiro, Montevideo, Lima and Santiago. They ran their businesses, but they also established newspapers, hospitals, schools and sporting clubs. They exploited South America's natural resources, and in return they gave football.

In Europe, it was a similar story. If there was a British community – whether centred on diplomacy, banking, trade or engineering – football soon followed. The first Budapest club was Újpest, established at a gymnasium in 1885, and MTK and Ferencváros soon followed. Vienna was the centre of the British presence in central Europe, and football, having initially been played among the staff of the embassy, banks and various trading and engineering companies, soon took hold. The first match in Austria took place on 15 November 1894, between the Vienna Cricket Club and gardeners from Baron Rothschild's estate, but local interest was so great that by 1911 the Cricket Club had become Wiener Amateure. Among Czechs, football had to compete with Sokol, a local variant of Turnen, the nationalistic gymnastics popular in Germany, but with increasing numbers of young intellectuals in Prague turning to London and Vienna for guidance, the game soon took root there as well. The inauguration of Der Challenge Cup in 1897, open to any side from the Habsburg Empire, prompted a further upsurge in interest.

Anglophile Danes, Dutch and Swedes were equally quick to adopt the game, Denmark proving good enough to take silver at the 1908 Olympics. There was never any sense, though, of trying to do anything different to the British, whether from a tactical or any other point of view. To look at photographs of Dutch sporting clubs of the late nineteenth century is to look at a pastiche of Victorian Englishness, all drooping moustaches and studied indifference. As a participant quoted by Maarten van Bottenburg and Beverley Jackson in *Global Games* put it, the purpose of sport was to play 'on English grounds, with all their English customs and English strategies ... amid the beautiful Dutch landscape'. This was about imitation; invention didn't come into it.

It was in central Europe and South America, where attitudes to the British were more sceptical, that football began to evolve. The 2-3-5 formation was retained, but shape is only part of the matter; there is also style. Where Britain, despite the acceptance of passing and the spread of 2-3-5, persisted in ruggedness and physicality, others developed subtler forms of the game.

△▽

What set football in central Europe apart was the speed at which it was taken up by the urban working class. Although tours by the likes of Oxford University, Southampton, Corinthians, Everton and Tottenham and the arrival of various coaches ensured a British influence remained, those playing the game had not been inculcated in the beliefs of the English public schools, and so had no preconceived notions of the 'right' way of doing things.

They were fortunate, also, that it was Scots who made the biggest impression, so ensuring that the focus of the game was on quick, short passing. In Prague, for instance, the former Celtic inside-left John Madden – 'the ball artist of his day with all the tricks' according to Jim Craig in *A Lion Looks Back* – coached Slavia between 1905 and 1938, while his compatriot John Dick, once of Airdrieonians and Arsenal, had two spells in charge of Sparta between 1919 and 1933. In Austria, meanwhile, a conscious effort was made to ape the style of the Rangers side that had toured in 1905.

The greatest teacher of the Scottish game, though, was an Englishman of Irish descent: Jimmy Hogan. Born and raised in Burnley in a staunchly Roman Catholic family, in his teens he toyed with the idea of entering the priesthood, but he turned to football and went on to become the most influential coach there has ever been. 'We played football as Jimmy Hogan taught us,' said Gusztav Sebes, the coach of the great Hungary side of the early fifties. 'When our football history is told, his name should be written in gold letters.'

Defying his father's desire for him to become an accountant, Hogan joined the Lancashire side Nelson as a sixteen year old and, developing into what he described as 'a useful and studious inside-right' went on to Rochdale and then Burnley. He was, by all accounts, a difficult character, haggling repeatedly for better wages and showing a wholly alien devotion to self-improvement. His team-mates nicknamed him 'the Parson' in recognition of his meticulous, almost Puritanical disposition. At one point Hogan and his father devised a primitive exercise bike – essentially a bicycle mounted on a rickety wooden stand – on which he would cycle 30 miles a day until he realised that far from making him quicker, he was merely tightening his calf muscles.

The ideal of effortless superiority may have belonged to the early amateurs, but it carried over into the professional game. Training, as such, was frowned upon. Players were expected to run, perhaps even practise their sprints, but ball-work was seen as unnecessary, possibly even deleterious. Tottenham's training schedule for 1904, for instance, shows just two sessions a week with the ball, and they were probably more enlightened than most. Give a player a ball during the week, ran the reasoning, and he would not be so hungry for it on a Saturday: a weak metaphor turned into a point of principle.

After one match, in which he had dribbled through a number of challenges to create an opportunity only to shoot disappointingly over the bar, Hogan asked his manager, Spen Whittaker, what had gone wrong. Had the position of his foot been wrong? Had he been off balance? Whittaker was dismissive, telling him just to keep trying, that to score one out of ten was a decent return. Others would have shrugged off the incident but, perfectionist that he was, Hogan dwelt on it. Surely, he thought, such things were not a matter of luck, but depended on technique. 'From that day I began to fathom things out for myself,' he said. 'I coupled this with seeking advice from the truly great players. It was through my constant delving into matters that I became a coach later in life. It seemed the obvious thing, for I had coached myself as quite a young professional.'

Hogan felt frustrated by Burnley's primitive approach, but it was a financial dispute that finally persuaded him, at the age of twenty-three, to leave Lancashire for the first time, enticed to Fulham by their manager Harry Bradshaw, whom he had known briefly at Burnley. Bradshaw had no playing pedigree and was a businessman and administrator rather than a coach, but he had clear ideas on how football should be played. No fan of kick-and-rush, he employed a series of Scottish coaches schooled in the close-passing game, ensured a hefty Scottish representation among the playing staff and left them to get on with it.

The policy was undeniably successful. Hogan helped Fulham to the Southern League championship in both 1906 and 1907 and, having joined the Second Division of the Football League in 1907–08, they reached the semi-final of the FA Cup, losing to Newcastle United. It was Hogan's last match for the club. He had been struggling for some time with a knee injury and Bradshaw, business head firmly in place, decided that to retain him was an unjustifiable risk. Hogan briefly joined Swindon Town, before representatives of Bolton Wanderers, having waited for him outside church after evensong one Sunday, persuaded him back to the north-west.

His career there was disappointing, ending in relegation, but a pre-season trip to the Netherlands made Hogan aware of the potential of Europe, and the desire of its players to learn. English football may have dismissed coaching as unnecessary, but the Dutch were begging for it. Following a 10-0 win over Dordrecht, Hogan vowed that one day he would 'go back and teach those fellows how to play properly'. He also, crucially, became good friends with James Howcroft, an engineer from Redcar who was a leading referee. Howcroft regularly took charge of games overseas and, as a result, knew several foreign administrators. One evening, Howcroft mentioned to Hogan that he had heard that Dordrecht were looking for a new coach, and hoped to employ somebody with an expertise in the British game. The coincidence was remarkable, and the opportunity not to be missed; Hogan applied, and, at the age of twenty-eight, a year after making his vow, he was back in Holland to fulfil it, accepting a two-year contract.

Hogan's players were amateurs, many of them students, but he began to train them as he felt British professionals should have been trained. He improved their fitness, certainly, but he believed the key was to develop their ball control. He wanted his team, he said, to replicate 'the old Scottish game', to play in 'an intelligent, constructive and progressive, on-the-carpet manner'. Crucially, because many of them came from the universities, his players were keen to study, and Hogan introduced lessons, explaining in chalk on a blackboard how he thought football should be played. Tactics and positioning began to be understood and explained not in an *ad hoc* manner on the pitch, but via diagrams in a classroom.

Hogan was successful and popular enough that he was asked to take charge of the Dutch national side for a game against Germany, which they won 2-1. Still only thirty, though, he felt he had more to give as a player, so, when his contract at Dordrecht was up, he returned to Bolton, who had retained his registration. He played a season there, helping them to promotion, but his future, he knew, lay in coaching. He began looking for work again in the summer of 1912, and again Howcroft proved instrumental, putting him in touch with the great pioneer of Austrian football, Hugo Meisl.

△▽

Meisl had been born in the Bohemian city of Maleschau in 1881 to a middle-class Jewish family, who moved to Vienna while he was still very young. He became obsessed by football, and turned out to limited success for the Cricket Club. His father, though, wanted him to go into business, and found him work in Trieste, where he became fluent in Italian and began to pick up other languages. Returning to Austria to perform his military service, he accepted his father's request that he should secure employment at a bank, but also started working for the Austrian football federation. Initially his job was concerned largely with fund-raising, but Meisl, like Hogan an intelligent inside-forward, had firm ideas on how the game should be played and was determined to shape the future of Austrian football. Slowly, his role expanded until, as the *de facto* head of the Austrian federation, he gave up banking altogether.

In 1912, Austria drew 1-1 against Hungary in a game refereed by Howcroft. Meisl was frustrated by the outcome, and asked Howcroft where his side was going wrong. Howcroft replied that he thought they needed a proper coach, somebody who could develop their individual technique, somebody, in other words, like his old mate Jimmy Hogan. Meisl promptly appointed him on a six-week contract, partly to work with leading Austrian clubs, but mainly to prepare the Austria national squad ahead of the Stockholm Olympics.

Hogan's first training session did not go well. The Austrian players found him difficult to understand, and felt he was focusing rather too much on basics. Meisl, though, was impressed, and he and Hogan talked long into the night about their vision of football. Tactically, neither saw anything wrong with the 2-3-5 – which had, after all, formed the basis of all football for over thirty years – but they believed that movement was necessary, that too many teams were too rigid and so predictable. Both believed that it was necessary to make the ball do the work, that swift combinations of passes were preferable to dribbling, and that individual technique was crucial, not for the slaloming individual runs that would become such a feature of the game in South America, but for the instant control of an incoming pass to allow a swift release. Hogan was also keen to stress the value of the long pass to unsettle opposing defences, provided it were well-directed and not an aimless upfield punt. Meisl was a romantic, but what is fascinating about Hogan is that his beliefs were, essentially, pragmatic. He was not an evangelist for the passing game through any quixotic notion of what was right; he simply believed that the best way to win matches was to retain possession.

Austria hammered Germany 5-1 in Stockholm, but went down 4-3 to Holland in the quarter-finals. Still, Meisl was convinced, and when the German football federation asked him to give Hogan a reference, he instead offered Hogan a job, putting him in charge of Austria's preparations for the 1916 Olympics. 'To leave my dark, gloomy, industrial Lancashire for gay Vienna was just like stepping into paradise,' Hogan said. He worked with the Olympic side twice a week, and spent the rest of the time coaching the city's top club sides, finding himself so much in demand that he was forced to begin his sessions with Wiener FC at 5.30 in the morning.

Austria warmed to Hogan, and Hogan warmed to Austria. Their

football, he said, was like a waltz, 'light and easy', and Meisl was optimistic of success in 1916. War, though, destroyed that dream. Realising the probability of conflict, Hogan approached the British consul and asked whether it would be advisable to return swiftly with his family to Britain. He was told there was no imminent danger, but within forty-eight hours, war had been declared. A day later, Hogan was arrested as a foreign national.

The American consul managed to get Hogan's wife and children back to Britain in March 1915, while Hogan was released the day before he was due to be sent to an internment camp in Germany after the Blythe brothers, who owned a department store in Vienna, agreed to act as guarantors for him. For almost eighteen months he worked for them, teaching their children how to play tennis, but, 130 miles to the east, moves were afoot to bring him back into football. Baron Dirstay, the Cambridge-educated vice-president of the Budapest club MTK, had heard of Hogan's plight and, after pulling various diplomatic strings, secured him a position coaching his side, provided he agreed to report regularly to the local police.

Hogan readily accepted. With most of the first team away at the front, his first task was to assemble a squad. He turned, naturally, to youth, picking up two of the club's most popular players, György Orth and Jozsef 'Csibi' Braun, after spotting them in a kickabout as he strolled through Angol Park. 'I pounced on them and said "they are mine, my very own",' he explained. 'They were both intelligent lads attending high school in Budapest. Every day after school I had them on the field, instructing them in the art of the game.' Clever and keen to learn, Orth and Braun were typical both of the sort of player central Europe produced and of the sort of player with whom Hogan loved to work; which is, of course, why he felt so at home in both Vienna and Budapest. 'The great advantage which continental football has over British soccer,' Hogan said, 'is that boys are coached in the art of the game at a very tender age.'

His methods brought spectacular success. MTK won the title in 1916–17, the first official championship after a brief hiatus for the war, and held on to it for nine years. As the war came to an end, a combined Budapest side gave notice of the growing strength of the continental game by hammering Bolton 4-1. Hogan, though, presided over just two of MTK's triumphs. As soon as he could when the war was over, he left for Britain. 'The time I spent in Hungary was almost as happy as my stay in Austria. Budapest is a lovely city – in my opinion, the most beautiful in Europe,' he said, but he had seen neither his wife nor his son in almost four years. Hogan was succeeded by one of his senior players, Dori Kürschner, who, twenty years later, would be crucial to the development of the game in Brazil.

Hogan returned to Lancashire and found a job in Liverpool, working as a dispatch foreman for Walker's Tobacco. Money, though, remained tight, and he was advised to ask for a hand-out from the Football Association, which had established a fund to support professionals financially disadvantaged by the war years. It proved a watershed in his career. Hogan believed he was due £200, and borrowed £5 to cover his travelling expenses to London. The FA secretary Frederick Wall, though, treated him with disdain. The fund, Wall said, was for those who had fought. Hogan pointed out that he had been interned for four years and so had had no chance to sign up. Wall's response was to give him three pairs of khaki socks, sneering that 'the boys at the front were very glad of those'. Hogan was furious, never forgave the FA and his talent – not that his ideas would have been well-received in conservative England anyway – was lost to English football.

In Vienna, Meisl retained Hogan's template, although his faith was tested by a 5-0 defeat Austria suffered to Southern Germany shortly after the end of the war. On a frozen, rutted pitch in Nuremberg, their close-passing game proved impractical, and a despondent Meisl spent the return journey discussing with his players whether they should abandon their approach for something more direct and physical. Absolutely not, came their response, and so were set in stone the principles from which grew the *Wunderteam* of the early thirties, the first of the great unful-filled national sides. Under Meisl, Brian Glanville wrote, 'soccer became almost an exhibition, a sort of competitive ballet, in which scoring goals was no more than the excuse for the weaving of a hundred intricate patterns.'

The pyramid remained as the basic shape, but the style of the game as a radicalised extension of the Scottish passing game was so different from that found in England that it became recognised as a separate model: 'the Danubian School'. Technique was prized over physicality, but was harnessed into a team structure. In South

America, the game came to diverge even more sharply from the original model. Again technique was prized, but in Uruguay and, particularly, Argentina, it was individuality and self-expression that were celebrated.

△▽

The Football Association's Laws of the Game arrived in Argentina in 1867, where they were published by an English-language newspaper, *The Standard*. Later that year the Buenos Aires Football Club was founded as an offshoot of the Cricket Club, but the seeds fell on stony ground, and six years later it switched to rugby. Only in the 1880s did football really take off, thanks largely to Alexander Watson Hutton, a graduate of the University of Edinburgh, who came to Argentina to teach at St Andrew's Scotch School. He resigned when the school refused to extend its playing fields, and established the English High School in 1884, where he employed a specialist games master to teach football. When the Argentinian Association Football League was reformed in 1893, Hutton was a central figure. Alumni, a team made up of old boys from the English High School, took their place in the first division and came to dominate it in the early part of the twentieth century, while the school team itself played lower down the league pyramid. They were far from the only school to take football seriously, and six of the first seven titles were won by teams based on the prestigious Lomas de Zamora boarding school.

It was a similar story across the River Plate in Uruguay, where young British professionals founded cricket and rowing clubs that developed football sections, and British schools pushed the game. William Leslie Poole, a teacher at the English High School in Montevideo, was the equivalent of Hutton, forming the Albion Cricket Club in May 1891, the football section of which was soon playing football against teams from Buenos Aires.

In those early days, as a quick glance at the team-sheets demonstrates, the players were largely British or Anglo-Argentinian, and so was the ethos. In his history of amateur football in Argentina, Jorge Iwanczuk speaks of the goal being 'to play well without passion' and of the importance of 'fair play'. In a game against Estudiantes, Alumni even refused to take a penalty because they believed it had been incorrectly awarded. It was all about doing things the 'right way', a belief that extended into tactics: 2-3-5 was universal. The *Buenos Aires Herald*'s extensive coverage of Southampton's 3-0 victory over Alumni in 1904 – the first game played on Argentinian soil by a British touring side – makes clear how public school values prevailed. Britain's pre-eminence, an editorial claimed, was the result of 'an inherent love of all things manly'.

Gradually, though, the British dominance waned. The Argentinian Football Association (AFA) adopted Spanish as its language of business in 1903 and the Uruguayan FA did likewise two years later. Alumni were wound up in 1911, and the following year AFA became the Asociación del Football Argentina, although it would take until 1934 before 'football' became '*fútbol*'. Uruguayans and Argentinians, uninfected by British ideals of muscular Christianity, had no similar sense of physicality as a virtue in its own right, no similar distrust of cunning. The shape may have been the same, but the style was as different as it was possible to be. The anthropologist Eduardo Archetti has insisted that, as the influence of Spanish and Italian immigrants began to be felt, power and discipline were rejected in favour of skill and sensuousness – a trend that was felt across a range of disciplines. 'Like the tango,' wrote the Uruguayan poet and journalist Eduardo Galeano, 'football blossomed in the slums.'

Different conditions necessitate a different style. Just as the game of the cloisters differed from the game of the playing fields in English public schools, so, in the tight, uneven, restricted spaces of the poorer areas of Buenos Aires and Montevideo, other skills developed and a new style was born: 'a home-grown way of playing football,' as Galeano put it, 'like the home-grown way of dancing which was being invented in the *milonga* clubs. Dancers drew filigrees on a single floor tile, and football players created their own language in that tiny space where they chose to retain and possess the ball rather than kick it, as if their feet were hands braiding the leather. On the feet of the first Creole virtuosos, *el toque*, the touch, was born: the ball was strummed as if it were a guitar, a source of music.'

Prioritising different virtues, the two styles could not comfortably coexist, and so, inevitably, when old and new met, there was conflict. That was apparent as early as 1905, when the physicality of Nottingham Forest against a representative XI – made up largely of Anglo-Argentinians – in the sixth game of their tour led to considerable ill-feeling. The *Herald*, pro-British as ever, even felt moved to issue a magnificently grand rebuke to those who had dared to criticise Forest's approach: 'a game especially intended to improve the stamina and try the strength of young men in the prime of life is not necessarily a parlour game.' Acrimony became a feature of subsequent tours, caused largely by a fundamental disagreement on the part the shoulder-charge had to play in the game.

Swindon Town's tour of 1912 was one of the few that could be judged a success, and from that came a realisation that the British might perhaps have something to learn. Samuel Allen, the Swindon manager, was generally approving, saying he had seen no better football between amateur sides, but even he expressed a concern that local players 'look on individual exploits as the main thing, and every time there was a chance to show clever work single-handed, it was taken'. Even traditionalists within Argentina were sceptical about the creolisation of the game. Jorge Brown, a former Alumni player of British origin, protested in the early 1920s that the new style of football 'was weakened by an excess of passing close to the goal. It is a game that is more fine, perhaps more artistic, even apparently more intelligent, but it has lost its primitive enthusiasm.' It was a criticism that would become increasingly familiar; until Hungary in 1953 settled the debate decisively at Wembley, Britain laboured under the delusion that the rest of the world suffered from a lack of directness in front of goal.

Nobody who watched Uruguay in the 1924 Olympics could have been so misguided. Argentina chose to stay at home, but Uruguay went to Paris and wrote one of the great stories of early football. Galeano has a tendency to over-romanticise, but his evident glee in his country's gold medal is hard to begrudge. This was, first and foremost, a team of workers, including, among other professions, a meat-packer, a marble-cutter, a grocer and an ice-salesman. They travelled to Europe in steerage, and played to pay for their board, winning nine friendlies in Spain before they even reached France. Uruguay were the first Latin American side to tour Europe, but they attracted little attention – at least initially – only around 2,000 turning up to watch them eviscerate Yugoslavia 7-0 in their opening game in the Olympics.

'We founded the school of Uruguayan football,' said Ondino Viera, who would go on to manage the national side and who had a turn of phrase only marginally less colourful than Galeano's, 'without coaches, without physical preparation, without sports medicine, without specialists. Just us alone in the fields of Uruguay, chasing the leather from the morning to the afternoon and then into the moonlit night. We played for twenty years to become players, to become what players had to be: absolute masters of the ball ... seizing the ball and not letting it go for any reason ... It was a wild football, our game. It was an empirical, self-taught, native style of football. It was a football that was not yet within the canons of the management of football in the Old World, not remotely ... That was our football, and that's how we formed our school of play, and that's how the school of play for the entire continent of the New World was formed.'

In Paris, word soon got around. 'Game after game,' Galeano wrote, 'the crowd jostled to see those men, slippery as squirrels, who played chess with a ball. The English squad had perfected the long pass and the high ball, but these disinherited children from far-off America didn't walk in their father's footsteps. They chose to invent a game of close passes directly to the foot, with lightning changes in rhythm and high-speed dribbling.'

Chess with a ball? Charles Alcock would scarcely have recognised it, although he would presumably have appreciated the goal-scoring ability of the centre-forward Pedro Petrone, even if he did refuse to head the ball for fear of disturbing his heavily brilliantined hair. Those who were there, though, were enraptured as Uruguay maintained their form through the competition, scoring a total of seventeen goals and conceding two in their four games before beating Switzerland 3-0 in the final. The reaction of the French essayist and novelist Henry de Montherlant was typical. 'A revelation!' he wrote. 'Here we have real football. Compared with this, what we knew before, what we played, was no more than a schoolboy's hobby.'

Gabriel Hanot, who would go on to edit *L'Équipe*, but was then coming to the end of a distinguished playing career, offered a less emotional response. Uruguay, he wrote, showed 'marvellous virtuosity in receiving the ball, controlling it and using it. They created a beautiful football, elegant but at the same time varied, rapid, powerful and effective.' As to the thought that British football might still be superior, Hanot was dismissive: 'It is like comparing Arab thoroughbreds to farm horses.'

Uruguay returned home and were promptly challenged to a game by Argentina, who insisted that their subsequent 3-2 aggregate win – achieved thanks to a 2-1 second-leg victory in Buenos Aires in a game halted early by crowd trouble – demonstrated that they would have been Olympic champions, if only they had turned up. Perhaps, perhaps not; it is impossible to say, but the Buenos Aires side Boca Juniors certainly impressed on a tour of Europe in 1925, losing just three of nineteen games.

Argentina did travel to Amsterdam for the Olympics four years later and, fittingly, met Uruguay in the final, losing 2-1 after a replay. Two years later, the two sides met again in the first World Cup final, and again Uruguay were triumphant, winning 4-2. As far as it is possible to judge from contemporary reports, Uruguay's advantage seems to have been that, for all their artistry and for all Viera's claims of a raw spontaneity, they were able to retain a defensive shape, whereas Argentina's individualism led at times to confusion. According to the Italian journalist Gianni Brera in *Storia critica del calcio Italiano*, the 1930 World Cup final was evidence that, 'Argentina play football with a lot of imagination and elegance, but technical superiority cannot compensate for the abandonment of tactics. Between the two *rioplatense* national teams, the ants are the Uruguayans, the cicadas are the Argentinians.' This is a fundamental: it could be said that the whole history of tactics describes the struggle to achieve the best possible balance of defensive solidity with attacking fluidity.

So grew up the theory of *la garra charrúa* – '*charrúa*' relating to the indigenous Charrúa Indians of Uruguay and '*garra*' meaning literally 'claw' or, more idiomatically, 'guts' or 'fighting spirit'. It was that, supposedly, that gave a nation with a population of only three million the determination to win two World Cups, and it was also that which gave a tenuous legitimacy to the brutality of later Uruguayan teams.

Romanticised as that theory may have been – there was, after all, next to no Charrúa involvement in football – what was obvious to everybody outside of Britain was that the best football in the world was being played on the River Plate estuary, and that it was a game far advanced from the predictable 2-3-5 as practised in Britain. 'The Anglo-Saxon influence has been disappearing, giving way to the less phlegmatic and more restless spirit of the Latin...' a piece in the Argentinian newspaper *El Grafi* in 1928 asserted.

Uruguay 4 Argentina 2, World Cup final, El Centenario, Montevideo, 30 July 1930

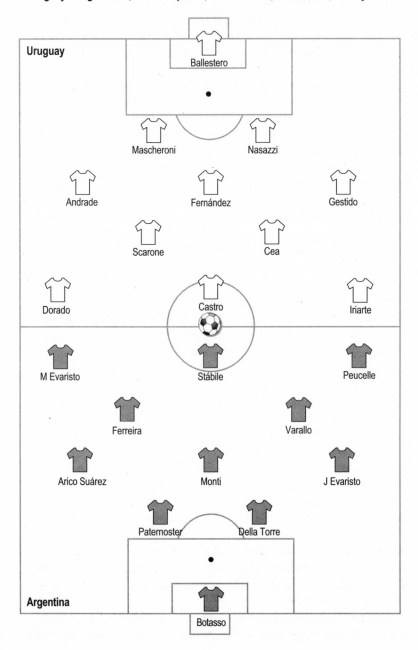

'They soon began modifying the science of the game and fashioning one of their own... It is different from the British in that it is less monochrome, less disciplined and methodical, because it does not sacrifice individualism for the honour of collective values... River Plate football makes more use of dribbling and generous personal effort, and is more agile and attractive.'

Imagination was prized to the extent that certain players were lionised as the inventors of certain skills or tricks: Juan Evaristo was hailed as the inventor of the '*marianella*' – the volleyed backheel; Pablo Bartolucci of the diving header; and Pedro Calomino of the bicycle-kick, although this last example is disputed. Some say the bicycle-kick was invented in Peru in the late nineteenth century; most seem to credit Ramón Unzaga Asla, a native of Bilbao who emigrated to Chile and first used it in 1914 (hence the use of term *chilena* throughout Spanish-speaking South America, unless that refers to David Arellano, a Chilean who popularised the technique on a tour of Spain in 1920); while others follow Leônidas, the Brazilian forward of the thirties, in attributing it to Petronilho de Brito. Weirdly, the former Aston Villa chairman Doug Ellis also claimed to have invented the bicycle-kick, even though he never played football to any level and was not born until ten years after the first record of Unzaga performing the trick. Who actually invented it is less important in this context than what the arguments show of the value set on imagination around the River Plate estuary in the twenties. The shaming thing for British football is that the game's homeland was so ill-disposed to innovation that it is just about conceivable that Ellis *was* the first man to perform a bicycle-kick on British soil.

Argentinian football developed its own foundation myth, based largely around the visit of the Hungarian side Ferencváros in 1922, which, exposing locals to the style of the Danubian School, supposedly revolutionised their thinking on the game. Given the process of creolisation had been going on for at least a decade, though, it seems probable that the tour simply confirmed changes that were already afoot, that in their early stages the Danubian and *rioplatense* games were similar and almost simultaneous shifts away from the physicality of the British style towards something based more on individual technique.

With the technical experimentation came a willingness to tinker – albeit gently – with tactics. 'South American teams treated the ball better and were more tactical in outlook,' said Francisco Varallo, Argentina's inside-right in the first World Cup final. 'It was the era when we had five forwards with the No.8 and the No.10 dropping back and wingers sending in passes.' Those inside-forwards came to be seen as the key to creativity, and the game developed a cult of the *gambeta*, the slaloming style of dribbling. In both Argentina and Uruguay the story is told of a player skipping through the opposition to score a goal of outrageous quality, and then erasing his footsteps in the dust as he returned to his own half so that no one should ever copy his trick.

Mythic, evidently, but indicative of the prevailing system of values, which became even more pronounced as Argentinian football drifted into reclusiveness. Undermined by the emigration of players ahead of the 1934 World Cup – there were four Argentinians in the Italy side that won it – they were beaten in the first round by Sweden, and then refused to send a team to France in 1938 after their own bid to host the tournament was turned down. As the Second World War took hold, and then Juan Perón led the country into isolation, Argentina did not appear again on the world stage until 1950, and in the interim enjoyed a golden age. A professional league began in 1931, big stadiums brought big crowds and newspaper and radio coverage both drew off, and fuelled, the nationwide interest in the game. So central did football become to Argentinian life that when Jorge Luis Borges, who hated the sport, and Adolfo Bioy Casares, who loved it, collaborated on the short story '*Esse est percipi*', it was football they chose to demonstrate how perceptions of reality could be manipulated, as they imagine a fan's disillusionment as he learns from a conversation with a club chairman that all football is staged, with results pre-ordained and players played by actors.

The style that had begun to emerge in the twenties developed into something even more spectacular, *la nuestra* – 'ours' or 'our style of play' – which was rooted in the *criolla viveza* – 'native cunning'. The term itself seems to have been popularised in the aftermath of Argentina's 3-1 victory over an England XI in 1953: '*la nuestra*', 'our style', it had been seen, could beat that of the *gringos* (although technically that was only a representative game, not a full international). What it describes, though, is the whole early philosophy of Argentinian football, which was founded on the joy of attacking. Between September 1936 and April 1938, there was not a single goalless draw in the Argentinian championship. Yet goals were only part of the story. In a much-cited anecdote from his novel *On Heroes and Tombs* (annoyingly missing from the English translation), Ernesto Sábato discusses the spirit of *la nuestra* as the character Julien d'Arcangelo tells the hero, Martín, of an incident involving two Independiente inside-forwards of the twenties, Alberto Lalín and Manuel Seoane (nicknamed both la Chancha and el Negro), who were seen as embodying the two different schools of thought on how football should be played. '"To show you what those two modalities were,"' D'Arcangelo says to Martín, "I am going to share with you an illustrative anecdote. One afternoon, at half-time, la Chancha was saying to Lalín: "Cross it to me, man, and I can go in and score." The second half starts, Lalín crosses and sure enough el Negro gets to it, goes in and scores. Seoane returns with his arms outstretched, running towards Lalín, shouting: "See, Lalín, see?!" and Lalín answered, "Yes, but I'm not having fun." There you have, if you like, the whole problem of Argentinian football.'

The tricks, entertainment, came to rival winning in importance. Half a century earlier, Britain had herself had the argument: to keep playing the 'right way', to keep dribbling (albeit in a far less flamboyant manner), or to adopt the style that won matches. In its twenty-year cocoon, in a culture obsessed by *viveza* and with few games against outsiders that might have brought defeat and a tactical rethink, the exuberant style flourished. It might not have been for the long-term good of Argentinian football, but it was fun while it lasted.

Chapter Three

△▽△▽△▽△▽△▽△▽

The Third Back

△▽   Part of football's enduring fascination is that it is a holistic game, that the slightest change in one part of the pitch can have unexpected and radical effects elsewhere. When the home associations persuaded the international board in 1925 to liberalise the offside law, it was to answer the specific issue of a lack of goals. Notts County had begun the trend, but by then several clubs, most notably Newcastle United with their full-back pairing of Frank Hudspeth and Bill McCracken, had become so adept at setting an offside trap that games would be compressed into a narrow sliver either side of the halfway line. When Newcastle drew 0-0 at Bury in February 1925, it came as the final straw. It was Newcastle's sixth goalless draw of a season that produced what at the time was an unthinkably low average of 2.58 goals per game. The football was boring, attendances were falling and the FA, for once, not merely recognised that something needed to be done, but set about doing it.

The offside law had remained unchanged since 1866, and demanded that, for a forward to be onside, three opposing players (usually a goalkeeper and two defenders) had to be between him and his opponent's goal. The FA came up with two possible solutions – either to require only two players to be in advance of the forward, or to add a line in each half 40 yards from goal behind which a forward could not be offside – and set about testing them in a series of exhibition games, with one half being played under one alternative, and the other under the other.

At a meeting in London in June, the FA decided they preferred the version requiring only two defending players to play a forward onside. The Scottish FA soon adopted the amendment as well, and it was they who presented the proposed rule change to the International Board, the new variant being implemented ahead of the 1925–26 season. Previously a side looking to play the offside trap had been able to retain one full-back as cover as his partner stepped up to try to catch the forward; the new legislation meant that a misjudgement risked leaving the forward through one-on-one with the goalkeeper.

On the face of it, the amendment was an immediate success, with the average number of goals per game shooting up to 3.69 the following season, but it brought about significant changes in the way the game was played, and led directly to Herbert Chapman's development of the 'third back' or W-M formation. And that, it is widely held, was what precipitated the decline and increasing negativity of English football.

The argument is put most strongly by Willy Meisl, the younger brother of Hugo, in *Soccer Revolution*, which was written in horrified response to England's 6-3 defeat at home to Hungary in 1953. Meisl, it should be said, had been a devout Anglophile even before he fled rising anti-Semitism in Austria to settle in London, and his book reads as a lament for a past he experienced only second-hand and probably idealised. He became a respected figure in sports journalism, writing mainly on English football for foreign publications, but *Soccer Revolution*, for all its fine phrase-making, is, to modern eyes at least, a strikingly eccentric work. For him, the change in the offside rule was football's version of the Fall; the moment at which innocence was lost and commercialism won out. Perhaps it was, but it was the very thin end of what is now a gargantuan wedge.

As he saw it, for he was no less a romantic than his brother, blinkered directors looking no further than their balance sheets had blamed the laws for football's failings without ever considering that they may be 'guilty of a wrong approach to the game'. And so they pressed ahead with a policy that 'might have appeared to the layman a slight revision in the Laws of the Game' but which 'turned out to be the crack of a shot that started an avalanche'.

And here again the divide is reached between those who seek to win, and those who wish simply to play well. These days the debate often feels perfunctory, but in the twenties it was sufficiently alive that the notion of a league itself – 'an incubus' roared Brian Glanville – began to be questioned. 'The average standard of play would go up remarkably if the result were not the all-important end of matches,' Chapman admitted. 'Fear of defeat and the loss of points eat into the confidence of players... What it comes to is that when circumstances are favourable, the professionals are far more capable than may be believed, and it seems that, if we would have better football, we must find some way of minimising the importance of winning and the value of points...' Winning and losing in football, though, is not about morality any more than it is in life. Even those who agree most wholeheartedly with Danny Blanchflower's dictum that 'the great fallacy is that the game is first and last about winning; it is ... about glory, it is about doing things in style and with a flourish' would surely not have it decided in the manner of figure-skating, by a panel of judges awarding marks out of ten. It is a simple but unfortunate fact that eventually those who are looking to win games will toy with negativity. After the glorious excesses of *la nuestra* it came to the Argentinians; and for all the self-conscious aestheticism of the Austrians, it would just have surely have come to them had fascism not got there first. Golden ages, almost by definition, are past: gleeful naivety never lasts for ever.

The most obvious immediate effect of the change in the offside law was that, as forwards had more room in which to move, the game became stretched, and short passing began to give way to longer balls. Some sides adapted better than others, and the beginning of the 1925–26 season was marked by freakish results. Arsenal, in particular, seemed unable to settle into any pattern of consistency and, after beating Leeds United 4-1 on 26 September, they were hammered 7-0 by Newcastle United on 3 October.

Charlie Buchan, the inside-right and probably the team's biggest star, was furious, and told Chapman he was retiring and wanted to stay in the north-east, where he had enjoyed considerable success with Sunderland. This Arsenal, he said, was a team without a plan, a team with no chance of winning anything. Chapman must have seen his life's project begin to crumble, and Buchan's words would have had a particular sting because, if nothing else, Chapman was a planner.

He had been born in Kiveton Park, a small colliery town between Sheffield and Worksop and, but for football, he would have followed his father into mining. He played first for Stalybridge, and then for Rochdale, then Grimsby, Swindon, Sheppey United,

Worksop, Northampton Town, Notts County and, finally, Totten-ham. He was a journeyman player, good enough to stay out of the pits, but little else, and if that part of his career was notable at all, it was for the pale yellow calf-skin boots he wore in the belief they made him easier for team-mates to pick out, an early indication of the inventiveness that would serve him so well as a manager.

His managerial career did not exactly begin with a fanfare. He was lying in the bath after playing in a friendly for Tottenham's reserve side in the spring of 1907 when his team-mate Walter Bull mentioned that he had been approached to become player-manager of Northampton, but wanted to prolong his full-time playing career. Chapman said that he would be interested, Bull recommended him and Northampton, after failing to attract the former Stoke and Manchester City half-back Sam Ashworth, gave him the job.

A fan, as apparently all those who gave the matter any thought were, of the Scottish passing game, Chapman wanted his side to reproduce the 'finesse and cunning' he saw as integral to that conception of football. After a couple of promising early results, though, Northampton faded, and a home defeat to Norwich in November saw them fall to fifth bottom in the Southern League. That was Chapman's first crisis, and he responded with his first grand idea, a recognition that 'a team can attack for too long'. He began to encourage his team to drop back, his aim being less to check the opposition forwards than to draw out their defenders and so open up attacking space. By Christmas 1908, Northampton were top of the Southern League; they went on to win the title with a record ninety goals.

Chapman moved on to Leeds City in 1912 and, in the two seasons before the First World War, took them from second bottom of Division Two to fourth. He also hit upon one of his most notable innovations, instituting team-talks after watching players arguing passionately over a game of cards. The war interrupted their progress there, but just as damaging to Chapman and the club were accusations that the club had made illegal payments to players. He refused to hand over the club's books, which led to Leeds City being expelled from the league and Chapman being banned from football for life in October 1919.

Two years later, though, while he was working for the Olympia oil and cake works in Selby, Chapman was approached by

Huddersfield Town to become assistant to their manager Ambrose
Langley, who had played alongside his late brother Harry before
the war. Chapman was intrigued and appealed to the FA, noting
that he had been away from the club working at the Barnbow arms
factory when the supposed illegal payments had been made.

The FA showed mercy, Chapman took up the post, and when
Langley decided a month later that he would rather be running a
pub, he found himself installed as manager. He advised the
directors that they had a talented young squad, but that they
needed 'a general to lead them'. Clem Stephenson of Aston Villa,
he decided, was just the man. Stephenson was thirty-three and,
crucially given Chapman's belief in the value of counter-attacking,
had developed a way of breaking the offside trap by dropping into
his own half before springing forward. Performances and gates
improved rapidly while Chapman, always looking at the bigger
picture, re-turfed the pitch and renovated the press seats at Leeds
Road. In 1922, despite their stuffed donkey mascot catching fire in
the celebrations that followed the semi-final victory over Notts
County, Huddersfield won the FA Cup, Billy Smith converting a
last-minute penalty in the final at Stamford Bridge to see off
Preston North End.

The authorities, though, were not impressed. The game had
been a poor one, littered with niggling fouls, leading the FA to
convey its 'deep regret' at the behaviour it had witnessed and to
express a hope that 'there will not be any similar conduct in any
future final tie'. Huddersfield asked what was meant, to which the
FA replied that the club should recognise indecency when it saw it,
the lack of clarification prompting many to believe that Chapman
was being censured for having deployed his centre-half, Tom
Wilson, deeper than usual so that, in the words of the *Huddersfield
Examiner*, he acted as 'a great spoiler'.

It is impossible at this remove to determine whether the FA had
anything so specific in mind, but again what is apparent is the
perception that there was a 'right way to play' from which
Chapman was deemed to have deviated. Equally, the deployment
of Wilson with a brief, if not to man-mark, then certainly to check
Billy Roberts, the opposing centre-forward, suggests that the
stopper centre-half was on its way, and may have come into
existence even without the change in the offside law.

There were other isolated incidents of clubs fielding their

centre-half with a specific defensive brief – Queen's Park, for instance, in danger of being overwhelmed by Rangers in a Glasgow Charity Cup tie in 1918, dropped Bob Gillespie back into what was effectively a central defensive role – but what was unique about Chapman's Huddersfield was less the willingness to deploy the centre-half defensively as the fact that they developed a distinctive style, based around their manager's distrust of the wing play that was so revered in Britain. Inside passing, Chapman argued, was 'more deadly, if less spectacular' than the 'senseless policy of running along the lines and centring just in front of the goalmouth, where the odds are nine to one on the defenders'. As the *Examiner* noted in 1924 after Huddersfield had wrapped up the league title, 'the low passing and the long-field play of the Leeds Road team has become famous.'

What was significant was not merely that Chapman had a clear conception of how football should be played, but that he was in a position to implement that vision. He was – at least in Britain – the first modern manager, the first man to have complete control over the running of the club, from signings to selection to tactics to arranging for gramophone records to be played over the public-address system to keep the crowd entertained before the game and at half-time. With Huddersfield on their way to defending their title in 1925, the *Sporting Chronicle* asked: 'Do clubs realise to the full today the importance of the man who is placed in control? They are ready to pay anything up to £4,000 and £5,000 for the services of a player. Do they attach as much importance to the official who will have charge of the player...? The man behind the scenes who finds players, trains talent, gets the best out of the men at his command is the most important man in the game from the club's point of view.'

The following year Huddersfield completed a hat-trick of league titles, but by then Chapman was gone, enticed south by what he saw as even the greater potential of Arsenal. It was not, it must be said, obvious. Arsenal were struggling to stay up and, in Sir Henry Norris, labouring under an idiosyncratic and domineering chairman. Leslie Knighton, Chapman's predecessor, had been forbidden to spend more than £1,000 on a player in an age in which £3,000 fees were becoming common, while there was also a ban on bringing in players measuring less than 5'8". When Knighton defied the height restriction to sign the 5'0" Hugh

'Midget' Moffatt from Workington in 1923, Norris had him offloaded to Luton Town before he had played a single league game. Knighton was dismissed at the end of the 1924–25 season, with Norris citing poor results, although Knighton claimed it was because the club wanted to avoid paying him a bonus he was due from a benefit match.

Chapman, warning that it would take him five years to win anything, took the job only on condition he would face no such restrictions, something to which Norris reluctantly agreed. His first signing was Charlie Buchan. Sunderland valued him at £4,000, which their manager, Bob Kyle, insisted represented value for money as the inside-forward would guarantee twenty goals a season. If he was so confident, Norris replied, then the fee should be structured according to Buchan's scoring record: a £2,000 initial payment, plus £100 for each goal scored in his first season. Kyle went along with it, Buchan scored twenty-one, and Sunderland gratefully accepted £4,100.

Not that such a thing seemed likely that September after the defeat at Newcastle. Buchan was an awkward character, who had walked out on his first day at Arsenal because he thought the kit was inadequate, and then refused to train on his second because he found a lump of congealed Vaseline in his supposedly freshly laundered sock. Some managers might have seen that as wilful obstructiveness or an unrealistic finickiness, Chapman seems rather to have regarded that as evidence of high standards. He also admired in Buchan an independence of thought about the game, something that was far from common in players of the age. John Lewis, a former referee, had noted in 1914 that 'our professionals evince no great anxiety to learn anything of the theory of the sport... In most teams there is no evidence of pre-conceived tactics or thought-out manoeuvres,' and, for all Chapman's efforts to encourage debate, not much had changed.

Buchan had argued from the beginning of the season that the change in the offside rule meant the centre-half had to take on a more defensive role, and it was notable that in Arsenal's defeat at St James' the Newcastle centre-half Charlie Spencer had stayed very deep. He had offered little in an attacking sense, but had repeatedly broken up Arsenal attacks almost before they had begun, allowing Newcastle to dominate possession and territory. Chapman, at last, was convinced, but the mystery is why, given his natural inclination to the counter-attack, he had not done so earlier. He was not a man readily cowed by authority, but perhaps the FA's words after the 1922 Cup final, coupled with his recognition of what they had done for him in lifting his life ban, had had an effect.

Arsenal were certainly not the first club to come to the conclusion that the centre-half had to become a third back, but where they did break new ground was in recognising the knock-on effect this would have at the other end of the pitch. Buchan argued, and Chapman agreed, that withdrawing the centre-half left a side short of personnel in midfield, and so proposed that he should drop back from his inside-right position, which would have created a very loose and slightly unbalanced 3-3-4.

Chapman, though, valued Buchan's goal-scoring abilities too highly to compromise them and so instead gave the role of withdrawn inside-forward to Andy Neil. Given Neil was a third-team player, that came as something of a surprise, but it proved an inspired choice and an emphatic endorsement of Chapman's ability to conceptualise and compartmentalise, to recognise what specific skills were needed where. Tom Whittaker, who went on to become Chapman's trusted number two, recalled his boss describing Neil as being 'as slow as a funeral' but insisting it didn't matter because 'he has ball-control and can stand with his foot on the ball while making up his mind'.

With Jack Butler asked to check his creative instincts to play as the deep-lying centre-half, the new system had an immediate effect and, two days after the debacle at Newcastle, Arsenal, with Buchan re-enthused by the change of shape, beat West Ham 4-1 at Upton Park. They went on to finish second behind Huddersfield that season, at the time the highest league position ever achieved by a London club. The next season, though, began poorly, partly because success had brought over-confidence, and partly because opposing sides had begun to exploit Butler's lack of natural defensive aptitude. Some argued for a return to the traditional 2-3-5, but Chapman decided the problem was rather that the revolution had not gone far enough: what was needed at centre-half was a player entirely without pretension. He found him, characteristically unexpectedly, in the form of Herbie Roberts, a gangling ginger-haired wing-half he signed from Oswestry Town for £200.

According to Whittaker, 'Roberts's genius came from the fact that he was intelligent and, even more important, that he did what he was told.' He may have been one dimensional, but it was a dimension that was critical. His job, Whittaker wrote, was 'to intercept all balls down the middle, and either head them or pass them short to a team-mate. So you see how his inability to kick a ball hard or far was camouflaged.' Bernard Joy, the last amateur to play for England and later a journalist, joined Arsenal in 1935 as Roberts' deputy. 'He was a straightforward sort of player,' Joy wrote in *Forward Arsenal!*, 'well below Butler in technical skill, but physically and temperamentally well suited to the part he had to play. He was content to remain on the defensive, using his height to nod away the ball with his red-haired head and he had the patience to carry on unruffled in the face of heavy pressure and loud barracking. This phlegmatic outlook made him the pillar of the Arsenal defence and set up a new style that was copied all over the world.' And that, in a sense, was the problem. Arsenal became hugely successful, and their style was aped by sides without the players or the wherewithal to use it as anything other than a negative system.

Arsenal lost the FA Cup final to Cardiff in 1927, but it was after Norris had left in 1929 following an FA inquiry into financial irregularities that success really arrived. Buchan had retired in 1928 and it was his replacement, the diminutive Scot Alex James, signed from Preston for £9,000, who made Chapman's system come alive. The club's official history cautions that nobody should underestimate James's contribution to the successful Arsenal side of the 1930s. He was simply the key man.' Economic of movement, he was supremely adept at finding space to receive the ball – preferably played rapidly from the back – and had the vision and the technique then to distribute it at pace to the forwards. Joy called him 'the most intelligent player I played with... On the field he had the knack of thinking two or three moves ahead. He turned many a game by shrewd positioning near his own penalty area and the sudden use of a telling pass into the opponents' weak point.'

By the time Arsenal won the FA Cup in 1930 – their first silverware, as Chapman had promised, coming in the fifth season after his arrival – the new formation had taken clear shape. The full-backs marked the wingers rather than inside-forwards, the wing-halves sat on the opposing inside-forwards rather than on the wingers, the centre-half, now a centre-back, dealt with the centre-forward, and both inside-forwards dropped deeper: the 2-3-5 had become a 3-2-2-3; the W-M.

'The secret,' Joy wrote, 'is not attack, but counter-attack... We planned to make the utmost use of each individual, so that we had a spare man at each moment in each penalty area. Commanding the play in midfield or packing the opponents' penalty area is not the object of the game... We at Arsenal achieved our end by deliberately drawing on the opponents by retreating and funnelling to our own goal, holding the attack at the limits of the penalty box, and then thrusting quickly away by means of long passes to our wingers.'

Trophies and modernisation tumbled on together, the one seeming to inspire the other. The FA, instinctively conservative, blocked moves to introduce shirt numbers and floodlit matches, but other innovations were implemented. Arsenal's black socks were replaced by blue-and-white hoops, a clock was installed at Highbury, Gillespie Road tube station was renamed Arsenal, white sleeves were added to their red shirts in the belief that white was seen more easily in peripheral vision than any other colour and, perhaps most tellingly, after training on Fridays, Chapman had his players gather round a magnetic tactics board to discuss the coming game and sort out any issues hanging over from the previous fixture. At Huddersfield he had encouraged players to take responsibility for their positioning on the field; at Arsenal he instituted such debates as part of the weekly routine. 'Breaking down old traditions,' a piece in the *Daily Mail* explained, 'he was the first manager who set out methodically to organise the winning of matches.'

It worked. Arsenal won the league in 1931 and 1933, and were beaten in the 1932 Cup final only by a highly controversial goal. Glanville wrote of them 'approaching the precision of a machine', and in their rapid transition from defence to attack, the unfussy functionalism of their style, there was a sensibility in keeping with the art deco surrounds of Highbury. The 'machine' analogy is telling, recalling as it does Le Corbusier's reference to a house as 'a machine for living in'; this was modernist football. William Carlos Williams, similarly, in a phrase that would become almost a slogan for his version of modernism, described a poem as 'a machine made of words ... there can be no part, as in any other machine, that is redundant.' Chapman's Arsenal were very much of their

Arsenal 2 Huddersfield Town 0, FA Cup final, Wembley, London, 26 April 1930

age. 'It was,' Joy said of their style, 'twentieth-century, terse, exciting, spectacular, economic, devastating.'

Perhaps that is not surprising. Chapman was, after all, part of the first wave of beneficiaries of Forster's Education Act of 1870, which made schooling compulsory to the age of twelve and allowed unprecedented numbers of working-class men to fill the managerial vacancies opened up by the First World War. They may not have had Ezra Pound's command to 'make it new' ringing in their ears, but it is fair to suggest that the new managerial class was more open to innovation than its tradition-bound predecessors. Chapman, it is worth remembering, was a near contemporary of another modernist genius of Nottinghamshire mining stock, D.H. Lawrence.

Within football there were doubters, perhaps the most astute of them Carruthers in the *Daily Mail*, who, after the 1933 championship, commented: 'If it were thought that other clubs would try to copy them, their example might, I'm afraid, be unfortunate. There is only one Arsenal today, and I cannot conceive another simply because no other club has players fit to carry on the same ideas.'

The ideas, anyway, were imperfectly understood, as was demonstrated when England's selection committee picked Roberts for a friendly against Scotland in 1931. He was the first stopper to be called up for his country, but neither of the full-backs, Fred Goodall and Ernie Blenkinsop, were accustomed to the W-M. As a result, Scotland 'picnicked happily in the open spaces' as L.V. Manning put it in the *Daily Sketch*, winning 2-0.

In Scotland, opinion was just as divided between those who recognised the efficacy of the more modern system, and those who remained romantically tied to the short passing game. The last hurrah of the pattern-weaving approach came on 31 March 1928 when the Scotland side who would become immortalised as the 'Wembley Wizards' hammered England, Alex Jackson scoring three and Alex James two in a 5-1 win. In his report in *The Evening News*, Sandy Adamson described Jackson's first goal as 'a zigzag advance which ought to go down in posterity as a classic of its kind' and went on to describe how 'exultant Scots engaged in cat-and-mouse cantrips... From toe to toe the ball sped. The distracted enemy was bewildered, baffled and beaten. One bit of weaving embraced eleven passes and not an Englishman touched the sphere until [Tim] Dunn closed the movement with a sky-high shot over the bar...'

The *Glasgow Herald* was more restrained. 'The success of the Scots,' its report said, 'was primarily another demonstration that Scottish skill, science and trickery will still prevail against the less attractive and simpler methods of the English style in which speed is relied upon as the main factor.' Jimmy Gibson and Jimmy McMullan, the wing-halves, and Dunn and James, the inside-forwards, clearly did combine to devastating effect on a wet pitch, but it should be borne in mind that the game was effectively a playoff for the wooden spoon in the Home International championship. The supposedly self-evident superiority of the Scottish style hadn't been apparent in the 1-0 defeat to Northern Ireland or the 2-2 draw against Wales.

It is significant too that eight of the Scotland eleven were based at English clubs: for all their passing ability, it evidently helped to have players used to the pace of the English game. Stylistically, anyway, this was not quite the throw-back some would suggest. Tom Bradshaw, the centre-half, was given a defensive role, marking Dixie Dean, so while they may not have been playing a full-blown W-M, nor was their system a classic 2-3-5.

The W-M's arrival in the club game was patchy. The former Rangers player George Brown recalls a charity game between a Rangers-Celtic XI and a Hearts-Hibs XI from 'about 1930': 'Davie Meiklejohn was at right-half, I was at left-half and Celtic's Jimmy McStay was at centre-half,' he said. 'Things did not go very well for us in the first half and by the interval we were one goal down. So during half-time, Meiklejohn said to McStay, "All the trouble is coming through the middle because you are too far up the field. We play with Jimmy Simpson well back and this leaves the backs free." McStay agreed to try this and we eventually ran out comfortable winners. So from then on he played the same type of game for Celtic.' Like Jack Butler at Arsenal, though, McStay was no natural defender, and a run of nine seasons without a title was brought to an end only when the stopper centre-half Willie Lyon was signed from Queen's Park.

And that, in a sense, was the problem: it was simply easier to be a good defensive centre-half than a good attacking one. The creative part of Chapman's equation was even harder to fulfil. Inside-forwards of the ability of Alex James were rare, but phlegmatic Herbie Roberts-style stoppers abounded. 'Other clubs tried to copy Chapman,' Jimmy Hogan said, 'but they had not the men, and the result was, in my opinion, the ruination of British football, with the accent on defence and bringing about the big kicking game which put to an end the playing of constructive football. Through this type of game our players lost the touch and feeling for the ball.'

The seeds of that decline may have pre-dated the change in the offside law, but they were nurtured by Chapman's response to it. The effect of the third-back game, as Glanville said, was 'to reinforce and aggravate weakness which already existed' because it encouraged a mental laziness on the part of coaches and players. It is far less arduous, after all, to lump long balls in the general direction of a forward than to endure the agonies of creation. Chapman, though, remained unapologetic. 'Our system, which is so often imitated by other clubs, has lately become the object of criticism and discussion...,' he told Hugo Meisl. 'There is only one ball in play and only one man at a time can play it, while the other twenty-one become spectators. One is therefore dealing only with the speed, the intuition, the ability and the approach of the player in possession of the ball. For the rest, let people think what they like about our system. It has certainly showed itself to be the one best adapted to our players' individual qualities, has carried us from one victory to another... Why change a winning system?'

Chapman himself never had to, nor did he have to deal with the transition from one generation of players to the next. On 1 January 1934, he caught a chill during a game at Bury, but decided to go anyway the next day to see Arsenal's next opponents, Sheffield Wednesday. He went back to London with a high temperature, but ignored the advice of club doctors and went to watch the reserves play at Guildford. He retired to bed on his return, but by then pneumonia had set in, and he died early on 6 January, a fortnight short of his fifty-sixth birthday.

Arsenal went on to win the title, and made it three in a row the following year. A few months after his death, a collection of Chapman's writings was published. In it, intriguingly, he too seemed to express regret for the passing of a less-competitive age. 'It is no longer necessary for a team to play well,' he said. 'They must get goals, no matter how, and the points. The measure of their skill is, in fact, judged by their position in the league table.'

This, now, seems all but axiomatic; it is a measure of how pervasive the amateur inclinations of the game remained that even Chapman seems to have felt it necessary to apologise for winning. 'Thirty years ago,' he went on, 'men went out with the fullest licence to display their arts and crafts. Today they have to make their contribution to a system.' And so, finally, resolved to winning, football recognised the value of tactics, the need for individuality to be harnessed within the framework of a team.

△▽△▽△▽△▽△▽

Chapter Four

How Fascism Destroyed the Coffee House

△▽ Herbert Chapman was one man, making one change to answer a specific problem. English football followed him because it saw his method worked, but the coming of the third-back game did not herald the coming of a generation of English tacticians. 'Unfortunately,' as Willy Meisl wrote, 'the plaster cast remained, no soccer sorcerer or professor was here to smash it to pieces and cast it in another mould.' If anything, the preference was to try to pretend the tactical change had not happened, that the sacred pyramid remained intact. When the FA made shirt numbering compulsory in 1939, they ignored later developments and stipulated that the right-back must wear 2, the left-back 3, right-half 4, the centre-half 5, the left-half 6, the right-winger 7, the inside-right 8, the centre-forward 9, the inside-left 10 and the left-winger 11, as though the 2-3-5 were still universal, or at least the basis from which all other formations were mere tinkerings. That meant that teams using the W-M lined up, in modern notation, 2, 5, 3; 4, 6; 8, 10; 7, 9, 11, which is why 'centre-half' is – confusingly – used as a synonym for 'centre-back' in Britain.

Newspapers, similarly, ignored the reality, continuing to print team line-ups as though everybody played a 2-3-5 until the 1960s. Even when Chelsea played the Budapest side Vörös Lobogó in 1954, and – alerted to tactical nuances by the fall-out from England's 6-3 defeat to Hungary at Wembley a year earlier – made the effort to print the Hungarian formation correctly in the match programme, they persisted with the delusion that their own W-M was actually a 2-3-5. So overwhelmingly conservative was the English outlook that the manager of Doncaster Rovers, Peter Doherty, enjoyed success in the fifties with his ploy of occasionally

Numbering in a 2-3-5

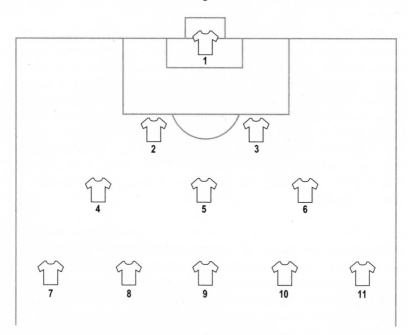

Numbering in a W-M (England)

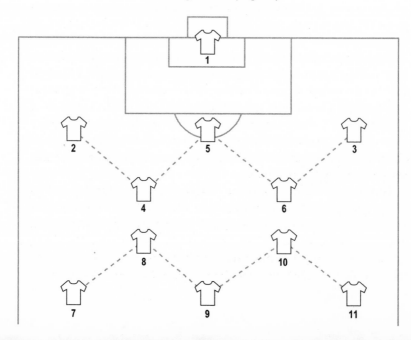

having his players switch shirts, bewildering opponents who were used to recognising their direct adversary by the number on their back.

For the importance of tactics fully to be realised, the game had to be taken up by a social class that instinctively theorised and deconstructed, that was as comfortable with planning in the abstract as it was with reacting on the field and, crucially, that suffered none of the distrust of intellectualism that was to be found in Britain. That happened in central Europe between the wars. What was demonstrated by the Uruguayans and Argentinians was explained by a – largely Jewish – section of the Austrian and Hungarian bourgeoisie. The modern way of understanding and discussing the game was invented in the coffee houses of Vienna.

△▽

Football boomed in Austria in the twenties, with the establishment of a two-tier professional league in 1924. That November the *Neues Wiener Journal* asked, 'Where else can you see at least 40–50,000 spectators gathering Sunday after Sunday at all the sports stadiums, rain or shine? Where else is a majority of the population so interested in the results of games that in the evening you can hear almost every other person talking about the results of the league matches and the club's prospects for the coming games?' The answer was easy: Britain aside, nowhere else in Europe.

But where in Britain the discussion of games took place in the pub, in Austria it took place in the coffee house. In Britain football had begun as a pastime of the public schools, but by the 1930s it had become a resolutely working-class sport; in central Europe, it had followed a more complex arc, introduced by the Anglophile upper middle classes, rapidly adopted by the working classes, and then, although the majority of the players remained working class, seized upon by intellectuals.

Football in central Europe was an almost entirely urban phenomenon, centred around Vienna, Budapest and Prague, and it was in those cities that coffee-house culture was at its strongest. The coffee house flourished towards the end of the Habsburg Empire, becoming a public salon, a place where men and women of all classes mingled, but which became particularly noted for its artistic, bohemian aspect. People would read the newspapers there; pick up mail and laundry; play cards and chess. Political candidates used them as venues for meetings and debates, while intellectuals and their acolytes would discuss the great affairs of the day: art, literature, drama and, increasingly in the twenties, football.

Each club had its own café, where players, supporters, directors and writers would mix. Fans of Austria Vienna, for instance, met in the Café Parsifal; Rapid fans in the Café Holub. The hub of the football scene in the inter-war years, though, was the Ring Café. It had been the hang-out of the anglophile cricket community, but by 1930 it was the centre of the broader football community. It was, according to a piece written in *Welt am Montag* after the war, 'a kind of revolutionary parliament of the friends and fanatics of football; one-sided club interest could not prevail because just about every Viennese club was present.'

The impact of football on the wider culture is made clear by the career of the Rapid centre-forward Josef Uridil. He came from the suburbs – in the Vienna of the time edgy, working-class districts – and his robust style of play was celebrated as exemplifying the proletarian roots of the club. He was the first football hero of the coffee house, and, in 1922, became the subject of a song by the noted cabaret artist Hermann Leopoldi, '*Heute spielt der Uridil*', which was so successful that it spread his fame even to those with no interest in football. He began advertising a range of products from soap to fruit juice and, by February 1924, he was appearing as a compère at a music hall while at the same time *Pflicht und Ehre*, a film in which he appeared as himself, was showing in cinemas.

It was into that environment that Hugo Meisl's *Wunderteam* exploded. The trend through the late twenties was upward and, despite a poor start, Austria narrowly missed out on the inaugural Dr Gerö Cup, a thirty-month league tournament also featuring Czechoslovakia, Hungary, Italy and Switzerland. After losing three of their opening four games, they hammered Hungary 5-1 and the eventual winners Italy 3-0, finishing runners-up by a point. In the Ring, they weren't satisfied, and agitated for the selection of Matthias Sindelar, a gifted, almost cerebral, forward from Austria Vienna, a club strongly associated with the Jewish bourgeoisie.

He was a new style of centre-forward, a player of such slight stature that he was nicknamed '*Der Papierene*' – 'the Paper-man'.

There was an air of flimsy genius about him that led writers to compare his creativity to theirs: a fine sense of timing and of drama, a flair for both the spontaneous and the well-crafted. In his 1978 collection *Die Erben der Tante Jolesch*, Friedrich Torberg, one of the foremost of the coffee-house writers, wrote that: 'He was endowed with such an unbelievable wealth of variations and ideas that one could never really be sure which manner of play was to be expected. He had no system, to say nothing of a set pattern. He just had ... genius.'

Hugo Meisl, though, was doubtful. He had given Sindelar his international debut as a twenty-three year old in 1926 but, for all that he stood in the vanguard of the new conception of football, Meisl was, at heart, a conservative. Everything he did tactically could be traced back to a nostalgic attempt to recreate the style of the Rangers tourists of 1905: he insisted on the pattern-weaving mode of passing, ignored the coming of the third back, and retained a sense that a centre-forward should be a physical totem, somebody, in fact, like Uridil.

Uridil and Sindelar were both from Moravian immigrant families, both grew up in the suburbs and both became celebrities (Sindelar too played himself in a film and supplemented his footballer's income by advertising wrist-watches and dairy products), but they had little else in common. As Torberg put it, 'They can only be compared as regards popularity; in terms of technique, invention, skill, in short, in terms of culture, they were as different from each other as a tank from a wafer.'

Finally, in 1931, Meisl succumbed to the pressure and turned to Sindelar, installing him as a fixture in the team. The effects were extraordinary, and on 16 May 1931, Austria thrashed Scotland 5-0. Two-and-a-half years on from the Wembley Wizards' 5-1 demolition of England, Scotland found themselves just as outmanoeuvred by the same game, taken to yet greater heights. They were, admittedly, without any Rangers or Celtic players, fielded seven debutants and lost Daniel Liddle to an early injury, while Colin McNab played on as a virtual passenger after suffering a blow to the head towards the end of the first half, but the *Daily Record* was in no doubt what it had witnessed: 'Outclassed!' it roared. 'There can be no excuses'. Only the heroics of John Jackson, the goalkeeper, prevented an even greater humiliation.

Given England had been beaten 5-2 by France in Paris two days earlier, that week now seems to stand as a threshold, as the moment at which it became impossible to deny the rest of the world had caught up with Britain (not that that stopped the British newspapers and football authorities trying). The *Arbeiter-Zeitung* caught the mood perfectly. 'If there was an elegiac note in watching the decline of the ideal the Scots represented for us, even yesterday, it was all the more refreshing to witness a triumph that sprang from true artistry,' it wrote. 'Eleven footballers, eleven professionals – certainly, there are more important sides to life, yet this was ultimately a tribute to Viennese aesthetic sense, imagination and passion.'

For the *Wunderteam*, that was just the beginning. Playing a traditional 2-3-5 with an elegant attacking centre-half in Josef Smistik – but with an unorthodox centre-forward who encouraged such fluidity that their system became known as 'the Danubian Whirl' – Austria won nine and drew two of their next eleven games, scoring forty-four goals and winning the second edition of the Dr Gerö Cup in the process. The coffee houses were jubilant: their way of doing things had prevailed, largely because of Sindelar, a player who was, to their self-romanticising eye, the coffee house made flesh. 'He would play football as a grandmaster plays chess: with a broad mental conception, calculating moves and countermoves in advance, always choosing the most promising of all possibilities,' the theatre critic Alfred Polgar wrote in his obituary in the *Pariser Tageszeitung*, an article remarkable for how many fundamental themes it drew together.

There was the analogy to chess Galeano had used to describe the Uruguayans of the twenties and, later still, Anatoliy Zelentsov would apply to Valeriy Lobanovskyi's Dynamo Kyiv. The influence of Hogan and his obsession with the instant control of the ball was apparent, as Polgar went on: 'He was an unequalled trapper of a ball, and a stager of surprise counter-attacks, inexhaustibly devising tactical feints which were followed by the true attacking move that his deception had made irresistible, the opponents having been cunningly fooled by a flash of skill.'

And, then, perhaps most strikingly, he pre-empts the thinking of the evolutionary biologist Stephen Jay Gould on 'the universality of excellence'. 'I don't deny the differences in style and substance between athletic and conventional scholarly performance,' Gould wrote, 'but we surely err in regarding sports as a domain of brutish intuition... The greatest athletes cannot succeed by bodily gifts alone... One of the most intriguing, and undeniable, properties of great athletic performance lies in the impossibility of regulating certain central skills by overt mental deliberation: the required action simply doesn't grant sufficient time for the sequential processing of conscious decisions.' 'In a way he had brains in his legs,' Polgar said of Sindelar, 'and many remarkable and unexpected things occurred to them while they were running. Sindelar's shot hit the back of the net like the perfect punch-line, the ending that made it possible to understand and appreciate the perfect composition of the story, the crowning of which it represented.'

And then, in December 1932, came the *Wunderteam*'s greatest test: England. They were not the best side in the world, far from it, but the world respected them for their influence over the development of the game and, at home, they remained unbeaten against foreign opposition. Spain had exposed England's vulnerability by beating them in Madrid in 1929, but two years later they felt the full force of the backlash, being hammered 7-1 at Highbury. Buoyed by the victory over Scotland, many in Austria were exuberantly hopeful, but Meisl, who always tended to pessimism, was concerned, and turned to his old friend and mentor, Jimmy Hogan.

Disenchanted with England, Hogan had moved to Switzerland in 1921, spending three years with Young Boys of Berne and then Lausanne, before returning to Budapest with MTK, in their new guise as FC Hungária. He then moved to Germany, working as an advisor to the football federation, coaching SC Dresden – where one of his pupils was Helmut Schön, who was assistant to Sepp Herberger when West Germany won the World Cup in 1954, and led them to victory himself in 1974 – and generally evangelising for a technically adept style of football that would ensure English football was soon overhauled by Europe.

He was initially greeted with suspicion and, when various local coaches complained about his lack of fluency in German, the German FA asked Hogan to prove himself by delivering a lecture without a translator. It began badly, as Hogan inadvertently presented himself as 'a professor of languages, not a master of football', and got steadily worse. Attempting to stress the importance of the mind in football, he told his bemused audience that it was a game not merely of the body, but also of the committee. Faced with laughter and derision, Hogan called for a ten-minute intermission and left the stage. When he returned, he was wearing his Bolton Wanderers kit. He removed his boots and his socks and, telling his audience that three-quarters of German players could not kick the ball properly, smashed a right-footed shot barefoot into a wooden panel 15 yards away. As the ball bounced back to him he noted the value of being two-footed and let fly with another shot, this time with his left foot. This time the panel split in two. His point proved, Hogan undertook a lecture tour, in one month alone speaking to 5,000 footballers in the Dresden area. When he died in 1974, the then secretary of the German Football Federation (DFB), Hans Passlack, wrote to Hogan's son, Frank, saying that Hogan was the founder of 'modern football' in Germany.

Uneasy about the political situation, Hogan left Germany for Paris, sewing his savings into the seams of his plus-fours to avoid restrictions on the export of currency, but he struggled to maintain discipline there among a team of stars and returned to Lausanne, where he never came to terms with a chairman who believed that players should be fined for missing chances. When Meisl came calling, he was desperate for a challenge.

Austria, it must be said, seem to have been in need of him, or at least in need of some outside confirmation of their talents. A fortnight before the game in London, with Sindelar unwell and playing far below his best, Austria had struggled to beat a scratch Vienna side 2-1. Nerves, evidently, were an issue, while there were fitness concerns over Adolf Vogl and Friedrich Gschweidl. Nonetheless, Austria was agog. Crowds gathered in the Heldenplatz to listen to commentary relayed over three loudspeakers, while the Parliamentary Finance Committee adjourned a sitting to listen to the game.

The *Wunderteam* did not begin well, and within twenty-six minutes England were two up, both goals coming from the Blackpool forward Jimmy Hampson. Austria pulled one back six minutes into the second half, Sindelar and Anton Schall combining to set up Karl Zischek. Walter Nausch hit a post amid a welter of pressure, but then, as England rallied, an Eric Houghton free-kick deflected off the ducking Schall and past Rudi Hiden in the Austria goal. Sindelar, with consummate control and a cool finish made it 3-2, but almost as soon as he had done so a long-range effort from Sam Crooks put England back in charge. With England baffled by their opponents' habit of dropping behind the ball when out of possession, Austria continued to dominate, spinning their webs of passes, but their lack of thrust was to cost them. Zischek bundled in a corner with five minutes remaining, but it was too late. They lost 4-3, but their performance captured the imagination. 'A revelation,' said the *Daily Mail*, while *The Times* awarded Austria the 'moral victory' and rhapsodised about their 'passing skills'.

Two years later, what was essentially the Austria national team played Arsenal at Highbury, although they were presented as a Vienna XI, matches between club and national sides being frowned upon by Fifa at the time. They lost 4-2, prompting Roland Allen to write in the *Evening Standard* that, 'It looks fine, it is fine: when the Austrians have learned how to turn all their cleverness into something that counts: when ... they have organised the winning of football matches as highly as they have organised the taming of a football, they will make [everyone] sit up and take notice.' The writing was on the wall, but nobody in England was minded to read it.

Instead the two games were taken as confirmation of the cliché that continental European teams lack punch in the final third. Applied to the Austrians, there was a certain truth to it, but the wider point about ball retention was obscured, a situation that wasn't helped by Meisl's habit of talking in idealistic terms. 'To us Middle Europeans,' he said, 'the attacking play of the British professional, seen from an aesthetic point of view, seems rather poor. Such play consists of assigning the job of scoring goals to the centre-forward and the wings, while to the inside-forwards is allotted the task of linking attackers and defenders, and more as half-backs than as attacking players... The centre-forward, who, among us in Europe, is the leading figure, because of his technical excellence and tactical intelligence, in England limits his activity to exploiting the errors of the opposing defence.'

He did, though, laud the pace at which the British played the game, saying it had left his own players 'confused and disoriented': 'Although their passing, swift and high, is rather lacking in precision, the English players compensate for this by the rare potency and great rapidity of their attacks.' The familiar battle-lines were drawn: England, physical, quick and tough; the continent, technical, patient and probably lacking in moral fibre.

Austria finally enjoyed the victory over England Meisl so craved in Vienna in May 1936. When he presented his team to Hogan, the Englishman questioned the stamina of the inside-forwards, to which Meisl replied that he expected to take a decisive lead in the first twenty minutes, and spend the rest of the game defending it. He was right. Sindelar repeatedly dragged the centre-half John Barker out of position – foreshadowing Harry Johnston's travails against Hungary's Nándor Hidegkuti seventeen years later – and England soon found themselves two down. George Camsell pulled one back early in the second half but, for all Meisl's bowler-hatted nervousness on the touchline, Austria's superiority was obvious. 'We didn't know whether we were coming or going,' Jack Crayston admitted. 'And it was disgustingly hot.' When the heat makes manic charging unsustainable and prioritises possession, British teams have never prospered.

By then, though, the *Wunderteam* was in decline, and the Austrians had ceded their European supremacy to Italy. In terms of formation, the Italians – almost inadvertently – took up a middle ground between the English W-M and the 2-3-5 of the Danubians, but what set them apart was their ethos. 'Technically less brilliant than its European rival,' Glanville wrote, Italian football 'compensated ... by its greater forcefulness and the excellent physical condition of its players'. A belief in the primacy of athleticism was perhaps natural under fascism, but it corresponded too to the inclinations of Vittorio Pozzo, the bushy-haired visionary who became the presiding genius of inter-war Italian football.

Born near Turin in 1886, Pozzo had shown great promise as a runner, winning the 400m at the Piedmont Student Games, but was converted to football after a friend of his, Giovanni Goccione, who would go on to play at centre-half for Juventus, mocked him for 'running like a motor car' and suggested he should try running with 'a ball in front of him'. No great player, Pozzo remained in academia, studying at the International School of Commerce in Zurich, where he learnt English, French and German, and then in London. Tiring of the ex-pat community in the capital, he moved north to Bradford, where his father's influence found him a post studying the manufacture of wool. England, and football, suddenly gripped him. So determined did he become to understand his new home that, although a Catholic, he began to attend Anglican services. His weeks soon fell into the English routine: church on Sunday, work for five days, football on Saturday. His parents recalled him to help with his brother's engineering firm, but he refused. His father cut off his allowance, but still he stayed, making ends meet by teaching languages.

Manchester United became Pozzo's favourite team, largely because of the style of their fabled half-back line of Dick Duckworth, Charlie Roberts and Alec Bell. He took to hanging around by the players' exit at Old Trafford after matches and, one week, having finally plucked up the courage, he approached Roberts, told him what an admirer he was and said how much he would appreciate the opportunity to talk with him about the game. It was the start of a lengthy friendship, from which grew the style Pozzo would have his Italy side play twenty years later. He abhorred the third-back game, and demanded his centre-half, like Roberts, be capable of sweeping long passes out to the wings. It was a belief he held fundamental and led, for instance, to his decision, having been reappointed *comisario tecnico* in 1924, immediately to drop Fulvio Bernadini, an idol of the Roman crowds, because he was a 'carrier' rather than a 'dispatcher'.

Pozzo finally went back to Italy to attend the marriage of his sister, after which his family prevented him from returning to England. He soon found a position as secretary of the Italian Football Federation, and was asked to take the national team to Sweden for the 1912 Olympics, becoming *comisario tecnico* for the first time. Having lost narrowly to Finland and then beaten Sweden, Italy were hammered 5-1 by Austria. The defeat was disappointing, if not unexpected, but was significant in precipitating a first meeting between Pozzo and Meisl. They became friends, and would be rivals for the rest of their lives.

Pozzo stood down after a 3-1 defeat to Austria the following December and resumed his travels. He served as a major in the Alpine Regiment during the First World War, and was made *comisario tecnico* for the second time following a 4-0 defeat to Austria shortly before the 1924 Olympics. They showed promise in Paris, beating Spain and Luxembourg before a narrow defeat to Switzerland, but Pozzo's wife died soon after, and he resigned again. For five years he served as a director of Pirelli, spending his spare time walking with his Alsatian in the mountains. Then, in

1929, the Italian Federation came calling again. He served for twenty years, turning Italy into the best side in Europe and probably the world.

When Pozzo had taken the job the first time, he had found a bloated league of sixty-four clubs, several of whom disestablished from the federation when he tried to form a more streamlined first division. By the time of his third coming, there was a professional league and the fascist government, having recognised the utility of sport as a propaganda tool, was eagerly investing in stadiums and infrastructure. 'Whether beyond or within the borders, sporting or not, we Italians ... shook and still shake with joy when seeing in these thoroughbred athletes, that overwhelm so many noble opponents, such a symbol of the overwhelming march of Mussolini's Italians,' as Londo Ferretti, Mussolini's press officer, put it in *Lo Sport Fascista* after Italy's 1938 World Cup triumph.

The level to which Pozzo bought into fascist ideology remains unclear. His associations with Mussolini led to him being shunned in the fifties and sixties and meant that the Stadio delle Alpi, the stadium built just outside Turin for the 1990 World Cup, was not named after him, but later in the nineties evidence emerged to suggest he had worked with the anti-fascist resistance, taking food to partisans around Biella and helping the escape of Allied prisoners of war.

What is certainly true is that he made full use of the prevailing militarism to dominate and motivate his side. 'More than one selector leads to compromise,' he said, 'and no great football team was ever built on that.' He was an astute man-manager, developing a stern, paternalistic style to deal with players often idolised by fans of their clubs. He would, for instance, referee all practice games played in training, and if he felt a player had refused to pass to a team-mate because of some private grudge, he would send him off. If he picked two players who were known not to get on, he would force them to room together. It was his nationalism, though, that was most controversial. On the way to Budapest for a friendly against Hungary that Italy won 5-0, to take just one example, he made his players visit the First World War battlefields of Oslavia and Gorizia, stopping at the monumental cemetery at Redupiglia. 'I told them it was good that the sad and terrible spectacle might have struck them: that whatever would be asked of us on that occasion was nothing compared with those that had lost their lives on those surrounding hills,' he wrote in his autobiography. At other times, he would march at the head of his players singing '*Il Piave*'.

For all that, Pozzo was Anglophile enough to hark back to a golden age of fair play, fretting about the deleterious effects of the win-bonuses that soon became a feature of the national league. 'It is win at all costs,' he said. 'It is the bitter grudge against the adversary, it is the preoccupation of the result to the ends of the league table.' He inclined, similarly, to a classical 2-3-5, but he lacked a centre-half of sufficient mobility and creativity to play the formation well. Pozzo turned instead to Luisito Monti, who had played for Argentina in the 1930 World Cup. He joined Juventus in 1931, and became one of the *oriundi*, the South American players who, thanks to Italian heritage, qualified to play for their adopted country. Already thirty when he signed, Monti was overweight and, even after a month of solitary training, was not quick. He was, though, fit, and became known as '*Doble ancho*' ('Double-wide') for his capacity to cover the ground. Pozzo, perhaps influenced by a formation that had already come into being at Juventus, used him as a *centro mediano*, a halfway house – not quite Charlie Roberts, but certainly not Herbie Roberts either. He would drop when the other team had possession and mark the opposing centre-forward, but would advance and become an attacking fulcrum when his side had the ball. Although he was not a third back – Glanville, in fact, says it was only in 1939 with an article Bernardini wrote after Pozzo's side had drawn 2-2 against England in Milan that the full implications of the W-M (the *sistema*, as Pozzo called it, as opposed to the traditional *metodo*) were fully appreciated in Italy – he played deeper than a traditional centre-half, and so the two inside-forwards retreated to support the wing-halves. The shape was thus a 2-3-2-3, a W-W. At the time it seemed, as the journalist Mario Zappa put it in *La Gazzetta della Sport*, 'a model of play that is the synthesis of the best elements of all the most admired systems.'

Shape is one thing, style is another, and Pozzo, despite his qualms, was fundamentally pragmatic. That he had a technically accomplished side is not in doubt, as they proved, before Monti had been called into the side, in a 3-0 victory over Scotland in 1931. 'The men are fast,' the *Corriere della Sera* reported of the hapless tourists, 'athletically well prepared, and seem sure enough in kicking and heading, but in classic play along the ground, they look like novices.' That would be stern enough criticism for any side, but for players brought up in the finest pattern-weaving traditions, it is damning.

Back then, the great centre-forward Giuseppe Meazza, who had made his debut in 1930, was regularly compared to a bull-fighter, while a popular song of the time claimed 'he scored to the rhythm of the foxtrot'. That sense of fun and élan, though, was soon to fade. Meazza remained a stylish forward, and there was no doubting the quality of the likes of Silvio Piola, Raimundo Orsi and Gino Colaussi, but physicality and combativeness became increasingly central. 'In the tenth year of the fascist era,' an editorial in *Lo Stadia* noted in 1932, 'the youth are toughened for battle, and for the fight, and more for the game itself; courage, determination, gladiatorial pride, chosen sentiments of our race, cannot be excluded.'

Pozzo was also one of the earliest exponents of man-marking, a sign that football had become not merely about a side playing its own game, but about stopping the opposition playing theirs. In a friendly against Spain in Bilbao in 1931, for instance, he had Renato Cesarini mark Ignacío Aguirrezabala on the logic that 'if I succeeded in cutting off the head with which the eleven adversaries thought, the whole system would collapse'.

That raised concerns among the purists, but it was at the 1934 World Cup that questions really began to be asked about the ethics of Pozzo's Italy. Having drawn 1-1 with England – who were still persisting in their policy of isolation – a year earlier, Italy, playing at home, were always going to be among the favourites, particularly given the sense that the *Wunderteam* was past its peak. For once Meisl's pessimism seemed justified as he complained of the absence of Hiden, his goalkeeper, and of players exhausted by foreign tours with their club sides, although he also claimed, apparently accepting the English criticism that his side lacked punch, that if he could have borrowed the Arsenal centre-forward Cliff Bastin, they could have walked to victory.

Italy and Austria, Pozzo and Meisl, met in the semi-final, but by then the tournament had already begun to slink into disrepute. Austria were far from innocent, having been involved in a brawl in their quarter-final victory over Hungary, but it was the 1-1 draw between Italy and Spain at the same stage that marked the descent of the tournament into violence. Monti, for all his ability, was quite prepared to indulge in the darker arts, while Ricardo Zamora, the Spain goalkeeper, was battered so frequently that he was unable to play in the replay the following day. Sources vary on whether three or four Spaniards were forced to leave the field through injury, but whichever, Spain were left feeling aggrieved as a diving header from Meazza gave Italy a 1-0 win.

The anticipated clash of styles in the semi-final was a damp squib. Sindelar was marked out of the game by Monti, Austria failed to have shot in the first forty minutes, and Italy won by a single goal, Meazza bundling into Hiden's replacement, Peter Platzer, and Enrique Guaita, another of the *oriundi*, forcing the loose ball over the line. It was left to Czechoslovakia, who had beaten Germany in the other semi, to defend the honour of the Danubian School. At times they threatened to embarrass Italy, and took a seventy-sixth minute lead through Antonín Puc. Frantisek Svoboda hit a post and Jirí Sobotka missed another fine chance but, with eight minutes remaining, Orsi equalised with a drive that swerved freakishly past Frantisek Plánicka. Seven minutes into extra-time, a limping Meazza crossed from the right, Guaita helped it on and Angelo Schiavio, who later spoke of having been driven by 'the strength of desperation', beat Josef Ctyroky to fire in the winner. Mussolini's Italy had the victory it so desired, but elsewhere the strength of that desire and the methods to which they were prepared to stoop to achieve it left a sour taste. 'In the majority of countries the world championship was called a sporting fiasco,' the Belgian referee John Langenus said, 'because beside the will to win all sporting considerations were non-existent and because, moreover, a certain spirit brooded over the whole championship.'

A meeting with England that November – the so-called 'Battle of Highbury' – only confirmed the impression, as Italy reacted badly after Monti broke a bone in his foot in a second-minute challenge with Ted Drake. 'For the first quarter of an hour there might just as well not have been a ball on the pitch as far as the Italians were concerned,' said Stanley Matthews. 'They were like men possessed, kicking anything and everything that moved.' England capitalised on their indiscipline to take a 3-0 lead, but after Pozzo had calmed his side at half-time, they played stirringly to come back to 3-2 in the second half.

Italy 1 Austria 0, World Cup semi-final, San Siro, Milan, 3 June 1934

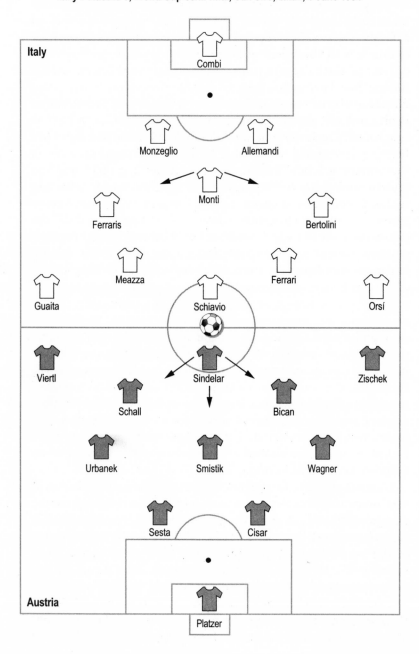

Beneath the aggression and the cynicism, Italy were unques-
tionably talented, and they retained the World Cup in 1938 with
what Pozzo believed was his best side. Again, the focus was on
defensive solidity. 'The big secret of the Italian squad is its capacity
to attack with the fewest amount of men possible, without ever
distracting the half-backs from their defensive work,' Zappa wrote.
Austria had been subsumed by Germany by then, but a team
formed by the two semi-finalists of the previous competition fared
poorly, and lost after a replay to Karl Rappan's Switzerland in the
first round. Czechoslovakia went out to Brazil in the last eight, but
Hungary progressed to the final for the last showdown between
the Danubian School and Pozzo. Italy proved too quick and too
athletic and, with Michele Andreolo, another *oriundo* who had
replaced Monti as the *centro mediano*, keeping a check on György
Sárosi, the Hungarian centre-forward, Meisl's conception of the
game was made to look sluggish and old-fashioned. It did not pass
without lament – 'How shall we play the game?' the French
journalist Jean Eskenazi asked. 'As though we are making love or
catching a bus?' – but pass it did.

△▽

As Sindelar reached the end of his career and with Meisl ageing,
the Danubian style of football may have faded away anyway, but
political developments made sure of it. With the Anschluss came
the end of the central European Jewish intelligentsia, the end of
the spirit of the coffee house and the death of Sindelar. As the
thirties went on, the great centre-forward had increasingly
withdrawn from the national team, but he allowed himself to be
picked for what was dubbed a 'Reconciliation Game' between an
Ostmark XI and an all-German line-up on 3 April 1938.

Football in Germany was not so advanced as in Austria, but it
was improving. Otto Nerz, first national coach, who was appointed
on 1 July 1926, was an early advocate of the W-M, but something of
Hogan's teaching lived on through Schalke 04, who reached nine
of the ten championship playoff finals between 1933 and 1942,
winning six. Their coach, Gustav Wieser, was an Austrian, and
under him they practised a version of the whirl that became
known as '*der Kreisel*' – the spinning-top. According to the defender
Hans Bornemann, it was not the man with the ball, but those out
of possession running into space who determined the direction of

their attacks. 'It was only when there was absolutely nobody left you could pass the ball to that we finally put it into the net,' he said. Hogan may have admired their style, but he would have questioned their ethos.

Such excess troubled Nerz, and he refused to pick both Schalke's feted inside-forwards, Ernst Kuzorra and Fritz Szepan, for the national team. (He did, in fact, call up Szepan for the 1934 World Cup, but bafflingly played him at centre-half.) 'Nerz,' Kuzorra explained, 'said to me: "Let me tell you something: your odds and ends football at Schalke, all that passing around, doesn't impress me one bit. If you and Szepan play together it'll just be fiddling and dribbling around."'

Germany were semi-finalists in Italy in 1934, which encouraged thoughts that they might win gold on home soil at the 1936 Olympics. Instead they lost, humiliatingly, 2-0 to Norway in what, unfortunately for Nerz, was the only football match Hitler ever attended.

Sepp Herberger, an assistant to Nerz and the man who would lead West Germany to victory at the 1954 World Cup, was not at the game, having gone to watch Italy play Japan in another quarter-final. He was eating a dinner of knuckle of pork and sauerkraut at the team camp when another coach brought him news of Germany's defeat. Herberger pushed his plate away and never touched knuckle of pork again. He succeeded Nerz after the tournament, and immediately switched to a more Danubian model, bringing in Adolf Urban and Rudi Gellesch from Schalke and deploying the elegant, hard-drinking Mannheim inside-forward Otto Siffling as a central striker. The result was a team of greater flexibility that reached its peak on 16 May 1937 with an 8-0 friendly victory over Denmark in Breslau (what is now Wroclaw). 'The robot style people like to pin on Germany sank into the realm of legend,' the journalist Gerd Krämer wrote. 'Artistic football triumphed.'

Still, they were neither as talented nor as artistic as the Austrians, and the Ostmark dominated the reconciliation game. Fact has become rather obscured by subsequent myths, but what is clear is that Sindelar missed a series of chances in the first half. Given how frequently he rolled the ball a fraction wide of the posts, even contemporary reports wondered whether he had been mocking the Germans – and supposed orders not to score – by missing on purpose. Eventually, midway through the second half, he knocked in a rebound, and when his friend Schasti Sesta looped a second from a free-kick, he celebrated by dancing in front of a directors' box packed with high-ranking Nazis.

In the months that followed, Sindelar, who never made any secret of his Social Democratic leanings, repeatedly refused to play for Sepp Herberger's united German team. In the August he bought a café from Leopold Drill, a Jew forced to give it up under new legislation – paying DM20,000, which was either a very fair price or disgracefully opportunistic, depending which account you choose to believe – and was censured by the authorities for his reluctance to put up Nazi posters. To claim he was a dissident, though, as some have done, is to take things too far.

On the morning of 23 January 1939, his friend Gustav Hartmann, looking for Sindelar, broke down the door of a flat on Annagasse. He found him, naked and dead, lying alongside the unconscious form of his girlfriend of ten days, Camilla Castignola. She died later in hospital, the victim, like Sindelar, of carbon monoxide poisoning caused by a faulty heater.

Or at least that was what the police said, as they ended their enquiries after two days. The public prosecutor, though, had still not reached a conclusion six months later when the Nazi authorities ordered the case be closed. In a 2003 BBC documentary, Egon Ulbrich, a friend of Sindelar, claimed a local official was bribed to record his death as an accident, which ensured that he would receive a state funeral. Others came up with their own explanations. On 25 January, a piece in the Austrian newspaper *Kronen Zeitung* claimed that 'everything points towards this great man having become the victim of murder through poisoning'. In his 'Ballad on the Death of a Footballer', Torberg suggested suicide by a man who felt 'disowned' by 'the new order'. There were later suggestions that Sindelar or Castignola or both were Jewish. It is true that Sindelar played for Austria Vienna, the club of the Jewish bourgeoisie, and had been born in Moravia, from where many Jews had emigrated to the capital, but his family was Catholic. It is just about conceivable that Castignola, an Italian, may have had Jewish origins, but they were well-enough hidden that she had been allowed to become co-owner of a bar in the week before her death. Most tellingly, neighbours had complained a few days earlier that one of the chimneys in the block was defective.

The available evidence suggests Sindelar's death was an accident, and yet the sense that heroes cannot mundanely die prevailed. What, after all, at least to a romantic liberal mind, could better symbolise Austria at the point of the Anschluss than this athlete-artist, the darling of Viennese society, being gassed alongside his Jewish girlfriend? 'The good Sindelar followed the city, whose child and pride he was, to its death,' Polgar wrote in his obituary. 'He was so inextricably entwined with it that he had to die when it did. All the evidence points to suicide prompted by loyalty to his homeland. For to live and play football in the downtrodden, broken, tormented city meant deceiving Vienna with a repulsive spectre of itself... But how can one play football like that? And live, when a life without football is nothing?'

To its end, the football of the coffee house remained heroically romantic.

Chapter Five

△▽△▽△▽△▽△▽

Organised Disorder

△▽ The football boom came late to the USSR and, perhaps because of that, it rapidly took on a radical aspect, uninhibited by historically rooted notions of the 'right' way of doing things. British sailors had played the game by the docks in Odessa as early as the 1860s, a description in *The Hunter* magazine giving some idea of the chaos and physicality of the game. 'It is played by people with solid muscles and strong legs – a weak one would only be an onlooker in such a mess,' their reporter wrote, apparently both bemused and disapproving.

It was only in the 1890s that the sport began to be properly organised. In Russia, as in so many other places, the British had a decisive role, first in St Petersburg, and later in Moscow, where Harry Charnock, general manager of the Morozov Mills, established the club that would become Dinamo Moscow in an attempt to persuade his workers to spend their Saturdays doing something other than drinking vodka. When Soviet myth-making was at its height, it was said that the Dinamo sports club, which was controlled by the Ministry of the Interior and ran teams across the USSR, chose blue and white as their colours to represent water and air, the two elements without which man could not live. The truth is rather that Charnock was from Blackburn, and dressed his team in the same colours as the team he supported: Blackburn Rovers.

Further west, the influence was naturally more central European. Lviv was still part of the Austro-Hungarian Empire when, in 1894, it hosted the first football match played on what is now Ukrainian soil, a brief exhibition during a demonstration of sports by the Sokol Sports Club.

By the time a national league was established in 1936, the

British were long gone (the expatriate dominance of Soviet football ended in 1908 when Sport, a Russian team, won the Aspeden Cup, the local St Petersburg competition), but the early 2-3-5 lingered as the default. The modification of the offside law in 1925 seems to have made little difference tactically and, with the USSR's isolation from Fifa restricting meetings with foreign opposition largely to games against amateur sides, there was little to expose how far the Soviets were falling behind.

All that changed in 1937. The coming of the national league perhaps would have led to more sophisticated analysis of the game anyway, but the trigger for development was the arrival of a Basque side on the first leg of a world tour aimed at raising awareness of the Basque cause during the Spanish Civil War.

Because of their rarity, matches against foreign sides were always eagerly anticipated, all the more so in 1937 after the release the year before of *Vratar* (*The Keeper*), Semyon Timoshenko's hugely popular musical-comedy about a young working-class boy – played by the matinee idol Grigori Pluzhnik – selected for a local side to play against a touring team having been spotted catching a watermelon as it fell from a cart. Predictably, if ridiculously, after making a series of fine saves, the hero runs the length of the field in the final minute to score the winner. The film's most famous song rams home the obvious political allegory: 'Hey, keeper, prepare for the fight/ You are a sentry in the goal./ Imagine there is a border behind you.'

The real-life tourists, though, featuring six of the Spain squad from the 1934 World Cup, were no patsies for Soviet propaganda and, employing a W-M formation, hammered Lokomotiv 5-1 in their first game. Dinamo were then beaten 2-1 and, after a 2-2 draw against a Leningrad XI, the Basques returned to Moscow to beat the Dinamo Central Council's Select XI 7-4. Their final game in Russia saw them face Spartak, the reigning champions. Determined to end the embarrassment, the head of Spartak's coaching council, Nikolai Starostin, called up a number of players from other clubs, including the Dynamo Kyiv forwards Viktor Shylovskyi and Konstantyn Shchehotskyi, who had starred in a Kyiv Select XI's 6-1 victory over Red Star Olympic – a rare game against professionals – on a tour of Paris in 1935.

Starostin decided to match the Basques shape-for-shape, converting his centre-half into a third back to try to restrict the influence of Isodro Langara, the Basque centre-forward. As Starostin records in his book *Beginnings of Top-level Football*, the move was far from popular, with the most vocal opponent being the centre-half, his brother Andrei. '"Do you want me to be famous across the whole Soviet Union?" he asked. "You are denying me room to breathe! Who will help the attack? You are destroying the tactic that has been played out for years..."'

This was not, though, Spartak's first experiment with a third back. A couple of years earlier, injuries on a tour of Norway had forced them to tinker with their usual 2-3-5. 'Spartak used a defensive version of the W-M by enhancing the two backs with a half-back,' Alexander Starostin, another of the brothers, said. 'When necessary, both the insides drew back.' Impressed by the possibilities of the system, Spartak briefly continued the third-back experiment as they prepared for the 1936 spring season. 'That thought, brave but unpopular in the country, was ditched after a 5-2 defeat to Dinamo [Moscow] in a friendly,' Nikolai Starostin said. 'Now came the second attempt, again in a friendly, but this time in a very important international encounter. It was a huge risk.'

And not just from a sporting point of view. The authorities took the game so seriously that in the build-up, Ivan Kharchenko, the chairman of the Committee of Physical Culture, Alexander Kosarev, the head of Comsomol (the organisation of young Communists) and various other party officials slept at Spartak's training base at Tarasovka. 'Spartak was the last hope,' Nikolai Starostin wrote in his autobiography, *Football Through the Years*. 'All hell broke loose! There were letters, telegrams, calls giving us advice and wishing us good luck. I was summoned to several bosses of different ranks and they explained that the whole of the country was waiting on our victory.'

The day did not begin auspiciously, as Spartak were caught in a traffic-jam, causing the kick-off to be delayed. Twice in the first half they took the lead, only for the Basques to level but, after Shylovskyi had converted a controversial fifty-seventh-minute penalty, they ran away with it, Vladimir Stepanov completing a hat-trick in a 6-2 win. Nikolai Starostin later insisted his brother's performance in an unfamiliar role had been 'brilliant', although the newspapers and the goalkeeper, Anatoly Akimov, disagreed, pointing out that Langara had dominated him in the air and scored one of the Basque goals.

That defeat proved an aberration. The Basques went on to beat Dynamo Kyiv, Dinamo Tbilisi and a team representing Georgia, prompting a furious piece in *Pravda*. Under the demanding headline 'Soviet Players should become Invincible', it laid down what had become obvious: 'The performances of Basque Country in the USSR showed that our best teams are far from high quality... The deficiencies of Soviet football are particularly intolerable as there are no young people like ours in other countries, young people embraced by the care, attention and love of the party and government.'

Amid the bombast, there was some sense. 'It is clear,' the piece went on, 'that improving the quality of the Soviet teams depends directly on matches against serious opponents. The matches against the Basques have been highly beneficial to our players (long passes, playing on the flanks, heading the ball).'

Four days later, the Basques rather proved *Pravda*'s point by completing the Soviet leg of their tour with a 6-1 victory over a Minsk XI. The lessons of the Basques, though, were not forgotten. It took time for the calls for increased involvement in international sport to be heeded, but it had been recognised that the W-M offered a number of intriguing possibilities.

The man who seized upon them most eagerly was Boris Arkadiev. Already highly regarded, he gradually established himself as the first great Soviet theorist of football. His 1946 book, *Tactics of Football*, was for years regarded as a bible for coaches across Eastern Europe.

Born in St Petersburg in 1899, Arkadiev moved to Moscow after the Revolution, where, alongside a respectable playing career, he taught fencing at the Mikhail Frunze Military Academy. It was fencing, he later explained, with its emphasis on parry-riposte, that convinced him of the value of counter-attacking. Having led Metallurg Moscow, one of the capital's smaller clubs, to third in the inaugural Supreme League in 1936, Arkadiev took charge of Dinamo Moscow, who had won that first title. There, his restless mind and fertile imagination – not to mention his habit of taking his players on tours of art galleries before big games – soon gained him a reputation for eccentric brilliance. His first season brought the league and cup double, but he had to rethink his tactics as the lessons of the Basques revolutionised Soviet football.

'After the Basque tour, all the leading Soviet teams started to reorganise in the spirit of the new system,' Arkadiev wrote. 'Torpedo moved ahead of their opponents in that respect and, having the advantage in tactics, had a great first half of the season in 1938 and by 1939 all of our teams were playing with the new system.' The effect on Dinamo was baleful, as they slipped to fifth in 1938, and a lowly ninth the year after. With Lavrenty Beria, the notorious head of the KGB and the patron of the club, desperate for success, drastic action was required.

Others might have gone back to basics, but not Arkadiev: he took things further. He was convinced that the key was less the players he had than the way they were arranged, and so, in February 1940, at a pre-season training camp in the Black Sea resort of Gagry, he took the unprecedented step of spending a two-hour session teaching nothing but tactics. His aim, he said, was a refined variant of the W-M. 'With the third-back, lots of our and foreign clubs employed so-called roaming players in attack,' Arkadiev explained. 'This creative searching didn't go a long way, but it turned out to be a beginning of a radical *perestroika* in our football tactics. To be absolutely honest, some players started to roam for reasons that had nothing to do with tactics. Sometimes it was simply because he had great strength, speed or stamina that drew him out of his territorial area, and once he had left his home, he began to roam around the field. So you had four players [of the five forwards] who would hold an orthodox position and move to and fro in their channels, and then suddenly you would have one player who would start to disrupt their standard movements by running diagonally or left to right. That made it difficult for the defending team to follow him, and the other forwards benefited because they had a free team-mate to whom they could pass.'

The season began badly, with draws against Krylya Sovetov Moscow and Traktor Stalingrad and defeat at Dinamo Tbilisi, but Arkadiev didn't waver. The day after the defeat in Tbilisi, he gathered his players together, sat them down and made them write a report on their own performance and that of their team-mates. The air cleared, the players seemed suddenly to grasp Arkadiev's intentions. On 4 June, playing a rapid, close-passing style, Dinamo beat Dynamo Kyiv 8-5. They went on to win the return in Ukraine 7-0, and then, in the August, they hammered the defending champions Spartak 5-1. Their final seven games of the season brought seven wins, with twenty-six goals scored and just three conceded. 'Our players worked to move from a schematic W-M, to breathe the Russian soul into the English invention, to add our neglect of dogma,' Arkadiev said. 'We confused the opposition, leaving them without weaponry with our sudden movements. Our left-winger, Sergei Ilyin, scored most of his goals from the centre-forward position, our right-winger, Mikhail Semichastny, from inside-left and our centre-forward, Sergei Soloviov, from the flanks.'

The newspapers hailed the 'organised disorder', while opponents sought ways of combating it. The most common solution was to impose strict man-to-man marking, to which Arkadiev responded by having his players interchange positions even more frequently. 'With the transition of the defensive line from a zonal game to marking specific opponents,' he wrote, 'it became tactically logical to have all the attackers and even the midfielders roaming, while having all the defenders switch to a mobile system, following their opponents according to where they went.'

It is important here to clarify exactly what Arkadiev meant by a 'zonal game'. What he did not mean was the integrated system of 'zonal marking' that Zezé Moreira introduced in Brazil in the early fifties and that Viktor Maslov would later apply with such success at Dynamo Kyiv. He was speaking rather of the transition from the simple zonal game of the 2-3-5, in which one full-back would take the left-side and one the right, to the strict system of the W-M, in which each player knew clearly which player he was supposed to be marking (the right-back on the left-wing, the left-half on the inside-right, centre-back on centre-forward etc). In England this had happened almost organically as the W-M developed; with the W-M arriving fully formed in the USSR, there was, inevitably, a period of confusion as the defensive ramifications were taken on board.

Very gradually, one of the halves took on a more defensive role, providing extra cover in front of the back three, which in turn meant an inside-forward dropping to cover him. It was a slow process, and it would be taken further more quickly on the other side of the globe, but 3-2-2-3 was on the way to becoming 4-2-4. Axel Vartanyan, the esteemed historian of Soviet football, even believes it probable that Arkadiev was the first man to deploy a flat back four.

As war caused the dissolution of the league, Arkadiev left Dinamo for CDKA (the forerunner of CSKA) in 1943, and went on to win the championship five times before the club was disbanded as Stalin held them responsible for the USSR's defeat to Yugoslavia at the 1952 Olympics. Dinamo, meanwhile, continuing to apply Arkadiev's principles, beguiled Britain with their short-passing style – *passovotchka*, as it became known – as they came on a goodwill tour following the end of hostilities in 1945.

The build-up to their first game, against Chelsea at Stamford Bridge, was marked by political concerns and, more practically, fears that 'charging' might become as great a source of dispute as it had been for British sides on those early tours of South America. Chelsea were only eleventh in the Southern Division – a full resumption of the league programme still being several months away – and struggled to a fortuitous 3-3 draw, but their comparative lack of sophistication was clear. Just as Sindelar had tormented England by dropping deep, just as Nándor Hidegkuti would, so Konstantin Beskov bewildered Chelsea by refusing to operate in the area usually occupied by a forward.

The most striking aspect of Dinamo's play, though, was their energy, and the intelligence with which they used it. 'The Russians were on the move all the time,' the Chelsea left-back Albert Tennant complained. 'We could hardly keep up with them.' Davie Meiklejohn, the former Rangers captain, wrote in the *Daily Record*: 'They interchanged positions to the extent of the outside-left running over to the right-wing and vice versa. I have never seen football played like it. It was a Chinese puzzle to try to follow the players in their positions as it was given [*sic*] in the programme. They simply wandered here and there at will, but the most remarkable feature of it all, they never got in each other's way.'

As Dinamo went on to thrash Cardiff 10-1, beat Arsenal 4-3 and draw 2-2 at Rangers, appreciation of their methods became ever more effusive. In the *Daily Mail*, Geoffrey Simpson spoke of them playing 'a brand of football which, in class, style and effectiveness is way ahead of our own. As for its entertainment value – well, some of those who have been cheering their heads off at our league matches must wonder what they are shouting about.' The question then was, was their style related to ideology?

There was talk – again – of their football being like chess, and suggestions that much of Dinamo's football was based around

Chelsea 4 Dinamo Moscow 4, friendly, Stamford Bridge, London, 13 November 1945

pre-planned moves. It may be an easy metaphor to speak of
Communist football being built around the team as a unit with
the players mere cogs within it, as opposed to the British game
that allowed for greater self-expression, but that does not mean
there is no truth to it. Alex James, the former Arsenal inside-
forward, wrote in the *News of the World* that Dinamo's success 'lies
in teamwork to which there is a pattern. There is no individualist
in their side such as a [Stanley] Matthews or a [Raich] Carter. They
play to a plan, repeating it over and over again, and they show little
variation. It would be quite easy to find a counter-method to beat
them. This lack of an individualist is a great weakness.' Or maybe
their great individuals – and nobody would have denied that the
likes of Beskov, Vsevolod Bobrov and Vasili Kartsev were fine,
technically gifted players – simply utilised their gifts in a different
way.

Mikhail Yakushin, who had replaced Arkadiev as coach of
Dinamo, seemed just as keen to peddle the ideological line as the
British press. 'The principle of collective play is the guiding one in
Soviet football,' he said. 'A player must not only be good in general;
he must be good for the particular team.' What about Matthews?
'His individual qualities are high, but we put collective football
first and individual football second, so we do not favour his style
as we think teamwork would suffer,' Yakushin replied.

In Britain, this was a revolutionary thought, and it raises an
intriguing theory. Broadly speaking, although Bob McGory
attempted to replicate the *passovotchka* style at Stoke City to little
success – perhaps not surprisingly, given the presence of Matthews
in his side – the lessons of the Dinamo tour were ignored. Now,
given British football had ignored or patronised developments in
South America and central Europe, it is unlikely – even in the
revolutionary years immediately following the war – it would ever
have cast off its conservatism entirely, but it may have been more
open to innovation if it hadn't been blessed at the time with a glut
of great wingers. Why change a formation that allowed the likes of
Matthews, Tom Finney and Len Shackleton in England, or Willie
Waddell, Jimmy Delaney and Gordon Smith in Scotland, to give
full rein to their talents?

Matthews' finest hour, perhaps the high point of English wing-
play, came in the 1953 FA Cup final, when his jinks and feints
inspired Blackpool to come from 3-1 down to beat Bolton 4-3. Six

months later, on the same pitch, Hungary destroyed England 6-3, and the *Daily Mirror*'s headline proclaimed the 'Twilight of the (Soccer) Gods'. In terms of the reliance on wingers to provide the artistry, it was right.

The irony, of course, is that Herbert Chapman, the progenitor of the W-M, had been deeply suspicious of wing-play. His system, the first significant tactical development in the English game in almost half a century, had initially circumvented wingers, and yet it ended up being set in stone by them: the very aspect with which his innovation had done away returned to preclude further innovation. For managers with such players, sticking with the tried and tested was the logical thing to do. England's record in the years immediately following the war was good; they went almost two years without defeat from May 1947, a run that included a 10-0 demolition of Portugal in Estoril and a 4-0 victory over Italy, still the world champions, in Turin. Scotland's form was patchier, but even they could take comfort from six straight victories from October 1948. The problem was that the glister of those wingers ended up blinding Britain to the tactical advances being made elsewhere, and it would be eight years after the Dinamo tour before England's eyes were – abruptly – opened.

△▽△▽△▽△▽△▽

Chapter Six

The Hungarian Connection

△▽ The experience of the *Wunderteam* and Dinamo Moscow's *passovotchka* tour had intimated at the future, but it was only in 1953 that England finally accepted the reality that the continental game had reached a level of excellence for which no amount of sweat and graft could compensate.

The visit of the *Aranycsapat*, Hungary's 'Golden Squad', to Wembley on 25 November that year – the Olympic champions, unbeaten in three years, against the mother of football, who still considered herself supreme – was billed as 'the Match of the Century'. That might have been marketing hyperbole, but no other game has so resonated through the history of English football. England had lost to foreign opposition before – most humiliatingly to the USA in the World Cup three years earlier – but, other than a defeat to the Republic of Ireland at Goodison Park in 1949, never at home, where climate, conditions and refereeing offered no excuse. They had certainly never been so outclassed. Hungary's 6-3 victory was not the moment at which English decline began, but it was the moment at which it was recognised. Tom Finney, injured and watching from the press-box, was left reaching for the equine metaphor Gabriel Hanot had used thirty years earlier. 'It was,' he said, 'like cart-horses playing race-horses.'

For the first half of the twentieth century, both from a footballing and a political point of view, Hungary had existed in the shadow of Austria. Their thinking had, inevitably, been influenced by Hugo Meisl and the Danubian Whirl, but the crucial point was that it was *thinking*. In Budapest, as in Vienna, football was a matter for intellectual debate. Arthur Rowe, a former Tottenham player who took up a coaching position in Hungary before being forced home by the war, had lectured there on the W-M in 1940, but, given his later commitment to 'push-and-run', it is safe to imagine he focused on rather more subtle aspects of the system than simply the stopper centre-half that so dominated the thoughts of English coaches of the time.

Aside from the negativity to which it leant itself, the major effect of the prevailing conception of the W-M was to shape the preferred mode of centre-forward. Managers quickly tired of seeing dribblers and darters physically dominated by the close attentions of stopper centre-halves, and so turned instead to big battering-ram-style centre-forwards of the kind still referred to today in Britain as 'the classic No. 9'; 'the brainless bull at the gate' as Glanville characterised them. If Matthias Sindelar represented the cerebral central European ideal; it was Arsenal's Ted Drake – strong, powerful, brave and almost entirely unthinking – who typified the English view.

But just as there would have been no place for *Der Papierene* in England in the thirties, so beefy target-men were thin on the ground in 1940s Hungary. That was troublesome, for 2-3-5 had yielded to W-M in the minds of all but a few idealists: there was a need either for Hungary to start developing an English style of centre-forward, or to create a new system that retained the defensive solidity of the W-M without demanding a brawny focal point to the attack.

It was Márton Bukovi, the coach of MTK (or Vörös Lobogó as they became after nationalisation in 1949), who hit upon the solution after his 'tank', the Romania-born Norbert Höfling, was sold to Lazio in 1948. If you didn't have the right style of centre-forward, rather than trying to force unsuitable players into the position, he decided, it was better simply to do away with him altogether. He inverted the W of the W-M, creating what was effectively an M-M. Gradually, as the centre-forward dropped deeper and deeper to become an auxiliary midfielder, the two wingers pushed on, to create a fluid front four. 'The centre-forward was having increasing difficulties with a marker around his neck,' explained Nándor Hidegkuti, the man who tormented England from his deep-lying role at Wembley. 'So the idea emerged to play the No. 9 deeper where there was some space.

'At wing-half in the MTK side was a fine attacking player with very accurate distribution: Péter Palotás. Péter had never had a hard shot, but he was never expected to score goals, and though he wore the No. 9 shirt, he continued to play his natural game. Positioning himself in midfield, Péter collected passes from his defence, and simply kept his wingers and inside-forwards well supplied with passes... With Palotás withdrawing from centre-forward his play clashed with that of the wing-halves, so inevitably one was withdrawn to play a tight defensive game, while the other linked with Palotás as midfield foragers.'

Hidegkuti played as a winger for MTK so, logically enough, when Gusztáv Sebes decided to employ the system at national level, it was Palotás he picked as his withdrawn striker. He retained him through Hungary's Olympic triumph of 1952, when Hidegkuti played largely on the right, but that September, Palotás was substituted for Hidegkuti with Hungary 2-0 down in a friendly against Switzerland. Sebes had made the switch before, in friendlies against Italy and Poland, leading the radio commentator György Szepesi to conclude that he was experimenting to see whether Hidegkuti, by then thirty, was fit enough to fulfil the withdrawn role. Hungary came back to win 4-2, and so influential was Hidegkuti that his position became unassailable. 'He was a great player and a wonderful reader of the game,' said Ferenc Puskás. 'He was perfect for the role, sitting at the front of midfield, making telling passes, dragging the opposition defence out of shape and making fantastic runs to score himself.'

Hidegkuti was almost universally referred to as a withdrawn centre-forward, but the term is misleading, derived largely from his shirt number. He was, in modern terminology, simply an attacking midfielder. 'I usually took up my position around the middle of the field on [József] Zakariás' side,' he explained, 'while [József] Bozsik on the other flank often moved up as far as the opposition's penalty area, and scored quite a number of goals, too. In the front line the most frequent goalscorers were Puskás and [Sándor] Kocsis, the two inside-forwards, and they positioned themselves closer to the enemy goal than was usual with ... the W-M system... After a brief experience with this new framework Gusztav Sebes decided to ask the two wingers to drop back a little towards midfield, to pick up the passes to be had from Bozsik and myself, and this added the final touch to the tactical development.'

It was Hidegkuti, though, who destroyed England. Their players had, after all, grown up in a culture where the number denoted the position. The right-winger, the No. 7, lined up against the left-back, the No. 3; the centre-half, the No. 5, took care of the centre-forward, the No. 9. So fundamental was this that the television commentator Kenneth Wolstenholme felt compelled in the opening minutes of the game to explain the foreign custom to his viewers. 'You might be mystified by some of the Hungarian numbers,' he said in a tone of indulgent exasperation. 'The reason is they number the players rather logically, with the centre-half as 3 and the backs as 2 and 4.' They numbered them, in other words, as you would read them across the pitch, rather than by archaic custom: how was an Englishman to cope? And, more pertinently, what was a centre-half to do if the centre-forward kept disappearing off towards the halfway line? 'To me,' Harry Johnston, England's centre-half that day, wrote in his autobiography, 'the tragedy was the utter helplessness ... being unable to do anything to alter the grim outlook.' If he followed him, it left a hole between the two full-backs; if he sat off him, Hidegkuti was able to drift around unchallenged, dictating the play. In the end Johnston was caught between the two stools, and Hidegkuti scored a hat-trick. Syd Owen, Johnston's replacement for the rematch in Budapest six months later, fared no better, and England were beaten 7-1.

It wasn't just Hidegkuti who flummoxed England, though. Their whole system and style of play was alien. It was, Owen said, 'like playing people from outer space'. Billy Wright, England's captain, admitted, 'We completely underestimated the advances that the Hungarians had made.' It says much about the general technical standard of English football at the time that Wolstenholme was enraptured by Puskás nonchalantly performing half-a-dozen keepie-ups while he waited to kick off. If that sends a shudder of embarrassment down the modern English spine, it is nothing to what Frank Coles wrote in the *Daily Telegraph* on the morning of the game. 'Hungary's superb ball-jugglers,' he asserted with a touching faith in the enduring powers of English pluck, 'can be checked by firm tackling.' Little wonder Glanville spoke of it as a defeat that 'gave eyes to the blind'.

And yet it wasn't just about technique, perhaps it wasn't even primarily about technique. Yes, Hungary had, in Puskás, Hidegkuti, Kocsis, Bozsik and Zoltán Czibor, five of the greatest players of the age and, in Sebes, an inspirational and meticulous coach but, as Hungary's right-back Jenő Buzánszky acknowledged,

'It was because of tactics that Hungary won. The match showed the clash of two formations and, as often happens, the newer, more developed formation prevailed.' Perhaps it is wrong to divide the two, for while the tactics permitted the technique to flourish, without the technique the tactics would have been redundant. England were slow to react to the problems (and certainly negligent in failing to address them ahead of the rematch in Budapest six months later), but it is hard to ar″e that their manager Walter Winterbottom picked the wrong tactics on the day. The problem, rather, was endemic.

England, Geoffrey Green wrote in *The Times* the following morning, 'found themselves strangers in a strange world, a world of flitting red spirits, for such did the Hungarians seem as they moved at devastating pace with superb skill and powerful finish in their cherry bright shirts. One has talked about the new conception of football as developed by the continentals and South Americans. Always the main criticism against the style has been its lack of a final punch near goal. One has thought at times, too, that perhaps the perfection of football was to be found somewhere between the hard-hitting, open British method and this other more probing infiltration. Yesterday, the Hungarians, with perfect teamwork, demonstrated this mid-point to perfection.'

Not that Sebes saw his Hungary as the mid-point of anything. Having organised a labour dispute at the Renault factory in Paris before the war, his Communist credentials were impeccable and, while he was assuredly saying what his government wanted to hear, there is no reason to believe he was not also voicing his own opinion as he insisted Hungary's success, so obviously rooted in the interplay of the team as opposed to the dissociated individuality of England, was a victory for socialism. Certainly that November evening, as the flags hung limp in the fog above the Twin Towers, themselves designed to reflect the work of Lutyens in New Delhi, it didn't take a huge leap of the imagination to recognise Empire's symbolic defeat.

△▽

Football, of course, is not played on the blackboard. However sound the system, success on the pitch requires compromise between – in the best case, stems from a symbiosis of – the theory and the players available. Bukovi's idea was perfect for Hungary, because four front men and a withdrawn centre-forward permitted a fluidity of attack that suited the mindset of their forwards. It is revealing watching a video of the game today that, midway through the first half, Wolstenholme observes, in a tone midway between amusement and amazement, that 'the outside-*left* Czibor came across to pick up the ball in the outside-right position'.

Fluidity is all very well, but, of course, the more fluid a team is, the harder it is to retain the structures necessary to defend. That is where Sebes excelled. He was so concerned with detail that he had his side practise with the heavier English balls and on a training pitch with the same dimensions as Wembley, and his notebook shows a similar care for the tactical side of the game. He encouraged the two full-backs, Buzánszky and Mihály Lantos, to advance, but that meant the centre-half, Gyula Lóránt, dropping even deeper, into a position not dissimilar to the sweeper in Karl Rappan's *verrou* system. Puskás had licence to roam, while Bozsik, notionally the right-half, was encouraged to push forwards to support Hidegkuti. That required a corresponding defensive presence, which was provided by the left-half, Zakariás, who, in the tactical plan for the game Sebes sketched in his notebook, appears so deep he is almost playing between the two full-backs. Two full-backs, two central defensive presences, two players running the middle and four up front: the Hungarian system was a hair's-breadth from 4-2-4.

And yet the *Aranycsapat* remained forever unfulfilled. After thirty-six games undefeated, Hungary threw away a two-goal lead to lose 3-2 to West Germany in the 1954 World Cup final, undone, in the end, by ill luck, a muddy pitch that hampered their passing game, a touch of complacency and the German manager Sepp Herberger's simple ploy of sitting Horst Eckel man-to-man on Hidegkuti. A system thought up to free the centre-forward from the clutches of a marker fell down when the marker was moved closer to him.

Perhaps, though, they paid as well for a defensive frailty. Even allowing for the attacking standards of the time, the Hungarian defence was porous. The three they conceded to West Germany meant they had let in ten in the tournament, while in 1953 they leaked eleven goals in a six-game run that culminated in the 6-3 win at Wembley. Just about everybody agreed that the three flattered England, an observation taken at the time to emphasise

England 3 Hungary 6, friendly, Wembley, London, 25 November 1953

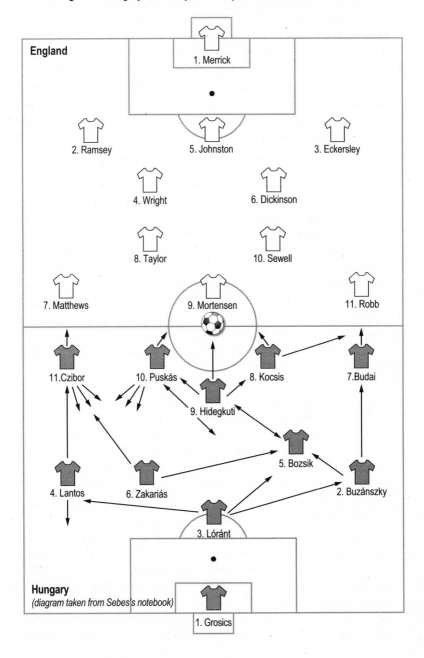

Hungary's superiority, but it could just as well be interpreted as a criticism of their laxity.

The problem with three at the back is that the defence operates on a pivot, with the left-back tucking in alongside the centre-back if attacks come down the right and vice versa, rendering it vulnerable to being 'turned' by a smart cross-field ball that, at the very least, gave the winger on the opposite flank acceleration room. Zakariás, still notionally a midfielder, did not play deep enough to provide the extra cover that would have allowed a full-back to remain tighter to the winger he was supposed to be marking.

Whatever the cause of the defeat in Berne, the response in Hungary was one of fury. When they had returned after beating England at Wembley, the *Aranycsapat* had been greeted by adoring crowds; after losing the World Cup final they had to be diverted to the northern town of Tata to avoid street demonstrations. Puskás was barracked at league games, Sebes's son was beaten up at school, and the goalkeeper, Gyula Grosics, was arrested. Through 1955, the management team Sebes had constructed was dismantled and, following a 4-3 defeat to Belgium the following year, he was replaced by a five-man committee headed by Bukovi. Amid the chaos of the Uprising and the subsequent defections of several players, though, his task was an impossible one. Sebes, meanwhile, lingered a while in sports administration as the deputy head of the National Physical Education and Sports Committee, before taking on a string of coaching positions, eventually retiring in 1970. 'When I was a kid, Sebes lived in the same area of Budapest as me,' remembers the great Ferencváros forward of the seventies, Tibor Nyilasi. 'He would come down to the square where I played football with my friends, and take us up to his flat, give us sandwiches, and show us Super-8 films of the 6-3 and 7-1 games. It was he who recommended me to Ferencváros. He was like a grandfather. He only lived for football.'

△▽

While it was the national team's performances that attracted the most attention at the time, it was probably Sebes's compatriot Béla Guttmann who had a more lasting influence on the game. To claim that he invented Brazilian football is stretching things, but that didn't stop him trying. What is beyond dispute is that he represented the final flowering of the great era of central European football; he was the last of the coffee-house coaches, perhaps even the last defender of football's innocence.

The two great Hungarian managers of the era could hardly have been more different. Where Sebes was a committed socialist, happy to spout the Party line and play the diplomatic game, Guttmann was a quick-tempered individualist, a man chewed up by circumstance and distrustful and dismissive of authority as a consequence. The end of his international playing career after three full caps was typical. Selected for the 1924 Olympics in Paris, Guttmann was appalled by Hungary's inadequate preparations. There were more officials than players in the squad, and the party accordingly was based in a hotel near Montmartre: ideal for the officials' late-night socialising, less good for players who needed to sleep. In protest Guttmann led a number of his team-mates on a rat-catching expedition through the hotel, and then tied their prey by the tails to the handles of the officials' room-doors. He never played for his country again. Guttmann lived life like the world's rejected guest, always on the lookout for a slight, always ready to flounce, irritating and irritated in equal measure.

Born in Budapest in 1899 to a family of dance instructors, Guttmann qualified as a teacher of classical dance when he was sixteen. It was football that really fascinated him, though, and, playing as an old-school attacking centre-half – contemporary accounts almost invariably describe him as 'graceful' – he impressed enough with the first-division side Torekves to earn a move in 1920 to MTK, a club seen as representing Budapest's Jewish middle-class and a club still playing in the style Jimmy Hogan had introduced.

At first, Guttmann was cover for Ferenc Nyúl, but he soon left for the Romanian side Hagibor Cluj, leaving the younger man to function as MTK's fulcrum as they won the championship in 1921, the sixth in a run of ten straight titles interrupted only by a three-year hiatus for the war. The following season, though, Nyúl returned and, ousted from the team, Guttmann did what he would go on to do throughout his career: he walked, following the route of many Jews fearing persecution from the Miklós Horthy regime and heading for Vienna. It was the first of twenty-three moves Guttmann would make across national borders.

Anti-Semitism was not exactly unknown in Vienna, but it was

there, amid the football intellectuals of the coffee houses, that
Guttmann seems to have felt most at home. 'Later,' the journalist
Hardy Grüne wrote in the catalogue of an auction of Guttmann
memorabilia held in the German town of Kassel in 2001, 'he would
often sit in São Paulo, New York or Lisbon and dream of enjoying a
Melange in a Viennese café and chatting to good friends about
football.' When, aged seventy-five, Guttmann finally gave up his
wandering, it was to Vienna he returned, living in an apartment
near the opera house on Walfischgasse.

He joined Hakoah, the great Jewish club of Vienna, late in 1921,
and supplemented the small income they were able to provide by
setting up a dancing academy. They too practised the Scottish
passing game, as preached by their coach Billy Hunter, who had
played for Bolton Wanderers – alongside Jimmy Hogan – and
Millwall. Although central Europe had never embraced the brute
physicality of the English approach, Hunter's ideas were to have a
lasting impact.

Hakoah turned professional in 1925 and, with Guttmann at
centre-half, won the inaugural professional Austrian championship the following year. Just as important to the club were the
money-making tours they undertook to promote muscular
Judaism in general and Zionism in particular. In 1926, billed as
'the Unbeatable Jews' (although they lost two of their thirteen
games), Hakoah toured the east coast of the USA. In terms of
money and profile, the tour was a tremendous success, and in that
lay Hakoah's downfall. The US clubs were richer than Hakoah and,
after agreeing a much-improved contract, Guttmann joined the
New York Giants. By the end of the year, half the squad was based
in the city.

From a football point of view, Guttmann prospered, winning
the US Cup in 1929, but, having bought into a speakeasy, he was
ruined as the economy disintegrated after the Wall Street Crash. 'I
poked holes in the eyes of Abraham Lincoln on my last five-dollar
bill,' he said. 'I thought then it wouldn't be able to find its way to
the door.' Always a man with an eye for the finer things in life – at
Hakoah he insisted his shirts be made of silk – he seems also to
have vowed then that he would never be poor again. He stayed with
the Giants until the US league collapsed in 1932, returning to
Hakoah to begin a coaching career that would last for forty-one
years.

He stayed in Vienna for two seasons and then, on the recommendation of Hugo Meisl, moved on to the Dutch club SC Enschede. He initially signed a three-month contract but, when they came to negotiate a new deal, he insisted upon a huge bonus should Enschede win the league. As the club was struggling to avoid relegation out of the Eastern Division, the directors readily agreed. Their form promptly revived and, after they had narrowly missed out on the national championship, their chairman admitted that towards the end of the season he had gone to games praying his side would lose: Guttmann's bonus would have bankrupted them.

He would have had little compunction about accepting it. Some managers are empire-builders, committed to laying structures that will bring their clubs success long after they have gone; Guttmann was a gun for hire. He bargained hard and brooked no interference. 'The third season,' he would say later in his career, 'is fatal.' He rarely lasted that long. After two years in Holland he returned to Hakoah, fleeing to Hungary after the Anschluss.

What happened next is unclear. Whenever he was asked how he survived the war, Guttmann would always reply, 'God helped me.' His elder brother died in a concentration camp, and it seems probable that contacts from Hakoah helped him escape to Switzerland, where he was interned. It was certainly there that Guttmann met his wife, but he refused always to speak of his wartime experiences, and his autobiography, published in 1964, contains a single paragraph on the subject: 'In the last fifteen years countless books have been written about the destructive years of struggle for life and death. It would thus be superfluous to trouble our readers with such details.'

By 1945, he was back in Hungary with Vasas, and the following spring he moved on to Romania with Ciocanul, where he insisted on being paid in edible goods so as to circumvent the food shortages and inflation afflicting most of Europe at the time. His departure was characteristic. When a director sought to interfere with team selection, Guttmann apparently turned to him, said, 'OK, you run the club; you seem to have the basics,' and left.

The following season he won the Hungarian title with Újpest, and then it was on to Kispest, where he replaced Puskás' father as coach. A row with Puskás, no shrinking violet himself, was inevitable, and it came in a 4-0 defeat to Győr. Guttmann, who was insistent that football should be played the 'right way', had spent the first half trying to calm the aggressive approach of the full-back Mihály Patyi. Furious with him, Guttmann instructed Patyi not to go out for the second half, even though that would leave Kispest down to ten men. Puskás told the defender to stay on. Patyi vacillated, and eventually ignored his manager, at which Guttmann retired to the stands for the second half, most of which he spent reading a racing paper, then took a tram home and never returned.

On he wandered: to Triestina and Padova in Italy, to Boca Juniors and Quilmes in Argentina, to Apoel Nicosia in Cyprus, and then, midway through the 1953–54 season, to AC Milan. He lifted them to third in that first season, and had them top of the table when he was dismissed nineteen games into 1954–55 following a series of disputes with the board. 'I have been sacked,' he told a stunned press conference convened to announce his departure, 'even though I am neither a criminal nor a homosexual. Goodbye.' From then on he insisted on a clause in his contracts stipulating he couldn't be dismissed while his team were top of the league.

He moved to Vicenza, but left twenty-eight games into the season, and was without a job for most of 1956, before the Budapest Uprising provided him with an opportunity. When Honvéd (as Kispest had become known after being taken over by the army), seeking to keep their players away from the fighting, accepted a long-standing invitation to tour Brazil and Venezuela, Guttmann, by this time reconciled with Puskás, was placed in charge. Finding himself in demand in South America, he decided to stay on, accepting a contract with São Paulo. And so it was, Guttmann claimed, that the Hungarian 4-2-4 was exported to Brazil, although the truth is rather more complex.

Guttmann led São Paulo to a Paulista title in 1957, but was quickly off, returning to Europe with Porto. A coach, he said, is like a lion tamer. 'He dominates the animals, in whose cage he performs his show, as long as he deals with them with self-confidence and without fear. But the moment he becomes unsure of his hypnotic energy, and the first hint of fear appears in his eyes, he is lost.' Guttmann never stayed long enough for that hint of fear to materialise.

He helped Porto overhaul a five-point deficit to pip Benfica to the title, at which Benfica promptly appointed him themselves. He sacked twenty players on his arrival but, promoting youth players, won the league in 1960 and 1961. Even more significantly, Benfica's free-flowing football saw off Barcelona 3-2 in the European Cup final in 1961, ending Real Madrid's five-year monopoly.

But that wasn't enough for Guttmann. A week after the final in Berne, he gave a debut to the player who would become the greatest in the club's history: Eusébio. The Mozambican would probably have joined Sporting had Guttmann not bumped into Carlos Bauer, who had played for him in São Paulo, in a Lisbon barber's shop. Bauer was leading a Brazilian side on a five-week tour of Africa, and Guttmann asked him to keep an eye out for fresh talent. Five weeks later, they met again in the same barber's shop. Bauer spoke of a forward with Sporting's feeder club in Lourenço Marques (as Maputo was then called), whom he wanted to sign but couldn't afford, and who was, anyway, destined for Sporting. Guttmann phoned the Mozambican club, hijacked the deal and had Eusébio's signature two days later. 'By signing Eusébio,' Guttmann said, 'I was able to play Mario Coluna deeper, more as a wing-half than an inside-forward. He did not like it at first because he did not score so many goals, but he became my best player.' He became, in other words, Benfica's Hidegkuti.

Benfica finished third that season, conceding more goals than Sporting and Porto – the two teams who had finished above them – put together. Perhaps that was a sign that Guttmann's attacking approach had had its day – 'I never minded if the opposition scored, because I always thought we could score another,' he said – but few thought that as Benfica came from 2-0 and 3-2 down to beat Real Madrid 5-3 in the European Cup final in Amsterdam. Puskás, having scored a hat-trick in a losing cause, sought out Eusébio at the final whistle and handed him his shirt, a gesture widely interpreted as a symbolic passing of the mantle of Europe's greatest player. Benfica, similarly, seemed to have supplanted Madrid as Europe's greatest team and, with Eusébio only twenty, there was little reason to believe that the club would not go on to dominate the sixties as surely as Real Madrid had the fifties. Had, that is, Guttmann stayed.

He did not. After the final, Guttmann approached Benfica's directors and asked whether he mightn't be due some kind of bonus. There was, the directors replied, no such provision in his contract. 'I got $4,000 less for winning the European Cup than the Portuguese championship,' Guttmann said. 'No attempt was made by the directors to change the situation, so I began to think about moving on.'

Two months later, he did, ignoring the overtures of Third Division Port Vale to return to South America with the Uruguayan side Peñarol. There he constructed a side that would go on to win the Copa Libertadores, although he left before the final to take charge of the Austria national team. Driven out by anti-Semitism after five games, he wandered on to Benfica – briefly – and then to Servette of Geneva, Panathinakos and Porto before a final return to the city he adored with Austria Vienna. He was never, though, quite the same after Benfica, and neither was the club. The story has grown up that he cursed them, vowing they would never win another European trophy until he was paid what he was due; nonsense, of course, but Benfica have been in five European finals since, and lost them all.

In truth, football has never been quite the same. Guttmann, more than anybody since Chapman, had defined the cult of the manager; the man who would take on his mantle was Helenio Herrera, whose conception of the game could hardly have been more different. Out went all romantic notions of scoring one more than the opposition, and in came cynicism and *catenaccio* and the theory of conceding one fewer.

Chapter Seven

△▽△▽△▽△▽△▽

Harnesssing the Carnival

△▽ The Brazil in which Béla Guttmann and Honvéd arrived in 1956 was far from the tactical wilderness he liked to portray. Individual technique and improvisation were prized, certainly, but having come to the W-M late, the 4-2-4 was already well developed – perhaps because the rigidity of the W-M, with its tight marking structure, did not sit easily with local demands for flair and self-expression.

If Brazilian football's foundation myth is to be believed, and there seems little reason to doubt its fundamentals, the sport had arrived in Brazil with Charles Miller. The son of an English father and a Brazilian mother, members of the coffee and commerce elite of São Paulo, he was sent back to England to be educated. While there he learned the game at school, going on to represent Hampshire and play a handful of games for St Mary's, the forerunner of Southampton. When he returned to São Paulo in 1894, he brought two footballs with him. The legend has him disembarking with a ball in each hand.

'What are those, Charles?' his father is supposed to have asked.

'My degree,' he replied. 'Your son has graduated in football.'

The specifics of the story are almost certainly untrue, but it is not hard to see why it would gain currency. Here, from its origins, was Brazilian football as happy, smiling, impertinent and disrespectful of authority.

The sport spread quickly, both among the Anglo elite and the indigenous population. By 1902 there was a thriving league programme in São Paulo, while the game had been imported to Rio de Janeiro by another Anglo-Brazilian, Oscar Cox, who had picked up the game during his schooling in Switzerland. He founded Fluminense with some friends and, like the early Dutch and Danish clubs, it seems to have become almost a parody of Englishness, all hats and moustaches, hurrahs and manliness. Miller, equally, was an old-school advocate of dribbling, and there is no reason to believe the game among the ex-pat community was any different in style to the game in Britain at the time.

Among the Anglo-Brazilian clubs, as elsewhere, dribbling soon began to give way to passing. Jock Hamilton, one of the many Scottish coaches employed by Harry Bradshaw at Fulham – a first, albeit tenuous, link between Jimmy Hogan and Brazil – was appointed at CA Paulistano, and pronounced himself 'surprised to find the game so advanced... their combination is really clever'. It got cleverer thanks to the influence of the Scottish Wanderers, a team of Scottish ex-pats formed in São Paulo in 1912. They practised the pattern-weaving approach, which, confusingly, became known as the *'systema ingleza'* – 'the English system'.

Wanderers' most noted player was Archie McLean, a left-winger who had spent two seasons with Ayr United in the Scottish Second Division. He 'was an artist, a worthy exponent of the Scottish school,' wrote Tomás Mazzoni in his 1950 history of football in Brazil. 'His scientific football became more prominent when he formed a partnership on the left wing with another of his compatriots Hopkins.' The pair later moved to São Bento, where their trick of rapidly exchanging short passes became known as the *'tabelinha'* (literally, 'little chart').

As Aidan Hamilton details in *An Entirely Different Game*, the British influence remained strong in Brazil far longer than it had in Uruguay or Argentina. Mazzoni speaks of Harry Welfare, a centre-forward who had played for Liverpool before accepting the offer of a teaching role in Rio de Janeiro, 'adapting' to 'our style of play' after joining Fluminense, but he also disseminated his own ideas. Max Valentim, in *On Football and its Technique*, says that Welfare taught the inside-forwards at the club how to play the through-ball, and describes two of his dribbling techniques: 'This break or feint of the body which the English call "swerving" and the jump to one side while running with the ball.'

The real divergence from the old model, though, began when locals got involved. Barred from Fluminense, they watched the Anglo-Brazilians from nearby rooftops, and saw a sport that was both far easier to comprehend and far easier to replicate than cricket. In the informal kickabouts in the streets, often using balls made of rags, a wholly different conception of the game developed. It was based on the unorthodox and individual skills required to thrive in such conditions and – crucially – was uninhibited by any proscriptions against showing off. McLean was not impressed. 'There were great players there,' he said of football in São Paulo, 'but they were terribly undisciplined. Their antics would not have been tolerated in Scotland.'

Various parallels have been drawn between Brazilian football and samba – Brazilian fans at the 1958 World Cup chanted 'Samba, samba' as they celebrated their country's first win in the tournament – while Simon Kuper in *Football against the Enemy* compares Pelé to a *capoerista*, an exponent of a martial art invented by Angolan slaves that was disguised as a dance to fool their masters.

The anthropologist Robert DaMatta came up with the theory of '*jeitinho*' – literally, 'the small way' – to explain the creativity on which Brazilians so pride themselves, positing that because the laws and codes of behaviour in Brazil, even after the abolition of slavery in 1888, were designed to protect the rich and powerful, individuals had to find imaginative ways of getting round them. *Jeitinho*, he wrote in *What makes Brazil, Brazil*, 'is a personal mediation between the law, the situation in which it should apply and the persons involved in such a way that nothing really changes, apart from a considerable demoralisation of the law itself... In the USA, France and England, for example, the rules are either obeyed or do not exist. In these societies, it is well known that there is no desire to establish new laws that are not in line with the common good or with the other laws of society, so creating room for bureaucratic corruption and diminishing the trust in the public institutions... So ... the Americans, the French and the British stop in front of a "Stop" sign, which seems to us a logical and social absurdity...'

Brazilians, by contrast, find a way around such restrictions; they come to rely on themselves rather than on external structures. It is not hard to see the imaginativeness that has historically characterised Brazilian football as a particular expression of that trait. Individuals find their own way to master situations, and that means both high levels of creativity, and a distrust of teamwork.

Much of DaMatta's work develops the thinking of Gilberto

Freyre, a sociologist who began writing in the late thirties. Freyre was among the first to promote Brazil's racial diversity as a positive, celebrating the Carioca figure of the *malandro*, typically a mixed-race trickster or con man, who used his wits to best those who in theory had authority over him. 'Our style of playing football,' Freyre wrote in 1938, 'contrasts with the Europeans because of a combination of the qualities of surprise, malice, astuteness and agility, and at the same time brilliance and individual spontaneity... Our passes ... our dummies, our flour-ishes with the ball, the touch of dance and subversiveness that marks the Brazilian style ... seem to show psychologists and sociol-ogists in a very interesting way the roguery and flamboyance of the mulatto that today is every true affirmation of what is Brazilian.'

For writers of the time, the *malandro* spirit found its personifi-cation in two of the greatest Brazilian players of the thirties, the centre-forward Leônidas and the defender Domingos da Guia, both of whom were black. Domingos openly acknowledged that his creative abilities, the technical skills that allowed him to carry the ball out from the back, were rooted initially in the need for self-preservation. 'When I was still a kid I was scared to play football,' he said, 'because I often saw black players ... get whacked on the pitch, just because they made a foul or sometimes for less than that... My elder brother used to tell me: the cat always falls on his feet... Aren't you good at dancing? I was and this helped my football... I swung my hips a lot... That short dribble I invented imitating the *miudinho*, that type of samba.'

However it came about, by 1919 there was a discernibly Brazilian style of play, as was outlined that November in an article headed 'Brazilian Innovation' in the first issue of the São Paulo magazine *Sports*. 'As opposed to the British school, which dictates that the ball be taken by the forwards right up to the opposition's goal and put in from the closest possible range, the Brazilian school states that shots be taken from any distance, the precision of the shot being worth more than the fact that it is made close to the target. And it further states that the collective advance of the whole forward line is not necessary; it's enough for two or three players to break away with the ball, which, by its devastating speed, completely unexpected, disorientates the entire rival defence.'

The perception that British football was insufficiently direct in front of goal rings strangely given how critical British commentators would become of the over-elaboration of central European sides. Perhaps it is simply that all things are relative, perhaps the Scottish ex-pats who made up the Wanderers did over-pass and that coloured the judgement, or perhaps the British game at the time, six years before the change in the offside law, was more intricate than it became. Whatever the truth, it is clear that the Brazilian game was focused more on self-expression than on team-play.

Football in Brazil, though, was nowhere near as developed at that stage as it was on the River Plate. Their first ten internationals – all against Argentina, Uruguay or Chile – brought just three victories, and in the 1917 Copa América they conceded four against both Argentina and Uruguay. In 1919, though, they fared rather better, winning the tournament thanks largely to the ploy of having one of the full-backs retain a purely defensive role, while the other was given licence to join the attack. It was far from sophisticated, but it was the first time the Brazil national team acknowledged the need for some sort of structure of defence.

That success, though, was far from the start of any continental domination. Brazil won just six of the twenty matches they played against Argentina before 1940, and five of thirteen against Uruguay. They won the Copa again in 1922, but it would be 1949 before they won it for a third time (astonishingly, it wasn't until 1997 and their fifth success that Brazil won the competition on foreign soil).

Internal disputes within the federation meant that Brazil were represented only by Carioca players at the 1930 World Cup. They lost their opening game 2-1 against Yugoslavia – 'Brazil were individually cleverer, collectively inferior,' Glanville wrote – and were eliminated despite a subsequent 4-0 victory over Bolivia.

Professionalism was formally sanctioned in 1933, which at least helped persuade Brazilian players on tours of Europe with their clubs to return home, but it would take time before it had an impact either on the results of the national side or on their style.

Having been knocked out of the 1934 World Cup after one game, beaten 3-1 by Spain, Brazil travelled on to Belgrade for a friendly against Yugoslavia, who had failed to qualify for the World Cup, and were hammered 8-4. This was a side featuring such talents as Domingos, Leônidas and Waldemar de Brito, but tactically they were humiliatingly exposed, even more so than they had been in Montevideo four years earlier. 'There was a lot of space between the lines,' the football historian Ivan Soter explained. 'The Yugoslavs were able to exploit that, showing up the faults of the old-fashioned system.' Something, evidently, had to change.

△▽

The first attempt to import the W-M to Brazil was made by Gentil Cardoso, but he was beset by two major difficulties: he had next to no background as a player, and he was black. He had been a bootblack, a waiter, a tram driver and a baker, and had then joined the merchant navy. That entailed frequent voyages to Europe, and while there he seems to have spent most of his free time watching football. He became a particular fan of the English game, and later claimed to have watched first-hand Herbert Chapman's development of the W-M formation at Arsenal. 'He was a larger than life character,' said Soter, 'somebody who loved telling tales of his travels.' Often they were embellished, but what is undeniable is his capacity for tactical analysis. He saw the W-M, recognised its possibilities, and realised that this, vastly different as it was to Brazilian football, was the future.

Cardoso was given his chance to coach in the thirties, when he divided his time between football and the sea. He implemented the W-M at the small Carioca side Sírio Libanês, where he oversaw the emergence of Leônidas. 'He was a thoroughly Brazilian player,' the playwright Nélson Rodrigues wrote of the forward. 'Full of the fantasy, improvisation, childishness and sensuality that have marked out all the Brazilian greats.' He was not, in other words, much like the centre-forwards the English preferred to employ in the W-M. Shape could be copied; style, it seems, was rather harder to implement.

Sírio Libanês was too small a club for Cardoso's innovation really to reverberate, and even after he'd moved to Bonsucesso, a slightly larger club, taking Leônidas with him, he found it hard to find an audience for his ideas. He became noted for quoting Socrates, Cicero and Gandhi in team-talks, and enhanced Brazil's footballing vocabulary – 'snake' to mean good player, for instance; or 'zebra' for a shock result – but, as a tactician, as Soter said, 'People just didn't take him seriously.'

It took a European, Dori Kürschner, to implant the W-M firmly in Brazil, although he died before his ideas really took hold. 'When Kruschner [*sic*] arrived in Brazil, Gentil was talking a lot about the W-M,' Flávio Costa, Kürschner's predecessor and successor at Flamengo, said in an interview with Aidan Hamilton, 'but he never had the prestige to apply it. Kruschner was the one who tried to apply *futebol sistema*.'

Kürschner has become a mythic figure in Brazil, a wise man from a distant land who brought great knowledge and, like all true prophets, went unheralded in his own lifetime. He is portrayed as an evangelist without a history, a man from nowhere. 'We don't even know if he was Hungarian, Czech, Bohemian...' said Roberto Assaf, the television pundit and great chronicler of Flamengo. The confusion is understandable. At some stage, the 'R' and the 'U' became transposed, and so in Brazil Kürschner's name is spelt and pronounced 'Kruschner'; anyone looking up 'Kruschner', of course, finds that the record is blank. As Alex Bellos notes in his introduction to *Futebol*, 'Brazil is not big on facts... It is a country built of stories, myths and Chinese whispers.'

That explains Kürschner's aura of mystery, but it does not explain why the Flamengo president José Bastos Padilha settled upon him as the man to further his plans for Carioca domination, which had already included funding the construction of a new stadium. Whatever his intentions, what he got when he appointed him was somebody with a fine pedigree in Danubian football, and somebody, moreover, who provided a direct link to Jimmy Hogan. Hogan is regularly hailed as the father of Hungarian, Austrian and German football; what is trumpeted rather less is that he was also the grandfather of the Brazilian game.

Kürschner was born in Budapest, and as a player enjoyed success with MTK, winning the Hungarian title in 1904 and 1908, and earning a handful of international call-ups. A left-half who occasionally operated in the centre, he was known for his unfussy acuity in possession, and was particularly noted for his heading ability. In his later days, he was coached by Hogan, and he succeeded him as MTK coach in 1918. Kürschner won a title there, but within a year he had left for Germany.

There he had minor success with Stuttgarter Kickers, won a national German title with Nürnberg, and, after a brief stint with Bayern Munich, was their coach as they shared the title the following season after the so-called 'eternal final' against SV

Hamburg. In his early career, Kürschner seems, like Guttmann, never to have been able to settle, and he moved on to Eintracht Frankfurt and then to Switzerland with Nordstern Basel, where he won promotion at the first attempt. He promptly left, and joined up with Hogan and the nominal head coach Teddy Duckworth, another Englishman, to prepare the Switzerland national side for the Paris Olympics. There, they achieved the greatest success in the history of Swiss football, reaching the final where they were beaten by defending champions Uruguay.

Kürschner moved back to Germany with Schwarz-Weiss Essen then, in 1925, he joined Grasshoppers in Zurich. He spent the next nine years there, winning three league titles and four cups, before being replaced by Karl Rappan. Had he stayed in Germany or gone back to Hungary, where the classic Danubian 2-3-5 still held sway, things might have been different, but it seems that in Switzerland Kürschner became convinced of the merits of the W-M, or at least a variant of it. So when Padilha approached him in 1937, he took with him to Rio de Janeiro the formation that would kick-start the Brazilian revolution.

Perhaps it is most charitably described as a slow-burner, for in its own way Brazilian football was just as conservative as the English game. Flamengo's centre-half when Kürschner arrived was Fausto dos Santos, 'the Black Wonder', an elegant stylist who was used to dominating games. There was a clear hierarchy of positions in Brazilian football, with centre-half at the top and the full-backs at the bottom and there was no way, he told Kürschner, that he was going to drop back and become a defensive player. Fans and journalists were divided on the issue, which was only resolved when Padilha intervened, fined Fausto, and told him to get on with doing what he was paid to do. That, at least, is the legend, which paints Kürschner as an unyielding moderniser, deaf both to the appeals of tradition and to the individual characteristics and concerns of his players.

It is not, though, quite as simple as that. Ideas rarely spring fully formed from the minds of their creators, and here too circumstance seems to have played its part. According to Assaf, Kürschner was appalled by the medical facilities he found at the club and his first significant decision, far from being an act of tactical fundamentalism, was to send his players to see a doctor. Fausto, it transpired, was suffering from the early stages of the tuberculosis that would kill him two years later, and the decision to push him into a deeper role seems to have been taken as much with his declining health in mind as for reasons of ideology. Whether, had Fausto been well, Kürschner would have retained the old 2-3-5, or whether he might have used him as a half-back and deployed another player as a defensive centre-half in a W-M, it is impossible to say.

Kürschner's notion of the W-M, anyway, seems to have been rather different to that common in Britain. As a Danubian, even one schooled in Swiss football, it is improbable he would have countenanced a Herbie Roberts-style stopper, either at centre-half or anywhere else on the pitch. And even if he had, Fausto dos Santos was absolutely not the right man to replicate that style. What Kürschner and the Brazilians call a W-M, it seems probable, is actually rather closer to Vittorio Pozzo's *metodo*, more of a W-W shape, with the centre-half playing behind his half-backs, but in advance of the two full-backs. As Soter acknowledges, although the system seemed shockingly defensive in the context of Brazilian football of the time, it was nowhere near as negative or as rigid as the British model.

While his background is not as obscure as is made out, what certainly is true is that Kürschner disappeared into nothing. Flávio Costa, the former Flamengo player he had replaced as coach, remained as his assistant and, taking advantage of the fact that Kürschner had no Portuguese, undermined him at every opportunity, pouring scorn on the W-M and backing Fausto during the dispute. Results were disappointing. Despite scoring eighty-three goals in twenty-two games, Flamengo finished second in the Carioca championship behind their arch-rivals Fluminense and Kürschner found himself and his methods widely derided in the local press. The first game of the 1938 campaign was also the inaugural game at the Estádio da Gávea, and when Flamengo lost 2-0 to Vasco da Gama, Kürschner was sacked – and replaced by Flávio Costa.

Widely misunderstood and far from popular, Kürschner might have been expected to return to Europe but, presumably fearing anti-Semitism back in Budapest where Miklos Hórthy's regime had declared a formal alliance with Nazi Germany, he stayed in Rio. He was appointed coach of Botafogo in 1939, but left the following year and died of a mystery virus in 1941.

For all the suspicion with which he was treated, Kürschner was asked to work as an advisor to the national coach, Adhemar Pimenta, at the 1938 World Cup in France. Before the tournament began, Tomás Mazzoni, then working as a newspaper reporter, went to watch a friendly between France and England at the Stade de Colombes in Paris. England were comfortably superior, winning 4-2, and yet, Mazzoni wrote in shocked tones, they retained three defenders throughout. This, he concluded, would never catch on in Brazil.

Things were changing, though, and while Brazil at that tournament used Martim Silveira as an attacking centre-half, the two inside-forwards, Romeu and Peracio, were withdrawn into what became known as the *ponta da lança* position (literally, the point of the lance), formalising a process that had been going on for some time. By the late thirties, even those nations who ostensibly practised the 2-3-5 had found five forwards strung out in a row too much. Matthias Sindelar dropped off the front line to give the Austrians flexibility, while in Argentina and Uruguay it was common for the inside-forwards to probe from deep. Silveira was a far more attack-minded player than Luisito Monti but, that aside, Brazil's formation in 1938 was little different from the *metodo* of Pozzo's Italy.

It evidently helped as Brazil reached the semi-finals. In a later study of the tournament, though, João Saldanha, the journalist who became national coach in 1969, was critical, concluding they would have gone further with a third back. They did, after all, let in ten goals in their five games, three of them from penalties, which he took as an indication of an over-manned defence panicking under pressure.

△▽

Back at Flamengo, Flávio Costa did not, as it had been assumed he would after Kürschner's dismissal, revert to a 2-3-5, but rather tweaked the W-M, creating what he termed 'the *diagonal*'. Essentially all he did was to nudge the square that lay at the centre of the W-M so it became a parallelogram. Crucially, it retained three defenders – which had been the bone of contention with Fausto – and three forwards, but rather than simply two half-backs and two inside-forwards, as in the British model, the *diagonal* featured a deep-lying half-back – in Flávio Costa's initial conception, which had crystalised by 1941, the right-half, Volante (the term '*volante*' is now used in Brazil to mean 'defensive midfielder') – with a more advanced player to his left – Jayme. The right of the two inside-forwards – Zizinho – then played slightly deeper so as not to leave too large a space behind him, with the inside-left – Perácio – more advanced in the classic *ponta da lança* role.

The formation could just as well be flipped, so that the right side was more attacking. Ondino Viera, part of Uruguay's World Cup-winning squad of 1930, for instance, employed the *diagonal* at Fluminense, but with Spinelli, the left-half, operating defensively, and Romeu providing the *ponta da lança*.

How new the *diagonal* was is debatable. According to the author and former Portugal coach Cândido de Oliveira in his book *The W-M System*, when Flávio Costa was later taken to Europe by a director of Vasco da Gama to explain his formation, it was laughed off as a cheap imitation of the W-M. Perhaps the truth is rather that Flávio Costa formalised an unspoken process that was inherent in the W-M. One inside-forward would always be more creative than the other; one half-back more defensive. At Arsenal in the thirties, as Bernard Joy explains in *Soccer Tactics*, the left-half Wilf Copping played deep, with the right-half Jack Crayston given more freedom. When the Wolves and England captain of the late forties and early fifties, Billy Wright, who could play as a centre-half, played as a half-back, did he not play deeper than Billy Crook or Jimmy Dickinson? As Richard Williams points out in *The Perfect 10*, it was usual – perhaps giving credence to theories linking left-sidedness with creativity – for the inside-left to be more attacking than the inside-right, which is why the No. 10 rather than the No. 8 became lionised as the playmaker.

It is easy, as for instance the Paulista commentator Alberto Helena Junior is, to be cynical about Flávio Costa, suggesting he was doing nothing more than repackaging Kürschner because, having been so critical of him, he could not simply re-use his methods, but the effect was of huge significance. Flávio Costa's tinkering made apparent that the W-M was no more inviolable than the pyramid had been. Once the square has become a parallelogram, it doesn't take much more of a nudge for it to become a diamond, and when that has happened, what is left is 4-2-4. Before that could take place and be widely accepted, though, Brazil had first to go through the agonies of 1950.

The Diagonal (Pela Direita) : Flamengo 1941

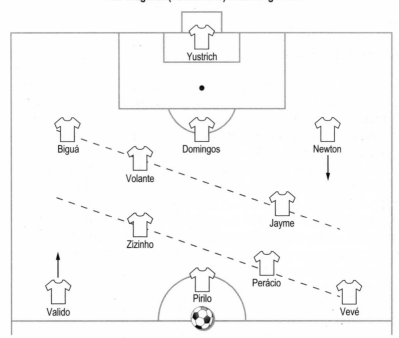

The Diagonal (Pela Esqueroa) : Fluminense 1941

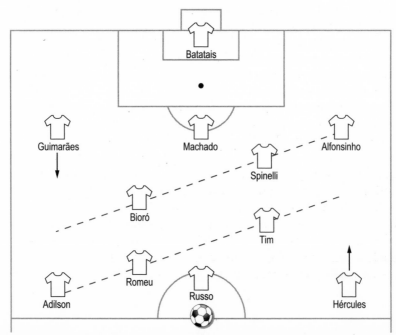

△▽

Brazil are almost universally recognised as having been the best side at the World Cup finals they hosted, but they did not win it. Rather they suffered a defeat in their final game so stunning that Nélson Rodrigues wrote of it as 'our catastrophe, our Hiroshima'.

The *diagonal* imposed by Flávio Costa had undergone a minor modification, with Ademir, really an inside-forward, acting as the centre-forward, Jair, the inside-left, as the *ponta da lança* and Zizinho the deeper-lying inside-forward. The result was an enhanced fluidity and flowing triangles of passes. Brazil swept to victory in the 1949 Copa América scoring thirty-nine goals in seven games before a playoff, in which they demolished Fleitas Solich's Paraguay 7-0.

Zizinho was injured for the start of the World Cup, but Brazil were still overwhelming favourites, and lived up to that billing in their opening match, hitting the post five times on their way to a 4-0 win over Mexico in the inaugural game at the Maracanã. Their problems began when they left Rio for their second match, against Switzerland in São Paulo. As was common at the time, Flávio Costa made several changes, bringing in three Paulista midfielders to appease local fans. Perhaps that disrupted the side, perhaps it was the 1-3-3-3 *verrou* system favoured by Switzerland, but Brazil were nowhere near their usual fluency and, despite twice taking the lead, could only draw 2-2, meaning they had to beat Yugoslavia in their last group game to qualify for the final group.

Fit again, Zizinho returned in place of the robust centre-forward Baltazar, allowing Ademir to resume his role as a mobile No. 9. That would have allowed a return to the side that had won the Copa so impressively the previous year, but the draw against Switzerland seems to have caused Flávio Costa to lose faith with the *diagonal* and switch to a more orthodox W-M, perhaps reasoning that with such an adventurous and fluid central attacking three, his two half-backs, Danilo and Carlos Bauer, could both play deeper and offer additional defensive solidity.

Initially, the change worked. Yugoslavia began with ten men as Rajko Mitić received treatment after gashing his head on an exposed girder shortly before kick-off, and by the time he had made it onto the field, Ademir had given Brazil the lead. Zizinho sealed an otherwise tight game in the second half.

Yugoslavia were physically tough, technically adept opponents and, having seen them off, confidence appears to have been restored. In the opening two games of the final group, Brazil were sensational. As they hammered Sweden 7-1 and Spain 6-1, Glanville wrote of them playing 'the football of the future... tactically unexceptional but technically superb'.

They may have been unexceptional tactically, but they were far more advanced than Uruguay, who were still playing a version of Pozzo's *metodo*, with a ball-playing centre-half in Obdulio Varela. They had equalised late to draw 2-2 with Spain in their opening game of the final stage, and had required two goals in the final quarter hour to beat Sweden 3-2 in their second. Brazil needed only a draw in the final match to be champions, but nobody in Rio expected anything other than victory. The early editions of *O Mundo* on the day of the final even carried a team photograph of the Brazil side under the headline 'These are the world champions'. Varela, Teixeira Heizer recounts in *The Tough Game of the World Cups*, saw the newspaper on display at the newsstand in his hotel on the morning of the final, and was so enraged that he bought every copy they had, took them back to his room, laid them out on his bathroom floor and then encouraged his team-mates to urinate on them.

Before the game, Ângelo Mendes de Moraes, the state governor, gave an address in which he hailed, 'You Brazilians, whom I consider victors of the tournament... You players who in less than a few hours will be acclaimed champions by millions of your compatriots.... You who have no equals in the terrestrial hemisphere... You who are so superior to every other competitor.... You whom I already salute as conquerors.'

Only Flávio Costa seemed at all concerned by the possibility of defeat. 'The Uruguayan team has always disturbed the slumbers of Brazilian footballers,' he warned. 'I am afraid that my players will take to the field on Sunday as though they already had the Championship shield sewn on their jerseys. It isn't an exhibition game. It is a match like any other, only harder than the others.'

What made it particularly hard was the acuity of Juan López, the Uruguay coach. The war in Europe had meant an end to the tours, so, playing largely South American opposition the *Rioplatense* School had had little chance to witness tactical developments elsewhere. López, though, saw how Switzerland had unnerved Brazil, and drew inspiration from their system. He instructed the full-back Matias Gonzalez to stay deep, almost as a sweeper, which meant that Eusebio Tejera, the other full-back, became effectively a centre-back. The two wing-halves, Schubert Gambetta and Victor Andrade, were set to man-mark the Brazilian wingers, Chico and Albino Friaça, while Varela and the two inside-forwards played deeper than usual in a system approaching Rappan's 1-3-3-3.

Officially there were 173,850 at the Maracanã that day; in reality there were probably over 200,000. So overcome by nerves was Julio Pérez, Uruguay's inside-right – or right-half, in the revised formation – that he wet himself during the anthems. Gradually, though, the pressure shifted. Brazil controlled the early stages – López's tactics perhaps subdued Brazil, but they did not neutralise them – but the opening goal would not come. Jair hit the post; Roque Máspoli, in Glanville's words, 'performed acrobatic prodigies in goal'; but at half-time it was still goalless. Home nerves were mounting.

Hindsight suggests the turning point came after twenty-eight minutes, when Varela punched Bigode, Brazil's left-back. Both players agree it was barely more than a tap, but in the mythology of the game it was at that moment that the fear enveloped Bigode, at that moment that he became 'a coward', the taunt that would pursue him for the rest of his life.

Two minutes after half-time, a reverse ball from Ademir laid in Friaça. He held off Andrade and, with a slightly scuffed cross-shot, gave Brazil the lead. In the first half, it might have been devastating, but having held out for so long, Uruguay knew they could live with Brazil, that they would not be overwhelmed.

Whether it was a deliberate policy or not is difficult to say, but Uruguay seemed to prefer to attack down their right. That was the side that, when Brazil had played the *diagonal*, had been the more vulnerable, with Danilo the more advanced of the two half-backs. In a W-M, he couldn't help himself but push forwards, which created a fatal space, because Bigode was now operating as an orthodox left-back rather than in the slightly advanced role he would usually have adopted. Alcide Ghiggia, Uruguay's frail, hunched right-winger, could hardly have dreamed he would have been granted so much room.

Brazil 1 Uruguay 2, World Cup final pool, Maracanã, Rio de Janeiro, 16 July 1950

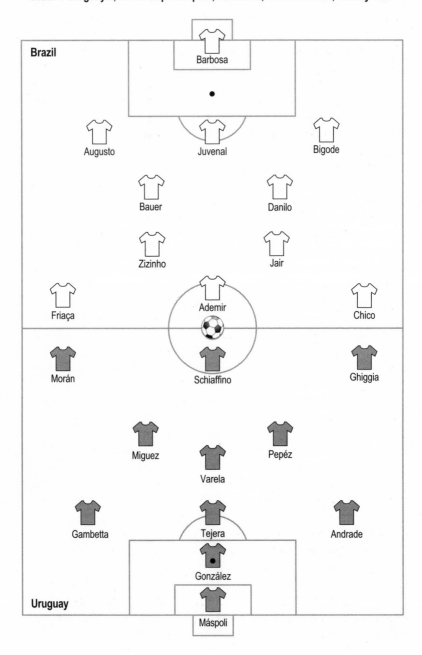

Brazil were twenty-four minutes from victory when the first blow fell. Varela, who was becoming increasingly influential, advanced, and spread the ball right to Ghiggia. He had space to accelerate, checked as Bigode moved to close him down, then surged by him, crossing low for Juan Schiaffino to sweep the ball in at the near post. 'Silence in the Maracanã,' said Flávio Costa, 'which terrified our players.' As blame was apportioned after the game, even the crowd did not escape. 'When the players needed the Maracanã the most, the Maracanã was silent,' the musician Chico Buarque observed. 'You can't entrust yourself to a football stadium.'

A draw would still have been enough for Brazil, but the momentum had swung inexorably against them. Thirteen minutes later, Ghiggia again picked up the ball on the Uruguayan right. This time Bigode was closer to him, but isolated, so Ghiggia laid it back to Perez. Nerves forgotten, he held off Jair and slipped a return ball in behind Bigode. Ghiggia ran on, and with Moacyr Barbosa, the Brazilian goalkeeper, anticipating a cross, struck a bobbling shot in at the near post. The unthinkable had happened, and Uruguay, not Brazil, were world champions.

Brazil, only founded as a nation in 1889, has never been in a war. When Rodrigues spoke of the 1950 World Cup final as his country's 'Hiroshima', he meant it was the greatest single catastrophe to have befallen Brazil. Paulo Perdigão expresses the same point less outrageously in *Anatomy of a Defeat*, his remarkable meditation on the final, in which he reprints the entire radio commentary of the match, using it as the basis for his analysis of the game almost as though he were delivering exegesis upon a biblical text. 'Of all the historical examples of national crises,' he wrote, 'the World Cup of 1950 is the most beautiful and most glorified. It is a Waterloo of the tropics and its history our *Götterdämmerung*. The defeat transformed a normal fact into an exceptional narrative: it is a fabulous myth that has been preserved and even grown in the public imagination.'

Bigode, Barbosa and Juvenal – probably not by coincidence Brazil's three black players – were held responsible. In 1963, Barbosa, in an effort to exorcise his demons, even invited friends to a barbecue at which he ceremonially burned the Maracanã goalposts, but he could not escape the opprobrium. The story is told of how, twenty years after the final, he was in a shop when a woman pointed at him. 'Look at him,' she said to her young son. 'He's the man who made all of Brazil cry.'

'In Brazil,' he said shortly before his death in 2000, 'the maximum sentence is thirty years, but I have served fifty.' Yes, it was a mistake, but if a reason is to be found for the defeat, Zizinho insists, it is the use of the W-M. 'The last four games of the World Cup were the first time in my life I played W-M,' he explained in an interview with Bellos. 'Spain played W-M, Sweden played W-M, Yugoslavia played W-M. The three that played W-M we beat. But Uruguay didn't play W-M. Uruguay played with one deep back and the other in front.' They played, in other words, a system whose defensive base was the same as that used by Brazil to win the Copa América in 1919.

Just as England reacts to any set-back by lamenting technical inadequacy, so Brazil blames defensive frailties. Perdigão's reference to *Götterdämmerung*, of course, echoes the *Mirror*'s 'Twilight of the Gods' headline after England's 6-3 defeat to Hungary, and that is not coincidence. The plaintiveness comes from the same source – a railing against habitual failings, an angry realisation that the traditional way of playing is not innately superior. The irony is that Brazil's traditions and England's could hardly be more different. There is no right way of playing; at some point every football culture doubts its own strengths and looks wistfully to the greener grass abroad.

No matter that twenty-two goals had been scored in six games; what was important was those two that had been conceded at the last. Clearly, Brazil's pundits decided, the defence needed bolstering. By the time of the 1954 World Cup, the attack-minded Flávio Costa had been supplanted by the more cautious Zezé Moreira. It was, a French journalist said, like replacing an Argentine dancer with an English clergyman.

The great trio of inside-forwards was gone, and a stopper centre-half was introduced in Pinheiro, a far more defensive player than Juvenal. Brazil swatted Mexico aside, but then drew with Yugoslavia before going out to Hungary in a vicious quarter-final, beaten 4-2 in the so-called 'Battle of Berne'. In his official report on the tournament, the head of the Brazilian delegation, João Lyra Filho, concluded that 'flashy trim lends artistic expression to the match, to the detriment of yield and results', something he blamed largely on black players. He was, fortunately, ignored, and

Jimmy Hogan, the father of central European football, demonstrating heading technique to the RAF in France, 1940

Vittorio Pozzo looks on nervously as Italy beat Czechoslovakia in the 1934 World Cup final

Herbert Chapman, the inventor of the W-M (*all pics © Getty Images*)

Boris Arkadiev outlines his theory of organised disorder to his CDKA players
(*Pavel Eriklinstev*)

Matthias Sindelar, the withdrawn centre-forward, whose genius lay at the heart of the Austrian Wunderteam

Sándor Kocsis beats Gil Merrick to the ball in Hungary's 6-3 victory over England at Wembley in 1953 (*both pics* © *PA Photos*)

Alicide Gigghia beats Moacyr Barbosa at his near post, to win the 1950 World Cup for Uruguay (*PA Photos*)

Jules Rimet hands over the trophy to Uruguay's captain, Obdulio Varela (*Getty Images*)

Three men who brought tactics to Brazil: Martim Francisco (top), Gentil Cardoso (bottom left) and Fleitas Solich (bottom right) (all pics © *Arquiro/Agência O Globo*)

Béla Guttmann, the wandering Hungarian, during his time as coach of Benfica (*PA Photos*)

Vicente Feola, the Brazil coach who introduced 4-2-4 to the world (*Getty Images*)

Garrincha, the winger whose anarchic style flourished in the 4-2-4 (*Getty Images*)

Stan Cullis devises another tactical masterplan for Wolves (*Getty Images*)

Viktor Maslov talks his Torpedo players through his latest stratagem (*Pavel Eriklinstev*)

the consensus agreed with Garrincha's complaint – or at least that ghosted for him in Stratton Smith's collection *The Brazil Book of Football* – that 'Brazil planned to win the World Cup by burying the individual in a general team plan. So they went to Europe to play like Europeans... What counted in Brazilian football was the ability of our players to improvise.'

Garrincha was never a player for tactical discipline, but improvisation couldn't be allowed to run anarchically unchecked. What was needed was a structure in which improvisation could flourish, without leaving the defence as exposed as poor Bigode had been. The answer, strangely, had been practised in Brazil almost since the beginning of the decade.

Just who invented the 4-2-4 is a matter of some debate: as Assaf says, 'it has many fathers'. Some credit Zezé Moreira, some Fleitas Solich, some Martim Francisco; there are even some who say it didn't emerge in its true form until Lula applied it at Santos. If Axel Vartanyan is right, it is possible that it is not even a Brazilian invention, but one of a number of variations employed by Boris Arkadiev at Dinamo Moscow. The truth is that Brazil, with the *diagonal*, and Hungary, with their withdrawn centre-forward (and correspondingly withdrawn left-half), had independently moved to a position from which the 4-2-4 was an inevitable development.

The Paraguayan coach Fleitas Solich certainly had a key role in promoting the 4-2-4, winning three Carioca titles in a row with it at Flamengo between 1953 and 1955, but the first man consciously to employ the system seems to have been Martim Francisco. He was coach of Vila Nova, a club from Nova Lima, a town about twenty miles from Belo Horizonte. He pushed his left-half, Lito, back to play as the '*quarto zagueiro*' – the 'fourth defender' – the term that is still used today in Brazil for the defender whose job it is to step up and join the midfield. Right from the start, though, there was a recognition that that wasn't enough to prevent a two-man midfield being swamped, and so one of the front four also had a brief to drop back. In Francisco's team, it was Osório, the right-winger. In practice, the 4-2-4 almost never appeared in that form. In possession, while attacking, it would be a 3-3-4; out of possession, a 4-3-3. The system was widely adopted, and soon developed two further modifications.

The first was a system of zonal marking, introduced by Zezé Moreira at Fluminense, which obviated the need for the strict

The 4-2-4: Vila Nova 1951

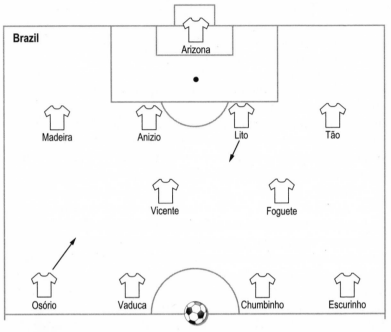

man-to-man marking of the W-M – the aspect that had failed so disastrously in 1950 – and also permitted a greater fluidity. When Arsenal toured Brazil in 1949, they had been struck by the willingness of Brazilian sides to attack from all positions, something they seem both to have feared and regarded as a weakness, a sign of tactical indiscipline. 'Suddenly, a bloke comes dashing through and he's had a shot at goal and the ball went wide,' said the full-back Laurie Scott, describing Arsenal's 5-1 win over Fluminense to Aidan Hamilton. 'And we started looking around to see who we'd got to blame for this. We couldn't find it. We found out it was their full-back. See, they didn't care. I never went up there like that.' Attacking full-backs would become an increasingly important part of the Brazilian game. Given the space in front of the full-backs, 4-2-4 was a system that encouraged them to advance, while at the same time providing immediate cover. Once marking had ceased to be man-to-man, it became a simple process for the 'fourth defender' to react to the forward movement of the full-back by not pushing out himself, leaving his side still with the three-man defensive cover they would have had in the W-M.

The second was the reintroduction of the *ponta da lança*, one of the two central forwards dropping slightly deeper than his partner, providing a natural link with the midfield. This was nothing particularly new – it was no different to the attacking inside-forward role in the *diagonal*, and Puskás had been performing a similar function for years in the Hungarian system – but it was a position that seems to have been naturally suited to the temperament of the Brazilian game. It soon found its apogee in a scrawny teenager from Três Corações. Pelé was sixteen when Lula gave him his debut at Santos; within a year he was inspiring his national side to their first World Cup.

△▽

For all Guttmann's claims, when he arrived with Honvéd in November 1956, their system caused few surprises. If anything, Brazil was further down the road to 4-2-4 than the Hungarians, although the similarity of shape was obvious. 'Basically, the only difference between Brazil's interpretation of the system and that of Hungary was in the number worn by the forward who withdrew into midfield,' said Nándor Hidegkuti. 'In 1958, the Brazilians opted for inside-right Didi, while for Hungary it was the centre-forward who fell back. In both teams the withdrawn forward operated in what we might call left midfield, and again in both teams the left-half fell back to play a more defensive role, while the right-half maintained the balance in midfield by playing a more open attacking game.'

Guttmann's impact was less to do with system than with style, and this is where the orthodoxy – or at least the British orthodoxy – about the great Hungary side requires a gloss. English observers tended to be overwhelmed by the *Aranycsapat*'s technical ability and the fluidity facilitated by the withdrawn centre-forward. Perhaps they differed marginally in degree, but had that been all they were about, they would not have been substantially different from the Austrian *Wunderteam*. Hungary, though, also had a briskness about them, a sense of purpose: their artistry was directed towards the end of winning, and in that they were very much Jimmy Hogan's heirs. Geoffrey Green perhaps flattered England when he spoke of the Hungary of 1953 as having hit a midpoint between British directness and continental elaboration, but the general point was sound. English advocates of the long-ball game would later see validation for their methods in the fact that, so often in that game at Wembley, Hungary transformed defence into attack with a counter of two or three passes. It was not 4-2-4 itself that Guttmann brought to Brazil, but that sense of purpose.

The difference in approach was perhaps best summed up by Nélson Rodrigues, who often wrote brief dramatic scenes featuring real-life personalities – effectively imaginary interviews. He responded to Honvéd's tour with a piece featuring Ferenc Puskás and Zizinho, still Brazil's great hero, ending by asking each what was the most magical thing for them to do during a game. Zizinho answered that it was setting up a team-mate to score a goal, while for Puskás it was, not surprisingly, scoring a goal. The example may be whimsical, but it does give an indication of Brazilian football's lack of pragmatism at the time.

São Paulo had had a poor season in 1956, finishing second in the Paulista championship, seven points behind the champions Santos, and they did not begin 1957 well, lying fifth after the first half of the championship, seven points behind the leaders Corinthians. Gradually, though, Guttmann's methods began to take effect.

He had a grid painted on a wall at the training ground, and in practice sessions would roll the ball to his forwards, shouting to them which square he wanted them to hit. He worked on long balls aimed for the centre-forward to flick on for the wingers. He discouraged dallying on the ball, drilling his players in rapid passing to such an extent that his calls of 'tat-tat-tat' and 'ping-pang-pong' became catchphrases. Everything was about moving the ball at speed, about getting his side playing by instinct. Perhaps most crucially, he signed Zizinho, then thirty-four, from the Rio club Bangu, and – in a foreshadowing of what he would later do with Mario Coluna at Benfica – installed him as the more creative of the midfield two, with Dino Sani, who had been the playmaker, dropping into the more defensive midfield role. 'It was only then,' he said, 'that I really began to play.'

São Paulo won the Paulista championship that year, at which Guttmann decamped for Europe. His influence, though, was carried on by Vicente Feola. Little more than an average player, Feola had led São Paulo to the Paulista championship in 1949, and had stayed on at the club after standing down as coach, serving as Guttmann's assistant. When he was appointed as national coach for the 1958 World Cup, it came as something of a surprise. Osvaldo Brandão had been forced to stand down after Brazil had finished third in the Copa América in 1957 and neither Silvio Pirilo nor Pedrinho, his two immediate successors, really impressed. There was a movement to have Solich appointed, but the fact he was Paraguayan counted against him, and so the Brazilian federation turned to Feola as a safe, uncontroversial choice. He was a *bon vivant* so relaxed, rumour said, that he was prone to cat-napping on the bench during training, although it is doubtful how true that is. Ruy Castro argues in his biography of Garrincha that Feola suffered coronary problems brought on by his excessive weight, and would occasionally suffer a stabbing pain in his chest. The best way to deal with it, he had learned, was to close his eyes, lower his head and wait for the spasm to pass, which a hysterical press supported by paparazzi photographs interpreted as sleeping.

Antonio Rattín, the Argentinian centre-half who played under Feola during his brief spell at Boca Juniors, though, insists that, on at least one occasion, he did drift off. 'Every training session we ended with a game,' he said. 'One day, a very hot day, we started playing, and kept playing, and kept playing. We were waiting for him to blow the whistle for half-time, but he just sat there. We kept looking at him, waiting for him to do something. So eventually I went over to him, and he was snoring. He'd been asleep all the time.'

Yet while Feola may have been a jovial fat man who enjoyed playing up to the stereotype, he was not the pushover the federation had imagined him to be. With funding from the Juscelino Kubitschek government, the squad for the 1958 World Cup was the best-prepared in Brazil's history. Officials visited twenty-five different locations in Sweden before selecting a training base, and then had all twenty-five female staff at that hotel replaced to minimise potential distractions. They even campaigned, without success, to have a local nudist camp closed for the duration of the tournament.

The backroom staff included a doctor, a dentist, a trainer, a treasurer, a psychologist and, in the former Fluminense coach Ernesto Santos, a spy, employed to gather information on opponents. After initial medical tests, the doctor prescribed the majority of the squad medication to tackle intestinal parasites, while one player had to be treated for syphilis. The dentist was just as busy, extracting a total of 470 teeth from the thirty-three players in the provisional squad. Feola was happy enough to go along with those measures, but he was openly dismissive of the psychologist Dr João Carvalhães.

Carvalhães, who usually assessed the psychological suitability of those applying to be bus drivers, had performed a series of tests on the squad, the most derided of which involved asking them to draw a picture of a man. The results were intriguing – the more instinctive the player, apparently, the more likely he was to draw a stick figure or something representational rather than attempting mimetic detail – but his conclusions were laughable. Pelé, he said, was 'obviously infantile' and did 'not possess the sense of responsibility necessary for a team game'. As Garrincha had scored just thirty-eight out of a possible 123 on his test – lower than the minimum required to drive a bus in São Paulo – Carvalhães suggested he was unsuited to high-pressure games. Feola ignored him and insisted both should be in his squad.

Neither, though, played in Brazil's opening game, an unexceptional 3-0 win over Austria. Pelé was injured, while Garrincha had fallen out of favour for showboating in a warm-up friendly against Fiorentina (having rounded the goalkeeper he decided not to roll the ball into an empty net, but to wait for him to recover, upon which he beat him again before walking the ball over the line). Yet Feola, it seems would have played him, had Santos not warned about the strength of the four midfielders in Austria's W-M. Feola could rely on Mario Zagallo to track back on the left – he, in effect, fulfilled the Orsório role – but that was not Garrincha's natural game, and so he turned instead to the more disciplined Joel of Flamengo.

They were also omitted against England, who were themselves experimenting with backroom staff – an indication of the growing professionalism of the game across the world. The Tottenham manager Bill Nicholson was sent to scout Brazil, and he concluded the way to stop Brazil was to stop Didi. On his suggestion, the England manager Walter Winterbottom – in a move almost without precedent – made tactical changes to counter Brazil's threat. The lanky Don Howe, a full-back at West Bromwich Albion, was brought in to play as a second centre-half alongside Billy Wright, with Thomas Banks and Eddie Clamp, a right-half at Wolves, operating as attacking full-backs on either side of them, and Bill Slater deputed to sit tight on Didi. Vavá hit the bar, Clamp cleared one off the line and Colin McDonald twice produced fine saves to keep out headers from José Altafini (who was still going by the nickname of Mazzola), but the system dulled Brazil, and England got away with a goalless draw.

That left Brazil needing to beat the USSR in their final group game to be sure of progression to the last eight. Carvalhães conducted further tests, asking the players to draw the first thing that came into their heads. Garrincha produced a circle with a few spokes radiating from it. It looked vaguely like a sun, but when Carvalhães asked what it was supposed to be, Garrincha replied that it was the head of Quarentinha, a team-mate at Botafogo. Carvalhães promptly ruled him out. In total, of the eleven who would eventually start against the USSR, he judged nine unsuitable for such a high-pressure game. Fortunately Feola trusted his own judgement, and selected both Pelé and Garrincha. 'You may be right,' Pelé recalls him saying to Carvalhães. 'But the thing is, you don't know anything about football.'

Feola was concerned by reports of the Soviets' supreme fitness, and had decided that his side had to intimidate them with Brazilian skill from the off. 'Remember,' he said to Didi just before he left the dressing room, 'the first pass goes to Garrincha.'

It took a little under twenty seconds for the ball to reach the winger. Boris Kuznetsov, the experienced Soviet left-back, moved to close him down. Garrincha feinted left and went right; Kuznetsov was left on the ground. Garrincha paused, and beat him again. And again. And then once again put him on the ground. Garrincha advanced, leaving Yuri Voinov on his backside. He darted into the box, and fired a shot from a narrow angle that smacked against the post. Within a minute Pelé had hit the bar, and a minute after that, Vavá gave Brazil the lead from Didi's through-ball. Gabriel Hanot called them the greatest three minutes of football ever played.

Brazil won only 2-0, but the performance was every bit as special as the demolitions of Spain and Sweden had been eight years earlier. Wales offered surprising resistance in the quarter-final, even without the imposing presence of the injured John Charles, and lost only 1-0, but this Brazil side could not be denied. France, hampered by an injury to Bob Jonquet, were brushed aside 5-2 in the semi-final, and Sweden went down by the same score in the final. 'There was no doubt this time,' Glanville wrote, 'that the best, immeasurably the finest, team had won.'

It was, Feola said, Zagallo's role, balancing the anarchic brilliance of Garrincha, that had proved key. Initially an inside-forward, Zagallo had converted himself into a winger because he realised that was his only chance of getting into the national side, and so was ideally suited to the role of tracking back and forth on the left flank. By the 1962 World Cup, he had taken to playing so deep that the system began to be referred to as a 4-3-3. 'The age factor, in Chile, was one we had always to take into consideration,' explained Aimoré Moreira, who replaced Feola as his health deteriorated but picked a similar squad for the following World Cup. 'That was responsible for our tactics being less flexible than some, remembering the team's sparkle in Sweden, expected. In Chile we had strictly to employ each player in accordance with what we knew about the yield of the whole team. For example, Didi was more and more a player good at waiting in midfield, and blocking the centre to the opponents... Zito, quicker, more dynamic, was able to shuttle backwards and forwards, and could last out a full ninety minutes while doing this. This meant, because of the need carefully to relate the role of one to the other, the elasticity of attacks was limited – with this one great compensation, that every player was free and had the ability to use his own initiative, and make variations.'

The greatest compensation of all was Garrincha. Opponents regularly set two or even three men to mark him, and he simply bypassed them. Pelé played only the opening two matches in Chile before injury ended his involvement, but Garrincha was enough. He missed a penalty but scored twice as England were seen off 3-1 in the quarter-final, and scored two more and was sent off in a 4-2 victory over Chile in the semi. Reprieved for the final, he was relatively subdued, but it didn't matter: 1962 had been his tournament, the final triumph of the winger before the culls of the mid-sixties.

In a piece in *A Gazeta* in 1949, Mazzoni wrote that, 'For the Englishman, football is an athletic exercise; for the Brazilian it's a game.

'The Englishman considers a player that dribbles three times in

Brazil, 1958 World Cup

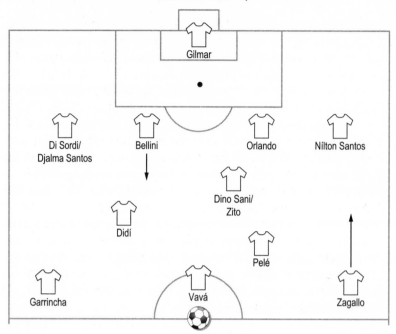

Brazil, 1962 World Cup

succession is a nuisance; the Brazilian considers him a virtuoso.

'English football, well played, is like a symphonic orchestra; well played, Brazilian football is like an extremely hot jazz band.

'English football requires that the ball moves faster than the player; Brazilian football requires that the player be faster than the ball.

'The English player thinks; the Brazilian improvises.'

There was nobody who exemplified the difference more than Garrincha. At São Paulo, Guttmann had had a left-winger called Canhoteiro, who was regarded as the left-footed Garrincha (the name translates as 'left-footed'). 'Tactics,' Guttmann once said after seeing Canhoteiro ignore him brilliantly once again, 'are for everybody, but they are not valid for him.' The beauty of playing four at the back was that, although it wasn't predicated on such players – as Viktor Maslov and Alf Ramsey would prove – it provided an environment in which they could thrive. The world soon got the message, and by the time of the 1966 World Cup, the W-M had all but passed into history.

△▽△▽△▽△▽△▽

Chapter Eight

The English Pragmatism (1)

△▽ 'You in England,' Helenio Herrera announced at an
impromptu press conference at Birmingham Airport in March
1960, 'are playing in the style we continentals used so many years
ago, with much physical strength, but no method, no technique.'
No one who had seen his Barcelona side deconstruct
Wolverhampton Wanderers, the English champions, the night
before could have been in much doubt that he was right.
Barcelona, already 4-0 up from the first leg, had dazzled in the
second, completing a 9-2 aggregate victory. The days of the floodlit
friendlies, in which Wolves had beaten the likes of Honvéd and
Spartak Moscow, seemed an awfully long time ago.

Wolves, in fairness, were more direct than most, but Herrera
believed the fact they had been so dominant domestically was
evidence of a more general weakness in the English game. 'When
it came to modern football, the Britons missed the evolution,' he
said, mocking their instinctive conservatism. 'The English are
creatures of habit: tea at five.' The irony of that is that Stan Cullis,
the Wolves manager, was actually one of England's more
progressive thinkers.

The heavy defeats to Hungary had made clear that any notion of
English superiority was a myth, and there was at least a recognition that the English style had to change, as is demonstrated by
the publication of a slew of books lamenting the passing of a
golden age. The problem was that nobody seemed too sure how to
go about it. The W-M was widely blamed, but remained the default.
In as much as solutions were suggested, they tended to follow the
course prescribed by Willy Meisl in *Soccer Revolution*: go back to the
golden age and readopt the 2-3-5; which tended, of course, rather

to prove Herrera's point: as the rest of the world became increasingly tactically sophisticated, there were serious and influential football writers in Britain advocating a return to a formation that had looked outmoded twenty years earlier.

The option of copying Hungary was something that was only really considered at Manchester City. Johnny Williamson had had success playing as a deep-lying centre-forward in the reserve side at the end of the 1953–54 season and, the following year, the manager Les McDowall had Don Revie play there for the first team. Revie subsequently devoted twenty pages of his memoir, *Soccer's Happy Wanderer*, to explaining the system. After an uncertain start – they were beaten 5-0 by Preston on the opening day of the season – and some difficult times on the heavy pitches of the winter, City went on to reach the Cup final and finish seventh, while Revie was named Footballer of the Year. That summer, though, Revie took a family holiday in Blackpool against the wishes of the club and, after being suspended for the opening fortnight of the season, remained on the periphery. Injuries restored him to the line-up for the FA Cup final, in which City beat Birmingham, but Revie had become disillusioned and joined Sunderland the following season.

City reverted to more traditional methods, while Revie struggled to settle at Roker Park. Locked in a spiral of reckless spending, Sunderland then tumbled into an illegal payments scandal, as they were found to be offering win bonuses of £10, when the stipulated maximum was £4. Amid the chaos, as their manager Bill Murray was replaced by Alan Brown, Sunderland were relegated. Revie, anyway, may not have adapted. 'There was only one way he could play,' said Sunderland's inside-right Charlie Fleming. 'He did a lot of things foreign to us... Don's system was alright in Manchester, but everybody knew about it when he came to Sunderland and how to play against it. Don couldn't change.' Or perhaps it was that British players couldn't change. Either way, Revie soon departed for Leeds, where he was used as an inside-forward, and the momentum of his experiment was lost.

Even those British teams who enjoyed success in the early European Cup tended simply to prosper not through innovation but because they were very good at applying the old model. Hibernian for instance, semi-finalists in the first European Cup, were famed for their Famous Five front line of Gordon Smith, Bobby Johnstone, Lawrie Reilly, Eddie Turnbull and Willie

Ormond. The Manchester United of Bobby Charlton, Dennis Viollet and Duncan Edwards, for all their youth and vibrancy, were a side rooted in the W-M. 'By a combination of short and long passes,' Geoffrey Green wrote, '[they] have discarded a static conventional forward shape and, with the basic essential of a well-ordered defence, have found success by the sudden switching and masking of the final attacking thrust by their fluid approach. This aims at producing a spare man – or "man over" – at the height of the attack.' Busby's United may have been fluid in British terms, and their brilliance is not in doubt, but they were still orthodox by European standards.

The most successful radicalism came at Tottenham Hotspur, where Hungarian thinking had taken hold even before the watershed of 1953. Arthur Rowe had lectured in Budapest in 1940, but education had proved a two-way process; after giving the sport to the world, finally there was cross-pollination back into Britain. Thanks to Peter McWilliam, an enlightened coach of the twenties and thirties (Scottish, of course), Tottenham had a historical preference for a close-passing game, something of which Rowe had been part. Although he had played as a deep-lying centre-half for Spurs, Rowe had been a far more rounded player than Herbie Roberts and his many imitators, preferring to hold possession and delay until he could play accurate passes rather than simply hoofing it forwards without design. Working with Hungarians, though, taught him just how far the practice could be extended and when, in 1949, he was appointed as manager of Tottenham, then a second-division side, he set about implementing that style: 'Make it simple, make it quick,' as he always urged.

Almost his first act was to sign Alf Ramsey, at the time noted as a forward-thinking right-back at Southampton. In *And the Spurs Go Marching On*, Rowe explains how he had admired Ramsey's willingness to attack, but encouraged him not to rely so heavily on long forward passes. 'Had he [Ramsey] ever thought how much more accuracy was guaranteed, how much more progress could be made if he pumped 15- or 20-yard passes to a withdrawn [outside-right Sonny] Walters. The opposing left-back would hesitate to follow Walters back into the Spurs half, which was definitely no man's land to the full-back then, thus giving Walters the vital gift of space. And Sonny could now make an inside pass if Alf followed up and made himself available.'

Almost uniquely in Britain, Spurs began building from the back, with Ramsey given licence to push on. 'There is no limit to where even a defender will go to attack,' he said. 'Maybe you have noticed how often I go upfield to cross a ball or even have a shot at goal. That a defender should not attempt to score a goal is something to which I can never subscribe.' He could only do that, though, because his centre-half, Bill Nicholson, as dour a player as he was a public speaker, was prepared to sit in and provide cover.

At times during that 1950–51 season, their first back in the top flight, Spurs were magnificent. After a 7-0 win over Newcastle in the November, for instance, the *Telegraph* was moved to write that 'Tottenham's method is simple. Briefly, the Spurs principle is to hold the ball a minimum amount of time, keep it on the ground and put it ahead into an open space where a colleague will be a second or two later. The result is their attacks are carried on right through the side with each man taking the ball in his stride at top pace, for all the world like a wave gathering momentum as it races to the far distant shore. It is all worked out in triangles and squares and when the mechanism of it clicks at speed, as it did on Saturday, with every pass placed to the last refined inch on a drenched surface, there is simply no defence against it.' They won the title by four points, and were still playig a similar style when they did the Double ten years later.

Such progressiveness was rare in England, though, and Spurs were regarded with suspicion, despite their success.

As the rest of the world developed technically, and worked out increasingly sophisticated defensive patterns or means of structuring fluidity, British football ploughed its own, less subtle, furrow. In its own way, it was just as rooted in fear – or, to its apologists, pragmatism – as the *catenaccio* Herrera would eventually adopt, but this was a very British insecurity. Skill, or anything that required thinking too much, was not to be trusted, while physical toughness remained the ultimate virtue. It is no coincidence that, the World Cup triumph of 1966 aside, the iconic image of English football remains a blood-soaked Terry Butcher, bandaged but unbowed after inspiring England to the goalless draw against Sweden that ensured qualification for the 1990 World Cup. Even the manner of that stalemate was characteristic. Italy might have set out to kill the game, passing the ball at deathly pace around midfield, wasting time, breaking the rhythm – as England in fact

Tottenham Hotspur 2 Leicester City 0, FA Cup Final, Wembley, May 6, 1961

Wolves 3 Honvéd 2, friendly, Molineux, Wolverhampton, 13 December 1954

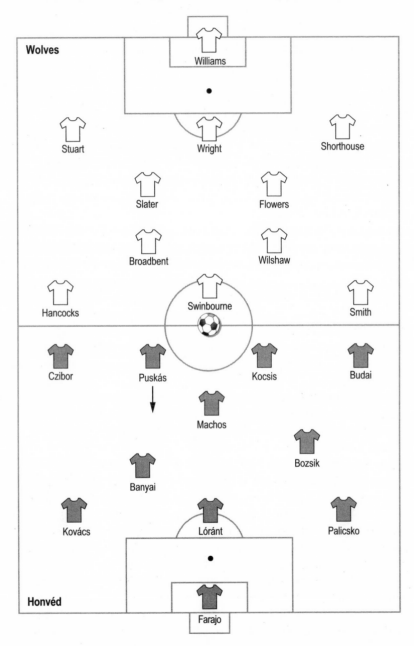

did in a scarcely credible role reversal against Italy in Rome in 1997. In Stockholm in 1989, though, England simply sat back, defended deep, and relied on courage under fire: what Simon Kuper has called the urge to recreate Dunkirk at every opportunity.

To blame Cullis for a trait that has run through English football from its earliest origins would be nonsensical, just as it was for writers in the fifties to blame Chapman (or even, as Willy Meisl did, on the basis of a hint supposedly dropped in a conversation with his brother, to persist in the wishful thinking that, had Chapman not died when he did, he would have reverted to a more classical system). Besides, if results rather than aesthetics are the goal, there is nothing necessarily wrong with functional physicality; thirteen years after the Hungary debacle, it would, after all, win England a World Cup. What is important, is the method and the thought behind it.

Cullis's side might have been overwhelmed by Herrera's Barcelona, but they had achieved notable results against elite sides only a few years earlier. Floodlights were installed at Molineux in the summer of 1953, and officially turned on for a game against a South Africa national side that September. Racing Club of Buenos Aires were beaten 3-1, a game in which 'Wolverhampton Wanderers efficiently demonstrated that English soccer played with speed and spirit is still world class', according to the ever-opinionated Desmond Hackett in *The Express*. Wolves then beat Dinamo Moscow 2-1 and Spartak 4-0, but the most memorable match, without question, was the meeting with the Honvéd of Puskás, Czibor, Bozsik and Kocsis on 14 December 1954. After the two humiliations Hungary had inflicted on England, this was a chance for revenge.

On the morning of the game, Cullis, remembering how Hungary had struggled in the mud in the World Cup final against West Germany that summer, sent out three apprentices – one of them a sixteen-year-old Ron Atkinson – to water the pitch. 'We thought he was out of his mind,' Atkinson said in an interview quoted in Jim Holden's biography of Cullis. 'It was December and it had been raining incessantly for four days.'

Honvéd struck twice in the opening quarter-hour, but the conditions soon began to take their toll. 'Honvéd gradually got bogged down,' Atkinson went on. 'Their tricks got stuck in the mud.' Cullis determined to bring the mud into play as little as possible and at half-time ordered his players to hit more long passes, to get the ball forward quickly to try to catch out the Honvéd full-backs, whom he felt were playing too square.

Four minutes into the second half, Wolves got the lifeline they needed as Johnny Hancocks converted a penalty. 'Bit by bit Wolves began to tighten the screws...' wrote Geoffrey Green. 'They seemed to double in number and swarm everywhere. The pitch, more and more churned up, resembled thick glue. And the Molineux crowd surged, tossed and roared like a hurricane at sea, and called for the kill.' With fourteen minutes remaining, Dennis Wilshaw, who had almost been ruled out through injury after crashing his bike on the way to the game, crossed for Roy Swinbourne to head an equaliser. Within ninety seconds the same pair had combined for the winner.

After a year of misery, English football revelled in the victory. 'I may never live to see a greater thriller than this,' wrote Peter Wilson in the *Daily Mirror*. 'And if I see many more as thrilling I may not live much longer anyway.' Charlie Buchan, in his column in the *News Chronicle*, hailed the affirmation of the English style. The *Daily Mail* captured the sense of ecstasy as it ran the headline: 'Hail Wolves, "Champions of the World".' It was a proclamation that so riled Gabriel Hanot he was inspired to institute the European Cup to disprove it.

Only Willy Meisl remained aloof, pointing out that only a few days earlier Honvéd had also lost to Red Star Belgrade, who at the time were seventh in the Yugoslav league, well adrift of the leaders Partizan. 'No one called Partizan champions of the world,' he said. 'Dare I also remark in passing that quagmires are not usually considered the best pitches on which world championships ought to be decided, not even neutral quagmires.' When it came to a battle of physique against technique, England could still mix it with the best of them, and yet the emptiness of such consolation was exposed in the years that followed. Wolves went on – admittedly in the void left by the Munich air crash – to win the league in 1958 and 1959, and the FA Cup in 1960, but the impression they made in formalised European competition, which began in 1955, was all but nil. Herrera's jibe stung because it was so accurate.

△▽

Like so many managers, Cullis's style as a coach bore little relation to the player he had been. He was generally regarded as a cultured, attack-minded centre-half. Even Puskás spoke of his reputation as 'the most classical centre-half of his time'. His leadership skills became apparent early and he captained Wolves at nineteen and England at twenty-two. So, too, did his meticulousness, as he kept a book in which he recorded his impressions of the centre-forwards against whom he played. Tommy Lawton said that to beat Cullis a forward needed 'the penetrative powers of a tank and the pace of a racing whippet'. Cullis also developed a reputation for scrupulous fairness, famously deciding against hacking down Albert Stubbins when the forward got behind him to score for Liverpool in a title-decider against Wolves. John Arlott referred to him as 'the passionate puritan'.

In terms of his coaching education, Cullis had the advantage of playing under the eccentric Major Frank Buckley, one of the more adventurous managers of the thirties. In the dressing room at Molineux, Buckley had installed a therapeutic diathermy machine, a universal machine for galvanism, sumsoidal and paradic treatments and a machine that gave out ultra-violet rays for irradiation. He also, notoriously, ahead of the 1939 FA Cup final had his players injected with 'animal secretions', supposedly taken from monkey's glands, although Cullis believed they were placebos designed more to enhance self-belief than muscle mass.

Encouraged to question the orthodoxy, Cullis went back to basics. 'There is no substitute for hard work,' he always insisted, and he was one of the first coaches in England to take fitness training seriously. He would have his players go on pre-season stamina-building runs across Cannock Chase, and employed Frank Morris, a former international runner, as a fitness coach. His players, he said, 'must have tremendous team spirit, they must be superbly fit, and they must use the correct tactics on the field.'

Those tactics mainly comprised a W-M in which every effort was taken to play the ball forward quickly. Wolves, Cullis insisted, as countless managers of similar philosophy would, did not hit aimless long balls, but rather attempted to transfer the ball swiftly to the two wingers, Jimmy Mullen and Johnny Hancocks. 'Some ill-advised critics called it kick and rush,' the centre-half and captain Billy Wright said. 'Nothing could be further from the truth. Every phase is strictly logical and, although placing unselfish coordination before individualism, Cullis has never scorned ball players.'

While he accommodated such gifted players as Peter Broadbent, Jimmy Murray and Bobby Mason in his side, skill, for Cullis, was to be harnessed for the ends of the team, and was certainly not an end in itself. Although he believed devoutly in the importance of fairness, notions of there being a 'right way' to play meant nothing to Cullis; for him the game was about winning. 'Because we insist that every player in possession of the ball makes rapid progress towards the business of launching an attack,' he said, 'our forwards are not encouraged to parade their abilities in ostentatious fashion, which might please a small section of the crowd at the cost of reducing the efficiency of movement.'

Where others praised Hungary's 6-3 victory at Wembley as a festival of passing and individual skill, Cullis instead saw a vindication of his own beliefs. The goalkeeper, Gyula Grosics, he pointed out, had a tendency to clear the ball long. Only one of Hungary's goals, he noted, came from a move begun in their own half of the field: three resulted from moves of one pass, one from a move of two passes and one from a free-kick. The pass-and-move football that was so admired, he said, came only in the second half when Hungary were keeping possession from England. 'The number of scoring chances which will arrive during the course of a match is in direct proportion to the amount of time the ball spends in front of goal,' he explained. 'If the defenders in the Wolves team delay their clearances, the ball will be in front of our goal for too long a period and the scoring chances will go to the other side. If too much time is spent in building up our own attacks, the ball will spend less of the game in the other team's penalty area and, of course, we shall score fewer goals.'

In that, Cullis found an ally in Wing-Commander Charles Reep, an RAF officer stationed at nearby Bridgnorth. Reep had been based at Bushy Park in south-west London in the thirties, and had become fascinated by the style of Herbert Chapman's Arsenal after attending two three-hour lectures given by their right-half, Charles Jones, in 1933. In them, Jones emphasised the need for the rapid transfer of ball from back to front, and explained Chapman's concept of the functional winger.

Reep was posted to Germany at the end of the war, and on his return in 1947, was disappointed to find that although the W-M shape had been adopted, Chapman's other ideas had not. The play, he felt, was too slow, while the winger had again become a figure who performed his tricks almost in isolation before sending over crosses that rarely produced goals. Reep became increasingly frustrated, until, as he wrote in an autobiographical article for the Scottish fanzine *The Punter* in 1989, he finally lost patience during a Swindon Town match at the County Ground on 19 March 1950.

There was no game on 19 March 1950, which is troubling given Reep's concern for statistical accuracy (although he may, in fairness, have been let down by a subbing error), but Swindon did beat Bristol Rovers 1-0 at home in Division Three (South) on 18 March, so it seems probable that that is the game to which he refers. After a first half in which he saw attack after attack come to nothing, Reep decided to record them in the second. Swindon, his notes showed, had 147 attacks in the second half. Reep, extrapolating this, and assuming 280 attacks per game and an average of two goals scored, realised this equated to a failure rate of 99.29 per cent, which meant that an improvement of only 0.71 per cent was necessary for a side to average three goals a game. That, he saw, would almost certainly guarantee promotion.

Reep made his analysis more sophisticated and began recording attacking moves for both sides. 'Back in 1950,' he wrote, 'these findings were by no means firmly established, but time was to prove them correct... Only two goals out of nine came from moves which included more than three received passes.' He also observed that a long pass from inside a team's own half appeared to make a move more effective; that possession regained either inside or just outside the opponents' box was the most effective way of scoring; and that it took roughly eight attempts on goal to produce a goal.

At the time, Reep was stationed at Yatesbury, and he began working with the RAF team there. He developed a theory about how wingers should play, and although no contemporary record survives, Øyvind Larson, in an essay on Reep's influence on Norwegian football, discusses a report Reep sent to the then Norway manager Egil Olsen in the nineties. It was initially produced for Walter Winterbottom (although there is no evidence Winterbottom ever read it), ahead of England's friendly against Uruguay in 1954, and was based on his observations of Uruguay's 7-0 victory over Scotland in the World Cup earlier that year. In it he argued that wingers should remain as high up the pitch as they could while remaining onside, almost on the touchline, waiting for long balls out of defence; that in possession they should head always for the near-post and then either shoot or cross; and that when out of possession they should make for the far post (in relation to the ball) in order to support their centre-forward. That, loosely, was how Chapman's wingers behaved and, if it was how Yatesbury's were performing, it brought them success, as they won the Army Southern Commands' knockout cup in 1950.

Reep was redeployed back to Bushy Park in 1950. While there, his theorising caught the attention of Jackie Gibbons, the manager of Brentford and, from February 1951, Reep was employed on a part-time basis by the club. When he arrived, with fourteen games of the season remaining, they were in danger of relegation, but with Reep advising, their goals per game ratio went up from 1.5 to 3, and they took 20 of 28 possible points to stay up comfortably. Later that year, though, Reep was transferred back to Bridgnorth.

Between 1953 and 1967, he and Bernard Benjamin, the head of the Royal Statistical Society, studied 578 games – taking in three World Cups, but mainly English league matches – and discovered that only five percent of all moves consist of four or more received passes and only one per cent of six or more. 'The reason for this is clear,' Ken Bray, a visiting Fellow in the Sport and Exercise Science group at the University of Bath, wrote in his book *How to Score*. 'Long chains of passes require repeated accuracy, very difficult to sustain as defenders move in to close down space – man-mark the targets as the sequence stretches out.' Reep's conclusion was that possession football was counterproductive and, at a low level, such as an RAF side or Brentford, there is probably a large element of truth to that. Reep never differentiated, but Bray is strangely uncritical of either him or Charles Hughes, the FA technical director who developed similar theories in the eighties. Just because long passing moves were rare in the English game of the fifties does not mean they were not desirable. Common does not necessarily equal good. From Chapman's time players had been encouraged to hit the ball long and early, and given the mudbaths that passed for pitches for the middle portion of the season, with good reason. Given long chains of passes were rare, it is hardly surprising so few goals resulted from them.

There is, anyway, a startlingly obvious flaw in the arguments of those who would use Reep's analysis to argue that direct football is more effective. His figures show that 91.5 percent of moves in the games he studied consisted of three received passes or fewer. If the number of passes in a chain before a goal made no difference, then logically the percentage of goals resulting from moves of three or fewer received passes would also be 91.5 percent. If direct football were more effective, this figure should be higher. Yet Bray concludes from Reep's figures that 'around 80 percent of all goals resulted from moves of three passes or fewer'. As has already been noted, Reep himself claimed that 'only two goals out of nine came from moves which included more than three received passes' (so seven out of nine, 77.8 percent, came from moves of three or fewer). Admittedly, Watford in 1981–82 scored 93.4 percent of their goals from moves of three received passes or fewer, but, then, only 72 of 106 goals at the 1982 World Cup (67.9 percent) resulted from moves of three passes or fewer.

If, as those figures suggest, roughly 80 percent of goals result from moves of three received passes or fewer, but 91.5 percent of moves consist of three received passes or fewer, then it surely follows – even within the unsubtle parameters Reep sets out – that moves of three passes or fewer are *less* effective than those of four or more. And these figures do not even take into account the goals scored when long chains of passes have led to a dead-ball or a breakdown; or even the fact that a side holding possession and making their opponents chase is likely to tire less quickly, and so will be able to pick off exhausted opponents late on. It is, frankly, horrifying that a philosophy founded on such a basic misinterpretation of figures could have been allowed to become a cornerstone of English coaching. Anti-intellectualism is one thing, but faith in wrong-headed pseudo-intellectualism is far worse.

One significant statistic does emerge from the article Reep published in the *Journal of the Royal Statistical Society*, although, as it runs counter to his thesis, it goes unremarked. At the 1958 World Cup, 1.3 percent of all moves comprised seven or more passes, as opposed to 0.7 percent in his selection of English league games (across all divisions) for 1957–58. At the 1962 World Cup, it was 2.3 percent compared to 1.3 percent in league games the previous season, and in 1966, 2.6 percent compared to 1.2 percent. That would seem to lead to two conclusions (in as much as any meaningful conclusions can be drawn from such a small sample). Firstly, that long chains of passes became increasingly common between 1958 and 1962, and secondly that international football – at the time surely still the pinnacle of the game – was roughly twice as likely to produce long chains of passes as club football. If long, direct play really were superior, surely there would be more of it the higher the level? Given the percentage of long chains of passes went up between the World Cups in Chile and England, it is not even that that disparity can be dismissed on the grounds of climate and the greater need to retain possession in hot weather (although Reep, anyway, shows no awareness of the possible implications of such outside agencies).

That is not to say that direct football is wrong at all times, merely that fundamentalism in tactics tends to be as misguided as in any sphere. Tactics must rather be conditioned by circumstances and the players available. Reep's apologists misinterpret the figures, but even if they had not, his method is so general as to be all but meaningless. Why would it follow that an approach suited to a Third Division match in Rotherham in December would be equally applicable to a World Cup game in Guadalajara in July? Part of the genius of the great tacticians is their ability to apply the right system at the right time. Even Alf Ramsey, adopting a more possession-based approach for the Mexico World Cup of 1970, acknowledged that.

Still, Reep's statistics supported Cullis's instincts, and – in the English league at least – the two enjoyed a fruitful working relationship. 'It helped me modify and improve points of tactics which were either costing us goals or reducing our scoring potential,' Cullis said. He was also much taken by Reep's isolation of the Position of Maximum Opportunity (POMO), an area a short distance from goal towards the back post from which a striking percentage of goals were scored, and into which Reep encouraged wingers to run. 'Reep's recordings of the Hungary match showed in exact detail the principles which I believed to be true,' Cullis said. 'He was able to establish in black and white the facts for which I was forced to trust my memory where, inevitably, some would become lost or confused.'

Just as convinced that the 6-3 defeat to Hungary was illusory was Alf Ramsey, who played at right-back in that game, and scored England's third goal from the penalty spot. He too noted how many of Hungary's goals had come from long passes, and suggested, in a veiled criticism of Gil Merrick, the England goalkeeper, that they'd just had one of those days when every shot they took flew in. That is disingenuous, ignoring the fact that

Hungary had thirty-five shots to England's five, and the almost embarrassing ease with which Hungary kept possession from England in the second half, but it is intriguing. Perhaps it was simply a function of Ramsey's blinkeredness when it came to foreigners (this, after all, was a man who once turned down the chance of watching *Sleeping Beauty* at the Bolshoi so as not to miss a screening of an Alf Garnett film at the British Embassy Club in Moscow), or perhaps, having developed as a player at a club whose style was not too far removed from that of the Hungarians, a side moreover in which forward players were encouraged to drop off to create space, he was simply not so awestruck as others by the technical and tactical mastery of his opponents. Ramsey, certainly, was not a man to be blinded by beauty.

Given he led England to their only success, it seems bizarre that the general assessment of him should be so ambivalent. While there are those who look back on 1966 – as others before them had looked back to Chapman, or to the 2-3-5 – and see it as the blueprint for all football to come, and there are those who seem somehow to blame Ramsey for having such devotees, as if it were his fault that, having been successful, others without the wit to evolve should seek to copy him. Even as England won the World Cup, respect for him was grudging. 'His detractors would point to his dissection of the game as though it were a laboratory animal, arguing that it robbed football of its poetry, reduced it to a science,' as his biographer Dave Bowler put it. 'It's an assessment he would not disagree with, one which he might well take as a compliment. For he saw football as a tactical exercise, a mental as much as a physical sport.' Not that he cared, but it did not help Ramsey's reputation that he was so wilfully cussed.

Ramsey was, at heart, a realist. That was apparent as soon as he took charge of Ipswich in August 1955. He may have approved of Rowe's methods with Spurs, but he soon realised that push-and-run had no place at a Third Division South team of whom little was expected. He began with the simple things, and although his first game in charge was lost 2-0 to Torquay United, the reporter for the *East Anglian Daily Times* admitted himself impressed by the range of corners on display.

Results soon picked up, but it wasn't until December that Ramsey made the switch that would set in motion a decade of evolution that ended in the World Cup. Jimmy Leadbetter was an inside-forward, a skilful, intelligent player whose major failing was his lack of pace. He had been signed in the summer by Ramsey's predecessor Scott Duncan and, having played just once in Ramsey's first four months in charge, was concerned for his future. Then, just before New Year, Ramsey asked Leadbetter to play on the left-wing. Leadbetter was worried he wasn't fast enough, but Ramsey's concern was more his use of the ball.

'I was supposed to be the left-winger, but I wasn't playing that game,' Leadbetter said. 'I was pulled back, collecting balls from defence – the other full-backs wouldn't come that far out of defence to mark me, so I had space to move in. As I went further forward, I could draw the full-back out of position. He wouldn't stay in the middle of the field marking nobody; he felt he had to come with me. That left a big gap on the left-hand side of the field. That was where [the centre-forward] Ted Phillips played. He needed space, but if you could give him that and the ball, it was in the back of the net.'

Promotion was won in 1957, and as the centre-forward Ray Crawford was signed from Portsmouth and the orthodox right-winger Roy Stephenson from Leicester City, Ramsey's plan took shape. This was 4-2-4, but like the formation with which Brazil won the World Cup, it was 4-2-4 with a twist. Where Brazil had Mario Zagallo shuttling deep from a high position, Ipswich had Leadbetter, whose lack of pace meant he sat deep naturally. If anything, it resembled in shape more the skewed 4-3-3 Brazil would adopt in 1962 than the 4-2-4 of 1958, although the style was very different.

'We believe in striking quickly from defence,' Ramsey said. 'A team is most vulnerable when it has just failed in attack. If I had to suggest an ideal number of passes, I would say three.' Three, perhaps not coincidentally, was also Reep's magic number, although there is no suggestion that the two ever met.

'Alf's idea was the less number of passes you take, the less chance there is of making a bad pass,' Leadbetter said. 'It's better to make three, good, simple ones, because if you try to make ten, as sure as anything you'll make a mess of one of them. You should be in a position to shoot with the third one. You could do that then because of the way teams played.'

The great weakness of the W-M was the pivot necessitated by the fact that there were only three defenders. If an attack came down the attacking side's left, the right-back would move to close the winger down, with the centre-half picking up the centre-forward, and the left-back tucking behind him to cover – and, if playing against a 4-2-4 or another system with two central strikers, picking up the other centre-forward. 'That was the only cover you got, so if you beat your full-back, your forwards had a good chance,' Leadbetter explained.

Ipswich went up again in 1961 and, to the bewilderment of many, went on to win the title the following year, despite having spent only £30,000 assembling their squad, less than a third of what Tottenham paid to bring Jimmy Greaves back from Italy. Ipswich, *The Times* said 'defy explanation – they do the simple things accurately and quickly; there are no frills about their play and no posing. They are not exciting; they do not make the pulses race... Maybe, after all, there is a virtue in the honest labourer.'

With little or no television coverage to expose the tactic, even the best defenders found it difficult to cope. 'Leadbetter laid so deep, I didn't know who the hell I was supposed to be marking,' said the Fulham and England full-back George Cohen. 'He pulled me out of position and started pumping the ball over me to Crawford and Phillips and they had two goals before we knew where we were... Substitute Phillips and Crawford for Hurst and Hunt and you have the England set-up.'

The next season, though, teams knew what to expect. Ipswich lost the Charity Shield 5-1 to Spurs as Bill Nicholson had his full-backs come inside to pick up the two centre-forwards, leaving the half-backs to deal with Leadbetter and Stephenson. Other teams did similarly and, by the end of October when Ramsey was appointed England manager, Ipswich had won just two of fifteen games.

Ramsey's predecessor in the national job, Walter Winterbottom, had been hamstrung by having his team selected by a committee of which he was only part; Ramsey demanded absolute control. Without that, tactical experimentation was impossible: if a group of men was simply voting for the best player to fill each position, the positions had to be laid out in advance, without much regard for balance or the interaction between players, and in the past that had meant unthinking faith in the merits of the W-M. 'People say Matthews, Finney, Carter and so on, they never needed a plan,' Ramsey protested.

'Well, I played with many of these players and I would say England's team was good then, but it would have been many times better if we had also had a rigid plan.'

Outright control, though, was only granted from the following May, so Ramsey faced two games in which he worked with the committee. In the first, they selected a W-M, and England lost 5-2 to France in Paris. That persuaded the committee to follow Ramsey's wishes and switch to a 4-2-4 and, although that brought a 2-1 home defeat to Scotland, he stuck with the formation for most of his early reign.

It was May 1964 and a post-season tour of South America that was to prove key to Ramsey's tactical development. England had hammered the USA 10-0 in New York – some revenge for Ramsey, having played in the side beaten 1-0 by the USA in Belo Horizonte in 1950 – but, exhausted by the effects of travel and scheduled to play Brazil just three days later, they were thrashed 5-1 by Brazil in their first game of a four-team tournament. A draw against Portugal followed, but it was the third game, against Argentina, that was crucial. Argentina knew a draw would be enough for them to win the competition, and so, the days of *la nuestra* a distant memory, sat men behind the ball, content to spoil, hold possession and see out time. England, like 'a bunch of yokels trying to puzzle their way out of a maze', as Desmond Hackett put it in the *Daily Express*, were nonplussed. They dominated the play, but never looked like scoring and, caught on the break, lost 1-0. 'We played 4-2-4 with Roberto Telch coming back, like Zagallo in 1962,' said the Argentina captain José Ramos Delgado. 'England had a great team with Moore, Charlton and Thompson, but we played intelligently. It's true that England had much more possession, but only because we gave up a midfielder so he could defend against certain players.'

As far as some players were concerned, Hackett went on, 'the triple lion badge of England could be three old tabby cats'. His reaction was typical: England may have been outwitted by disciplined opponents sticking to an intelligent plan, but the assumption was – as it so often had been, and would continue to be – that they hadn't tried hard enough, that they hadn't shown enough pride in the shirt. Brian James in the *Daily Mail*, while no less angry, came rather closer to a realistic assessment. 'If you do not give a damn about the game, and are prepared to leave enter-

tainment to music halls you can win anything,' he wrote.
'Argentina have simply taken logic and pushed it to the limit. Their
policy lays down that, "if they do not score, we do not lose"... Only
in their wildest moments of heady recklessness were they prepared
to open out.' Ramsey, of course, would rather have admitted to a
love of Tchaikovsky than to having been influenced by Argentina,
but he did acknowledge the 'tremendous gap' between the two
South American giants and England. Significantly, the FA's report
on the triumph of 1966 made a point of noting how important the
experience gained on that tour had been.

Over that summer, Ramsey rethought his strategy: system, he
seems to have decided, was more important than personnel.
Ramsey's taciturn nature makes it hard to be sure, but it is not
implausible to suggest that the two years that followed represent a
carefully controlled evolution towards winning the World Cup.

The players he had been playing wide in a 4-2-4, Bobby Charlton
and Peter Thompson, weren't the kind to track back, and neither
could Jimmy Greaves nor Johnny Byrne, the two centre-forwards,
realistically have been asked to drop in. George Eastham, who
commonly played as one of the central midfielders, was a
converted inside-forward, and his partner Gordon Milne was no
spoiler either. Ramsey realised that although 4-2-4 was a fine
formation for beating lesser sides, it was unsuitable for playing
stronger opponents, and could leave even a markedly better team
vulnerable if it had an off day. In short, the problem came down to
the fact that while 4-2-4 was potent when you had possession, it
didn't help you get the ball in the first place.

It is unclear when Ramsey's thoughts first turned to Nobby
Stiles, the combative Manchester United anchor, but what was
apparent as soon as he selected him was that Stiles could not play
in a 4-2-4. Do that, and it placed an undue creative burden, the
entire task of manoeuvring the ball from back to front, on one
man. The victim of that realisation was Thompson, even though he
had probably been England's best player in Brazil, being dubbed
'he 'White Pelé' by the local press. To Ramsey's new way of
thinking, the Liverpool winger was too much of an entertainer
and, as he turned to the likes of John Connelly, Ian Callaghan and
Terry Paine, Thompson slowly drifted out of the set-up.

England's first game of the new season was a Home
International away to Northern Ireland the following October.

Ramsey again picked a 4-2-4, but with Bobby Charlton moving back into Eastham's role in midfield and Paine selected on the right and encouraged to drop deep in the manner of Zagallo or Leadbetter. England were 4-0 up by half-time, but ended up winning only 4-3. The *Mail*, speaking of 'ninety minutes of shambles', called for Ramsey's head but, while he was furious at his side's sloppiness, he was not a man to allow adverse media reaction to divert him from his plan.

An unconvincing 2-2 draw against Belgium followed, but the real breakthrough came in a get-together the following February. Six players, including Gordon Banks, Bobby Charlton and Peter Thompson, withdrew because of FA Cup commitments, but Ramsey persisted in his programme, sending out a senior side for a practice game against the Under-23s in a 4-3-3 formation. He was delighted by the result. 'I played what amounted to a rather cruel trick on the younger players, in that I gave them no advance warning of the tactics the seniors were about to employ,' he said. 'The seniors, with three recognised outstanding footballers in midfield – Bryan Douglas on the right, Johnny Byrne in the middle and George Eastham on the left – ran riot with the young lads.' The 'Wingless Wonders' had been born. 'To have two players stuck out wide on the flanks,' Ramsey said, 'is a luxury which can virtually leave a side with nine men when the game is going against them.'

For Dave Bowen, the Wales manager between 1964 and 1974, Ramsey's genius had been to recognise earlier than anyone else in Britain that if sides played four at the back, the traditional winger was dead. 'With three defenders it was different,' he explained. 'The back on the far side was covering behind the centre-half so the winger always had space from the cross-field pass. With four defenders the backs can play tight on the winger and he's lost his acceleration space. Without that, the winger's finished.'

The formation clear, Ramsey then set about finding the best players to deploy within it. In April, Stiles and Jack Charlton made their debuts in a 2-2 draw against Scotland, and the following month Alan Ball came in for a 1-1 draw against Yugoslavia. It was only later than month, though, in a friendly against West Germany in Nuremberg, that Ramsey unveiled his 4-3-3 in public. Ron Flowers of Wolves replaced Stiles, with Ball in midfield, Leeds United's Mick Jones and Eastham up front and Paine and Everton's Derek Temple, in his only appearance for his country, alternating between the wing and offering support to the midfield. England won the game 1-0, then beat Sweden 2-1, with Stiles back in the side, leaving Ramsey convinced the switch to 4-3-3 was right. The key to the system was probably Ball, whose tremendous energy meant he could operate both as a winger and as an auxiliary midfielder – just as Zagallo had for Brazil in 1962.

Early performances in 1965–66 were less impressive, but in December, England, with Stiles, Ball and Charlton in midfield and Roger Hunt, Eastham and Joe Baker up front, beat Spain 2-0 in a performance of overwhelming quality. Ramsey, realising just how potent his system was, immediately decided to place it under wraps. 'I think it would be quite wrong to let the rest of the world, our rivals, see what we are doing,' he told Brian James of the *Mail*. 'I think it is my duty to protect certain players until the time we need them most. This was a step and a very big one in our education as a football party. My job will be to produce the right team at the right time and that does not always mean pressing ahead with a particular combination just because it has been successful.'

Ramsey went back to a 4-2-4 for a friendly draw against Poland and a 1-0 win over West Germany. Geoff Hurst made his debut that day, and immediately struck up an understanding with Hunt. A subsequent 4-3 victory over Scotland pleased the fans and the media, but it confirmed in Ramsey's mind what he already knew: that defensively the 4-2-4 was inadequate. And then, in a 2-0 win over Yugoslavia at Wembley in May 1966, Ramsey introduced the final piece of the jigsaw: the undemonstrative West Ham midfielder Martin Peters. Although Ramsey's designation of him as being 'ten years ahead of his time' would become a burden, Peters was, like Ball and Hurst, a modern multifunctional footballer, capable both of creativity and of doing his share of defensive leg-work.

In a friendly away to Finland, Ramsey played 4-3-3, with Ball, Peters and Charlton in midfield, and Callaghan as the sole winger. England won that game 3-0, and three days later they beat Norway 6-1 in Oslo, this time with two wingers: Connelly in orthodox mode and Paine dropping deeper in the Leadbetter role. Peters was still not considered a first choice – or not by the media anyway – but he was recalled for England's final warm-up game, against Poland in Katowice. This, at last, was the formation to which

Ramsey had been building, a fact acknowledged as he read out the line-up to the press, pausing with an uncharacteristic sense of drama before revealing that he had given the No. 11 shirt to Peters. This was a side with no wingers, orthodox or otherwise. Although it continued to be referred to as 4-3-3, it was really, as Nobby Stiles pointed out in his autobiography, a 4-1-3-2, with him as the anchor and Peters, Charlton and Ball ahead of him, all given licence to break forward and support the front two of Hunt and, it seemed probable at the time, Greaves. England won 1-0, through a Hunt goal and, according to Ray Wilson, it was then that he began to accept that Ramsey might have been right when, three years earlier, he had insisted England would win the World Cup.

Yet against Uruguay in the first game in the World Cup, Ramsey opted for Connelly ahead of Peters and went back to the lopsided 4-3-3. Perhaps he was still playing his cards close to his chest, perhaps he felt a winger still had a role to play in overcoming a weaker side that was sure to pack its defence. Either way, it didn't really work, and as the midfield struggled to get forward to support the front three, Uruguay held out for a 0-0 draw.

Peters came in for the injured Ball in the second game, against Mexico, with Paine replacing Connelly. That reversed the skew, so the winger was on the right rather than the left, but the essentials were the same, Ramsey again using a winger against opposition he expected to beat. They did so, not exhilaratingly but well enough, winning 2-0. Callaghan was selected against France in the third group game, and England again won 2-0, although the match was more notable for a dreadful tackle by Stiles on Jacky Simon. Fifa warned him as to his future conduct, at which Ramsey received a message from the FA asking whether it were really necessary to carry on fielding Stiles. Ramsey, maybe partly on principle, but surely mainly because he knew how vital his midfielder spoiler was, threatened to resign.

At last, against Argentina in the quarter-final, he turned again to 4-1-3-2. Perhaps the tactical switch would have been enough, but Ramsey was aided by an injury to Greaves. That allowed him to include Hurst – a less spectacular forward, but one capable of winning the ball in the air and holding it – without fear of the reaction if he dropped the darling of the press. The game was grim and violent – 'not so much a football match as an international incident' as Hugh McIlvanney put it – but England were resolute

England 4 West Germany 2, World Cup Final, Wembley, London, 30 July 1966

and, after Antonio Rattín, the Argentina captain, had been sent off, a headed goal from Hurst gave them a 1-0 win. It had been no exhibition, but as far as Ramsey was concerned, the lessons of England's defeat in the Maracana two years earlier had been learned. Stiles, unusually, had been asked to man-mark Ermindo Onega, and had done so with discipline, while Ball, playing high on the right, was superb, not merely troubling Argentina offensively, but preventing their full-back, Silvio Marzolini, from advancing.

Stiles's role was crucial again against Portugal in the semi-final, as he neutralised Eusebio in a 2-1 win. Bobby Charlton scored both that day, and the efficacy of the system in allowing the three attacking midfielders to break was seen again in the final, as Peters got England's first, and then as Ball, tireless on the right, sent in the cross from which Hurst – controversially – made it 3-2 in extra-time. The decisive fourth, belted in by Hurst in the dying seconds after a long pass from Bobby Moore, was, as Leadbetter later noted, just the kind of goal Ramsey had delighted in at Ipswich: no fuss, just a simple ball and an emphatic finish. Perhaps that was fitting, but it was also a touch misleading, for England, as they would show even more conclusively in Mexico four years later, were perfectly capable of holding possession.

Nonetheless, as time went by, Ramsey's pragmatism became increasingly wearing. McIlvanney spoke for many when he noted caustically, after the 3-1 defeat at home to West Germany in 1972, that 'cautious, joyless football was scarcely bearable even while it was bringing victories. When it brings defeat there can only be one reaction.' As England, thanks to Jan Tomaszewski's heroics for Poland at Wembley, failed to qualify for the 1974 World Cup, Ramsey was sacked.

For all the terseness of his dealings with the media, the antipathy to Ramsey was rooted in a re-casting of the old tension between aesthetics and results. There was no question on which side Ramsey lay. He despised Argentina's approach, and his sides were certainly not guilty of the excesses of *anti-fútbol*, but he would have agreed with Osvaldo Zubeldía's thoughts on the role of a manager. 'I'm employed to win football matches,' Ramsey said. 'That's all.'

Chapter Nine

△▽△▽△▽△▽△▽

The Birth of the New

△▽ Perhaps all football pundits are condemned to reiterate the fears of their forbears. Take the following two examples: 'Speed was made a fetish. Quick was equal to good – no, better'; 'hurried clearances... the panicky power game... the terror of failure, the inability to keep the ball and stay calm, the howling from without that freezes the blood and saps all creativity'. The first is Willy Meisl writing in 1957, the second Martin Samuel in *The Times* two days after the 3-2 defeat to Croatia in 2007 that confirmed England would not qualify for Euro 2008. Both, of course, are right in highlighting the principle failing of the English game: if something goes wrong for England it tends to be rooted in a mistrust of technique, and that was as true a century ago as it is today and at all points in between.

And yet complaints about speed are relative. If the English game in the mid-fifties was too quick for Meisl's tastes, what on earth would he have made of the Premiership in the early years of the third millennium? To look at videos from the years immediately following the Second World War is to see a game played almost in slow motion by the standards of the modern game – and it is getting quicker. Watch the Hungarians of the fifties or the Brazilians of the sixties and what is noticeable to the modern eye is how long players have on the ball – and not just because their technical ability gave them instant control. It is simply that nobody closes them down. A player receiving the ball had time to assess his options. The dribbling technique of Garrincha or Stanley Matthews doesn't exist in today's game, not because the skills have been lost, but because no side would ever give them the three or four yards of acceleration room they needed before their feints became effective. Would they have been great players in today's game? Probably, but not by dribbling like that.

It is that diminution of space, that compression of the game – pressing, in other words – that marks out modern football from old. It is such a simple idea that once one side had started doing it, and had had success by doing so, it is baffling that everybody did not follow them, and yet the spread of pressing is curiously patchy. It arrived in Germany only in the nineties. When Arrigo Saachi imposed it on AC Milan in the late eighties, it was hailed as ground-breaking, yet Rinus Michels's Ajax and Valeriy Lobanovskyi's Dynamo Kyiv – even Graham Taylor's Watford – had been using it for years. It was central, too, to the success of the Argentinian side Estudiantes de la Plata under Osvaldo Zubeldía in the late sixties. It was invented, though, by a Russian working in Ukraine, by a coach virtually unknown today outside the former Soviet bloc. The game's evolution, of course, is not linear, and there are others who have had significant roles to play, but if there is a single man who can claim to be the father of modern football, it is Viktor Maslov.

He was an unlikely revolutionary, noted at the time less for his vision or any kind of explosive leadership than for his warmth. 'It always intrigued me that he was known as Grandad,' said Mykhaylo Koman, probably Dynamo's best forward of the fifties. 'The players who played under him could have been his sons, but he was far too young for them to have been his grandsons. It seems the nickname had stuck before he arrived in Kyiv, and that it had nothing to do with his age. Maybe the way he looked contributed to his grandfatherly image: he was of plump constitution, had a bald head, and thick, bushy eyebrows. Still, the main reason for the name was his colossal wisdom, humanity and kindness.'

Born in Moscow in 1910, Maslov had been one of the leading players of the early years of the Soviet league, a robust and author-itative half capable of a wide range of passing. He was in the Torpedo side that finished second in the Moscow championship in 1934 and 1935, and then captained the club between 1936 and 1939, leading them to victory in an international tournament in France in 1938. After ending his playing career in 1942, he took over as coach of Torpedo, and had four spells in charge of them before leaving for Rostov-na-Donu in 1962. The last of those, beginning in 1957, was by far the most successful, as Maslov led

Torpedo twice to second place in the Soviet league and, in 1960, to their first championship. It was after arriving at Dynamo Kyiv in 1964, though, that he really began to give free rein to his ideas, as he wrenched the centre of Soviet football from Moscow to the Ukrainian capital.

Avuncular he may have been, but a feat like that was not achieved without a certain toughness and an ability to play the political game. He, for instance, made the most of the love Volodymyr Shcherbytskyi, who ran the Ukrainian Communist Party central committee's ideological department, had for football (Lobanovskyi maintained the strong relations after Shcherbytskyi had become head of the party in Ukraine). Dynamo had always been able to recruit from across the republic – Dynamo's side in the fifties, for instance, included several players from Zakarpattya – but under Maslov almost all the best Ukrainian players gravitated to Dynamo, attracted by apartments in Kyiv and other benefits that could be conferred by the Party leadership.

At the same time, though, he was strong enough to maintain his independence. On one occasion, Kyiv legend has it, the assistant of a senior party official came to berate the team at half-time of a game in which they were playing badly. 'Tomorrow I have a free day,' Maslov is supposed to have said as he shepherded him to the door. 'I'll come and see your boss then and answer all his questions. As for today ... could you close the door on your way out?' The tale may be apocryphal – there is no agreement as to the game at which the incident happened or which functionary was involved – but the fact that it is widely repeated suggests a basic truth behind it.

'We appreciated Grandad first for his human qualities and only second as a coach,' said Andriy Biba, Dynamo's captain between 1964 and 1967. 'And for his part, he looked at us first of all as people with all our positives and negatives, and only after that as footballers. He managed his relations with the players in such a manner, and was so sincere with us that it was impossible to have any bad feelings against him. He trusted us and we responded in the same way.'

Perhaps that was true for those who were members of the inner circle, but Eduard Streltsov, the great star of Maslov's Torpedo side before his imprisonment in 1958 on a – possibly trumped-up – charge of rape, remembers a different side to him. 'If Maslov disliked any of his players,' he said, 'he could never hide his antipathy.'

Either way, there is no doubting that, to those with whom he did get on, Maslov was an inspirational figure. 'His pre-match instructions lasted no more than five minutes,' Biba went on. 'He could never remember things properly, and he distorted the names of opposing players hopelessly, but he was always precise in telling us how to counteract their strengths. He would always finish with an aphorism to touch our hearts: "Today you must be strong like lions, fast like stags, agile like panthers!" And we would always do our best...'

Certainly there was in him none of the authoritarianism that would later characterise Lobanovskyi, his greatest disciple. Rather, he was willing to discuss and compromise, and on occasions even seemingly to be over-ruled by his players, as Arkady Galinsky, one of the most popular football journalists of the sixties and seventies, recalled. 'At one of Torpedo's league matches I was sitting close to the pitch and the reserve bench,' he wrote. 'The team wasn't doing well and the coach decided to substitute one of his players... The substitute took off his coat and tracksuit and after a short warm-up, he went to the half-way line, waiting to replace one of his team-mates the next time the referee stopped the game.

'It was just as usually happens in football. But what happened next I found extremely interesting. The Torpedo captain, the well-known forward [Valentin] Ivanov, came running over to this player after the referee had whistled and told him the team needed no substitute. After spending some time in confusion, the reserve player returned to the bench. I glanced at the coach: how would he react? But he simply shrugged his shoulders, looking indifferent to what had happened.

'I supposed this to be an attempt to motivate the player who was to be substituted, pre-conceived by the coach and the captain, but it appeared after the match that the team had simply rejected the substitution proposed by the coach. I have never seen anything like this in football before. A few years later I witnessed the same episode once again. The match was played at the same stadium – the Central Lenin Stadium [now the Luzhniki] in Moscow – the coach was the same, only the team was different: Dynamo Kyiv. Once again Maslov expressed no emotion.'

During his time as the Kyiv correspondent of *Sovetsky Sport*,

Galinsky became noted for his pro-Moscow sympathies. He was critical of Dynamo's use of a zonal marking system, and seems to have had various personal spats with Maslov, who, however Biba saw it, had a tendency to be at times rather more 'sincere' than tactful. Galinksy's conclusion, though, was that the two incidents were indicative not of any weakness on Maslov's part, but rather of his strength. 'He understood that the players rejected the substitution not to undermine his authority,' he wrote, 'but for the benefit of the affair. Dynamo players – like the Torpedo ones formerly – were telling their coach: don't worry, everything is OK, we'll soon turn the game in our favour. And that was what happened in both cases.'

Consultation was a key part of the Maslov method. The evening before games he would gather together his squad – or the senior players at least – to talk through the next day's match, canvassing their thoughts before drawing up his final game plan. It was that level of trust and mutual understanding that allowed Maslov to implement his more radical tactical innovations. And they were radical, almost incomprehensibly so in the context of the times.

In the early sixties, the USSR, like most of the world, had begun to turn to the 4-2-4, a process pioneered by the national coach Gavriil Kachalin. He had led the USSR to victory at the 1956 Olympics and to success in the inaugural European Championship with a W-M, but he had seen in Brazil's performances in the 1958 World Cup the way football was headed. Several club coaches followed his lead and, for once, the habitually conservative Soviet establishment supported his experiments. The change, or at least the pace with which it had been imposed, was widely blamed for the USSR's disjointed showing at the 1962 World Cup, when they beat Yugoslavia and Uruguay but went out in the quarter-final against Chile, but the Brazilian method was so in vogue that Konstantin Beskov, Kachalin's successor, continued to insist he was using a 4-2-4 when he had actually reverted to a W-M for his eighteen months in the job.

Maslov was rather more astute than Beskov. Like Sir Alf Ramsey, he recognised how important Zagallo had been to Brazil's success, tracking back to become a third midfielder. Maslov went one further, and pulled back his right-winger as well. Ramsey is regularly given the credit (or the blame) for abolishing the winger and, given the lack of communication between the USSR and the

West in those days, there is no suggestion he did not come up with the idea independently, but the 4-4-2 was first invented by Maslov.

Like Ramsey, though, and unlike so many who followed, Maslov withdrew his wingers in such a way that it did not impinge upon his side's creative capacity. The likes of Andriy Biba, Viktor Serebryanykov and Josef Szabo all began their careers as forwards before being converted into midfielders by Maslov, and they and more orthodox halves such as Volodymyr Muntyan and Fedir Medvid retained a creative brief, functioning almost as a second line of attack. There were, though, casualties. Maslov may have coached by consensus, but he could be ruthless when he saw a player who did not fit his system. Former stars such as Viktor Kanevskyi and Oleh Bazylevych were swiftly dispensed with, and so too, most controversially, was Lobanovskyi.

Quite why Maslov and Lobanovskyi fell out – if indeed they did – remains unclear. Their conceptions of football were very different but, if Galinsky is to be believed, there was also a personal antagonism. Then again, it should be borne in mind that Galinsky was one of the prime movers in attempting to lure Lobanovskyi away from Ukraine to Moscow, so his evidence may not be entirely objective. According to his version of events, the problems flared after a training camp on the Caucasian Black Sea coast ahead of the 1964 season.

'Everything seemed to be going well,' Galinsky wrote. 'The players seemed to be fond of their new coach, the team had worked well, and Maslov seemed pleased with Lobanovskyi.' On the flight home, though, bad weather forced Dynamo's aeroplane to land at Symferopol. Their departure was repeatedly postponed, until eventually Maslov ordered lunch. To the amazement of the players, he also ordered them each a glass of *horilka* – Ukrainian vodka.

'They couldn't believe their eyes,' Galinsky. 'Nothing like this had been seen before at Dynamo. Maslov proposed a toast to good luck in the coming season. Everybody drank to it, apart from Lobanovskyi, who didn't even touch his glass. Seeing this, Maslov asked him to drink to the team's success. When Lobanovskyi again refused to do so, Maslov cursed him. Lobanovskyi swore back at him.' From then on, Galinsky claimed, there was bad blood between them.

Kanevskyi, though, insists Galinsky has exaggerated the episode. He was at the meal and agrees there was *horilka* and that everybody apart from the fastidious Lobanovskyi drank the toast, but he also maintains that Lobanovskyi's strict self-discipline was well known, even admired, and that Maslov was unconcerned by his abstinence. 'Maslov said nothing to him,' he recalled, 'and certainly he didn't use any insulting words.'

Others believe their relationship broke down during a game in Moscow against Spartak on 27 April 1964. Lobanovskyi had given Dynamo the lead, and they were still 1-0 up when he was substituted – for the first time in his career – with twenty minutes to go. Spartak then equalised and the game ended in a draw, leading to speculation that Maslov had arranged the result in advance with the Spartak coach Nikita Simonyan, and that Lobanovskyi was taken off because he had refused to go along with their agreement. True or not, the next game, away to Shinnik in Yaroslavl, was Lobanovskyi's last for the club.

Then again, it may be there was no falling out. Maslov was just as swift to get rid of Mikhail Gershkovich, David Pays and Grigory Yanets – all leading players – when he returned to Torpedo in 1971, apparently for no other reason than that they did not fit his system, and it is easy to see why Lobanovskyi would not have fitted Maslov's plans, whatever Galinsky may say. Nicknamed 'Cord' in the Moscow press because of the way the ball at times appeared to be tied to his boot-laces, Lobanovskyi was a genuine star, talented and popular with the crowd. On his death in 2002, several messages of condolence from fans recalled how they had gone to Dynamo games in the early sixties excited by the prospect of watching him take corners packed with backspin so they dropped almost vertically in the box – a variant of the 'falling leaf' free-kicks devised by Didi a few years earlier. The problem was that he was a left-winger, and wingers had no place in Maslov's plan.

'I'd not call what happened between Maslov and Lobanovskyi a conflict,' Biba explained. 'It was just that Valeriy often opposed the coach's directions. Maslov was seeking new forms of football and footballers who held on to the ball for too long didn't suit him. Even the "banana shot" invented by Lobanovskyi couldn't persuade him. But then, after becoming a coach, Valeriy acknowledged that Lobanovskyi the player could not have played in his team.' This was the debate raised by Mihkail Yakushin's preference for the collective over the individualism of a Stanley Matthews taken to its logical extreme. No matter how talented the individual, if they did not function as part of the collective, they had no place within it.

That is not to say that Maslov was opposed to great individuals *per se*. On the contrary, Biba was one of the most gifted midfielders Ukraine has ever produced, functioning in Maslov's system as Bobby Charlton did in Ramsey's England side. 'When he gets the ball, he knows in advance what his team-mates and his opponents are going to do,' said Iosif Betsa, who was part of the USSR team that won gold at the 1956 Olympics and who went on to become a respected coach. 'He has a plan of his next actions and with his first touch puts the ball in a comfortable position to execute it quickly. And if the opponent has guessed his intentions, he changes the direction of the attack immediately. At the same time, Biba possesses a magnificent long shot and can finish off attacks arriving in the right place at just the right time.'

Biba reached his peak in 1966. In the spring he beat Lev Yashin with a 40-yard drive in a game against Dinamo Moscow; he was superb in the crucial 4-0 victory over CSKA in the autumn, setting up two of Dynamo's goals; and he rounded off the year with the decisive goal in the Cup final victory over Torpedo as Dynamo won the double. He was the creative hub of the team and, to widespread agreement, he was named Soviet Player of the Year.

Soviet football seems to have become obsessed by Didi after the 1958 World Cup and, more particularly, by the lack of such playmakers in their own game. In the sixties there were only two: Biba and Gennady Gusarov of Dinamo Moscow.

Crucially, Maslov was able to develop in his side an under-standing of how best to make use of a playmaker, something that wasn't always clear. Galinsky, for instance, recalls Beskov in 1968 responding to Gusarov's retirement by attempting to retrain the forward Yuri Avrutsky as a playmaker. 'He treated the role quite seriously,' Galinsky wrote. 'He was always finding space, offering himself to his team-mates, moving, and when he got the ball, executing good passes, but when he found space again he almost never got the ball back. I don't know whether the players didn't follow Beskov's directions, or whether they weren't clear enough, but often when Avrutsky was free of his marker the other players preferred to dribble with the ball or pass it forwards themselves. But in such a situation a playmaker is pointless. Even worse, he becomes a burden for his team because he isn't marking any specific opponent while they are attacking.'

It remains a common complaint, and the distrust of 'luxury players' remains widespread, at least in northern Europe. Galinksy was scathing of the special treatment granted them, but in his mockery he happened upon the truth. 'Some coaches in football,' he wrote, 'interpret the playmaker to be something like a patient at a health resort. It might be all right to release one or two forwards from their defensive obligations, but to do the same with a midfielder? Is he Charlton or Didi?'

Maslov's solution was exactly that which had allowed Didi such freedom. It was the forgotten innovation, the one devised by Zezé Moreira and used by Brazil for the first time at the World Cup in 1954: zonal marking. It was the theory that had prepared the ground for Brazil's blossoming in 1958 and 1962, but it didn't find immediate favour in the USSR. The difficulty with zonal marking is that it requires organisation and understanding between defenders. It is not quite so easy as a defender merely picking up any player in his area. Two forwards could come into his zone, or over-manning in another zone could require him to track a forward outside his zone, which then requires another defender to pick up anybody coming into the zone the original defender has just vacated, and that is not something that can simply be improvised.

An attempt by Nikolai Morozov to introduce zonal marking with the national team ahead of the 1966 World Cup was a failure. After six goals were conceded over the course of pre-World Cup friendlies against France and CSKA, Morozov became so paranoid that he ended up fielding five defenders, with a sweeper picking up the pieces behind the other four and the midfielders encouraged to drop deep whenever possession was lost, attacking only on the counter. The USSR reached the semi-final of that tournament, their best placing in a World Cup, but the ultra-defensive approach, which mimicked that of Helenio Herrera's Internazionale, was never seen as anything other than a one-off solution to a particular problem.

Maslov, though, remained convinced zonal marking was the right way to proceed, something that seems almost to have been for him almost an ethical principle. 'Man-marking,' he once said, 'humiliates, insults and even morally oppresses the players who resort to it.'

Biba didn't pick up any specific opponent, but then neither did any other Dynamo midfielder. 'Only Biba retains full rights of democracy,' Maslov said. 'He is a very clever and honest player, who would never allow himself any excess and never abuses his skills. Andriy will do exactly what is necessary. He has the right to construct the game as though he were the coach himself during the match, making decisions as to how to shape it. The others then grasp his ideas and develop them as far as they can.'

Maslov believed that through good organisation, it was possible to over-man in every part of the pitch, an idea the journalist Georgiy Kuzmin suggested in *Kiyevskiye Vedomosti* that he took from basketball. With Biba in a free role, though, to do that he needed a fixed defensive point in his midfield to allow the full-backs to step up from the back four as required. That was provided by the veteran defender Vasyl Turyanchyk, who was deployed in front of the back four, becoming the first holding midfielder in Soviet football. His job, as Maslov put it, was to 'break the waves', presenting the first line of resistance to opposing forwards, while also to initiating Dynamo's attacks. In other words, he played almost as József Zakariás had for Hungary. In that context, it helped that he had begun his career as a forward, but it is perhaps just as significant that, like Szabo and Medvid, he came from Zakarpattya, where the Hungarian influence was strong.

Most crucially of all, though, Turyanchyk was instrumental in the application of the pressing game. Would Maslov have tried it – would he even have thought of it? – if he hadn't had a player as commanding and with such a fine grasp of the geometry of the game? Given the absence of a diary or journals, it is impossible to say. As in his use of Biba, his genius was, having spotted the possibilities offered by Turyanchyk's ability to step out from the back, to teach the rest of the team how best to make use of it. By the time Dynamo won their first title under Maslov in 1966, their midfield was hunting in packs, closing down opponents and seizing the initiative in previously unexpected areas of the pitch. The Moscow press was appalled, one newspaper printing a photograph of four Dynamo players converging on an opponent with the ball with the caption: 'We don't need this kind of football.'

Pressing, demanding as it did almost constant movement from the midfielders, required supreme physical fitness, which may explain why it had not emerged earlier. Full-time professionalism was a prerequisite, as was a relatively sophisticated understanding

Dynamo Kyiv 1 Celtic 1, European Cup First Round Second Leg, Olympyskyi, Kyiv, 4 October 1967

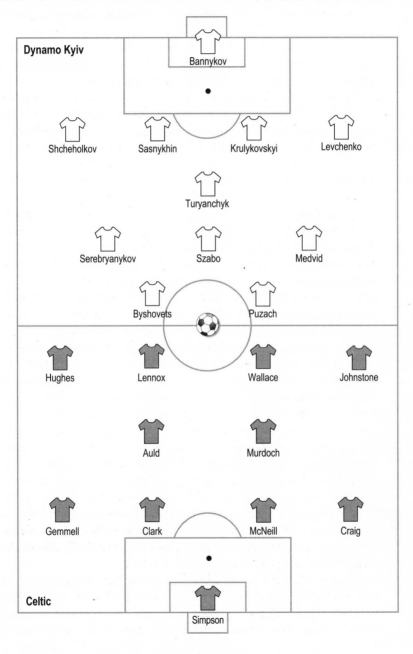

of nutrition and condition. Dynamo had been noted for their physical fitness when they had won the title for the first time under Vyacheslav Solovyov in 1961, but Maslov took things to a new level. 'He was the first Dynamo coach really to put an emphasis on the physical preparation of players,' the midfielder Volodymyr Muntyan said. 'Not Lobanovskyi as is often thought, but Maslov, although he did what felt right, whereas Lobanovskyi was acting on a scientific basis.'

The statistics are telling. When Dynamo won the title in 1961, they conceded twenty-eight goals in thirty games, so they had a history of defensive soundness. The following season, when they were fifth, they let in forty-eight in forty-two, and in 1963, as they slipped to ninth, forty-eight in thirty-eight. Maslov arrived the following season, and twenty-nine goals were conceded in thirty-two games as Dynamo came sixth. They were runners-up in 1965, letting in twenty-two in thirty-two, and it got better in their three championship seasons: seventeen in thirty-six games in 1966, a staggering eleven in thirty-six in 1967 and twenty-five in thirty-eight in 1968. Not surprisingly, the debate over Maslov's tactics soon abated. In his review of the 1967 season, Martin Merzhanov, the doyen of Soviet football journalism and the founder of *Futbol* magazine, wrote that 'zonal defence, when defenders base their play on mutual understanding and mutual securing, and are dealing with not one concrete opponent but whoever comes into their zone, has proved far more efficient [than man-marking].'

It was not, though, foolproof, and Dynamo's 2-1 defeat to Shakhtar Donetsk in 1967 hinted at things to come. After leaving Dynamo, Lobanovskyi spent two seasons with Chornomorets Odessa before moving east to Shakhtar. In that time, his tactical thinking had evolved and, with the coach Oleg Oshenkov, he came up with a plan to combat Dynamo's system. Where most sides sought to do no more than contain the champions, Lobanovskyi insisted Shakhtar should attack them, and so they adopted a 4-2-4, but with their two midfielders man-marking Muntyan and Szabo. That left Medvid, a less creative player, free, but that didn't bother Lobanovskyi: although he wanted to blunt Dynamo's cutting edge as far as possible, his greater concern was to overwhelm their defence by weight of numbers. The pattern was repeated in the European Cup that year when Dynamo, having beaten the holders Celtic in the first round, lost 3-2 on aggregate to the Polish champions Górnik Zabrze in the second, undone by the pace and mobility of Włodzimierz Lubański and Zygfryd Szołtysik.

Still, those were rare examples, and Dynamo, regularly changing their approach according to the opposition – something extremely rare at the time – proved adept at dealing with the many stylistic variations presented by the Soviet League. 'This team has something like two different squads,' Galinsky wrote. 'One is fighting, engaging in a frank power struggle if that is offered by the opponent, while the other plays in the "southern" technical, combinational style, at an arrhythmic tempo. But the transformation from one squad to the other happens very simply at Dynamo. One or two changes before the match and sometimes even one substitution in the course of it is enough. They can go straight from the southern style to a much more simple game with runs down the flanks, crosses, shots and long aerial balls.'

Maslov would have gone further. Having instigated the move to just two forwards, he speculated that a time would come when sides only used one up front. 'Football,' he explained, 'is like an aeroplane. As velocities increase, so does air resistance, and so you have to make the head more stream-lined.' In terms of range, novelty and success, his work is extraordinary enough as it is, but there was one more step he wanted to take. His conception would be realised soon enough by Dynamo and by Ajax, but it never quite came to fruition under his management, although, by instituting zonal marking and pressing he had lain the groundwork.

In October 1981, Lobanovskyi's Dynamo beat Zenit Leningrad 3-0 to win the Soviet title for the tenth time. A piece in *Sportyvna Hazeta* eulogising their fluidity of movement in that game and over that season makes the progression clear: 'Viktor Maslov dreamt once of creating a team that could attack with different groups of players. For instance [Anatoliy] Byshovets and [Vitaliy] Khmelnytskyi would start the match battering the opposition defence, but then at some point they could drop back into midfield and their places could be taken by, say, Muntyan and Serebryanykov. But at that time such a way of playing didn't come together. It is an achievement of the present day.'

And yet every now and again Maslov's players did, by chance or by instinct, switch positions. 'The 4-4-2 system introduced by Grandad was only a formal order; in the course of the game there was complete inter-changeability,' Szabo said. 'For example, any defender could press forward without fear because he knew that a team-mate would cover him if he were unable to return in time. Midfielders and forwards could allow themselves a much wider variety of actions than before. This team played the prototype of Total Football. People think it was developed in Holland, but that is just because in Western Europe they didn't see Maslov's Dynamo.'

Maslov was eventually sacked in 1970 as Dynamo slipped to seventh in the table. In 1966, with several members of the squad away at the World Cup, he had managed to maintain Dynamo's league form because of the emergence of a number of players from the youth team. In 1970, he found no such reserves. 'Any coach's fate depends on results,' said the defender Viktor Matviyenko. 'After the spring half of the season we were second in the table, and I'm sure Grandad would have kept his job if we'd have maintained that position to the end. He just needed to repeat the experience of 1966 when the outstanding youth players kept the players who had come back from England out of the squad. It was a similar situation in 1970. The Dynamo players who were at the World Cup in Mexico were absent for a month and a half, and played only a couple of games. They lost more there than they gained simply because they had no match practice. But Grandad didn't take it into account and brought straight back players who had lost their sharpness, and so we began to fall in the standings.'

Perhaps that was understandable. Maslov had, after all, been at the club for seven years, and the feeling was that he had perhaps gone stale. The manner of his dismissal, though, leaves a sour taste; Koman called it 'the most disgraceful episode in Dynamo's history'. It was decided that it was more politically expedient to dismiss him away from Kyiv, and so when, towards the end of the 1970 season, Dynamo travelled to Moscow for a game against CSKA, they were joined by Mizyak, the deputy head of the Ukrainian SSR State Sport Committee. He usually had a responsibility for winter sports, but in the Hotel Russia before the game, he made the official announcement that Maslov had been removed from his position.

With Maslov sitting in the stand and no replacement appointed, Dynamo lost 1-0. After the game, as the team bus carried the players to the airport for the flight back to Kyiv, they stopped at the Yugo-Zapadnaya metro station and dropped Maslov off. As he walked away, he looked back over his shoulder and slowly raised a hand in farewell. 'If I hadn't seen it myself,' Koman said, 'I'd never have believed a giant like Maslov could have wept.'

Maslov returned to Torpedo, and won the cup with them, and then had a season in Armenia with Ararat Yerevan, where he again won the cup, but he never had the resources – or perhaps the energy – to repeat the successes of Dynamo. By the time he died, aged sixty-seven, in May 1977, Lobanovskyi, the player he had exiled, was ensuring his legacy lived on. His impact was perhaps less direct than that of Jimmy Hogan, but no coach since has been so influential.

Chapter Ten

△▽△▽△▽△▽△▽

Catenaccio

△▽ There is no tactical system so notorious as *catenaccio*. To generations, the word – which means 'chain', in the sense of a chain on a house door – summons up Italian football at its most paranoid, negative and brutal. So reviled was it in Britain that when Jock Stein's Celtic beat Helenio Herrera's Internazionale, its prime exponents, in the European Cup final of 1967, the Liverpool manager Bill Shankly congratulated him by insisting the victory had made him 'immortal'. It later emerged that he had instructed two Celtic coaches to sit behind the Inter bench and abuse Herrera throughout the game. Herrera would always insist he was misunderstood, that his system, like Herbert Chapman's, had acquired an unfavourable reputation only because other, lesser sides attempting to copy his team's style implemented it so badly. That remains debatable but, sinister as *catenaccio* became, its origins were homely.

It began in Switzerland with Karl Rappan. Softly-spoken, understated and noted for his gentle dignity, Rappan was born in Vienna in 1905, his professional career as a forward or attack-minded half coinciding with the golden age of Viennese football in the mid-to late twenties. So rooted was he in coffee-house society that later in life he ran the Café de la Bourse in Geneva. He was capped for Austria and won the league with Rapid Vienna in 1930, after which he moved to Switzerland to become player-coach at Servette. His players there were semi-professional and so, according to Walter Lutz, the doyen of Swiss sportswriting, Rappan set about devising a way of compensating for the fact that they could not match fully professional teams for physical fitness.

'With the Swiss team tactics play an important role,' Rappan said in a rare interview with *World Soccer* magazine shortly before the World Cup in 1962. 'The Swiss is not a natural footballer, but he is usually sober in his approach to things. He can be persuaded to think ahead and to calculate ahead.

'A team can be chosen according to two points of view. Either you have eleven individuals, who owing to sheer class and natural ability are enabled to beat their opponents – Brazil would be an example of that – or you have eleven average footballers, who have to be integrated into a particular conception, a plan. This plan aims at getting the best out of each individual for the benefit of the team. The difficult thing is to enforce absolute tactical discipline without taking away the players' freedom of thinking and acting.'

His solution, which was given the name *verrou* – bolt – by a Swiss journalist, is best understood as a development from the old 2-3-5 – which had remained the default formation in Vienna long after Chapman's W-M had first emerged in England. Rather than the centre-half dropping in between the two full-backs, as in the W-M, the two wing-halves fell back to flank them. They retained an attacking role, but their primary function was to combat the opposition wingers. The two full-backs then became in effect central defenders, playing initially almost alongside each other, although in practice, if the opposition attacked down their right, the left of the two would move towards the ball, with the right covering just behind, and vice versa. In theory, that always left them with a spare man – the *verouller* as the Swiss press of the time called him, or the *libero* as he would become – at the back.

The system's main shortcoming was that it placed huge demands on the centre-half. Although on paper the formation – with four defenders, a centre-half playing behind two withdrawn inside-forwards, and a string of three across the front – looks similar to the modern 4-3-3 as practised by, say, Chelsea in José Mourinho's first two seasons at the club, the big difference is how advanced the wingers were. They operated as pure forwards, staying high up the pitch at all times rather than dropping back to help the midfield when possession was lost. That meant that when the *verrou* faced a W-M, the front three matched up in the usual way against the defensive three and inside-forwards took the opposition's wing-halves, leaving the centre-half to deal with two inside-forwards. This was the problem sides playing a *libero* always

Rappan's Verrou, 1938

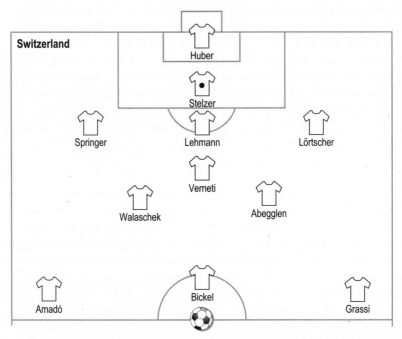

faced: by creating a spare man in one part of the pitch, it necessarily meant a shortfall elsewhere.

Against a 2-3-5, the situation was even worse. The side playing the *verrou* had a man over at both ends of the pitch, but that meant the centre-half was trying to cope not only with the opposing inside-forwards, but also the other centre-half. That was all but impossible, so Rappan's team tended to drop deep, cede the midfield to their opponents and, by tight marking, present a solid front to frustrate them so they ended up passing the ball fruitlessly sideways. As the system developed, the burden was taken off the centre-half as an inside-forward gradually fell back to play alongside him, but the more striking change was that made to the defensive line as one of the two full-backs (that is, the *de facto* centre-backs) dropped behind the other as an orthodox sweeper.

Rappan won two league titles with Servette and five more with Grasshoppers, whom he joined in 1935, but it was his successes with the Switzerland national side that really demonstrated the efficacy of his system. Rappan became national coach in 1937, with a brief to lead Switzerland into the 1938 World Cup. At the time, Switzerland were regarded as the weakest of the central European nations, and their record in the Dr Gerö Cup was correspondingly poor: played 32, won 4, drawn 3, lost 25. Using the *verrou*, though, they beat England 2-1 in a pre-World Cup friendly, and then beat Germany – by then encompassing Austria – in the first round of the tournament itself, before going down 2-0 to Hungary. That was an honourable exit – far more than Switzerland had achieved previously, but the *verrou* was considered little more than a curiosity; perhaps a means for lesser teams to frustrate their betters, but no more.

△▽

Perhaps not surprisingly given the rethink of defensive tactics necessitated by Boris Arkadiev's organised disorder, a similar system sprang up, seemingly independently, a few years later in Russia. Krylya Sovetov Kuibyshev (now Samara), a team backed by the Soviet Air Force, were founded in 1943, winning promotion to the Supreme League in 1945. They soon became noted for their defensive approach, specifically a tactic known as the *Volzhskaya Zashchepka* – the 'Volga Clip'. It may not have been so flexible as the *verrou*, and it was a development of the W-M rather than the 2-3-5, but the basic principle was the same, with one of the half-backs dropping deep, allowing the defensive centre-half to sweep behind his full-backs.

Its architect was Krylya's coach, Alexander Kuzmich Abramov. 'Some people were amazed because he wasn't a football professional in the usual sense of the term,' the former Krylya captain Viktor Karpov said. 'He came from the world of gymnastics, so maybe because of that he wasn't directed by dogma, but had his own opinions on everything. He paid a lot of attention to gymnastic exercises, using training sessions to improve our coordination. An hour could go by and you wouldn't touch the ball, yet somehow it helped us to be more skilful. Kuzmich made us think on the pitch. Before each game he would gather the team together and we would discuss the plan for the match. As far as I'm aware, other coaches didn't do this.

'How we played depended on our opponents. If we were playing Dinamo, for instance, and their forward line was Trofimov, Kartsev, Beskov, Soloviov, Ilyin, then of course you had to take measures to counter such a star quintet. At that time most teams played with three defenders, but our half-backs would help them out more. Usually that meant me and [the left-half] Nikolai Pozdyanakov.

'We didn't man-mark as such. We tried to play flexibly, and the system meant that the range of action of each player became broader. Sometimes a reserve player would come in and he would try to chase his opponent all over the pitch – his man would go and have a drink and our novice would follow him. We would laugh at players like that, because we regulars had been taught that we should act according to the circumstances.'

As when Nikolai Starostin first had his brother operate as a third back, there were those who protested at Abramov's innovation, seeing it as a betrayal of the ideals of Russian football, but gradually the system became accepted, as Lev Filatov puts it in *About Everything in an Orderly Manner*, as 'the right of the weak'. The forward Viktor Voroshilov, who also captained the side under Abramov, was scathing of the system's critics. 'Let's say we were playing against CDKA,' he said. 'In attack they had Grinin, Nikolaev, Fedotov, Bobrov and Doymin. So we're supposed to venture upfield? That's why we played closer to our own goal. Once against Dinamo Moscow we opened up, [their coach] Mikhey Yakushin outwitted us and we lost 5-0.'

The Volga clip's success as a spoiling tactic could hardly be faulted. After winning just three of twenty-two games in 1946, and finishing tenth of the twelve top-flight sides, Krylya climbed to seventh of thirteen in 1947, recording a famous win over Dinamo Moscow. They beat them again in 1948 and, in 1949, they won 1-0 both home and away against CDKA. 'Their famous opponents tried to make it a game,' Filatov wrote. 'They combined in passing moves, won corners and free-kicks, but every time they were denied and the ball flew into the sky or on to the running track that ran round the pitch. Eventually their spirits dropped, because they realised they were banging their heads against a wall.'

Essentially, though, the clip was seen as a small team's tactic, a means of countering superior sides rather than a pro-active strategy in its own right. Krylya finished fourth in 1951 and got to the Soviet Cup final two years later, and Karpov recalls man-marking the giant Hungarian forward Gyula Szilágyi as the USSR employed the clip to win a B-international 3-0 in Budapest in 1954, but it largely remained confined to Krylya. The bolt had to move to Italy before it became mainstream.

△▽

The fishing fleet lies dark against the sun-washed sea. Along the Tyrrhenian waterfront, a stressed football manager, unable to sleep, takes an early-morning walk. Oblivious to the shrieking of the gulls and the haggling of the dockside mongers, he strides on, asking himself again and again how he can get the best out of his side, ponders how he can strengthen a defence that, for all his best efforts, remains damagingly porous. As he paces the harbour, churning the problem over and over in his head, a boat catches his eye. The fishermen haul in one net, swollen with fish, and then behind it, another: the reserve net. This is his eureka moment. Some fish inevitably slip the first net, but they are caught by the second; he realises that what his side needs is a reserve defender operating behind the main defence to catch those forwards who slip through. That manager was Gipo Viani, his team was Salernitana, and his invention was *catenaccio*.

That, at least, is the story Viani told – and with its vaguely biblical overtones it is an attractive one – but it is, at the very least, over-romanticised. Nonetheless, among the many theories of how *catenaccio* developed in Italy, Viani's claim to be the originator seems strongest. Perhaps others did use it before him, but he was the first to employ the system on a regular basis and with a level of success. Again, it seems to have grown up independently of Rappan, although the historical influence of Switzerland on Italian football is significant. Vittorio Pozzo, for instance, spent two years playing for the reserve team of the Zurich club Grasshoppers, while Franz Cali, the first captain of Italy, was educated in Lausanne. Between the wars, it would have been unusual to find a leading northern Italian side without at least one Swiss ex-pat, their presence being felt particularly strongly at Genoa, Torino and Internazionale.

Whether it was inspired by a dawn walk by the sea or not, it seems that Viani, recognising the limited resources at his disposal, decided the most fruitful policy was to try to stop the opposition playing – to exercise 'the right of the weak'. One of the notional half-backs, Alberto Piccinini, who went on to win two *scudetti* with Juventus, dropped in to mark the opposing centre-forward, with the central of the three defenders in the W-M, which had come by then to supplant Pozzo's *metodo* as the default formation in Italy, falling back as the sweeper. Viani then had his team sit deep, drawing out the opposition, leading them to commit extra men to the attack and so rendering them vulnerable to the counter. The shape may have been different, but the thinking behind his innovation was no different to Herbert Chapman's at Northampton in 1907.

Salernitana's use of what became known as the *vianema*, though, was not *catenaccio*'s breakthrough. They were a small side, and although the system helped them to promotion in 1947, when they had the best defensive record of any team in the three parallel second divisions, they failed to win an away game in their one season in Serie A, and were immediately relegated.

Viani's relative success at Salernitana made *catenaccio* fashionable, and it began to spring up in varying guises across the country. 'Smaller teams began realising that they stood no chance if they turned the game into a series of individual battles,' explained Lodovico Maradei, the former chief football writer of the *Gazzetta della Sport*. 'And so, while maintaining the W-M, many made small adjustments so they could have a spare man at the back. Usually this was done by pushing one of the wingers back and letting the full-back slide across behind the defence. Still, this was not something that was done systematically, but was rather extemporaneous. Many would disagree, but the reason I say this is that, because it was smaller teams doing this, most of the time they were pegged back anyway and, therefore, even if the full-back wanted to slide across, often you wouldn't even notice it, since the whole side was further back defending.'

The most striking exponent of the new style was Nereo Rocco, who rapidly transformed Triestina. He would go on to lead AC Milan to two European Cups, but it was his unfashionable home-town club that formed him and his way of thinking about the game. He had worked in his grandfather's butcher's shop before Triestina offered him a contract and, after pursuing a modest playing career that took him to Padova and Napoli – and, crucially, earned him the international cap necessary at the time in Italy to become a manager – he returned home to the city he loved. Aside from television appearances, when he affected something more neutral, he spoke always with a strong Trieste accent and became a Christian Democrat councillor there in 1948. It was his achieve-ments with the local football club, though, that cemented his place in local folklore.

When Rocco was appointed in 1947, Triestina were in a mess. They had just finished bottom of Serie A, avoiding relegation only through an exemption granted because, with British and American troops still occupying the city, they were unable to play any matches at home. Few saw much reason to believe things would have been much better had they not always been forced to travel. In Rocco's first season, though, they remained unbeaten at home, and finished joint second. That was as good as it got, but successive eighth-placed finishes in the following two seasons were still respectable for a club of Triestina's limited means, and when Rocco then left following a disagreement with the club's board, to be replaced by Béla Guttmann, they slumped immediately to fifteenth.

Still, *catenaccio* was seen as 'the right of the weak', and it was only when Internazionale adopted it under Alfredo Foni that it began to be seen as a system with which big clubs could win trophies. He had Gino Armano, the right-winger, drop back to mark the opposing left-winger, allowing Ivano Blason, the right-back, to shift across as a sweeper. Armano was the first of what are known in Italy as *tornanti* – 'returners' – wingers who track back and help with the defence.

Blason, meanwhile, became lionised as the first great *libero*. When he had joined the club from Triestina in 1950, he had been a clumsy full-back, but in his new role became noted for his long clearances and his uncompromising nature. Legend has it that before kick-off he would scratch a line on the pitch and tell opposing forwards they were not allowed beyond it, hacking them down if they tried. 'Blason was not the elegant *libero* some may imagine,' Maradei said. 'He was basically a hacker who just belted the ball into touch whenever he could. That's why the *libero* was originally known as *battitore libero* – "free hitter" – because more often than not he would simply hit the ball into touch.'

In 1952–53, Inter scored just forty-six goals in thirty-four games, twenty-seven fewer than Juventus, yet still pipped them to the *scudetto* by virtue of having conceded only twenty-four (to put that in context, Juventus had won the league the previous season scoring ninety-eight and conceding thirty-four). Describing their style, Gianni Brera said Inter would defend, then 'suddenly, Blason fired off a mortar shot: seventy metres away there were not many players around and a lot of empty space that Inter's individual players could exploit.' Eight times that season they won 1-0, four times drew 0-0. 'They were harshly criticised by the press at the time because their football was generally very defensive and lacklustre, despite a stellar frontline which included Benito Lorenzi, Nacka Skoglund and István Nyers,' Maradei said. 'It was quite revolutionary: you have to remember that, at the time, the *scudetto* winners regularly scored around a hundred goals.'

Variations on the theme sprung up. Fiorentina, for instance, won the title in 1956 under Fulvio Bernardini, the centre-half discarded by Pozzo, using a variant of *catenaccio* in which the left-half, Armando Segato, played as the *libero*. Maurilio Prini, the left-winger, retreated as a *tornante*, with the added twist that the inside-left, Miguel Angel Montuori, would push on into the position vacated by Prini, effectively becoming a spare centre-forward. Unpopular it may have been, but the template for Italian football had been set.

△▽

Inter may have become the most noted practitioners, but it was the red half of Milan that first showed the rest of Europe how potent *catenaccio* could be, thanks to the genius of Rocco. Square-faced and plump, with short legs, he cut a vaguely comical figure, but he dominated his players almost absolutely, even having them watched after they'd left the training ground so he could be sure their private lives would not interfere with their football. So controlling was he that at Torino in the mid-sixties, the forward Gigi Meroni went through a spell of pretending his girlfriend was his sister to deflect Rocco's attentions. He was ebullient and charismatic, quick-tempered and charming, an enthusiastic drinker who would use a local restaurant as his office. Once, in a fury, he kicked out at what he thought was a bag full of spare shirts lying on the dressing-room floor, discovering too late that it was actually a tool-kit. Players who were there remember staring desperately at the ground, terrified to laugh until he was out of earshot.

At Torino, Rocco would often drop into the bar at the training ground, have a couple of drinks, and then sleep them off on top of the lockers in the dressing room. He liked nothing better than sitting up late into the night downing bottle after bottle of wine with Brera, another northern Italian who shared his views on the how the game should be played. 'The perfect game,' Brera once wrote, 'would finish 0-0.' Rocco perhaps did not go quite that far, but he did have a fanatical aversion to the ball being lost in midfield with meaningless sideways passes, and insisted that all his players should track back, even the forwards. The idea was not always well received. The Brazilian forward José Altafini (or Mazzola, as he was known during his early career in Brazil), for instance, although he had a fruitful time at Milan, struggled to accept it, while it was one of the major sources of Jimmy Greaves's dissatisfaction with life in Italy. It is often forgotten that Greaves, who returned home after just five months in *Serie A* in 1961–62, scored nine goals in the ten games he played for Milan, but for Rocco that was not enough. 'Those two,' he said, 'need to understand that during a football match you get kicked, not just well paid.'

After a brief spell with Treviso, Rocco returned to Triestina, but it was only when he moved to Padova in 1953 that the success of his methods became apparent again. They were far from being giants, but between 1956–57 and 1959–60, they finished third, seventh, fifth and sixth, by some distance the best run in the club's history. And then came Rocco's big chance, as he was called upon to take over at AC Milan after Viani, who had won the *scudetto* in 1959, suffered a heart attack. Viani stayed on as sporting director, and later claimed it was then that he persuaded Rocco of the merits of the sweeper. Perhaps there were some discussions over the finer details of the system, but Rocco had, without question, been using a form of *catenaccio* since he first took over at Triestina.

His form of it, though, was far removed from the negative stereotype. In winning the *scudetto* in 1961–62, for instance, Milan scored eighty-three goals in thirty-four games, twenty-two more than Roma, the next most prolific side. Although Cesare Maldini, who was also born in Trieste and began his career with Triestina, was as resolute a defender as there has been, he was not the bogeyman the sweeper became in the popular imagination. Rather when he left for Torino in 1966 after twelve years of service, he left behind, in the words of the club's official history, 'the memory of a gentleman footballer, a player with a clean game, with a sense of style, who nevertheless always observed his defensive duties.'

Rocco was also able to accommodate such a languid creative presence as Gianni Rivera, compared by Richard Williams in *The Perfect 10* to 'Camus's existential stranger, palely loitering on the fringe of life'. On the subject of Rivera, Brera could never agree, calling the issue the 'Stalingrad' in his relationship with Rocco. A fundamentalist for what he liked to term 'defensivist' football, Brera saw Rivera as a luxury, dismissing him as *l'abatino* – 'the monk' – a term that hinted at a lack of courage. Yet Rivera's importance to Rocco's side can be seen from their two European Cup final successes. Twice in the space of eight second-half minutes he laid on goals for Altafini as Milan came from behind to beat Benfica in 1963, and he set up another two in Milan's 4-1 victory over Ajax in the 1969 final.

Rocco's *catenaccio* may not have been so defensive as some suggested, but it was still a very different game to that practised by Guttmann's Benfica. They shared a cantankerous disposition, but Guttmann's notion of football remained essentially romantic; Rocco simply wanted to win. Ahead of an Intercontinental Cup game against the notorious Argentinian side Estudiantes de la Plata in 1969, Rocco is supposed to have issued the instruction, 'kick anything that moves; if it's the ball, so much the better'. The story may be apocryphal, but it was not uncharacteristic.

When Ipswich Town were beaten by Milan in the second round of the European Cup in 1962–63, their captain Andy Nelson was left complaining that Rocco's side 'were up to all the cynical stuff – pulling your hair, spitting, treading on your toes'. In the final, the winger Paolo Barison, despite having scored freely throughout the tournament, was dropped and, with Bruno Mora switching from the right to the left flank, was replaced by Gino Pivatelli, who was given a specific brief to nullify Benfica's majestic inside-forward, Mario Coluna. Perhaps it was bad luck or mistiming, but when Coluna was left hobbling following a heavy challenge by Pivatelli a minute after Altafini had equalised, nobody was too surprised.

△▽

Whatever the excesses of Rocco's team, they were nothing compared to those perpetrated by their city rivals. *La grande Inter*, the side created by Helenio Herrera, was hugely gifted, undeniably successful and thoroughly ruthless. They were the supreme exponents of *catenaccio* and came, in the popular imagination, to embody all that was seen as wrong with football. It was hard to deny them respect, but equally it would be hard to deny that that respect – in Britain most particularly – was grudging.

Herrera claimed to have invented the sweeper independently of Rappan during a game in France in 'around 1945'. He was playing at left-back in a W-M, and his side led 1-0 with quarter of an hour remaining. Realising they were coming under increasing pressure, Herrera instructed the left-half to drop back into his position, while he moved in-field to cover behind the defensive centre-half. 'Already when I was a player, I thought like that,' he said. 'And we won, and when I became manager I remembered that.' That may or may not be true – and Herrera was certainly not averse to polishing his own myth – but what is beyond dispute is that he became the godfather of the system, and it brought him two European Cups. Rocco, with his rotund stature and his love of wine, always seemed at odds with the ethos of his system; Herrera, erect, cadaverous and rigorously disciplined, was its personification, even if his hair always 'seemed a bit too black' as the journalist Camilla Cederna put it.

Herrera was born in Buenos Aires, although exactly when remains unclear. It is said that his father, a Spanish migrant, falsified his date of birth so as to avoid a fine for late registration of his son's arrival in the world, while Herrera, at least according to his wife, later altered the date on his birth certificate, changing 1910 to read 1916. His father was a carpenter – 'like Jesus', he said in his autobiography – and an anarchist trades unionist, while his mother, whom he described as 'illiterate but with extraordinary intelligence', worked as a cleaner.

At the age of four, perhaps fleeing the authorities, the family moved to Morocco where Herrera only just survived a bout of diphtheria. Later, shortly before becoming manager of Barcelona, he narrowly avoided death in a plane crash. The escapes seem to have convinced him of his own specialness, his status as a chosen one, a leader with a mission. That manifested itself in the asceticism of his life: the only adornment in his room at Inter's training camp was a crucifix. Having recovered from diphtheria, he gained in strength sufficiently that by his teens he was recognised as a physically imposing full-back. 'From fourteen or fifteen years old, I played with the Arabs, Jews, with the French, with Spaniards,' he told Simon Kuper in an interview given five years before death finally caught up with him in 1997. 'That is the school of life.'

He began his formal playing career with Racing Casablanca, but, discovered by 'scouts looking under the rocks in poor countries', as he put it in his autobiography, soon moved to Paris. There he played for Red Star 93 and Racing Club, and won two caps for France at full-back. His career had never threatened to be much more than average, but it was brought to an end anyway at the age of twenty-five after he suffered a serious knee injury. Typically, given his acute sense of his own destiny, Herrera later in life drew a positive from the setback. 'As a player I was a very sad thing,' he said. 'My advantage is that big-star players are monuments of presumptuousness when they become managers. They do not know how to teach someone what they naturally did with so much grace. Not in my case.'

As the war came to an end, Herrera was appointed coach of the amateur side Puteaux and, after impressing there, he moved to Stade Français while working part-time with the national team as an assistant to Gaston Barreau. It was there that he first acquired the nickname '*Le Sorcier*' ('The Wizard' – it was later translated to become '*Il Mago*' in Italy). Herrera hated the title, believing it detracted from his achievements. 'The word wizard doesn't belong to football,' he said. '"Passion" and "strength" are football words. The greatest compliment I've ever had was someone saying I worked thirty hours a day.' He was similarly dismissive of the concept of luck in football. 'I hate it when they ask about being fortunate,' he said towards the end of his career, with sixteen major titles to his name. 'I don't believe in good luck. When someone has won so much in twenty years, can it be fortune? Modestly, I've won more than any other manager in the world. My case is unprecedented.' For him, everything was controllable, everything could be made better. In that regard he was the first modern manager. Guttmann might have followed Chapman in establishing the cult of the manager, but it was Herrera who defined his role, he who showed just what an effect a manager could have. 'When I started, managers carried the teams' bags,' he said. 'I put them in the place they deserved to be, earning what they should earn.'

Herrera was not just a fine tactician; he was a perfectionist, involving himself in all aspects of team affairs. He would control his players' diets, developed the system of the *ritiro*, whereby players would be confined to the team's training base the evening before games, and was a pioneer of sports psychology. Every morning he would rise before seven to practise yoga, reciting to himself the phrase, 'I am strong, I am calm, I fear nothing, I am beautiful.' He would pin motivational notices to the dressing-room walls: 'Fighting or playing? Fighting and playing,' read one; another insisted: 'He who plays for himself plays for the opposition. He who plays for the team, plays for himself.' He encouraged his players to sleep twelve hours a day, and rarely stayed up later than nine o'clock himself. He was, Brera said, 'a clown and a genius, vulgar and ascetic, voracious and a good father, sultan and believer ... boorish and competent, megalomaniac and health freak.'

As Stade Français's president sold the club's franchise in 1949, Herrera moved to Spain, becoming manager of Atlético Madrid after a brief spell with Real Valladolid. He won two championships there, and continued through Málaga, Deportivo la Coruña, Sevilla and the Portuguese side Belenenses before arriving at Barcelona, where he enjoyed his first European success. It was his predecessor, Domènec Balmanya, who took them to the final of the Fairs Cup, even overseeing the first leg, a 2-2 draw at Stamford Bridge against a London XI, but he was sacked as Barcelona's league form faltered, allowing Herrera to arrive, inspire a 6-0 win in the second leg, and take the glory.

Herrera acknowledged he had inherited an 'extraordinary group of players'. 'All one could do was win every competition in which the team participated,' he said. 'Until now the triumphs achieved by Real Madrid at home and abroad have intimidated the team.' And so he set about bolstering their self-belief, not only with motivational slogans, but with a series of rituals that played on his exotic heritage. 'Too many managers,' he said, 'limit their role to little taps on the players' shoulders as they are about to go on to the pitch, or making the occasional patriotic speech, which, while maybe warming up the hearts of some players, only serves to cool the muscles of the whole team.'

Players were given herbal tea before kick-off, supposedly a magic potion of South American or Arab origin. Herrera would gather his team in a circle before they went on the field and throw them each the ball in turn, staring into their eyes and asking: 'How are we

going to play? Why are we going to win?' When he had been round
every player, they would link arms over each others' shoulders and
affirm, 'We are going to win! We are going to do this together!' The
forward Luis Suárez had a belief that if wine was spilled during a
meal, he would score in his next game; Herrera made a point
before key games of knocking over his glass during the team meal,
at which Suárez would damp his finger on the wine-soaked table-
cloth, before touching it to his forehead and his foot.

By the time he got to Inter, the rituals had become even more
complex, as he sought to improve what he saw as the cold atmosphere surrounding the club. There, before the game, Herrera
would hold a ball in the centre of the circle, and the players would
reach towards it, calling out: 'I must have it! I must have it!' 'It is
important to touch the ball before the match,' he explained. 'The
players are nervous. It is a big match, a big crowd, but the ball: that
is their life. Then I made the players hug each other. Not kiss, just
hug! And I told them, "We are all in the same boat!"... Then they
would get changed and I would say, "Speak to each other! Defence,
speak among yourselves!" *Une équipe, une famille.*'

Herrera's style at Barcelona spoke of his great self-confidence, as
he deployed inside-forwards in the wing-half positions, giving
them creativity throughout the midfield square. They scored
ninety-six goals in thirty games in winning the league by four
points in 1958–59, and eighty-six goals in 1959–60 as they edged
out Real Madrid on goal difference. Herrera, though, was sacked
before the end of that season after a 6-2 aggregate defeat to Real
Madrid in the European Cup semi-final. He departed, as he had
arrived, between the two legs of a Fairs Cup final in which Barca
overcame English opposition. Fans had attacked him at his hotel
after the European Cup defeat, but after his sacking they carried
him on their shoulders down the Ramblas. By then, only
Guttmann could challenge him as the most wanted coach in
Europe.

After receiving a number of offers, Herrera opted for the most
lucrative, and moved to Milan with Inter. Their president, Angelo
Moratti, had sacked twelve coaches in the previous five years.
Herrera promised he would provide the success Moratti so desperately sought, but demanded a then-record annual salary of
£35,000. 'Sometimes an expensive choice can be a cheap one, a
cheap one very expensive,' he said, and was vindicated as gate

receipts went up fivefold in his first season at the club.

A few weeks after his arrival he met the players' wives and explained to them the importance of nutrition and the routines he wanted his players to follow. Herrera wanted his control to be all-encompassing, even if his implementation of the *ritiro*, confining players to their Appiano Gentile headquarters before games, was far from popular. 'The idea was that we would focus on the upcoming match and nothing else,' said the defender Tarcisio Burgnich. 'During the retreat, you couldn't leave; you would just train, eat and sleep. When we did get a free moment, there was nothing to do beyond playing cards. So you ended up doing nothing but thinking about the next game. The problem with such retreats is that they're OK once in a while, but if you do them too often it's really tough on the players.'

Everything, from sleep to training to diet to the courses of oxygen players were given the night before each game, was strictly regulated. The English forward Gerry Hitchens described leaving Herrera's Inter as being 'like coming out of the bloody army', and told the story of how he, Suárez and Mario Corso were once left behind at the training ground by the team bus after lagging on a cross-country run and had to make the six-mile journey back into town themselves. Even Sandro Mazzola, the great star of the side, admitted there were times when Herrera's obsession with preparation became too much. 'After beating Vasas in the European Cup [in 1966–67],' he said, 'we were in the showers chatting about the chance of a couple of days off because we literally lived in our camp. Unfortunately he was listening. He said to me: "No matter how successful you think you are, you always have to keep you feet on the ground." Nobody said a thing and we all returned to the Appiano Gentile.'

Discipline was absolute, and any challenge to his authority was pitilessly suppressed. At Barcelona, Herrera described the Hungarian forward Ladislao Kubala as 'the greatest player I have ever known', but ostracised him because, he said, his bouts of heavy drinking were undermining his form and destabilising the team. Kubala's apologists suggest Herrera was rather trying to break the cult of *kubalismo* that had given him disproportionate influence at the club. Similarly, when he arrived at Inter, Herrera jettisoned the Argentinian forward Antonio Angelillo, who had scored thirty-three goals in thirty-three games in the 1958–59 season, because of his turbulent social life. Even Armando Picchi, the renowned *libero*, wasn't safe, being sold on to Varese in 1967 after questioning Herrera's judgement. 'I've been accused of being tyrannical and completely ruthless with my players,' Herrera said, 'but I merely implemented things that were later copied by every single club: hard work, perfectionism, physical training, diets and three days of concentration before every game.'

That preparation extended to dossiers on the opposition. Players came to know their opponents so well that it was said they could recognise them from Herrera's descriptions without recourse to photographs. Suárez, who became the world's most expensive player when he joined Inter from Barca in 1961, regarded Herrera's approach as unprecedented. 'His emphasis on fitness and psychology had never been seen before. Until then, the manager was unimportant. He virtually slapped the best players, making them believe they weren't good enough, and praised the others. They were all fired up – to prove him right or wrong.'

Inter hammered Atalanta 5-1 in Bergamo in Herrera's first game in charge, won their next away game 6-0 at Udinese, then put five past Vicenza. They ended up third in the table, but scored seventy-three goals in thirty-four games – more than anybody but the champions Juventus. They were second the following year, but that was not enough for Moratti. That summer, the president even invited Edmondo Fabbri to the Appiano Gentile to offer him Herrera's job, only to have second thoughts at the last minute and send him home, telling Herrera he had one more season to deliver the success he had promised. It was then that Herrera decided he had to change. 'I took out a midfielder and put him sweeping behind the main defenders, liberating the left-back to attack,' he said. 'In attack, all the players knew what I wanted: vertical football at great speed, with no more than three passes to get to the opponents' box. If you lose the ball playing vertically, it's not a problem – but lose it laterally and you pay with a goal.'

Picchi, who scored just once in his Serie A career, proved a diligent sweeper, described by Brera as 'a defensive director ... his passes were never random, his vision was superb'. Aristide Guarneri operated as a stopper central-back, with Burgnich, the right-back, sitting alongside him. 'By this point,' said Maradei, 'many teams were employing a *tornante*, usually the right-winger, which meant that effectively the left-winger was the more

La Grande Inter

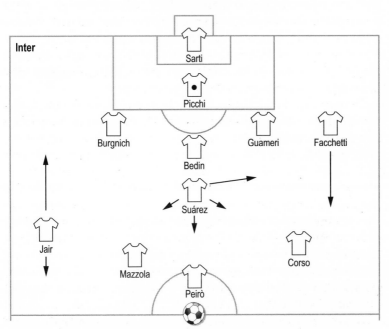

attacking, often cutting inside to shoot on goal. Many great Italian forwards – most notably Gigi Riva and Pierino Prati – started like that.'

That gave the left-back, Giacinto Facchetti, who had arrived at the club as a forward, greater licence to push forwards, because the man he was marking tended to sit deeper. 'Jair was in front of Burgnich,' Maradei went on. 'He was not a great defender, but dropped deep because he was the kind of player who liked to run at people and needed space in front of him. On the left, in front of Facchetti, you had Corso, a very creative player, not the quickest or the most attacking, but a man capable of unlocking opposing defences. He was the link man with the front guys. Carlo Tagnin and, later, Gianfranco Bedin, sat in front of the defence and did most of the running and defending. Alongside him was Suárez who had great vision and the ability to hit very accurate long passes. That was the typical way Inter restarted after winning possession. They would either get the ball to Jair, who would run into space, or leave it for Suárez, who would hit it from deep over the midfield for Mazzola or the centre-forward – Beniamino Di

Giacomo or Aurelio Milani, neither of whom was particularly gifted – or Jair cutting in from the right to run on to.'

Facchetti was the key, and it was he who gave Herrera his best defence against the accusations of negativity. 'I invented *catenaccio*,' Herrera said. 'The problem is that most of the ones who copied me copied me wrongly. They forgot to include the attacking principles that my *catenaccio* included. I had Picchi as sweeper, yes, but I also had Facchetti, the first full-back to score as many goals as a forward.' That is a slight exaggeration – Faccchetti only once got into double figures in the league – but his thrusts down the left give the lie to those who suggest Herrera habitually set up his team with a *libero* and four defensive markers.

The effectiveness of Herrera's system could hardly be questioned. They won Serie A in 1963, 1965 and 1966 – missing out in 1964 only after losing a playoff to Bologna, were European champions in 1964 and 1965 and reached the final again in 1967. Success alone, though, does not explain why Shankly so hated Herrera and *catenaccio*, even allowing for their perceived defensiveness. The problem was the skulduggery that went along with it.

Even at Barcelona there had been dark rumours. Local journalists who felt aggrieved by Herrera's abrasive manner began referring to him as 'the pharmacy cup coach' and, although players of the time deny the allegations, they are given credence by what followed. 'He was serious at his job, but had a good sense of humour, and knew how to get the best out of his players,' said the Spain midfielder Fusté, who came through Barcelona's youth ranks during Herrera's reign. 'All that stuff about him giving us all drugs is all lies. What he was, was a good psychologist.'

That he certainly was, but the suggestion he was also a decent pharmacologist never went away. Most notorious were the claims made in his autobiography by Ferruccio Mazzola, Sandro's younger and less talented brother. 'I've seen with my eyes how players were treated,' he said. 'I saw Helenio Herrera providing pills that were to be placed under our tongues. He used to experiment on us reserve players before giving them to the first-team players. Some of us would eventually spit them out. It was my brother Sandro that suggested that if I had no intention of taking them, to just run to the toilet and spit them out. Eventually Herrera found out and decided to dilute them in coffee. From that day on "*Il Caffè Herrera*" became a habit at Inter.' Sandro vehemently denied the allegations, and was so angered by them he subsequently broke off relations with his brother, but the rumours were widespread. Even if they were not true, their proliferation further sullied the image of the club, and the fact that they were so widely believed is indicative of how far people thought Herrera would go in his pursuit of victory.

At Inter, tactics, psychology and ethos became commingled. Herrera might have had a case when he argued that his side's tactical approach was not necessarily defensive, but it can hardly be denied that there was a negativity about their mentality. In *The Italian Job*, Gianluca Vialli and Gabriele Marcotti speak at length of the insecurity that pervades Italian football; in Herrera's Inter it revealed itself as paranoia and a willingness to adopt means that would have appalled Chapman, never mind an idealist like Hugo Meisl. Brera, eccentrically, always maintained that Italians had to play defensive football because they lacked physical strength. Gamesmanship became a way of life. Ahead of the 1967 European Cup final against Celtic, for instance, Herrera arrived in Glasgow by private jet to watch Celtic play Rangers at Ibrox. Before leaving Italy, he had offered to give Jock Stein a lift back so he could see Inter's match against Juventus. Stein, wisely, did not cancel the tickets he had booked on a scheduled flight, and his caution was justified when Herrera withdrew the invitation on arrival in Glasgow, saying the plane was too small for a man of Stein's girth. The taxi and tickets Inter had promised to lay on in Turin similarly failed to materialise, and Stein ended up seeing the game only because a journalist persuaded gatemen to admit him with a press card.

They were minor examples, but even leaving aside the accusations of drug-taking and match-fixing, there were times Herrera appeared monstrously heartless. When Guarneri's father died the night before a match against AC Milan, for instance, Herrera kept the news from him until after the game. In 1969, when he had left Inter and become coach of Roma, the forward Giulano Taccola died under Herrera's care. He had been ill for some time and, after an operation to remove his tonsils brought no relief, further medical examination revealed he had a heart murmur. Herrera played Taccola in a Serie A game at Sampdoria, but he lasted just forty-five minutes before having to be taken off. A fortnight later

Herrera had him travel with the squad to Sardinia for an away game against Cagliari. He had no intention of playing him, but on the morning of the game, he made Taccola train on the beach with the rest of the squad, despite a cold and gusting wind. Taccola watched the match from the stands, collapsed in the dressing room after the game and died a few hours later.

Then there were the allegations that Herrera habitually rigged games. The suggestions Inter manipulated referees first surfaced – at international level at least – after their European Cup semi-final against Borussia Dortmund in 1964. They had drawn the first leg in Germany 2-2, and won the return at the San Siro 2-0, a game in which they were significantly helped by an early injury to Dortmund's Dutch right-half Hoppy Kurrat, caused by a kick from Suárez. The Yugoslav referee Branko Tesanić took no action. That might have passed without notice, but then a Yugoslav tourist met Tesaniç on holiday that summer, and claimed the official had told him that his holiday had been paid for by Inter.

In the final in Vienna, Inter met Real Madrid. Tagnin was detailed to man-mark Di Stefano, Guarneri neutralised Puskás, and two Mazzola goals gave them a 3-1 win. The Monaco forward Yvon Douis had criticised Inter's approach earlier in the tournament, and Madrid's Lucien Müller echoed his complaints after the final. Herrera simply pointed to the trophy. They were more attacking in Serie A the following season, scoring sixty-eight goals, but they had lost none of their defensive resolve. Leading 3-1 from the first leg of their quarter-final against Rangers, they conceded after seven minutes at Ibrox, but held out superbly. That was the legitimate side of *catenaccio*; what followed in the semi-final against Liverpool was rather less admirable.

Liverpool took the first leg at Anfield 3-1, after which, Shankly said, an Italian journalist told him, 'You will never be allowed to win.' They weren't. They were kept awake the night before the game by rowdy local fans surrounding their hotel – a complaint that would become common in European football – but it was when the game started that it became apparent something was seriously wrong. Eight minutes in, Corso struck an indirect free-kick straight past the Liverpool goalkeeper Tommy Lawrence, and Ortiz de Mendibil, the Spanish referee, allowed the goal to stand. Two minutes later Joaquin Peiro pinched the ball from Lawrence as he bounced it in preparation for a kick downfield, and again De

Mendibil gave the goal. Facchetti sealed the win with a brilliant third.

De Mendibil was later implicated in the match-fixing scandal uncovered by Brian Glanville and reported in the *Sunday Times* in 1974, in which Dezso Solti, a Hungarian, was shown to have offered $5,000 and a car to the Portuguese referee Francisco Lobo to help Juventus through the second leg of their European Cup semi-final against Derby County in 1973. Glanville believes he was in the pay of Juventus's club secretary, Italo Allodi, who had previously worked at Inter. He showed that the games of Italian clubs in Europe tended to be overseen by a small pool of officials, and that when they were, those Italian clubs were disproportionately successful. In so doing, Glanville simply proved what anecdotal evidence had suggested all along: referees were being paid off. It was that that Shankly could not forgive.

The 1965 final against Benfica – played, controversially, at the San Siro – was almost a case study in the classic Hererra match. Inter took the lead three minutes before half-time as Jair's shot skidded through Costa Pereira in the Benfica goal, but even after he had been injured, leaving his side down to ten men and with Germano, a defender, in goal, even though they were effectively playing at home, Inter continued to defend, happy to protect their lead. Was it pragmatism, or was it that, for all Herrera's efforts at building self-confidence, they didn't quite have faith in their own ability? Was it even that they had come to rely not just on their own efforts, but on those of the referee?

Benfica, losing their second final in three years, blamed the curse of Guttmann, but the truth was that their attacking approach had become outmoded; at club level at least, *catenaccio* – by means both justified and illegitimate – had superseded the remnants of the classic Danubian style that still lingered in their 4-2-4. When all else was equal, though – when referees had not been bought off – *catenaccio* could still come unstuck against talented attacking opposition. Inter won the *scudetto* again in 1965–66, but were beaten by Real Madrid in the semi-final of the European Cup. The referee for the second leg of that tie was the Hungarian György Vadas. He officiated with scrupulous fairness as Madrid secured a 1-1 draw that took them through by a 2-1 aggregate, but years later he revealed to the Hungarian journalist Peter Borenich that he too had been approached by

Solti. He, unlike an unknown number of others, turned Inter down.

It was the following year, though, that Herrera's Inter disintegrated, and yet the season had begun superbly, with a record-breaking run of seven straight victories. By mid-April they were four points clear of Juventus at the top of Serie A, and in Europe had had their revenge on Real Madrid, beating them 3-0 on aggregate in the quarter-finals. And then something went horribly wrong. Two 1-1 draws against CSKA Sofia in the semi-final forced them to a playoff – handily held in Bologna after they promised the Bulgarians a three-quarter share of the gate-receipts – and although they won that 1-0, it was as though all the insecurities, all the doubts, had rushed suddenly to the surface. They drew against Lazio and Cagliari, and lost 1-0 to Juventus, reducing their lead at the top to two points. They drew against Napoli, but Juve were held at Mantova. They drew again, at home to Fiorentina, and this time Juve closed the gap, beating Lanerossi Vicenza. With two matches of their season remaining – the European Cup final against Celtic in Lisbon, and a league match away to Mantova – two wins would have completed another double, but the momentum was against them.

Herrera was said to have fallen out with Allodi, and was being courted by Real Madrid; Suárez was reported also to be considering a return to Spain, the homeland of his fiancée; and Moratti was believed to be keen to give up the presidency to devote more time to his business interests. Worse, Suárez was ruled out of the final with what was variously described as a thigh strain or cartilage damage, while Mazzola had suffered flu in the days leading up to the game.

Celtic had dabbled with a defensive system, away to Dukla Prague in the semi-final, but although they got away with a goalless draw, that game had made clear that their strength was attacking. Their basic system was the 4-2-4 that had spread after the 1958 World Cup, but the two centre-forwards, Stevie Chalmers and Willie Wallace, took turns dropping deep, trying to draw out Inter's central defensive markers. The two wingers, Jimmy Johnstone and Bobby Lennox, were encouraged to drift inside, creating space for the two attacking full-backs, Jim Craig and Tommy Gemmell. If Inter were going to defend, the logic seemed to be, Celtic were going to attack with everything in their power.

And Inter were set on defending, particularly after Mazzola gave them a seventh-minute lead from the penalty spot. They had done it against Benfica in 1965, and they tried to do it again, but this was not the Inter of old. Doubts had come to gnaw at them, and as Celtic swarmed over them they intensified. 'We just knew, even after fifteen minutes, that we were not going to keep them out,' Burgnich said. 'They were first to every ball; they just hammered us in every area of the pitch. It was a miracle that we were still 1-0 up at half-time. Sometimes in those situations with each minute that passes your confidence increases and you start to believe. Not on that day. Even in the dressing room at half-time we looked at each other and we knew that we were doomed.'

For Burgnich, the *ritiro* had become by then counter-productive, serving only to magnify the doubts and the negativity. 'I think I saw my family three times during that last month,' he said. 'That's why I used to joke that Giacinto Facchetti, my room-mate, and I were like a married couple. I certainly spent far more time with him than my wife. The pressure just kept building up; there was no escape, nowhere to turn. I think that certainly played a big part in our collapse, both in the league and in the final.'

On arriving in Portugal, Herrera had taken his side to a hotel on the sea-front, half an hour's drive from Lisbon. As usual, Inter booked out the whole place. 'There was nobody there, except for the players and the coaches, even the club officials stayed elsewhere,' Burgnich said. 'I'm not joking, from the minute our bus drove through the gates of the hotel to the moment we left for the stadium three days later we did not see a single human being apart from the coaches and the hotel staff. A normal person would have gone crazy in those circumstances. After many years we were somewhat used to it, but by that stage, even we had reached our breaking point. We felt the weight of the world on our shoulders and there was no outlet. None of us could sleep. I was lucky if I got three hours a night. All we did was obsess over the match and the Celtic players. Facchetti and I, late at night, would stay up and listen to our skipper, Armando Picchi, vomiting from the tension in the next room. In fact, four guys threw up the morning of the game and another four in the dressing room before going out on the pitch. In that sense we had brought it upon ourselves.'

Celtic, by contrast, made great play of being relaxed, which only made Inter feel worse. In terms of mentality, it was *catenaccio*'s *reductio ad absurdum*, the point beyond which the negativity couldn't go. They had created the monster, and it ended up turning on its maker. Celtic weren't being stifled, and the chances kept coming. Bertie Auld hit the bar, the goalkeeper Giuliano Sarti saved brilliantly from Gemmell, and then, seventeen minutes into the second half, the equaliser arrived. It came thanks to the two full-backs who, as Stein had hoped, repeatedly outflanked Inter's marking. Bobby Murdoch found Craig on the right, and he advanced before cutting a cross back for Gemmell to crash a right-foot shot into the top corner. It was not, it turned out, possible to mark everybody, particularly not those arriving from deep positions.

The onslaught continued. 'I remember, at one point, Picchi turned to the goalkeeper and said, "Giuliano, let it go, just let it go. It's pointless, sooner or later they'll get the winner,"' Burgnich said. 'I never thought I would hear those words, I never imagined my captain would tell our keeper to throw in the towel. But that only shows how destroyed we were at that point. It's as if we did not want to prolong the agony.'

Inter, exhausted, could do no more than launch long balls aimlessly forward, and they succumbed with five minutes remaining. Again a full-back was instrumental, Gemmell laying the ball on for Murdoch, whose mishit shot was diverted past Sarti by Chalmers. Celtic became the first non-Latin side to lift the European Cup, and Inter were finished.

Worse followed at Mantova. As Juventus beat Lazio, Sarti allowed a shot from Di Giacomo – the former Inter forward – to slip under his body, and the *scudetto* was lost. 'We just shut down mentally, physically and emotionally,' said Burgnich. Herrera blamed his defenders. Guarneri was sold to Bologna and Picchi to Varese. 'When things go right,' the sweeper said, 'it's because of Herrera's brilliant planning. When things go wrong, it's always the players who are to blame.'

As more and more teams copied *catenaccio*, its weaknesses became increasingly apparent. The problem Rappan had discovered – that the midfield could be swamped – had not been solved. The *tornante* could alleviate that problem, but only by diminishing the attack. 'Inter got away with it because they had Jair and Corso in wide positions and both were gifted,' Maradei explained. 'And, also, they had Suárez who could hit those long

Internazionale 1 Celtic 2, European Cup Final, Estadio Nacional, Lisbon, 25 May 1967

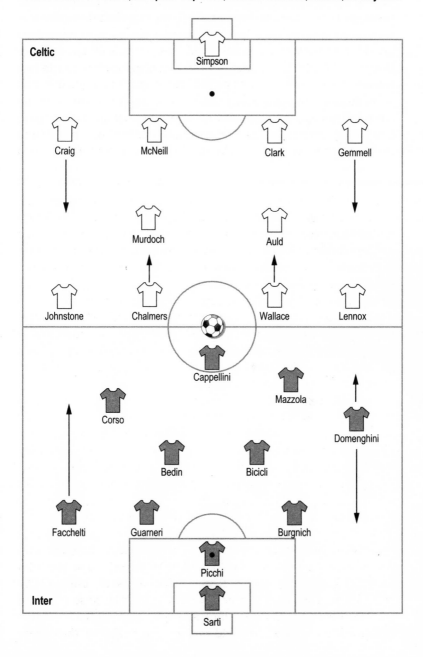

balls. But for most teams it became a serious problem. And so, what happened is that rather than converting full-backs into *liberi*, they turned inside-forwards into *liberi*. This allowed you, when you won possession, to push him up into midfield and effectively have an extra passer in the middle of the park. This was the evolution from *catenaccio* to what we call "*il giocco all' Italiano*" – "the Italian game".'

In 1967–68, morale and confidence shot, Inter finished only fifth, thirteen points behind the champions Milan, and Herrera left for Roma. *Catenaccio* didn't die with *la grande Inter*, but the myth of its invincibility did. Celtic had proved attacking football had a future, and it wasn't just Shankly who was grateful for that.

△▽△▽△▽△▽△▽

Chapter Eleven

After the Angels

△▽ The World Cup in 1958 was, in a very different way, just as significant in shaping the direction of Argentinian football as it had been for Brazilian. Where for Brazil success, and the performances of bright young things such as Pelé and Garrincha, confirmed them in their individualist attacking ways, for Argentina a shocking failure left them questioning the fundamentals that had underpinned their conception of the game for at least three decades. Tactical shifts tend to be gradual, but in this case it can be pinpointed to one game: the era of *la nuestra* ended with Argentina's 6-1 defeat to Czechoslovakia in Helsingborg on 15 June 1958.

The change in the offside law in 1925 had passed all but unnoticed in Argentina, and an idealistic belief in 2-3-5 – or, perhaps more accurately, simply in playing, for the notion that there could be another way seems never to have occurred – carried them right through until Renato Cesarini took charge of River Plate in 1939. Even the Hungarian Emérico Hirschl, who arrived at Gimnasia de la Plata in 1932 and moved to River in 1935, and was accused of importing European ideas, seems to have favoured a classic Danubian pyramid, although probably by then with withdrawn inside-forwards. Certainly his philosophy was an attacking one, as a record 106 goals in thirty-four games in the double championship-winning year of 1937 indicates. Cesarini played in that side, but it was after he had succeeded Hirschl that River reached their peak.

Cesarini was one of the original *oriundi*, who left Argentina for Italy in the late 1920s. He had been born in Senigallia, Italy, in 1906, but his family emigrated to Argentina when he was a few months old. He began his playing career with Chacarita Juniors, but, in 1929, Juventus enticed him back to the land of his birth. He was spectacularly successful there, winning five consecutive Serie A titles and developing such a knack of scoring crucial late goals that even now in Italy last-minute winners are said to have been scored in the *zona cesarini*.

Juve developed the *metodo* at roughly the same time as the national coach Vittorio Pozzo, but Cesarini had a very specific role in it, often man-marking the opponents' most creative player. Not surprisingly, when he returned to Argentina in 1935 – initially as a player with Chacarita, and then with River – he brought those ideas with him. Cesarini is often described as having introduced the W-M to Argentina, but, like Dori Kürschner in Brazil, his version of it would not have been recognised as such in Britain. Rather what he brought was the *metodo*, as he deployed Néstor Rossi, a forward-thinking centre-half, slightly deeper than the wing-halves, in the manner of Luisito Monti (himself, of course, an *oriundo*). Although Rossi had to provide defensive cover, the 'Howler of the Americas' – as fans dubbed him for the ferocity of his organisational shouting – was also expected to initiate attacks. 'Rossi was my idol,' said the great holding midfielder Antonio Rattín, who was Argentina's captain at the 1966 World Cup. 'I tried to do everything Rossi did. Not just the way he played, but the way he yelled, the way he moved, the way he did everything. My first game for Boca Juniors was against River. I was nineteen, he was thirty-one. The first thing I did after that first match, which we won 2-1, was to get a picture with him.'

From the late twenties, inside-forwards in both Uruguay and Argentina had begun pulling deep from the front line, but under Cesarini, River took such movement to extremes. The front five of – reading from right to left – Félix Loustau, Ángel Labruna, Adolfo Pedernera, José Moreno and Juan Carlos Muñoz became fabled (although they only played as a quintet eighteen times over a five-year period). Rather than the two inside-forwards withdrawing, it was Moreno and Pedernera who dropped off into the space in front of the half-line. Loustau, meanwhile, patrolled the whole of the right flank, becoming known as a *'ventilador-wing'* – 'fan-wing' (*'puntero-ventilador'* is used, but the half-English term seems more common) – because he was a winger who gave air to the midfield by doing some of their running for them.

La Máquina

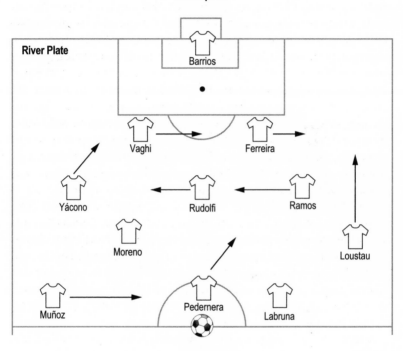

Loustau's running meant that Norberto Yácono, the nominal right-half, could be given a more defensive brief, and he became known as 'The Stamp' for the way he would stick to the player he was marking. (Everybody and everything at the time, it seems, had nicknames, an indication perhaps of how central football was to popular culture and everyday conversation in Argentina at the time.) As other teams replicated Yácono's role, Argentinian football gradually developed what was effectively a third-back, but rather than it being the centre-half, the No. 5, dropping in between the two full-backs (Nos. 2 and 3), it was the right-half, the No. 4, operating to the right of them. When 4-2-4 was adopted in the aftermath of 1958, it was – as elsewhere – the left-half, the No. 6, who moved back into a central defensive position, alongside the No. 2 and with the No. 3 to his left, while the centre-half, the No. 5, remained as a holding midfielder. (Even today in Argentina, positions tend to be known by their numbers, so Rattín, for instance, was a 'five', while Osvaldo Ardiles was an 'eight'.) So, where a typical English back four would read, from right-to-left, 2, 5, 6, 3, an Argentinian one would read 4, 2, 6, 3.

In Uruguay, meanwhile, where there was no corresponding movement of the right-half backwards, and so no consequent shuffle of the two full-backs to the left. When the 2-3-5 (or the *metodo*) became 4-2-4, the two wing-halves simply dropped straight in as wide defenders (what would in Britain today be called full-backs), and a back-four there would read, 4, 2, 3, 6, although the 2 would often – as Matías González had in the 1950 World Cup final – play behind the other three defenders as a sweeper, thus replicating the numbering system in the Swiss *verrou*.

Cesarini's River side, *la Máquina*, became the most revered exponents of *la nuestra*. 'You play against *la Máquina* with the intention of winning,' said Ernesto Lazzatti, the Boca Juniors No. 5, 'but as an admirer of football sometimes I'd rather stay in the stands and watch them play.' As befits the self-conscious romanticism of the Argentinian game at the time, though, River were not relentless winners. Although they were, by general consent, the best side in the country, between 1941 and 1945 River won just three titles, twice finishing second to Boca. 'They called us the "Knights of Anguish" because we didn't look for the goal,' said Muñoz. 'We never thought we couldn't score against our rivals. We went out on the pitch and played our way: take the ball, give it to

Numbering in the 4-2-4

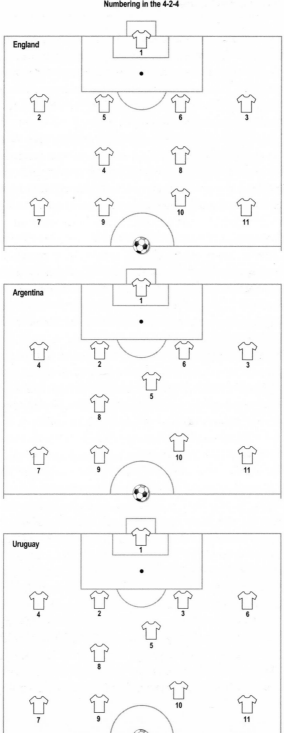

me, a *gambeta*, this, that and the goal came by itself. Generally it took a long time for the goal to come and the anguish was because games were not settled quickly. Inside the box, of course, we wanted to score, but in the midfield we had fun. There was no rush. It was instinctive.' *La Máquina* was a very different machine to that of Herbert Chapman's Arsenal.

As such, they were the perfect representatives of the Argentinian golden age, when football came as close as it ever would to Danny Blanchflower's ideal of the glory game. Isolation – brought about by war and Perónist foreign policy – meant there were no defeats to international sides to provoke a re-think, and so Argentinian football went ever further down the road of aestheticism.

It may have been insular, but that is not to say that the impression of superiority was necessarily illusory. On the odd occasion when foreign opposition was met, it tended to be beaten. Over the winter of 1946–47, for instance, San Lorenzo toured the Iberian peninsular, playing eight games in Spain and two in Portugal. They won five, lost just once, and scored forty-seven goals. 'What would have happened if Argentina had played in the World Cup at that time?' asked the forward René Pontoni. 'I feel like I have a thorn stuck in my side that has not gone away over the years. I don't want to be presumptuous, but I believe that if we'd been able to take part, we'd have taken the laurels.'

Victory in the representative game over England in 1953 seemed only to confirm what everybody in Argentina had suspected: that their form of the game was the best in the world, and that they were the best exponents of it. Who, after all, was leading Real Madrid's domination of the European Cup but Alfredo di Stéfano, brought up in the best traditions of *la nuestra* at River? That conclusion was corroborated as Argentina won the Copa América in 1955 and retained it in Peru two years later.

That latter side bubbled with young talent, the forward-line of Omar Corbatta, Humberto Maschio, Antonio Angelillo, Omar Sívori and Osvaldo Cruz playing with a mischievous verve that earned them the nickname 'The Angels with Dirty Faces'. They scored eight against Colombia, three against Ecuador, four against Uruguay, six against Chile and three against Brazil. They lost their final game to the hosts, but by then the title was won and Argentina's isolation emphatically over. They weren't just back:

they were the best side in South America, and possibly the world.

By the time of 1958 World Cup, though, Maschio, Angelillo and Sívori had moved to Serie A, and all three ended up playing international football for Italy. Di Stéfano, similarly, had thrown in his lot with Spain. Come Sweden, Argentina were so desperate for forwards that for cover they were forced to turn to Labruna, who was by then approaching his fortieth birthday. A 3-1 defeat to the defending champions West Germany was no disgrace, but it did suggest Argentina weren't quite as good as they had believed themselves to be. 'We went in wearing a blindfold,' Rossi admitted.

Still, self-confidence was restored as they came from behind to beat Northern Ireland 3-1 in their second game. They ended with party-pieces – 'taking the mickey' said the Northern Ireland midfielder Jimmy McIlroy – but the warning signs were there. Northern Ireland had been told of Argentina's great tradition, of the skill and the pace and the power of their forward play, but what they found, McIlroy said, was 'a lot of little fat men with stomachs, smiling at us and pointing and waving at girls in the crowd'.

That left Argentina needing a draw in their final group game against Czechoslovakia to progress. Czechoslovakia didn't even make it to the quarter-finals, losing in a playoff to Northern Ireland, but they blew Argentina away. 'We were used to playing really slowly, and they were fast,' said José Ramos Delgado, who was in the squad for the tournament but didn't play. 'We hadn't played international football for a long time, so when we went out there we thought we were really talented, but we found we hadn't followed the pace of the rest of the world. We had been left behind. The European teams played simply. They were precise. Argentina were good on the ball, but we didn't go forwards.'

Milan Dvorák put Czechoslovakia ahead after eight minutes with an angled drive, and before half-time Argentina were three down as individual errors handed two goals to Zdenek Zikán. Oreste Corbatta pulled one back from the penalty spot, but Jiri Feureisl had restored the three-goal margin within four minutes, before two late strikes from Václav Hovorka completed a 6-1 humiliation.

'If I had to look for an explanation to explain such a bad performance, I would sum it up with one word: disorganisation,' said the goalkeeper Amadeo Carrizo. 'We travelled to Sweden on a flight that took something like forty hours. It was not the best way to start. Compare that to Brazil, who went in a private plane and after making a tour in which the team adapted their tactics. The football was disorganised as well. We didn't know anything about our rivals. The Czechs scored four goals past me that were identical. They pulled a cross back and it was a goal. They pulled another cross back and it was another goal. They grew tired of scoring in that way. We stepped off the plane thinking it would all be easy for us. We came back having made it all easy for everybody else.'

The reaction was furious. Players were pelted with coins and vegetables at Buenos Aires airport, and the coach, Guillermo Stábile, who had been in charge since 1941, was dismissed. 'He didn't know about tactics,' said the historian Juan Presta. 'He just picked the best players and told them to play. He was a romantic.'

'It was terrible,' Ramos Delgado recalled. 'In every stadium, we were abused by everyone; even those of us who had not played. The national team had to be modified. A different kind of player was looked for, players who were more about sacrifice than play. Football became less of an art after that.'

The reaction against *la nuestra* was brutal. There was a realisation that the *metodo* was outdated, but the backlash went far further than a simple switch to a 4-2-4. Crowds for league matches fell sharply, partly because of a sense of disillusionment, and partly because the growing middle-class began watching games on television rather than at the stadiums. Clubs, which had enjoyed state support under Perón, lost their subsidies. Many turned to foreign talent in an attempt to woo back spectators with exoticism, further diluting the culture of *la nuestra*, but, most crucially of all, the ethos changed. With the financial stakes raised, football became less about the spectacle than about winning, or at least, not losing. As in Italy in the late twenties, the result was that tactics became increasingly negative.

'It was then that European discipline appeared,' said the philosopher Tomás Abraham. 'That was the way that modernity, which implies discipline, physical training, hygiene, health, professionalism, sacrifice, all the Fordism entered Argentinian football. There came these methods for physical preparation that gave importance to defence – and who had cared about defence before? It's a strange thing that it should come then, in parallel with the Brazilian triumph, which really should be an argument for our own local football.'

Boca, at least, did try to repeat the Brazilian success, appointing Vicente Feola, although he lasted only a season before being replaced by José D'Amico. Feola brought with him two Peruvians and six Brazilians, the most significant of whom was probably Orlando, his World Cup-winning central defender from 1958. 'It was Orlando who introduced us to the idea of a caged No. 6, sitting in defence rather than in midfield,' said Rattín. 'Feola was unlucky. Under him we kept hitting the post or missing penalties, and then D'Amico won the championship with the same team.'

The triumph of 1962, sealed with a 1-0 victory over River as Antonio Roma saved a late penalty, was achieved with a 4-3-3, but with Alberto González operating as a *ventilador*–wing (or *tornante*, as the Italians would have called him), tracking back to become a fourth midfielder to add solidity. That defensive resolve reached its apogee two years later as, under Pedernera, Boca won the title again, conceding just fifteen goals in thirty games – only six in their final twenty-five – and scoring a mere thirty-five. Pedernera may have been a member of *la Máquina*, but he was unapologetic about his side's approach. 'The Bohemian from before doesn't exist anymore,' he said. 'Today the message is clear: if you win, you are useful, if you lose, you are not.' Significantly, Boca proved just as useful overseas, going unbeaten through an eight-game tour of Europe in 1963.

The Independiente coach Manuel Giúdice, who led his side to the league title in 1960 and 1963, and then to successive Libertadores triumphs, was more of a traditionalist, but even his side were known for their *garra* – their 'claw', forcefulness or fighting spirit. 'Independiente and Boca in the early sixties were very strong marking sides and played a lot on the counter-attack,' said Ramos Delgado.

'There's a first modernity there,' said Abraham. 'For many years this would divide Argentinian football between those who want to keep the tradition and those who insist that we've been left behind.' That would find its most famous manifestation in the disputes between Carlos Bilardo and César Luis Menotti, but it existed earlier, most notably in the tension between Labruna, who coached at River and Rosario Central, and Juan Carlos Lorenzo, who led the Spanish side Real Mallorca to successive promotions and then interspersed spells with San Lorenzo with several years in Italy. He was unequivocal about his methods. 'How do you beat a team that has a great forward?' Lorenzo asked. 'Very simple. If you don't want somebody to eat, you have to stop the food coming out of the kitchen. I don't send somebody to mark the waiter; I have to worry about the chef.'

When Lorenzo was appointed as national coach ahead of the 1962 World Cup, the football federation was explicitly seeking a European approach. He tried to install a *catenaccio* system – even having the *libero* wear a different coloured shirt in training so the players could better see his role – but found he had too little time to implement something wholly alien and returned to a 4-2-4 for the tournament itself.

He was reappointed in 1966, and during the tournament instituted for the first time what would become the classic Argentinian formation: the 4-3-1-2, essentially a midfield diamond, with Rattín at its base, Jorge Solari and Alberto González, the *ventilador*–wing of Boca, shuttling up and down on either side of him as what were known as *carrileros*, and Ermindo Onega given the playmaking brief at the diamond's point. Width was provided by forward surges from the two full-backs, Roberto Ferreiro and Silvio Marzolini. Once it became apparent that there was no need for out-and-out touchline-hugging wingers, the midfield four became far more flexible. England's shape was essentially similar, the major difference being that where England had a designated defensive midfielder in Nobby Stiles, Argentina had a designated attacking midfielder in Onega. English and Argentinian sources agree on little about their quarter-final meeting in that tournament, but both accept that the major reasons for England's victory – once the refereeing conspiracies and Fifa's supposed financial need for the home team to reach the final in the days before satellite television are put to one side – were that Stiles silenced Onega, and that Alan Ball, attacking from the right side of midfield, prevented Marzolini getting forward.

The major change in the Argentinian game in the years following 1958, though, was less the system than the style. Their football became increasingly violent, as Celtic discovered against Racing Club in the Intercontinental Cup final of 1967. Celtic won the first tie in Glasgow 1-0, but then walked into a storm in Buenos Aires. As far as Argentinian football was concerned, there was a

Argentina 1966

score to be settled after the national side's controversial defeat to England in the World Cup quarter-final a year earlier, and distinctions between the component parts of Great Britain meant little.

Celtic took to the field amid a hail of missiles. Ronnie Simpson, their goalkeeper, was struck on the head by a stone during the warm-up and had to be replaced. An intimidated referee denied them a clear penalty before he finally did award one and, although that was converted by Tommy Gemmell, Norberto Raffo levelled for Racing before half-time with a header from what Celtic claimed was an offside position. Celtic were further unsettled when they returned to their dressing room at half-time to find there was no water. It got worse in the second half. Juan Carlos Cárdenas scored early to give Racing the lead, after which they set about wasting time, with the crowd hanging onto the ball for long periods.

A win apiece meant a playoff in Montevideo, and this time Celtic decided to fight back. 'The time for politeness is over,' said Jock Stein. 'We can be hard if necessary and we will not stand the shocking conduct of Racing.' The game was even more brutal than the first. It was settled by another Cárdenas goal, but the result hardly mattered amid the violence. Celtic had three men sent off and Racing two, but it could easily have been many more. Celtic fined their players, Racing bought theirs new cars: victory was everything.

Racing may have been representative of the way things had gone in Argentina, but they certainly weren't the worst exponents of the win-at-all-costs mentality. That prize, without question, went to the Estudiantes de la Plata of Osvaldo Zubeldía.

Juan Carlos Onganía seized power in a coup in June 1966 and, realising the power of sport, made money available to the clubs to clear their debts. In return, the championship was revised, being split into two – the Metropolitano and the Nacional – the aim being to encourage the development of sides from outside Buenos Aires. The stranglehold of the big five was broken and, in 1967, Estudiantes became the first Metropolitano champions.

When Zubeldía arrived at the club in 1965, having been dismissed from the national side, his initial target had simply been avoiding relegation. As a player with Boca Juniors, Vélez Sársfield, Atalanta and Banfield, he had been noted for his intelligence and his positional sense, and that awareness of shape and space was the cornerstone of his management. 'He was a right-half, so he played just alongside me at Boca,' said Rattín. 'Even as a player he was a real studier of the game. He would look at the law, and he would stand right there on the border of it.'

Zubeldía led Atalanta to two respectable finishes, but found things rather more difficult with Argentina, perhaps because, as Valeriy Lobanovskyi later discovered with the USSR, it is a much harder thing to impose a vision on a team at national level, where the time available to work with players is so brief, than it is at club level where the involvement is day-to-day.

'He came to the club a month before starting,' said Juan Ramón Verón, who is generally acknowledged to have been the most naturally gifted player in that Estudiantes side. 'He looked at the first team and he looked at the third team and he saw the third team was playing better, and asked himself what was the point of keeping the old players.'

He retained only four of them, preferring to try to mould young minds. 'Zubeldía was a very simple man, and work was his goal,' Verón went on. 'He was very fond of teaching, of spending time with and working with the players. He came here with another trainer, Argentino Genorazzo, who was a very crazy guy, who was never at any club for long because he was always falling out with people. But when they got here they had a plan, and they already knew what they wanted to do.

'We had a pre-season, which had not happened before. Coaches started to get heavily involved in daily training, which before then had not been usual. When Zubeldía came here, we started going into concentration the day before the game. We lived at the training ground. We learnt tactics on a blackboard and then practised them on the pitch.'

No club from outside the capital had ever won the title before, so there were no expectations, no demands for instant success. 'The fans here were more patient, so Zubeldía could work here for three years without having to win championships, which he would not have been able to do at, for instance, Boca,' Verón said. 'We were really young and didn't really notice what was happening. Things just started growing, and we realised one day that we had a great team.'

In *El Gráfico*, the journalist Jorge Ventura wrote of their style as 'a football that is elaborated over a hard week of laboratory work, and explodes on the seventh day with an effectiveness that consecrates the tale of positions. Because Estudiantes continue to manufacture points just as they manufacture football: with more work than talent... Estudiantes keep winning.'

They trained harder and more meticulously than any Argentinian side ever had before. 'All the possibilities afforded by the game were foreseen and practised,' Bilardo said. 'The corners, the free-kicks, throw-ins were used to our best advantage and we also had secret signs and language which we used to make our opponents fall into the trap.'

Estudiantes finished second in Group A of the Metropolitano championship in 1967, qualifying them for the last four. That in itself was some achievement, but they went on to come from 3-0 down to beat Platense 4-3 in the semi-final before a comfortable 3-0 win over Racing in the final. 'Their victory has been a triumph for the new mentality, so many times proclaimed from Sweden until here, but rarely established in facts,' the columnist Juvenal wrote in *El Gráfico*. 'A new mentality served by young, strong, disciplined, dynamic, vigorous, spiritual and physically upright people.

It is clear that Estudiantes didn't invent anything. They followed the path already traced by Racing the previous year... Estudiantes won after the thirty-six-year "ban" of championships on ambitious "small" teams. Estudiantes defeated their convictions and their limitations as an ultra-defensive-destructive-biting team. Estudiantes defeated the intoxication of a unique week in their club history, claiming the most exemplary of their attributes in the hour of victory: humility.'

Just as Pozzo's Italy side had been hailed as representing the militaristic side of fascism, so too Estudiantes became poster-boys for Onganía's new Argentina. Juvenal made the point even more clearly in January 1969, by which time Estudiantes were on their way to a third successive Copa Libertadores success. He praised their 'defensive structures, dynamics, temperament, sacrifice, aggression in defence, fighting spirit, team thinking, organisation. We eliminate improvisation. We improve and evolve into what had caused our inferiority according to some critics.' They were, in other words, being praised very specifically for what they did differently to *la nuestra*; moreover they were hailed for defying the European stereotype of South Americans as stylish but indolent.

Estudiantes may have been following Racing in their style and their absolutist rejection of the tenets of *la nuestra*, but in certain key regards what they were doing was new. The shape was the 4-3-3 that was gaining in popularity across the continent, but what they did within that was unique not only in Argentina, but in South America as a whole: they pressed, and played an aggressive offside trap. 'It was something unknown in Argentina,' said Verón, 'and it was that that allowed a humble team like Estudiantes to have such success.'

The question then is where the idea came from. Zubeldía was noted for his curiosity and his study of coaching practices from around the world, and most of his squad seem to agree that pressing was something he picked up from, as Verón put it, 'some European team'. Others go further and insist it was an eastern European side, but none can remember which one. As far as they were concerned, at least when the idea was introduced, it was just another one of Zubeldía's schemes, just another video he was showing them. It is tempting to believe that Zubeldía was influenced by Viktor Maslov – and given that at that stage his Dynamo Kyiv were the only side really proficient at pressing it is even probable – but there is no direct evidence. Even, though, if it were some other eastern European side from which Zubeldía picked up pressing, they logically must themselves have picked it up from Maslov. Maslov's influence was global.

Pressing and the high offside line were their legitimate innovations, but there was also a more sinister side. It was the violence of Estudiantes that shocked Europeans, but, according to Presta, in that they were no different to any other Argentinian side of the time. Where they stood out was in their use of dirty tricks. 'You don't,' Zubeldía said, 'arrive at glory through a path of roses.' It is difficult now to separate fact from fiction, but the stories are too widespread for them not to have at least some basis in actuality. The story has grown up that Bilardo would carry pins with him on the field to jab into opponents. 'A myth,' Verón said, but Rattín insisted it was true, although he admitted he had not seen it himself. 'Bilardo was sneaky,' Rattín said. 'He was always up to something. Tricky: he'd pull your shirt, pretend to be hit, anything.'

Although he was reluctant to go into specifics, Verón acknowledges that Estudiantes 'tried to find out everything possible about our rivals individually, their habits, their characters, their weaknesses, and even about their private lives so we could goad them on the field, get them to react and risk being sent off.'

'They used psychology in the worst possible way,' said Presta. 'There was a player from Independiente who had accidentally killed a friend on a hunting trip – when he played Estudiantes, all game long they chanted "murderer" at him. Or there was a goalkeeper for Racing who had a really close relationship with his mother. She didn't want him to marry, but eventually he did, and six months later his mother died. Bilardo walked up to him and said, "Congratulations, finally you've killed your mother."'

It has even been alleged that Bilardo, who was a qualified doctor, drew on his contacts in the medical profession. The Racing defender Roberto Perfumo, for instance, was sent off for kicking Bilardo in the stomach, supposedly because Bilardo had taunted him about a cyst his wife had recently had removed.

Unpalatable their methods may have been, but Estudiantes were undeniably effective and, at least at first, that was enough for commentators to overlook their excesses. There was, after all, more to them than thuggishness. 'They were really well constructed,' said Delgado, who played against them after his move to Santos. 'Aside from marking, they knew how to play. Verón was the key player. He gave them a flow. The two central midfielders – Pachamé and Bilardo – were not really talented. Pachamé was really defensive, and Bilardo was not talented but really really smart. Bilardo was the least talented of them all.'

Estudiantes won the Libertadores in 1968, beating Racing in a brutal three-game semi-final, and then opening up to beat Palmeiras of Brazil in a final that also went to a third-game playoff. It was during that run that the term '*anti-fútbol*' was coined to describe their methods, but *El Gráfico* remained supportive, although acknowledging that their style was 'more solid than beautiful'.

Later in the year they faced Manchester United in the final of the Intercontinental Cup over two games of predicable violence. In the first leg in Buenos Aires, Denis Law complained of having his hair pulled, George Best was punched in the stomach and Bobby Charlton was left requiring stitches following a foul by Bilardo. Nobby Stiles received a cut eye from a head-butt and then, having been goaded all game, was sent off late on for flicking a V-sign at a linesman. Amid it all, Marcos Conigliaro headed in a Verón corner to give Estudiantes the win. In was a similar story back in Manchester, where Law needed four stitches in a leg wound and Best and José Hugo Medina were sent off after throwing punches at each other. Willie Morgan cancelled out a Verón header late on, but a 1-1 draw gave the title to Estudiantes.

'That was the high point,' said Verón, but others were less convinced. The United midfielder Paddy Crerand called Estudiantes 'the dirtiest team I've played against', and the press reaction was just as bitter. 'The night they spat on sportsmanship,' read the *Daily Mirror*'s headline after the first leg, while Brian Glanville in the *Sunday Times* was despairing. 'Some of their tactics...' he wrote, 'draw us again to question how football, at the highest level, can survive as a sport. Tactical fouls as practised tonight by Estudiantes, by Racing last year and by Argentina in 1966 at Wembley, simply make it impossible to practise the game.'

The *El Gráfico* columnist Osvaldo Ardizzone defended Estudiantes after that victory – explaining it away as a natural product of England's World Cup quarter-final win over Argentina, but by the time Estudiantes had won a second Libertadores, beating Nacional of Uruguay in both legs of the final, he was beginning to sound doubtful. 'Estudiantes go out to destroy, to dirty, to irritate, to deny the show, to use all the illegal subterfuges in football...' he wrote. 'If it is good to win, it must be good.'

The tide was turning and, David Goldblatt points out in *The Ball is Round*, not merely against Estudiantes. There were insurrections against the military regime in Cordoba and Rosario in 1969, suggesting that tolerance for an ends-justifies-the-means philosophy was diminishing. There were also, though, simple football reasons for the backlash against Estudiantes. Verón speaks of how delight in the triumph of a 'humble' team soon developed into resentment among clubs and press from the capital, while defeats away to Bolivia and Peru in the middle of 1969 effectively eliminated Argentina from the 1970 World Cup.

Besides, that July there was a new underdog to cheer as Chacarita Juniors, a team from San Martín, a poor suburb of Buenos Aires, beat River Plate 4-1 in the Metropolitano final. In *El Gráfico*, Juvenal's position had clearly changed. 'Chacarita's victory validates the values that made Argentinian football great...,' he wrote. 'Those values seemed to have been forgotten by many teams, players and coaches... Because Chacarita is not an "enlarged small" team that enjoys its greatest historical victories by running and playing roughly, by biting and fighting, by sweating and continuous rough play. Chacarita run, bite, sweat, give, sacrifice, but they also play football. Rather: they want to play, taking care of the ball throughout the park, and they also fight.'

It was the failure to qualify for the Mexico World Cup, though, that really focused minds. An editorial in *El Gráfico* proclaimed 'the school of Argentinian football' as a 'great victim' of the revolution that followed the embarrassment of 1958. 'The desire to erase the memory of those six Czechoslovakian goals propelled us towards a more defensive game, towards the eternal fear of losing, making us forget the necessity and pleasure of scoring more goals than our opponents to win,' it said. 'The desire to overcome our lack of speed and physical power before the Europeans induced in us an indiscriminate imitation, a contempt for ability and intelligence.'

Estudiantes soon gave their critics further ammunition. Later in September they lost the first leg of the Intercontinental final 3-0 away to AC Milan, which raised doubts about the efficacy of their style, but it was the return in la Bombonera that really hardened opinion against them. Estudiantes won 2-1, but far more significant was the violence of the game. Aguirre Suárez elbowed Néstor Combin, breaking his cheekbone, the goalkeeper Alberto Poletti punched Gianni Rivera, an assault Eduardo Manera followed up by kicking him to the ground.

A wave of revulsion was unleashed. 'Television took the deformed image of a match and transformed it into urban guerrilla warfare all over the world,' said the match report in *El Gráfico*, and the watching president was just as unimpressed. 'Such shameful behaviour has compromised and sullied Argentina's international reputation and provoked the revulsion of a nation,' Onganía said. All three were sentenced to thirty days in jail for disgracing a public spectacle.

Zubeldía was vilified, which immediately led his defenders to claim that he sanctioned only the system, not the gamesmanship. A more credible argument in mitigation might be that his side weren't that much worse than anyone else in Argentina at the time, merely more effective. 'Those who attribute a dimension of Mephistophelean leadership in regards to the roguery,' Walter Vargas wrote in *Football Delivery*, 'should know that on the sadly famous night in 1969, at the Bombonera against Milan, he went on to the pitch himself to try to stop the violent incidents and, once they had been committed, he condemned them and cautioned his players. Does that mean that 100 percent of the sins attributed to that Estudiantes are purely myths? Of course not. But the one suffered by Rivera, Combin and co was the most unjustifiable stain, the one that is impossible to expunge. Then, as is well known, [Juan] José [Pizzuti]'s Racing, the Independiente of 68, Rattín's Boca and the rest were not exactly a monastery of Trappist monks.'

Although Estudiantes went on to win the Libertadores the following year, losing to Feyenoord in the Intercontinental final, the mood was set against them. 'The Estudiantes that we admired, applauded and defended, were a very different thing,' another editorial in *El Gráfico* proclaimed. 'When they won their first finals, their play was not *anti-fútbol*, but authentic football suffused with effort, vitality and sacrifice.' Perhaps, like Herrera's Inter, they pursued their idiosyncrasies so far that they ended up becoming a parody of themselves.

As physicality and gamesmanship became unfashionable, so

there awoke a nostalgia for the lost age of la nuestra. Three weeks after the Milan game, El Gráfico ran a piece claiming la Máquina would have beaten Estudiantes. A need developed for a side to take on their mantle, to reintroduce the old style. It emerged in Rosario with Newell's Old Boys under the management of Miguel Antonio Juarez. It was his assistant, though, who would become far more acclaimed: César Luis Menotti.

Menotti was an ineffably romantic figure. A pencil-thin chain-smoker with collar-length hair, greying sideburns and the stare of an eagle, he seemed the embodiment of Argentinian bohemi-anism. He was left-wing, intellectual, a philosopher and an artist. 'I maintain that a team is above all an idea,' he said, 'and more than an idea it is a commitment, and more than a commitment it is the clear convictions that a coach must transmit to his players to defend that idea.

'So my concern is that we coaches don't arrogate to ourselves the right to remove from the spectacle the synonym of festival, in favour of a philosophical reading that cannot be sustained, which is to avoid taking risks. And in football there are risks because the only way you can avoid taking risks in any game is by not playing...

'And to those who say that all that matters is winning, I want to warn them that someone always wins. Therefore, in a thirty-team championship, there are twenty-nine who must ask themselves: what did I leave at this club, what did I bring to my players, what possibility of growth did I give to my footballers?

'I start from the premise that football is efficacy. I play to win, as much or more than any egoist who thinks he's going to win by other means. I want to win the match. But I don't give in to tactical reasoning as the only way to win, rather I believe that efficacy is not divorced from beauty...'

Under Menotti, beauty and efficacy went hand in hand. In 1973, he won the Metropolitano title with Huracán, playing glorious attacking football. 'To watch them play was a delight,' an editorial in Clarín asserted. 'It filled Argentinian fields with football and after forty-five years gave the smile back to a neigh-bourhood with the cadence of the tango.' So beguiling were they, that when they beat Rosario Central 5-0, the opposing fans applauded them. 'The team was in tune with the popular taste of Argentinians,' said their forward Carlos Babington. 'There were gambetas, one-touch moves, nutmegs, sombreros [a trick involving lifting the ball over the opponent's head], one-twos, overlaps.'

After the 1974 World Cup, in which Argentina had been humil-iated by Holland, Menotti was appointed national coach. The irony, of course, was that the great validation of that ideological shift was played out in a political environment with which it could hardly have been more at odds. Isabel Perón had been deposed as president in a coup in 1976 and replaced by a right-wing military junta that savagely repressed dissent. Onganía's right-wing dicta-torship had led to a ruthlessness in sport and a disregard for the woolly virtues of artistry, but the relationship between football and the military government of the late seventies was far more complex. In that Menotti self-consciously harked back to a lost golden age – 'our victory is a tribute to the old and glorious Argentinian football,' he said after the 1978 World Cup – he appealed to the conservatism of the generals and that, plus the fact that he was successful, compensated for a worldview wholly opposed to the ideology of the junta.

The way the triumph of 1978 was exploited clearly made Menotti uncomfortable, and he addresses the issue at length in his autobiography *Football without Tricks*. What should he have done, he asked, 'To coach teams that played badly, that based everything on tricks, that betrayed the feelings of the people? No, of course not.' Instead, he argued, his football, being free and creative, offered a reminder of the free, creative Argentina that existed before the junta.

Yet that is to idealise his side. It is notable that his belief in artistry did not extend so far as giving a seventeen-year-old Diego Maradona a place in his squad, even though he had handed him an international debut almost a year earlier. Perhaps the comparison with Feola and his treatment of Pelé twenty years before is unfair, but it is hard to avoid. Yes, an aggressive 4-3-3, the direct running of Mario Kempes, Leopoldo Luque and Oscar Ortiz, along with the more cerebral plotting of Osvaldo Ardiles and the erratic brilliance of René Houseman, meant that their football was at times thrilling, but it was not *la nuestra*.

Abraham goes so far as to suggest a level of duplicity on the part of Menotti. 'He spoke a traditional discourse,' he said, 'but in 1978 he shut the players in a laboratory for months, without women, eating vitamins ... [and playing] ... a pace of game that when they went out on River's pitch, even the Hungarians said looked desperate.' Hungary, beaten 2-1 at El Monumental in Argentina's first game of the tournament, became so frustrated by a series of niggling fouls that Tibor Nyilasi and András Töröcsik were both sent off for retaliation in the final three minutes – almost the only thing that united the two great rivals in their careers. 'Menotti prepared the players physically with technical advances,' Abraham went on, 'but his discourse was this: the important thing is to feel the ball, to pass it, to knead it, to dribble with it.'

Given the developments in defensive organisation and physiological preparation perhaps a certain level of compromise between the scientific and the artistic is only realistic, but it can hardly be denied that Argentina's success came with a measure of chicanery. Most notoriously, there was the second-phase game against Peru. Moronic scheduling meant Argentina went into that match knowing that they needed to win by three, while scoring at least four, to make it to the final. They did that, and more, winning 6-0, but the result has always been tainted by suspicion.

In 1986, the *Sunday Times* cited an anonymous civil servant claiming that the Argentinian government shipped 35,000 tons of grain – and possibly some arms – to Peru and that the Argentinian central bank released $50million of frozen Peruvian assets, but proof is hard to come by and the fact that the story was published on the day England met Argentina in the World Cup quarter-final does not suggest meticulously researched, impartial journalism.

It is doubtful that anybody watching the video of the game with no knowledge of context would see anything untoward. Juan José Muñante hit the post for Peru early on, while their goalkeeper Ramón Quiroga, who had been born in Argentina and would later take much of the blame, made a number of scrambling saves. If the game really were fixed, it looked as though nobody had told Peru until midway through the first half. Certainly Peru wilted after Alberto Tarantini's diving header made it 2-0 just before half-time, but that is hardly surprising. They were already out of the tournament, there were 37,000 rammed into the Arroyito creating a fearsome atmosphere, and Argentina's passing was at times sensational. The Kempes volley that made it 3-0 and Luque's late sixth both followed bursts of magnificent football.

Where there was clear malpractice – *viveza*, gamesmanship, cheating, whatever term is used – was ahead of the final against Holland. The bus carrying the Dutch team took a deliberately

Argentina 2 Holland 1, World Cup Final, El Monumental, Buenos Aires, 25 June 1978

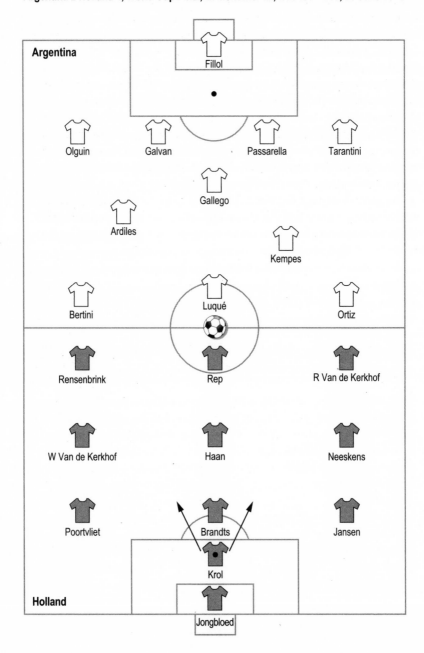

circuitous route from their hotel to the stadium, and fans were allowed to crowd around it, hammering on the windows, chanting and being generally intimidating. Argentina then delayed their arrival on the pitch before kick-off, leaving Holland standing around, exposed to the full fury of the crowd, and when they finally did emerge, they protested about the cast on René van der Kerkhof's arm. Given he had been wearing it without controversy all tournament, their only purpose can have been to try to unsettle their opponents. The refereeing of the Italian Sergio Gonella was weak, and Argentina seemed to get the benefit of a number of decisions, but, after Rob Rensenbrink's last-minute effort had come back off the post, extra-time goals from Kempes and Daniel Bertoni gave them the title.

Victory for Argentina, victory for the junta, victory for Menotti and, slightly tarnished, slightly modified for the modern age, victory for the ideals of *la nuestra*.

△▽△▽△▽△▽△▽

Chapter Twelve

Total Football

△▽ Sometimes the world is simply ripe for innovation. Just as Newton and Liebniz happened upon calculus independently and roughly simultaneously, so, on opposite sides of Europe, Rinus Michels and Valeriy Lobanovskyi each came to the same realisation about how football should be played. The game, as they saw it, was about space and how you controlled it: make the pitch big when you have the ball and it is easy to retain it; make it small when you do not and it becomes far more difficult for the opposition to keep it.

Both encouraged their players to interchange positions, both relied on team-mates being able to cover, and both produced sides that were capable of exhilarating football. In that, they were the logical next step from the *passovotchka* of the forties or the Hungarian style of the fifties – certainly it was to the latter that the Dutch were frequently compared – but what allowed Ajax and Dynamo to do that was their implementation of an aggressive offside trap. Pressing was the key, but it was probably only in the mid- to late-sixties that it became viable.

In an amateur context, pressing is all but impossible. It is hugely demanding physically, requiring almost constant motion and thus supreme levels of fitness. By the time of Michels and Lobanovskyi, the shortages of the war years were over, nutrition was good, and sports science (both legal and illicit) had advanced sufficiently that players could keep running for ninety minutes. This was a stage of football's development that stemmed as much from enhanced physical possibility as from advances of theory.

△▽

It is difficult now, given its modern reputation for liberalism and excess, to imagine how Amsterdam must have been in the years immediately following the war. There has been an undeniable commodification of its bohemian nature, but it is still readily comprehensible that the city should nurture revolutionary ideas. Back in the fifties, it was not. In *The Fall*, which was published in 1955, Albert Camus writes of how bored he was by Amsterdam, a city where 'for centuries, pipe smokers have been watching the same rain falling on the same canal'.

Dutch football was similarly staid. The moustaches and the Victorian stylings of the early Anglophile clubs may have gone by the fifties, but the style was still backward-looking, and the result was a national side that was barely even a joke. Between a 4-1 win over Finland in June 1949 and a 1-0 win over Belgium in April 1955, Holland played twenty-seven internationals, winning just two, and twice contriving to lose to Norway. When England hammered Holland 8-2 at Huddersfield in 1948, the Dutch, long after the W-M had become the default across Europe, were still using a classic 2-3-5 formation, leading the England centre-forward Tommy Lawton, who scored four that day, to marvel that he'd 'never had so much room'.

The coming of a limited form of professionalism in 1954 was the main stimulus for the rise of Dutch football in the sixties, but it does not explain why the upsurge took the form it did. It helped that the Netherlands all but skipped the W-M phase of evolution, meaning that the notion of rigid one-to-one marking never became instilled, and they were fortunate also that their earliest teachers themselves seemed to flourish outside the pressures of the league structure. It may strike modern readers as eccentric when Brian Glanville writes of the 'incubus of the league', but it does explain why so many European nations found their football development enhanced by enlightened British coaches. Perhaps it was not so much that they themselves were forward thinkers – although the fact they were prepared to emigrate in itself suggests a level of open-mindedness – but that the new environments in which they found themselves allowed them to pursue experiments that back home would have been dismissed as hopelessly idealistic.

Dutch football's founding father was Jack Reynolds. Although he had once been a second-string player at Manchester City he, like so many influential coaches, pursued a far from stellar playing career, moving from Grimsby Town to Sheffield Wednesday and then Watford. In 1912, Reynolds moved to Switzerland to become manager of St Gallen, and he was set to take charge of the Germany national side when war broke out in 1914. He sought refuge in the Netherlands, and was appointed manager of Ajax – for the first time – in 1915. Over the following thirty-two years, he would spend twenty-five years at the club in three separate spells. His first departure was caused by a row with directors; his second by the Second World War, during which he was interned in the Tost detention centre in Upper Silesia, a former lunatic asylum. There he was held with PG Wodehouse, who had been picked up in the French resort of Le Touquet. 'An Associated Press man, who came down to interview me later,' Wodehouse said, 'wrote in his piece that Tost Lunatic Asylum was no Blandings Castle. Well, it wasn't of course, but still it was roomy. If you had had a cat, and wished to swing it, you could have done so quite easily...'

When Reynolds returned to Amsterdam in 1945, Michels came under his tutelage, and the similarities in their styles of management are obvious. Reynolds was a strict disciplinarian, and believed in the primacy of technique, encouraging his players to work with a ball in training. He also laid the foundations of the Ajax youth system, commonly working a fourteen-hour day to ensure that teams at each level played the same style of football. He transformed what had been a minor team into one of national importance, while maintaining an attacking ethos. 'For me,' he said in an interview in 1946, 'attack is and remains the best form of defence.' Ajax's philosophy was encapsulated by a couplet of the thirties: 'Open game, open game/You can't afford to neglect the wing.'

Those were the seeds, but it wasn't until Vic Buckingham arrived in 1959 that they began to sprout. He had played in the same Tottenham Hotspur side as Arthur Rowe, and inherited similar ideas about the value of pass-and-move football, retaining possession rather than endlessly lumping it long. 'Possession football is the thing, not kick and rush,' he said in a 1993 interview with David Winner quoted in *Brilliant Orange*. 'Long-ball football is too risky. Most of the time what pays off is educated skills. If you've got the ball, keep it. The other side can't score...'

His own beliefs, he discovered, gelled with what he found at Ajax. 'Dutch football was good,' he said. 'It wasn't a rough-tough, got-to-win-things mentality. Their skills were different, their intellect was different and they played proper football. They didn't get this from me; it was there waiting to be stirred up ... it was just a case of telling them to keep more possession. I've always thought possession is nine-tenths of the game and Ajax played possession football... I influenced them, but they went on and did things above that which delighted me. For instance, two of them would go down the left side of the field passing to each other – just boom-boom-boom – and they'd go 30 yards and two men would have cut out three defenders and created a vast acreage of space.'

Buckingham was a devotee of W-M, and it was with that formation – albeit a far more fluid version of it than would have been found in Britain at the time – that Ajax won the Dutch league title in 1960, playing an attacking style that brought them an average of 3.2 goals per game. Buckingham left after two seasons to join Sheffield Wednesday, and when he returned in 1964, he struggled to replicate his earlier success. By January 1965, Ajax were struggling near the relegation zone, and Buckingham was sacked.

He was replaced by Michels who, after retiring in 1958, had studied at the Amsterdam sports academy and taught gymnastics at a local school before becoming coach of the amateur side JOS. Like Lobanovskyi, by the time he returned to the club at which he had spent the bulk of his playing career, his outlook had undergone a radical overhaul. Michels the player, Winner says, had been 'an easy-going artist on the pitch with a taste for practical jokes off it'. As a coach, he was completely different, as the long-time Ajax assistant coach Bobby Haarms recalls. 'The main thing with him was now discipline,' he said. 'Fantastic discipline. Even with the assistant coaches he was like an animal trainer.'

Michels kept Ajax up in his first season; the next, they won the league. Although they played attractive and fluent football in doing so, there was no talk of Total Football at that stage, and certainly Michels did not turn up clutching a blueprint of how he believed football should be played. 'In starting,' he said, 'you have no exact idea about the aims after which you are going to strive.' His immediate task was to avoid relegation. 'To do that I especially needed to change the team spirit, and I had to change the team tactically,' he explained. 'Of course, the team-spirit development, the team's tactical development, that just went on.'

He altered the nature of training, prioritising ball-work even more than Reynolds had and so putting in place the structures that would produce the technical proficiency that became such a key feature of the Ajax style. Crucially, he modernised the management of the club so that by the end of his second full season every player in his squad was fully professional and could commit absolutely to his training schedule. Tactically, his first change was to abandon the W-M for a 4-2-4, with Piet Keizer, Johan Cruyff, Sjaak Swart and Henk Groot up front and the combative Bennie Muller alongside the more technical Klaas Nuninga in midfield.

That in itself was not especially radical – rather, it was part of a wider trend that swept Europe in years that followed the 1958 World Cup – but there was a radicalism in the air. Amsterdam in the sixties was, as the British anarchist Charles Radcliffe said, 'the capital of the youth rebellion'. The establishment after the war of the welfare state, and the growing prosperity of Europe, had led, as elsewhere, to a blurring of society's traditional divisions. Art and culture became increasingly *avant garde* and, in December 1962, Amsterdam witnessed its first 'happening' with the poet Simon Vinkenoog's 'Open the Grave' event, which insisted that 'the victory over old ways begins in Magic Centre Amsterdam'.

By the middle of the decade, the whole atmosphere of Amsterdam was surreal and anarchic, with the 'Provos', dressed all in white, holding regular anti-consumerist demonstrations. Most significant was their reaction in 1966 to the wedding of Princess Beatrix to Claus von Amsberg, a German aristocrat who had served in the Wehrmacht. They announced they would attempt to disrupt the ceremony, and encouraged the circulation of rumours listing a series of ingenious ways by which they would do so. It was said that LSD would be introduced to the water supply, that lion dung would be spread on the streets to spook the horses pulling the wedding-carriages, and that laughing-gas would be pumped into the church through the organ pipes. In the end, the protest amounted to nothing more than setting off smoke bombs on the Raadhuisstraad, but that was enough. The police panicked and, over-reacting as they had repeatedly through the Provos' campaign, set about protestors with batons. Similar incidents had happened before, but never on this scale, and never live on national television. Viewers were horrified and, when a strike over holiday pay three months later led to further rioting, public attitudes were set on the way to change.

An inquiry into the riots led to the dismissals of the mayor and the chief of police, and the authorities decided that the best way to deal with the youth rebellion was simply to tolerate it. Within a couple of years Dam Square had become a camp for foreign hippies and the Amsterdam police had a reputation as the most easy-going in Europe. It is no coincidence that it was in the Amsterdam Hilton in 1969 that John Lennon and Yoko Ono celebrated their marriage with a week-long 'Bed-In'.

Most of Michels's Ajax side are dismissive of the links between the cultural and football revolutions, but it is difficult to disagree with Winner when he concludes that they are there, even if they extend no further than a self-confidence that was prepared to question the orthodoxy. Structures and traditions were not to be accepted, but to be challenged.

At the centre of that lay Cruyff, even at that stage very obviously the leader of the team. Young, iconoclastic and unselfconscious about ensuring he was paid what he was worth – itself a product of the new classlessness – he became an icon of the burgeoning Dutch youth movement of the time, the equivalent, the former Ajax youth coach Karel Gabler said, of Lennon in Britain. In 1997, in a piece in *Hard Gras* magazine marking Cruyff's fiftieth birthday, the journalist Hubert Smeets wrote that: 'Cruyff was the first player who understood that he was an artist, and the first who was able and willing to collectivise the art of sports.'

Cruyff was not a Provo – his conservatism in such matters as family values was diametrically opposed to their beliefs – and yet he shared with them an awkwardness, an anarchic attitude and a love of provoking the establishment. Most famously, he refused to wear the three Adidas stripes on his shirt during the 1974 World Cup, honouring his contract with Puma by insisting on wearing only two. 'The Dutch,' Smeets went on, 'are at their best when they can combine the system with individual creativity. Johan Cruyff is the main representative of that. He made this country after the war. I think he was the only one who understood the sixties.'

The notion of individuality within a system, Winner argues, is characteristic of the Netherlands at the time. The structuralist architect Aldo van Eyck, for instance, wrote that, 'All systems should be familiarised, one with the other, in such a way that their combined impact and interaction can be appreciated as a single complex system.' He was speaking specifically of architecture, but he could just have well have been describing the football of Michel's Ajax.

The term '*totaalvoetbal*' itself appeared only in response to performances of the national side in the 1974 World Cup, but the prefix '*totaal*' was used across a range of disciplines. Another architect, JB Bakema, who wrote for the influential *Forum* magazine, spoke of 'Total Urbanisation', 'Total Environment' and 'Total Energy'. 'To understand things,' he said in a lecture given in 1974, 'you have to understand the relationship between things... Once the highest image of interrelationship in society was indicated by the word "God" and man was allowed to use earth and universal space under condition that he should care for what he used. But we have to actualise this kind of care and respect since man came by his awareness nearer the phenomenon of interrelationship called the relation of atoms. Man became aware of his being part of a total energy system.' As in architecture, as across a range of disciplines at the time – the literary theory and semiology of Roland Barthes, the anthropological theory of Claude Lévi-Strauss, the psychoanalytic theory of Jacques Lacan – so in football. Within the Ajax model, players derived their meaning, their significance, from their interrelationship with other players. To suggest that could not have occurred without a decline in faith is probably a theoretical leap too far, but again, it is hard not to see a link between Dutch football and the intellectual spirit of the time – and it is a beguiling coincidence that the two greatest exponents of system as an attacking force, Ajax and Dynamo Kyiv, sprang up in the Netherlands and the USSR, arguably the two most secular societies in the world at the time.

The first signs that something special was coming together at Ajax came in 1966, when Liverpool were hammered 5-1 at De Meer in the second round of the European Cup. The result came as such a surprise that Bill Shankly's boast that Liverpool would win 7-0 at Anfield was taken seriously, but two Cruyff goals helped Ajax to a comfortable 2-2 draw in the second leg. In the quarter-final against Dukla Prague, though, their weaknesses were exposed as a 1-1 draw at De Meer was followed by a 2-1 defeat in Czechoslovakia. It was then that Michels showed his ruthlessness for the first time. Tonny Pronk, who had conceded a penalty in the away leg, was moved from defence into midfield, while Ajax's captain and centre-back, Frits Soetekouw, having scored an own-goal, was sold to PSV Eindhoven.

Although Ajax eventually became renowned for their attacking flair, Michels began his construction of it from the back, bringing in the experienced sweeper Velibor Vasović from Partizan Belgrade to replace Soetekouw alongside Hulshoff. Ajax won the league four times between 1966 and 1970, and also lost in the final of the European Cup to AC Milan in 1969. It was that achievement that captured the imagination of the Dutch public, with over 40,000 travelling to Paris to watch a playoff against Benfica after Ajax had overcome a 3-1 deficit from the home leg to draw 4-4 on aggregate in the quarter-final.

The system at that stage was still a modified 4-2-4, but with Vasović both dropping behind the other defenders and then stepping out to provide a third man in midfield. They still, though, could be overmanned in midfield. Bertie Mee, after seeing his Arsenal side beat Ajax 3-0 at Highbury in the semi-final of the Fairs Cup in 1970, described Ajax as 'amateurish'; there was an idealism about them that bordered on naivety. Later that month Ajax drew 3-3 against Feyenoord, at which Michels came to the conclusion Brazil had reached eight years earlier and Viktor Maslov and Alf Ramsey a little later: playing four forwards could make it very hard for a team to regain possession.

Feyenoord themselves were on their way to a European Cup, under Ernst Happel, who had been part of the Austria side that had finished third in the 1954 World Cup. That side had been the last to use an attacking centre-half to any level of success, but Happel was no nostaligist and had already made the move to 4-3-3. Rinus Israel was a ferocious sweeper, while the creative duties in midfield fell to Wim van Hanegem. He was flanked by the Austrian Frank Hasil and Wim Jansen, with the rapid Coen Moulijn providing attacking thrust from the left wing. 'Michels was an expert in planning the tactics before the match and preparing players physically and mentally, but Happel was a fine dissector of the game,' explained Theo van Duivenbode, who had played at left-back for Ajax when they lost the 1969 European Cup final to AC Milan, before being sold to Feyenoord because Michels judged him too flimsy. 'He saw things so quickly that he would make changes from the bench after only a few minutes' play. Happel did not have at Feyenoord the outstanding individual players that Michels had at Ajax, so he went into greater tactical detail and produced more of a cooperative team. Not so much flair, perhaps, but very thorough teamwork.'

That makes them sound stodgy, which they were not – merely less fluent than Ajax. Nonetheless, that draw convinced Michels, and Ajax's 4-2-4 became 4-3-3, with Vasović pushing up whenever possible to make a 3-4-3, which still left two markers to deal with the two opposing centre-forwards, plus a spare man as cover. 'I played the last man in defence, the *libero*,' said Vasović. 'Michels made this plan to play very offensive football. We discussed it. I was the architect, together with Michels, of the aggressive way of defending.'

Vasović was never a man to hide his light under a bushel, and his claims should be treated with a degree of scepticism, but he was certainly pioneering as a defender who advanced up from the back line to become an additional midfielder, an idea that has remained constant in Dutch football through such sweepers as Horst Blankenburg, Arie Haan (in his later days) and Danny Blind. It was the combination of that with pressing that made it such an effective weapon.

Pressing for Ajax stemmed largely from Johan Neeskens's aggression. He was usually deputed to pick up the opposing playmaker and Haarms described him as being 'like a kamikaze pilot' as he pursued him, often deep into opposition territory. At first other Ajax players hung back, but by the early seventies they had become used to following him. That meant they were playing a very high defensive line, squeezing the space in which the opposition had to play. That was risky, but Vasović was adept at stepping out to catch opposing forwards offside.

It required a particular skill to be able to do that. Captaining Brazil in their 2-0 defeat to Holland in the 1974 World Cup, the centre-back Marinho Peres had seen at first hand just how devastating the Dutch way could be, but he nonetheless found it hard to adjust after his 1974 move to Barcelona, who were by then under Michels's management and had bought Cruyff and Neeskens. 'Defenders in Brazil would never be able to push up like that,' he said. 'When I went to Barcelona, Michels wanted the centre-backs to push out to make the offside line. In Brazil this was known as the donkey line: people thought it was stupid. The theory was that if you passed one defender, you passed all the others.' This had been a constant in Brazilian football since the full-backs were first split for the 1919 Copa América, and remained in the concept of the *quarto zagueiro* as developed by Lito at Vila Nova: as one defender went to the ball, another dropped off to provide cover.

'What Cruyff said to me was that Holland could not play Brazilians or Argentinians, who were very skilful, on a huge pitch,' Marinho went on. 'The Dutch players wanted to reduce the space and put everybody in a thin band. The whole logic of the offside trap comes from squeezing the game. This was a brand new thing for me. In Brazil, people thought you could chip the ball over and somebody could run through and beat the offside trap, but it's not like that because you don't have time.'

The pressing had a dual function, though: it wasn't just about frustrating the opposition. 'In one training session,' Marinho recalled, 'I pushed up and we caught four or five players offside. I was pleased, because it was still new to me and I was finding it difficult, but Michels came and shouted at me. What he wanted was for us then to charge the guy with the ball with the players we had spare because they had men out of the game in offside positions. That's how offside becomes an offensive game. If when we got the ball like this, we couldn't create a chance, the defenders dropped back and made the pitch bigger. It was all about space.'

The theory Winner sets out in *Brilliant Orange* that the Dutch are particularly adept at the manipulation of space because of the way their flat, frequently flooded landscape forces them to manipulate space in everyday life is persuasive (and just as the Viennese coffee-house writers saw a connection between Sindelar's genius and their own literary output, it doesn't seem a huge leap to see a relationship between the precise, glacial brilliance of Dennis Bergkamp and that of, say, Piet Mondriaan), but that is not to say Total Football was thought out in advance.

Buckingham spoke of how even in his day Ajax players were capable of what he called 'habit football': 'They could find each other by instinct. They'd have a rhythm; go from the left side of the field to the right but make progress of 30 or 40 or 50 yards as well.' The eventual flowering of Dutch football, first with Ajax and then with the national side, seems to have been less the result of any plan than the harnessing of a process that occurred naturally among a group of intelligent players who played with each other often enough for long enough that they were capable of 'habit football'. 'When I saw Suurbier going forward, I knew I had to go back,' Swart said. 'I didn't have to be told. And after two years everybody knew what to do.'

To call it serendipitous would be unfairly to downplay the roles of Cruyff and Michels, but they were reacting to circumstance rather than, as Lobanovskyi did, imposing a vision. Even the rapid interchanging of positions, which became the defining feature of Ajax's play, had developed initially as a measure to overcome the packed defences with which opponents attempted to combat their attacking style. This, in a sense, was the lesson learned from Celtic's victory in the 1967 European Cup final: massed defences were best overcome by massed attacks, which meant defenders advancing to provide attacking options from deep.

'In the fourth or fifth year,' Michels said, 'I tried to find guide-lines that meant we could surprise a little those walls. I had to let midfield players and defensive players participate in the building up and in the attacking. It's easy to say, but it's a long way to go because the most difficult thing is not to teach a full-back to partic-ipate in attacking – because he likes that – but to find somebody else who is covering up. In the end, when you see they have the mobility, the positional game of such a team makes everyone think "I can participate too. It's very easy." And then you have reached the top, the paramount of the development.'

The move to 4-3-3 made that switching of positions rather easier to structure, because it tended to happen either down one flank or down the middle. So Suurbier, Haan and Swart interchanged on the right; Vasović (or Blankenburg or Hulshoff), Neeskens and Cruyff down the middle; and Ruud Krol, Gerrie Mühren and Keizer on the left. 'People couldn't see that sometimes we just did things automatically,' said Hulshoff. 'It comes from playing a long time together. Football is best when it's instinctive. This way of playing, we grew into it. Total Football means that a player in attack can play in defence – only that he can do this, that is all. You make space, you come into space. And if the ball doesn't come, you leave this space and another player will come into it.'

What was revolutionary was that the interchanging of positions was longitudinal rather than lateral. In Boris Arkadiev's Dinamo

Moscow side, wingers had moved into the centre, and inside-forwards had played on the wing, but the three lines of defence, midfield and attack had, broadly speaking, remained constant. The great Hungarians, by withdrawing their centre-forward and sitting the left-half so deep, had blurred the lines, and with 4-2-4 came attacking full-backs, but Michels's Ajax were the first to encourage such whole-scale interchanges, and what allowed them to do so was pressing. Suddenly it didn't matter if there were 40 yards of space behind the deepest outfield player because if an opponent received the ball he would be hounded so quickly it would be almost impossible for him to craft an accurate pass.

'We could play sixty minutes of pressing,' Swart said. 'I've never seen any other club anywhere who could do that.' Within a few years, Lobanovskyi's Dynamo certainly could, but there was no one else, which raises the question of how they were able to maintain that intensity for so long. Both Ajax and Dynamo invested significantly in the science of preparation, working on nutrition and training schema, but both also looked to pharmaceutical means.

In an interview he game to the magazine *Vrij Nederland* in 1973, Hulshoff spoke of having been given drugs ahead of a match against Real Madrid six years earlier: 'We took the pills in combination with what we always called chocolate sprinkles,' he said. 'What it was I don't know, but you felt as strong as iron and suffered no breathlessness. One disadvantage was you lost all saliva, so after thirty-five minutes of the game I was retching.'

Salo Müller, who was Ajax's masseur between 1959 and 1972, admitted as much in his autobiography, published in 2006, and revealed that Hulshoff and Johnny Rep had both come to him with concerns over pills given them by John Rollink, the club doctor. Over time, Müller collected pills Rollink had distributed from other sportsmen and had them analysed. 'The results were not a surprise to me,' he wrote. 'They ranged from painkillers, muscle relaxants and tranquilising pills to amphetamine capsules.'

Even before joining Ajax, Rollink had form. The first drugs scandal to hit Dutch sport came at the 1960 Rome Olympics, when a female swimmer took two prescriptions from a team-mate's bag and gave them to the press. A doctor said one was indicative of doping, pure and simple, and that the other was likely to be part of a programme of drug use: Rollink's signature was on one of the prescriptions. He later left the Dutch Cycling Union when doping controls were instituted, and said that Ajax would have refused to comply had doping controls been brought in to Dutch football. He even admitted to taking amphetamines himself if he was working late. It may have been the systematic drugs programmes of the Soviet bloc that attracted the greatest attention, but they were certainly not the only ones at it.

△▽

Michels was the father of Total Football, and he carried it on at Barcelona, but it was only after he had left Amsterdam that Ajax reached their peak. Ajax, it is said, responded to his departure by drawing up a shortlist of fifteen names to replace him. They ended up with the cheapest, Ştefan Kovacs, a Romanian of Hungarian ethnicity who had led Steaua Bucharest to a league title and three Romanian Cups in the previous four years. He had had a brief spell with the Belgian side Charleroi during his playing career, but he was far from well-known in the Netherlands, and most greeted the arrival of the squat, grey-haired raconteur with a mixture of bewilderment and scepticism. He even, it is said, bought a return ticket to Amsterdam from Romania because he couldn't quite believe himself that his stay would be a long one.

'How do you like the length of our hair?' one player is supposed to have asked at Kovacs's first training session, seeing a soft target after the stringent days of Michels. 'I've been employed as a coach, not a hair-dresser,' Kovacs replied. A few minutes later, as he stood on the touchline, a ball fizzed towards him at knee-height. In one movement, he trapped and returned it. The test was passed, but the questions about his temperament would never go away.

'Kovacs was a good coach,' Gerrie Mühren said, 'but he was too nice. Michels was more professional. He was very strict, with everyone on the same level. In the first year with Kovacs we played even better because we were good players who had been given freedom. But after that the discipline went and it was all over. We didn't have the same spirit. We could have been champions of Europe for ever if we'd stayed together.'

Well, perhaps. Or perhaps the side's eventual disintegration was simply built into its emotional make-up. It is easy to see familiarity breeding discontent, particularly given the unusually confrontational atmosphere of the Ajax dressing room. Others, anyway, believed the slackening of the reins was necessary after the rigours of Michels. 'The players were fed up with the hardness and discipline of Michels,' Rep insisted. Liverpool, similarly, blossomed after the avuncular Bob Paisley had succeeded Bill Shankly and his more abrasive approach.

Certainly it was in 1971–72 that Ajax were at their most fluent, as Kovacs replaced Vasović with Blankenburg and encouraged him, Suurbier and Krol to advance, safe in the knowledge that Neeskens, Haan and Mühren could drop in to cover. Vasović himself always insisted Kovacs's impact was minimal. 'Those who say Total Football started with Kovacs are wrong,' he said shortly before his death in 2002. 'Kovacs had nothing to do with it. He simply took over a very good team, the champions of Europe, and let them continue the way they had already been playing.' As Kovacs's supporters point out, though, sometimes the hardest thing for a manager to do is to sit back and do nothing.

Doubts always pursued Kovacs. His record was extraordinary – two European Cups, an Intercontinental Cup, two European Super Cups, two Dutch championships and a Dutch Cup in two seasons – and yet there was always a sense that he was only a caretaker. In April 1972, shortly after a goalless draw away to Benfica had confirmed their progress to a second successive European Cup final, Ajax's board members held an emergency meeting and decided to fire him. At the time, Ajax were five points clear in the league, had just hammered Feyenoord 5-1 in Rotterdam and had reached the Dutch Cup final. The sense, though, was that beating the Portuguese champions 1-0 over two legs was somehow not worthy of Ajax, and there were continual rumours of ill-discipline, with the assistant coach Han Grijzenhout and Rollink suggesting to the board that Kovacs had lost control of his squad.

If he had, though, the players evidently enjoyed the freedom. They rebelled, and Kovacs stayed. 'The results show that Kovacs was not wrong,' Cruyff said. 'Our team was ready to take part in making decisions.' They may not have impressed in the semi-final against Benfica, but the 2-0 victory over Internazionale in the final, with Cruyff getting both goals, confirmed the superiority of their method, and hammered yet another nail into the coffin of old-school *catenaccio*. 'Ajax proved that creative attack is the real lifeblood of the game,' the report in *The Times* read the following morning; 'that blanket defence can be outwitted and outmanoeuvred, and by doing so they made the outlines of the night a little sharper and the shadows a little brighter.'

The following year, by winning the European Cup again, Ajax became the first side since Real Madrid to complete a hat-trick of titles. Appropriately, having hammered Bayern Munich 4-0 in the first leg of the quarter-final, it was Real Madrid whom Ajax beat in the semi. The aggregate score of 3-1 barely does justice to their superiority, and the tie is better remembered for Mühren's keepie-ups in the second leg at the Bernabéu, a moment of arrogance and *joie de vivre* that encapsulated the ethos of Kovacs's Ajax. 'I knew I was going to give the ball to Krol, but I needed some time until he reached me,' Mühren recalls. 'So I juggled until he arrived. You can't plan to do something like that. You don't think about that. You just do it. It was the moment when Ajax and Real Madrid changed positions. Before then it was always the big Real Madrid and the little Ajax. When they saw me doing that, the balance changed. The Real Madrid players were looking. They nearly applauded. The stadium was standing up. It was the moment Ajax took over.'

In Belgrade in the final, they beat Juventus 1-0, but it was as emphatic as a one-goal victory can be as, having taken a fourth-minute lead, Ajax taunted the Italians with long strings of passes. A year later, Holland tried something similar in the World Cup final after going ahead in the first minute, and were beaten by West Germany.

Winner claims that that Ajax side was 'probably as close as anyone has ever come to running a major football team like a workers' cooperative', although there is no doubt that there was one major figure within that. 'Cruyff was a big influence,' Haarms said, 'especially as he grew older and talked more and more about tactics with other players.' Kovacs was close to Cruyff, but he wasn't entirely cowed by him. On one occasion, it is said, when Cruyff complained of pains in his knee before a game, Kovacs, knowing his captain's reputation for loving money, took a 1,000-guilder note and rubbed the afflicted area. With a smile Cruyff agreed he was feeling better, and played without any ill effect.

He was not, though, tough enough. Where a ruthlessness lay beneath Paisley's shabby cardigan, it seems probable that Kovacs was too nice, lacking the steel to rein in Cruyff as he took on an increasing prominence in that second season. Rep accuses Kovacs of 'not having the guts' to promote him in place of Swaart until

Ajax 2 Juventus 1, European Cup Final, Marakana, Belgrade, 30 May 1973

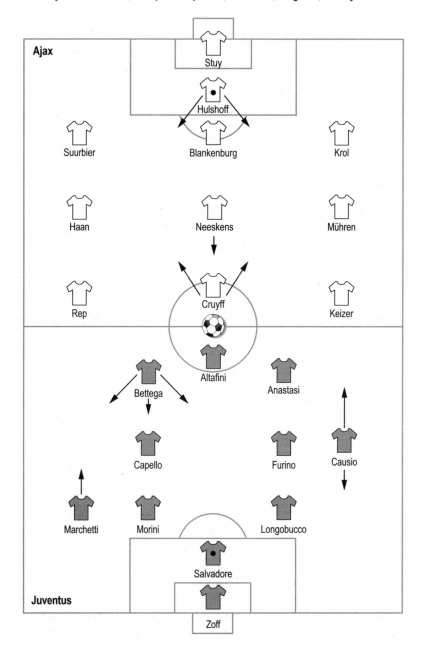

Cruyff gave his approbation, and the players in time came to resent Cruyff's influence.

Kovacs left after that second European Cup success to become manager of France, and when his replacement George Knobel held a vote on whom the club captain should be in the 1973–74 season, Cruyff was deposed in favour of Piet Keizer. Cruyff played only two more games for Ajax before joining Barcelona. The team rapidly disintegrated, and Knobel was sacked in 1974, shortly after a newspaper interview in which he accused his players of drinking and womanising – what many saw as the licence of the Kovacs days taken too far.

Kovacs's subsequent career never approached the same heights. He managed just one win in the qualifying competition for the 1976 European championship and was replaced by Michel Hidalgo, and although a subsequent spell with Romania saw him take them to the brink of qualification for the 1982 World Cup, it ended shamefully as the Communist authorities – ludicrously – accused him of throwing a game against Hungary. 'We must accept,' the veteran Romanian coach Florin Halagian said, 'that Ajax was his opera. It was one of the greatest football has known.' The paradox was that by giving that squad the freedom to reach its peak, Kovacs also paved the way for its destruction.

Total Football itself, meanwhile, lived on under Michels at Barcelona.

Chapter Thirteen

△▽△▽△▽△▽△▽

Science and Sincerity

△▽ Valeriy Lobanovskyi was a twenty-two-year-old winger when, in 1961, Dynamo Kyiv won the Soviet Supreme title for the first time. They had come so close so often that their fans had begun to despair of it ever happening, and the joy at their victory was heightened by relief. Amid the jubilation, though, Lobanovskyi wasn't happy, as he made clear on what was supposed to be a celebratory visit to the Science and Research Institute of the Construction Industry with his team-mates Oleh Bazylevych and Vladimir Levchenko. '"Yes, we have won the league,"' Volodymyr Sabaldyr, a Kyivan scientist and long-time amateur footballer, remembers him saying in the face of excited congratulations. '"But so what? Sometimes we played badly. We just got more points than other teams who played worse than us. I can't accept your praise as there are no grounds for it."'

Sabaldyr asked him how it felt to have achieved something that had been a dream for Kyivans for decades. 'A realised dream ceases to be a dream,' Lobanovskyi replied. 'What is your dream as a scientist? Your degree? Your doctorate? Your post-doctoral thesis?'

'Maybe,' Sabaldyr replied. 'But a real scientist dreams about making a contribution to scientific development, about leaving his mark on it.'

'And there you have your answer.'

Lobanovskyi the player was dilettantish, and opposed to Viktor Maslov's strictures, and yet the perfectionist rationalism, the ambitious and analytic intelligence, was there from the start. Perhaps that is no great surprise. He was, after all, gifted enough as a mathematician to win a gold medal when he graduated from high school, while the era in which he grew up was obsessed by scientific progress. Born in 1939, Lobanovskyi was a teenager as the USSR opened its first nuclear power station and sent Sputnik into space, while Kyiv itself was the centre of the Soviet computer industry. The first cybernetic institute in the USSR was opened there in 1957, and quickly became acknowledged as a world leader in automated control systems, artificial intelligence and mathematical modelling. It was there in 1963 that an early prototype of the modern PC was developed. At the time Lobanovskyi was studying heating engineering at the Kyivan Polytechnic Institute, the potential of computers and their possible applications in almost all spheres was just becoming apparent. It was exciting, it was new, and it is no great surprise that Lobanovskyi should have been carried along by the wave of technological optimism.

In him was acted out the great struggle between individuality and system: the player in him wanted to dribble, to invent tricks and to embarrass his opponents, and yet, as he later admitted, his training at the Polytechnic Institute drove him to a systematic approach, to break down football into its component tasks. Football, he explained, eventually became for him a system of twenty-two elements – two sub-systems of eleven elements – moving within a defined area (the pitch) and subject to a series of restrictions (the laws of the game). If the two sub-systems were equal, the outcome would be a draw. If one were stronger, it would win.

So much is obvious, even if the manner of addressing it is not. But the aspect that Lobanovskyi found truly fascinating is that the sub-systems were subject to a peculiarity: the efficiency of the sub-system is greater than the sum of the efficiencies of the elements that comprise it. This, as Lobanovskyi saw it, meant that football was ripe for the application of the cybernetic techniques being taught at the Polytechnic Institute. Football, he concluded, was less about individuals than about coalitions and the connections between them. 'All life,' as he later said, 'is a number.'

It took time for Lobanovskyi, though, to come to that conclusion. As Maslov's Dynamo wrapped up a third straight title in 1968, the Shakhtar side for whom he was playing finished a poor fourteenth. Thoroughly disillusioned, he decided to give up football altogether. His frustration, though, was less to do with their poor form than the reasons for it. As he saw it, they played 'anti-football' – although that had nothing to do with the term '*anti-fútbol*' as applied to Zubeldía's Estudiantes. 'It's impossible to play as we do,' he wrote in his autobiography, *Endless Match*. 'It is impossible to rely on luck or on accidents in modern football. It is necessary to create the ensemble, a collective of believers who subordinate themselves to the common playing idea.'

Lobanovskyi contemplated a move back into plumbing, but he found himself unable to turn down Dnipro Dnipropetrovsk, then in one of the four parallel second divisions, when they offered him the position of coach in 1969. There, he set about applying the scientific methods he had become convinced represented the future. 'If you want to be a good coach, you must forget the player you were,' he said. 'My relationship with Maslov didn't turn out well, but that's not important. He was a great tactician who taught his players how to play football.' By that stage, if he had a disagreement with Maslov's philosophy, it was purely method-ological. Maslov had worked by his instincts; Lobanovskyi wanted proof.

In his third season with Dnipro, Lobanovskyi led them to promotion. The following season they finished sixth in the Supreme League, just a point behind Dynamo. 1972 was more significant, though, as the year in which Lobanovskyi met Anatoliy Zelentsov. Lobanovskyi had for some time been frustrated by the difficulties of evaluating the physical condition of his players and the strains placed on them by his attempts to institute a system of pressing. Zelentsov, a specialist in bioenergetics, he realised, was the solution.

'Lobanovskyi and I became really inseparable,' Zelentsov said. 'He once told me in public at a party: "You know, if not for you, I might not have come off as a coach. I owe you my formation, my knowledge, skills, understanding and realisation of football."' The two of them would meet regularly with Bazylevych, who had become manager of Shakhtar. 'We would analyse in detail our new training regimes,' Lobanovskyi said. 'It seemed to us that we were taking the process of training to a completely new level. In the course of one of these heated debates (Bazylevych and I were always questioning Zelentsov's statements, believing them to be only theories) somebody suddenly exclaimed, "Wouldn't it be great to do this at a higher level than Shakhtar or Dnipro?"'

They soon got their chance. After Maslov's dismissal in 1970, Dynamo turned to Alexander Sevidov, who had served a long apprenticeship with Dinamo Minsk before leading the Kazakh side Kairat Almaty to promotion. He won the title in his first full season in Kyiv, but his style was very different to Maslov's as he abandoned both pressing and zonal marking. 'The team played some really bright football that season,' Oleh Blokhin, who was just beginning to emerge from the youth ranks, wrote in *Full-life Football*. 'Synchronisation of the actions and thoughts of players, arrhythmia (a combination of fluent play with sudden bursts into the box), and an intensity of attacking action – they were the main principles of Dynamo in 1971. The team stopped physical pressing almost completely, and also aerial balls into the box. We strove for sharp combinations, and the creation of unexpected chances.'

In contrast with the frank and emotional Maslov, Sevidov was always calm and business-like, even in defeat. A devotee of high culture, he preferred his players to continue their education, whereas Maslov had been committed to football and football alone. He was no great evangelist for his style of play, though, and admitted freely that part of the reason for Dynamo's success was that their opponents expected them to play in a quite different way. 'We need two or three years of planned work to consolidate our grip on first place,' he said at the ceremony at which Dynamo were presented with the trophy. 'We'll have to spend time coming up with new combinations that our opponents aren't used to. But that's the law of any sport: to defend and counterattack is easier than to attack.'

Over the next two seasons, Sevidov could not reproduce the same success, as Dynamo finished as runners-up up each year. As early as the end of 1972, it seems, the Party hierarchy had lost faith in him, and Lobanovskyi was offered the Dynamo job. The problem was probably less that Dynamo finished second than the identity of the team who finished first. Zorya, from the eastern Ukrainian city of Luhansk (or Voroshylovhrad, as it then was), had never threatened to win the title before, and never would again, but, as Volodymyr Shevchenko, the first secretary of the regional Communist Party, encouraged the local mines to back the club financially, they finished five points clear of Dynamo. That was a huge embarrassment to Shcherbytskyi, and Shevchenko was soon sacked, narrowly escaping prosecution for alleged financial malpractice. Zorya immediately fell away and finished in the bottom half of the table the following season.

Lobanovskyi turned the job down then, but Sevidov was sacked with three games of the 1973 season remaining. Quite why he was dismissed at that particular moment remains unclear. Dynamo finished second behind Ararat Yerevan – another provincial side with no great history of success – but that was largely because they dropped three points in those final three matches. The official reason was that Sevidov had been removed 'because of a collapse of pedagogical work in the team', but no details were given. Arkady Galinsky claims that Shcherbytskyi had been persuaded by an administrator at Dnipro that the calm and reliable Lobanovskyi was just the man to help his son, Valeriy, a huge football fan, get over his problems with drug abuse. That sounds outlandish, but even if there is some truth to the theory, it does not adequately explain why Sevidov was dismissed just then, when a far smoother handover could have been enacted a couple of weeks later.

Whatever the reason, Lobanovskyi returned to Kyiv late in 1973 to become Dynamo's first Kyivan manager since Viktor Shylovskyi had been replaced by Vyacheslav Solovyov in 1958. By that stage, he saw a football team as a dynamic system, in which the aim was to produce the optimal level of energy in the optimal pattern. He had come to the conclusion that, to win titles, what happened off the field in terms of physical preparation and, particularly, rehabilitation, was just as important as what happened on it.

Lobanovskyi arrived at Dynamo as part of a team of four. He had specific responsibility for modelling playing systems; Zelentsov was in charge of the individual preparation of players; Bazylevich, having been prised from Shakhtar, took care of the actual coaching; while Mykhaylo Oshemkov dealt with what was known as 'informational support' – that is, the collation of statistical data from games.

Everything was meticulously planned, with the team's preparation divided into three levels. Players were to have individual technical coaching so as to equip them better to fulfil the tasks Lobanovskyi set them during a game; specific tactics and tasks for each player were drawn up according to the opponents; and a strategy was devised for a competition as a whole, placing each game in context by acknowledging that it is impossible for a side to maintain maximal levels over a protracted period. Dynamo, accordingly, would regularly lose late-season games with the title already won, and habitually killed games away from home, looking only for a draw while attempting to conserve their energy.

'When we are talking about tactical evolution,' Lobanovskyi and Zelentsov wrote in their book, *The Methodological Basis of the Development of Training Models*, 'the first thing we have in mind is to strive for new courses of action that will not allow the opponent to adapt to our style of play. If an opponent has adjusted himself to our style of play and found a counter-play, then we need to find a new strategy. That is the dialectic of the game. You have to go forward in such a way and with such a range of attacking options that it will force the opponent to make a mistake. In other words, it's necessary to force the opponent into the condition you want them to be in. One of the most important means of doing that is to vary the size of the playing area.'

Like Michels's Ajax, Lobanovskyi's Dynamo could press, seeking to pen their opponents in and win the ball high up the field, but they were equally capable of sitting deep and striking on the counter-attack. As Lobanovskyi was always at pains to make clear, it all depended on circumstance. One thing remained central: keep the preferred playing area as large as possible while in possession, and as small as possible while out.

'Sometimes people say that football's meaning is only in attack,' Lobanovskyi and Zelentsov went on. 'But it is nearer the truth to say that when we possess the ball, we are attacking; when our opponents possess the ball, we are defending. From this fundamental, football strategy is derived: how, where and when to attack or defend.' Possession was everything; their approach could hardly have been more different from that preached by the likes of Charles Hughes and Egil Olsen.

On the wall at Dynamo's training-base were hung lists of the demands Lobanovskyi placed on players. Significantly, of the fourteen defensive tasks, four concerned the distribution of the ball and the establishment of attacking positions once the ball had been won. There was no notion of simply getting the ball clear, for that would have been to surrender possession and thus place their side back on the defensive. The thirteen demands on forwards, as well as including a line about pressing and attempting to regain possession high up the field, are also dominated by calls for movement and the search for ways to shift the ball away from areas in which the opponent has a high concentration of players.

Perhaps nobody had compiled such lists before, but their

content, even if the emphasis on possession was extreme, was far from revolutionary. Far more radical was the list of twenty items concerning what Lobanovskyi and Zelentsov called 'coalition actions'. These concerned both defensive applications, such as the setting of an offside trap, and attacking, such as the creation of overlaps. 'To attack,' Lobanovskyi said, 'it is necessary to deprive the opponent of the ball. When is it easier to do that – with five players or with all eleven? The most important thing in football is what a player is doing on a pitch when he's not in possession of the ball, not vice-versa. So when we say that we have an excellent player that comes from the following principle: one percent talent and 99 percent hard work.'

Lobanovskyi's goal was what he termed 'universality'. He wanted his forwards to defend and his backs to attack, and saw no contradiction in the instruction because, to him, attacking and defending were related not to position on the pitch, but possession. 'No other coach ever demanded that I should chase opponents even back into my own penalty box,' said the former Russia forward Serhiy Yuran, who began his career at Dynamo under Lobanovskyi. 'For example, Oleg Romantsev, both with the national team and Spartak Moscow, told me to work hard, but only in the opponents' half. He told me to do everything in my area, but not to intervene where others should be playing.'

Set moves were practised, to be used, Zelentsov said, not roboti-cally, but like a chess player adapting set gambits according to circumstance. These were the key to their conception of football, and it was through their models of training to develop among players a better understanding of the structures of the game that they carried football forwards. The classic example of such principles in action, perhaps, came in the Cup-Winners' Cup final of 1986, with Dynamo's second goal in their 3-0 win over Atlético Madrid. Vasyl Rats advanced down the left, drew two men, and played the ball inside to Ihor Belanov. He then took two touches, and, as the centre-back moved across to close him down, he, without so much as a glance, laid the ball right for Vadym Yevtushenko. He took one pace forward, forcing the opposing left-back inside to close him down, then instinctively flicked the ball right for the overlapping Oleh Blokhin, who ran onto his pass and lifted his finish over the goalkeeper. It was a move so quick and instinctive as to be virtually unstoppable, resembling less football

Lobanovskyi's three great teams
3-0 v Ferencváros, Cup-Winners' Cup Final, St Jakob Stadium, Basle, 14 May 1975

3-0 v Atlético Madrid, Cup-Winners' Cup final, Stade Gerland, Lyon, 2 May 1986

3-3 v Bayern Munich, Champions League semi-final, first leg, Olympyskyi, Kyiv, 7 April 1999

than a rugby team working the ball along a line of backs until the overlap is created.

Critics often suggest that Lobanovskyi stifled individuality, but the truth is rather that he made his players aware that they were not individuals, that individual skill was only of use within the context of the system. 'The tactics are not chosen to suit the best players,' Lobanovskyi explained. 'They must fit our play. Everybody must fulfil the coach's demands first, and only then perform his individual mastery.'

In *Methodological Basis*, Lobanovskyi and Zelentsov give as an example of their preparation for a specific game the European Cup semi-final against Bayern Munich in 1977. 'The play,' they wrote, 'was constructed on attacking actions, with the obligatory neutral-isation of the opponent's players, the intention being to deprive him playing space and to defend against the attacks from wide at which Bayern were so strong. The objective was a draw, but we ended up losing 1-0. In the match in Kyiv, we chose a playing model based on squeezing the play and fighting for the ball in our opponents' half of the pitch, trying to create a numerical advantage in various areas. Eventually we won 2-0.'

Their other great advance was to work out a method of recording and analysing games far more sophisticated than the shorthand of Charles Reep. Each element of the game was broken down and targets set according to the style Lobanovskyi had adopted. (see table on page 244)

The day after matches, the statistical breakdown of the game would be posted on the notice-boards at the training ground, an innovation that gave Lobanovskyi great power. 'When I was a player,' he said, 'it was difficult to evaluate players. The coach could say that a player wasn't in the right place at the right moment, and the player could simply disagree. There were no videos, no real methods of analysis, but today the players cannot object. They know that the morning after the game the sheet of paper will be pinned up showing all the figures characterising his play. If a midfielder has fulfilled sixty technical and tactical actions in the course of the match, then he has not pulled his weight. He is obliged to do a hundred or more.'

The attitude, inevitably, led to conflict and, while most players seem to have respected Lobanovskyi – most notably Andriy Shevchenko, who insisted 'he made me as a player' – he inspired

Action	Target actions per game		
	Squeezing (pressing only in opponent's half)	Counter-attacking (pressing only in own half of pitch)	Combination of both models
Short passes:			
Forwards	130	80	30–130
Sideways	100	60	40–100
Backwards	70	40	20–70
Medium passes:			
Forwards	60	80	40–90
Sideways	50	25	30–80
Backwards	25	15	10–30
Long passes:			
Forwards	30	50	15–40
Sideways	20	30	10–30
Backwards	0	0	0
Headed passes	20–40	20-40	15–70
Runs with the ball	140	80	70–150
Beating the opponent	70	50	20–70
Interceptions	80	110	70–140
Tackles	50	70	30–80
Shots on goal	10–20	15–35	10–35
Headers on goal	10–15	5–10	5-15
Returning the ball to play	10–30	10–30	10–40
Error percentage	20–35	15–30	25

little warmth. 'My relationship with Lobanovskyi wasn't hostile, but it wasn't friendly either,' said Belanov. 'It was simply professional. But he did a lot for me. He invited me to Dynamo and persuaded me to play his way. We had quarrels, but we were aware that we were doing a great thing.' As if to prove there were no hard feelings, Belanov named his son Valeriy.

Oleksandr Khapsalys, who played for Dynamo in the late

seventies and early eighties, recalled how Lobanovskyi would simply shout down any perceived criticism. 'It was better not to joke with Lobanovskyi,' he said. 'If he gave an instruction, and the player said: "But I think…" Lobanovskyi would look at him and scream: "Don't think! I do the thinking for you. Play!"'

With Dynamo, he was hugely successful, winning eight Soviet titles, six Soviet Cups, five Ukrainian titles, three Ukrainian Cups and two European Cup-Winners' Cups, and defining Ukrainian football. In his various stints with the USSR, though, Lobanovskyi was less successful. Twice in 1975 – against Turkey and the Republic of Ireland – his demand for 'a star-team' rather than 'a team of stars' led him to field a national team made up entirely of Dynamo players, and the squad he took to the 1976 Olympics in Montreal was similarly Dynamo dominated.

They had won successive league titles, and were undoubtedly one of the best teams in Europe, but Lobanovskyi still wasn't satisfied, and increased their training schedule yet further. The players were appalled, and many complained that they were too exhausted to perform to the full extent of their abilities. Matters came to a head in the semi-final as the Soviets produced a sluggish display in losing to East Germany. The players blamed Lobanovskyi, and went on strike. The incident was hushed up, and agreement eventually reached as Lobanovskyi stood down from the national job. 'The problem was that we were applying scientific methods to players who were semi-amateurs, and that led to conflict,' explained Zelentsov.

The dispute made Lobanovskyi aware that more training did not necessarily produce fitter players, and that was where Zelentsov made his great breakthrough as he constructed a training programme that managed to balance the twin but conflicting needs for speed and stamina; Zelentsov claims that Italy borrowed the model when they won the 1982 World Cup. Increasingly, he used computers in analysing games, and it was in through that development that they were able to revolutionise the game.

'In my laboratory, we evaluate the functional readiness of players and how their potential can best be realised,' Zelentsov explained. 'And we influence players in a natural way – we form them following scientific recommendations. With the help of modelling we assemble the bricks and create the skeleton of the team. It is true that not every player will fit the Dynamo system, but we don't just give a coach advice, we justify it with numbers. We recommend how to compose the training programmes, how to evaluate them, how to understand the actions of players on the field – all from a scientific point of view, no emotions.'

Lobanovksyi's conception became the default Soviet style, partly because it was successful, partly because of Lobanovskyi's domineering personality and partly because it felt ideologically right. For all that players of the time protest against the stereotype, the philosophy was rooted in the team: perhaps there is no such thing as the 'socialist football' to which Gusztav Sebes glibly referred, but the style of Lobanovskyi's teams was nonetheless a development of the 'collective play' of which Mikhail Yakushin had spoken during Dinamo Moscow's tour of Britain in 1945. Yet there was an internal opposition, and for a few years in the early eighties, Soviet football was torn between two radically different philosophies of how the game should be played.

Where Lobanovskyi was taciturn and analytical, his outbursts rooted in his desire to make his players conform to his system, Eduard Malofeev was loquacious and ebullient, frighteningly so. 'There is no one in Belarus with his energy or optimism,' said Gennadiy Abramovich, who played with Malofeev at Dinamo Minsk and then worked alongside him as an assistant coach. In the late nineties, Malofeev appeared on what Abramovich described dismissively as 'a women's programme' on television. Asked what he did each morning, he replied that first he thanked God he was alive, then he got out of bed and jumped up and down to celebrate the fact. His football, in conception at least, was similarly joyous.

Malofeev became a respected forward in twelve seasons with Dinamo Minsk, winning forty caps for the USSR and playing in the 1966 World Cup, and topping the scoring charts in the Soviet League in 1971. A cartilage injury brought his career to a close and, after a brief spell working in youth football, he graduated as a coach in 1975, being appointed manager of Dinamo Minsk in 1978. He led them to promotion in his first season, and they were sixth in his second. Even more remarkable, it was all achieved playing what Malofeev termed 'sincere football'. 'It was honest football,' explained Abramovich. 'No causing injuries, no bumping, no barging: just kicking the ball. No paying money to referees outside the ground. And attacking, pure football. Football of the heart, not of the head.'

Nereo Rocco, one of the pioneers of *catenaccio* (*PA Photos*)

Helenio Herrera, the grand wizard of *catenaccio* (*PA Photos*)

Ronnie Simpson claims a cross as Celtic beat Inter in the 1967 European Cup final (*Getty Images*)

César Luis Menotti, who won the World Cup with his reinterpretation of *la nuestra* ... (*Getty Images*)

... and his ideological opposite, Carlos Bilardo, who won the World Cup after devising 3-5-2 (*PA Photos*)

Rinus Michels on the
Dutch bench at the
1974 World Cup ...
... and Johan Cruyff,
with whom he
developed Total
Football (both pics
© *Getty Images*)

The two schools of Soviet football, Eduard Malofeev (left) and Valeriy Lobanovskyi (right) *(Igor Utkin)*

Sacha Prokopenko: playboy and player (both pics © *Dinamo Sports Society*)

Graham Taylor, who introduced pressing to the English game, and Elton John, his chairman at Watford (*Getty Images*)

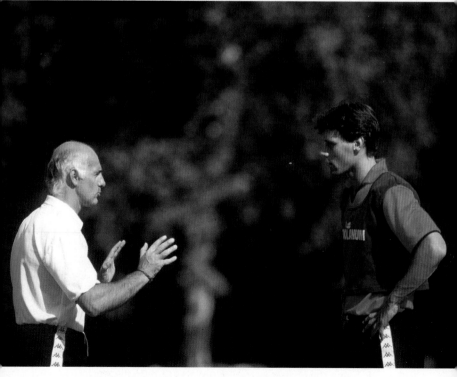

Arrigo Sacchi makes a point to Marco van Basten (*PA Photos*)

Pelé heads home the opener in the 1970 World Cup final (*Getty Images*)

Mario Zagallo, the coach who oversaw the greatest display of football's pre-systemic age (*Getty Images*)

The last of the old-style play makers, Juan Roman Riquelme ... *(Rex Pictures)*

... and Luka Modrić, the first of the new *(PA Photos)*

Malofeev's other great strength was his ability to handle players and get the best out of them. It is an over-simplification to say Lobanovskyi saw his payers as tools to be deployed, but not much of one; Malofeev, though, was concerned with individuality and self-expression. 'The main thing about Malofeev was his psychology,' explained Mikhail Vergeenko, Dinamo Minsk's goalkeeper in the early eighties. 'We would have a team-talk three hours before each game. He would gather everyone together and read out the team. He looked into the players' eyes, at each one, eye to eye. He was always looking, searching to discover something. He was like a doctor. He analysed players and he knew straightaway their strong points and their weak points. He was a person who could get to your heart, your soul. He knew how to talk to people.' Malofeev's failure at Hearts in 2006 – statistically, he is their worst ever manager, taking two points from his four games in charge – Vergeenko puts down to the absence of a good translator.

It didn't take long for comparisons to be made with what was going on 270 miles to the south-east. 'The rivalry between Minsk and Kyiv was the rivalry between two minds,' Vergeenko explained. 'Lobanovskyi was a coach by mathematics; Malofeev was more romantic. The main thing he wanted from the players was that they should express themselves on the pitch. If you give your all, he said, the fans will love you.'

The player the fans loved most was a man whose lifestyle would have disbarred him from getting anywhere near a Lobanovksyi side: Alexander Prokopenko. He was a heartbreak of a midfielder, a genius whose talent was as unbridled as his capacity for alcohol. A painfully shy man, he was so tormented by a speech impediment that he refused ever to be interviewed. It didn't matter: Dinamo fans knew what he thought because he drank with them. More than that, he was one of them, just another worker from Minsk who happened to be a superb instinctive footballer, and an industrious one at that. 'The tribune knew he would go for ninety minutes,' the journalist Vasily Sarychev wrote in *The Moment and the Destiny*, his book celebrating Belarus's top sportsmen. 'He would sooner die than cease his motion on the pitch through tiredness or laziness.'

His drinking after the USSR team of which he had been a part finished third in the 1980 Olympics led him to miss the end of the season, but he returned in glory and scored the iconic goal of the

1982 campaign, a backheel against Dynamo Kyiv. As Dinamo's form slid in the mid-eighties, his alcoholism got worse, and he was forced to spend time at LTP, a state-sponsored rehab clinic. The club, acting under the instructions of the local Communist Party, refused to take him back, but Abramovich, whom he came to refer to as a second father, persuaded the second division side Dnepr Mogilev to take him on. After a season there he moved to Azerbaijan with Neftchi Baku, playing against Dinamo Minsk and scoring against Spartak.

It was only a brief respite, though, and he began drinking heavily again. He was readmitted to the LTP in 1989, but died two months later, aged just thirty-five. 'He was followed by the smell of grass and of skin, by the joy of his goals and by empty cans,' Sarychev wrote. 'When the need for football went, the urge died in him, the urge he was born to fulfil.'

Brilliant but unpredictable, his demons masked by the charm of his play, Prokopenko was the model of a Malofeev footballer. Lobanovskyi, predictably, was scathing of Malofeev's idealism. As he pointed out, for all Dinamo Minsk fans raved about the Prokopenko backheel, the match had ended in a draw and a valuable away point for Dynamo. 'When somebody mentioned it,' Abramovich recalled, 'he slapped his hand to his head and said, "In my life I have seen many things, but never *sincere* football."'

Nonetheless, at least for one glorious season, it worked. 'What happened with Dinamo in 1982 was about the harmony of youth and experience,' the midfielder Sergei Aleinikov wrote in his autobiography. 'Everybody, whether they were veterans or novices, played every game like it was the last of his career. But the main thing was that Malofeev was the head of the team, the unique and only one. That was his victory, the triumph of his principles and his understanding of football.'

That year, every ploy Malofeev initiated paid off. Vergeenko remembers in particular the game away to Pakhtakor Tashkent, who went on to finish sixth that season. 'It was forty degrees plus in the shade,' he said. 'The game was at 6 p.m., but at noon, Malofeev said, "OK, let's go and train." Everybody was stunned. Even in the hotel it was over thirty-five at night, no air-conditioning. Imagine: we were just thinking how to escape the heat; then Malofeev says we're training at noon. "But afterwards," he said, "you will see – just thirty minutes, you will sweat, but you

Dinamo Minsk 1982

will be OK." We had thirty minutes training. The workers in the ground were shocked. They were sitting there out of the heat drinking water, and Malofeev brings his team for training. But that evening, we knew we could deal with the heat and we won 3-0, and they were a good team at that time.'

Malofeev's team talks were equally eccentric. Dinamo went into their final league game away to Spartak Moscow needing a win to clinch the title. Twenty-nine years earlier, it was widely believed in Belarus, Spartak had cheated Dinamo Minsk out of second place in the league with a bout of late-season match-fixing, and the fear was they would do something similar to hand the title to Dynamo. Malofeev knew he had to break down his side's cynicism, to persuade them that defeat was not inevitable, and so came up with something that sounds like the rejected draft of a Just So story.

'"Imagine there is a troop of monkeys crossing a field,"' Vergeenko remembers him telling a hushed dressing room. '"On the other side of the field is a group of lions. Many different things could happen. Maybe the lions will tear the monkeys to pieces. Or maybe one of the monkeys will go first, and will distract the lions, and will sacrifice himself so the other monkeys will live. Today, as monkeys, we must sacrifice ourselves for the victory."

'I thought: I am the goalkeeper, maybe I will be injured, but the main thing is that the team will win.' And they did, by the typically Malofeevan score of 4-3. 'When the team got back from Moscow to Minsk, it was amazing,' Vergeenko went on. 'There were people with flowers and kisses and love: nothing organised, just love.'

Malofeev promptly left for Moscow to take charge of the USSR Olympic side, leaving him ideally placed to step in when Lobanovskyi's second spell in charge of the main national team came to an end. All had seemed to be progressing well for him, particularly after a 5-0 demolition of Portugal in Moscow in qualifying for Euro 84. Away in Lisbon, though, Lobanovskyi – as he always did in tough away games – set out for the draw, only to be undone by a penalty awarded for a foul that clearly took place outside the box. Portugal won 1-0, the USSR failed to qualify, and Lobanovskyi, blamed for his pragmatism, was dismissed.

Lobanovskyi's star had never been lower, and only the personal intervention of Scherbytskyi saw him reinstated at Dynamo. Even that looked an error when Dynamo finished that 1984 season tenth. Lobanovskyi, though, stuck to his guns. 'A path always remains a path,' he said. 'It's a path during the day, it's a path during the night and it's a path during the dawn.' The next season, Dynamo did the double, before adding the Cup-Winners' Cup.

Malofeev, meanwhile, was faltering. The USSR won just one of their opening five qualifiers for the Mexico World Cup, but salvaged a place in the finals by winning their last three games. 'Malofeev became very nervous, and there was no clear pattern to our football, but Mexico was waiting,' Aleinikov wrote in his autobiography. 'The media was attacking both the players and the coaches. The final straw was the grey 0-0 draw against Finland [in a friendly] at the Luzhniki Stadium. It was rumoured that Malofeev might be replaced, and Lobanovskyi had just won the Cup-Winners' Cup, but I didn't believe it would come to reality before the start of the World Cup.'

Nonetheless, it did, as Malofeev was called away from a training camp in Novogorsk and didn't return. 'There was a strange atmosphere in the squad,' Aleinikov went on. 'The Kyiv boys liked the decision, as you can imagine, because most of them were not in favour of Malofeev's ideas. On the other hand, there were the boys who understood there were no positions for them in the squad under Lobanovskyi. They were prepared for Mexico, but they knew they would not be going.

'Lobanovskyi made us train harder. To say it was difficult would be an understatement. In the evening I was just looking to get to bed as soon as possible. For Lobanovskyi the game was about the result, not about fun. Football had to be rational. For him, 1-0 was better than 5-4.'

For all the doubts, Lobanovskyi received immediate vindication as his side hammered the much-fancied Hungary 6-0. In the second round, though, the USSR, let down by poor refereeing and a catastrophic performance from defender Andriy Bal, were beaten 4-3 by Belgium in one of the greatest games the World Cup has known. 'As a coach you can't account for individual errors and you certainly can't account for refereeing blunders,' said Lobanovskyi said – an acknowledgement that there were factors beyond the control of even a system as scientific as his.

Two years later at the European Championship in West Germany, the USSR came as close to glory as they ever would under Lobanovskyi. They beat Holland and England in the group stage, and then outplayed Italy in the semi-final. So impressed was the former Italy coach Enzo Bearzot by the USSR's 2-0 win that he sought out Lobanovskyi after the final whistle. 'I realised once again that you are a great team,' he told him. 'You play modern football at 100km/h. The pressing you showed today is the sign of great ability, and the physical shape of the Soviet players is clearly the result of great self-sacrifice and professionalism.'

The only flaw in an otherwise awesome performance was the booking collected by the sweeper Oleh Kuznetsov, which ruled him out of the final against Holland. 'Have you seen how bees fly?' asked Zelentsov. 'A hive is in the air, and there is a leader. The leader turns right and all the hive turn right. It turns left and all the hive turn left. It is the same in football. There is a leader who takes a decision to move, say, here. The rest need to correct their motion to follow the leader. Every team has players who link coalitions; every team has players who destroy them. The first are called on to create on the field, the latter to destroy the team actions of the opponent.' Without their leader, the USSR missed a penalty, suffered Marco van Basten's preposterous volley and lost 2-0.

After a disappointing World Cup in 1990, Lobanovskyi left the USSR for the Middle East, but he was persuaded back to Dynamo in 1996, partly by the riches promised by new investors, but mainly by the potential of the generation of Shevchenko, Oleh Luzhny, Serhiy Rebrov and Vyacheslav Vashchuk. He inspired them to a Champions League semi-final in 1999 – his third great team – but, by the time of his death from a stroke in 2002, the suspicion was that he was struggling as, having been forced to sell the majority of his better players, he was forced to turn to imports. According to Serhiy Polkhovskyi, the Dynamo vice-president, it had become apparent in his final months that he was having difficulty dealing even with local players who had not been brought up under Communism. 'He had internal torments,' Polkhovskyi said. 'Previously a word, a glance, was enough to assert his authority and explain what he wanted. Maybe it was typical of the Communist system, but now players have a greater freedom and an individuality.'

Still, his legacy is secure. As Marcello Lippi, who coached Juventus to the Champions League and Italy to the World Cup, said, 'Everybody plays a pressing game now.'

Chapter Fourteen

△▽△▽△▽△▽△▽

Fly Me to the Moon

△▽ The 1970 Mexico World Cup now stands, mythically and perhaps in fact, as the apogee of football. In the popular consciousness, it was a festival of attacking football, and the Brazil side that won the tournament – Pelé, Tostão, Gérson, Rivellino *et al* – is regarded as some unmatchable paradigm, the greatest side the world has known, and probably will ever know. And yet there is also an acceptance that their style of play would be impossible today, their achievement was an achievement of the old football, before system had taken charge.

As part of their build-up for the tournament, Brazil's squad underwent a NASA training programme, the metaphorical significance of which seems to have been lost on nobody. The *Jornal do Brazil* is usually an austere newspaper, but on 22 June 1970, it made an observation that was startling in its boldness. 'Brazil's victory with the ball,' it said, 'compares with the conquest of the moon by the Americans.'

At first the comparison seems ludicrous, and yet there is something there, some grain of truth. To begin with, there is the use of abstract terms: 'victory with the ball... conquest of the moon'. The Americans beat the Soviets in the space race, and Brazil beat Italy in the World Cup final, yet neither opponent is mentioned. Rather the triumphs, which happened less than a year apart, come to be regarded as a greater endeavour, a victory attained less against corporeal rivals than over external, non-human elements, as though to play football of that majesty were somehow a victory for all of humanity.

It is surely significant that all the most memorable moments of the 1970 tournament are essentially non-competitive: Pelé's lob from the halfway line against Czechoslovakia did not go in; having extravagantly dummied the Uruguay goalkeeper Ladislao Mazurkiewicz in the semi-final, he then missed an open goal. Even Carlos Alberto Torres's famous goal in the final came with four minutes to go when the outcome was already decided. This was *futebol arte* in a very literal sense: celebrating not events that determined the result, but passages of play that transcended the immediate context of the matches of which they were part – although, that said, had Brazil not won the tournament, they may be remembered not with the fondness that they are, but as counter-productive extravagances.

Whether the moon landing was the supreme technological achievement of the twentieth century, whether Brazil's 1970 World Cup success was the supreme sporting achievement, is debatable, but what is sure is that no other event in either sphere had such an immediacy of impact, such a universal symbolic importance. The reason for that is simple: television. Instantly, to a watching audience of millions across the world, Neil Armstrong's one small step and Carlos Alberto's thunderous strike became icons, destined from the moment of their happening to be reproduced again and again in a multiplicity of forms. These were the first two great global events of the telecultural age. As if to seal the symbolic link, the second moon landing happened on the same day that Pelé converted a penalty for Santos against Vasco da Gama to reach 1,000 career goals.

It helped that Brazil played in vibrant yellow with shorts of cobalt blue: they were perfect for the new age of colour television. Under the iridescent heat of the Mexican sun, it seemed as though this was the future: bright and brilliant. Brazil kept just one clean sheet in the tournament, but it didn't matter. Fallibility was part of their charm: there was a naivety about them that gave them a universal appeal – apart, perhaps, from in Argentina. 'Those last minutes,' Hugh McIlvanney wrote in his match report of the final, 'contained a distillation of their football, its beauty and élan and almost undiluted joy. Other teams thrill us and make us respect them. The Brazilians at their finest gave us pleasure so natural and deep as to be a vivid physical experience... the qualities that make football the most graceful and electric and moving of team sports were being laid before us. Brazil are proud of their own unique abilities but it was not hard to believe they were anxious to say something about the game as well as themselves. You cannot be the best in the world at a game without loving it and all of us who sat, flushed with excitement, in the stands of the Azteca sensed that we were seeing some kind of tribute.'

The moon landing was the culmination of a project in which the USA had concentrated their scientific, technological, financial and emotional resources. Once Kennedy had acknowledged the start of the space race in 1962, conquering the moon became the USA's great goal. In 1962, Brazil won their second World Cup, and set about directing their resources into winning a third. By 1970, as the military government became involved in football, players underwent preparatory programmes of previously unimaginable sophistication. 'We knew we needed to do something to improve our physical condition,' Gérson said, noting that was where the European nations had progressed. 'In 1966 we were in good physical condition, but not as good as theirs.' Each Brazilian player went to Mexico with pairs of individually fitted handmade boots, while a fortnight before departure they began living on Mexican time with a strictly controlled programme of diet and sleep. Even their kit was redesigned so as not to become weighed down by sweat. Brazil's triumph was one of imagination and spontaneity, but it was backed up by science and preparation – and by economic circumstance.

The long economic boom that lasted from the end of the Korean War to the mid-seventies – and so effectively funded the space programme in the USA – created a wider market for Brazil's raw materials, leading to rises in employment and wages through the fifties. That prompted a rise in consumption among the working-classes and the creation of an urban middle-class, but the gap between city and country widened, leading to an influx of migration and the escalating growth of *favelas*. Put bluntly, the conditions were perfect for football. As David Goldblatt notes in *The Ball is Round*, 'Too little wealth and the football infrastructure cannot be maintained. Too much wealth and the social production line of *malandros* and *pibes* cannot be maintained.'

An ageing side was found out at the 1966 World Cup in England, their cause not helped by lax refereeing that allowed Pelé effectively to be kicked out of games. Hugely frustrated, he retired from international football, only returning to the national side two years later. 'I had found the violence and the lack of sportsmanship as dispiriting as the weak refereeing that had allowed it to go unchecked for so long,' he explained in his autobiography. Even in Brazil, though, football had become increasingly violent, mirroring the trend in a society in which guerrilla groups regularly launched attacks against the military regime, and met with savage reprisals in their turn.

When General Médici took control in October 1969, football had an advocate in power. Dissent had been quelled, and the general, a staunch Flamengo fan, quickly realised that football could give him the popular legitimacy he desired. That was good news for Brazilian football generally, in that it ensured there would be significant investment in the 1970 campaign, but it was bad news for the national coach João Saldanha. He had been a member of the Communist Party in his youth and, with his habitual candour, he made little secret of his ideological opposition to the regime.

Saldanha had played for Botafogo, and became a journalist after his playing career had come to an end. He gained the nickname 'João sem Medo' – 'Fearless João' – for his outspoken style and, after regularly criticising his former side, he was appointed manager in 1957. He promptly led them to the Carioca championship and, although his subsequent lack of sustained success meant a return to journalism, he was given the national job in 1969. He was, Pelé said, 'smart and sharp-tongued and he brought a new directness to the job of national coach'. There, the refusal to play the diplomatic game that had made him so popular as a columnist proved his undoing. His demise, though, was precipitated by a tactical issue.

Saldanha's side had cruised through World Cup qualifying, totalling twenty-three goals in winning six games out of six against Colombia, Venezuela and Paraguay in 1969. In those days he would proudly announce, 'what I want is goals', but he went on a scouting trip to Europe that October and was troubled by the muscular, defensive football, the 'brutal play and lenient referees' he saw there. 'The finals,' he announced, after the draw had grouped Brazil with England, Czechoslovakia and Romania, 'will develop into a brawl if we are not vigilant and the European teams with the best boxers and wrestlers will win it.'

Although emotionally opposed to negativity, Saldanha recognised that it had been a naive faith in improvisational football that had led to Brazil's underperformances in the thirties, and he was terrified of making the same mistake again. On his return, he tried to set Brazil up to deal with increasingly physical opponents, changing personnel so as to raise the average mass of his defence by five pounds and their average height by three inches. His modifications, though, led only to confusion. 'He couldn't take criticism and the relationship between him and his former colleagues in the press deteriorated,' Pelé said. 'He liked a drink and started to behave erratically.'

Matters came to a head in March 1970 as Brazil faced back-to-back warm-up games against Argentina. He dropped Dario, a forward whose move from Atlético Mineiro to Flamengo had been engineered by Médici. That probably would not have mattered had a journalist not asked whether he were aware that Dario was a favourite of the general. 'I don't choose the president's ministry,' Saldanha said, 'and he doesn't choose my forward line.' Médici had already been offended by Saldanha's refusal to adjust his training schedule to allow the players to attend a banquet at the presidential palace, and from that moment the coach was living on borrowed time.

Defeat at home to Argentina, who had failed to qualify for the Mexico World Cup, pushed him closer to the edge, particularly when the Argentina defender Roberto Perfumo described Saldanha's side as 'the poorest Brazil team I have played against'. Wilson Piazza and Gérson had been swamped in the middle of the midfield, something for which Saldanha blamed Pelé, accusing him of having failed to follow his orders to track back and help. This was seen as insanity: criticising Pelé at all was bad enough, but to tell him to defend was heretical.

Saldanha's temper only made things worse. In 1967 he had twice fired a gun into the air after a confrontation with Manga, a Bangu goalkeeper he had accused of match-fixing, and he reacted similarly when Yustrich, the Flamengo coach, called him 'a coward' during a radio interview, storming into the lobby of the Rio hotel where Yustrich was staying and brandishing a loaded handgun. Yustrich, fortunately, had gone out.

Yet somehow, amid the madness, Saldanha pulled a master-stroke in the second game, as he brought on the nineteen-year-old Clodoaldo of Santos for Piazza. He immediately gave the midfield added zest and resolve, and Pelé scored a late winner. Still, though, Saldanha felt Pelé was not doing sufficient defensive work, and publicly admitted he was considering dropping him. He was promptly sacked amid accusations of emotional instability. Public sympathy was limited, and the little that remained was lost as he responded with a bizarre outburst in which he claimed that claimed Gérson had mental problems, Pelé was too short-sighted to play and that Emerson Leão, the reserve keeper, had short arms.

After Dino Sani and Oto Gloria had both turned down the job, Mário Zagallo, the shuttling left-winger of 1958 and 1962, was appointed as his replacement. He had been Saldanha's protégé at Botafogo, but, more importantly, he was seen as a safe pair of hands, unencumbered by any dangerously left-wing political beliefs. When the military government installed Captain Cláudio Coutinho to work as his fitness coach – it was he who went on the fact-finding mission to NASÃ – and added Admiral Jerônimo Bastos to the touring party, he raised no fuss. He did not, though, pick Dario.

In fact, Zagallo was faced with only two significant selection decisions. By the time he arrived, Pelé said, 'the team was more or less chosen but there were a few changes to be made'. Saldanha had based his squad around Santos and Botafogo, working on the same logic as Vittorio Pozzo and Gusztav Sebes: that players who play together on a regular basis will have a greater understanding. Zagallo, though, brought in Roberto Rivellino from Corinthians and confirmed the importance of Cruzeiro's Tostão. When critics suggested they were too similar to Gérson and Pelé, Zagallo replied, 'What this team needs is great players, players who are intelligent. Let's go with that and see where it takes us.'

It took them to heights that perhaps remain unsurpassed. 'Our team was the best,' said Gérson. 'Those who saw it, saw it. Those who didn't will never see it again.' The final against Italy was billed as a battle for football's soul, between the *futebol arte* of the Brazilians and the *futebol de resultados* – as the Brazilians had it – of the Italians. Art won, but never again would a side enjoy such success simply by throwing their best players on the field and asking them to play.

It was not, of course, quite so simple as that, although it is difficult to know just how central Zagallo was. Gérson, Pelé and Carlos Alberto formed a sub-committee of senior players – the *cobras*, as they became known – and it was they who suggested the line-up to Zagallo after a warm-up game against Atlético Mineiro had ended with them being booed off following an uninspiring

3-1 win. The back four was relatively straightforward, with Piazza
being used as the *quarto zagueiro*. So, too, was the selection of
Gérson, the elegant, deep-lying playmaker – playing as what the
Italians would call a *regista*. He needed protection, so Clodoaldo,
untouchable after that second Argentina game, operated alongside
him, a more physical, defensive presence – he may be best remembered for his part in Brazil's final goal in the final, dribbling
nonchalantly through three Italians in his own half, but that was
utterly uncharacteristic.

But what then? Could Pelé and Tostão really play together?
'Tostão was not a typical centre-forward,' said the historian Ivan
Soter. 'He was a *ponta da lança* like Pelé. So he would drop off and
Pelé would become the centre-forward. It was very fluid.' The
danger then was that there would be nobody in the box to take
advantage of their attractive approach play, but that was alleviated
by Jairzinho, a rapid right-winger (he more than lived up to his
nickname of '*Furacão*' – 'the Hurricane') with an eye for goal. His
strike against England, hurtling late into the box to hammer an
angled finish across Gordon Banks after Pelé had held up and then
laid off Tostão's cross was typical, and he finished the tournament
as the only man to score in every game in the finals. In training
Gérson spent hours practising clipping diagonal balls for Jairzinho
to run onto, in effect calibrating his left foot, making adjustments
for the thinness of the Mexican air. Jairzinho's forward surges left
space behind him, but that was no problem because Carlos Alberto
was an attacking right-back in the sprit of Nílton Santos. He
advanced and the defence shuffled over.

That still left two major issues: who to play on the left, and
where to fit Rivellino. He was another who favoured the *ponta da
lança* role, and there were question marks over his fitness. Everaldo
was a far more defensively-minded full-back, which balanced the
back-four, but that meant that if a flying left-winger – like Edu of
Santos – were selected, damaging space could appear on that
flank, just the sort of weakness Alcide Ghiggia had exploited in the
1950 final. Two problems became one solution, as Rivellino was
stationed vaguely on the left, although he often drifted infield,
asked to provide some sort of balancing counterweight to
Jairzinho's surges and encouraged to unleash his left foot
whenever possible. Was it 4-4-2, was it 4-3-3, was it 4-2-4, was it even
4-5-1? It was all of them and none of them: it was just players on a

pitch who complemented each other perfectly. In modern parlance, it would probably have been described as a 4-2-3-1, but such subtleties meant nothing then.

Italy's coach Ferruccio Valcareggi, meanwhile, dared not play both his great playmakers at the same time, Sandro Mazzola and Gianni Rivera, and so came up with the unhappy compromise of the *staffetta* – the relay – whereby one played the first half, and the other the second. The contrast could hardly have been more pronounced.

Fittingly, Brazil even completed their victory with a goal of supreme quality. No thought from them of sitting on a 3-1 lead, no question of running the clock down. Rather, they simply kept playing, and produced a goal still regularly voted the greatest ever scored, a wonderful parting gift from a wonderful team at a wonderful tournament.

It began with Clodoaldo and his unlikely dribble inside his own half, the thoughtless backheel that, forty-nine minutes earlier, had presented an equaliser to Italy apparently banished from his mind. He fed Jairzinho, now appearing on the left. As Giacinto Facchetti checked his run, the winger turned infield and laid the ball on to Pelé. He waited, and with the same languid precision that had produced goals against England and Uruguay earlier in the competition, he rolled it outside for Carlos Alberto, the full-back and captain, who charged through the space vacated by Jairzinho to flash a first-time shot into the bottom corner.

It was exuberant, it was brilliant and it wasn't just Brazil that reacted with euphoria, but it marked the end of the age of football's innocence. In club football, in Europe at least, that era had ended much earlier, but in Mexico, the heat and the altitude combined to make pressing or any kind of systematic closing down of opponents impossible. For the last time in major competition, there was space, and Brazil had a team perfectly equipped to make the best use of it. What had appeared, as satellites beamed it in vibrant technicolour around the world, as the beginning of a brave new world, actually sounded the last post for the old one. And there, perhaps, is the final parallel with the moon landing: the illusory nature of the bold future it seemed to herald. Just as there are no human settlements in outer space, so football has found itself restricted by earthly concerns.

Brazil 4 Italy 1, World Cup Final, Azteca, Mexico City, 21 June 1970

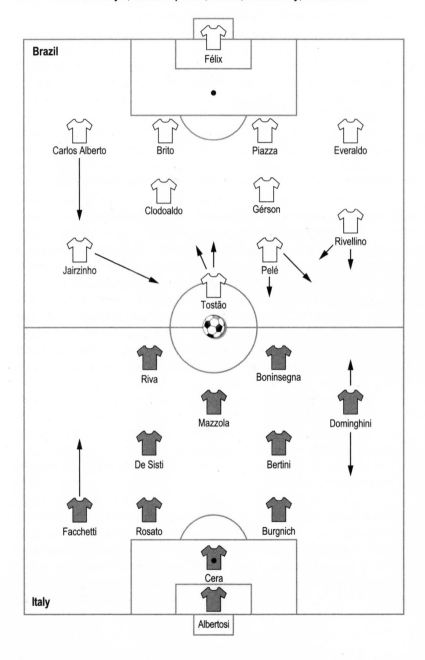

Even Brazil seem to have accepted that 1970 was a zenith never to be repeated. It may have cost him his job, but Saldanha's assessment of how football was going turned out to have been broadly right – just about twelve months premature. Although the cerebral and aesthetic qualities of the Dutch sides that dominated football in the early seventies were undeniable, they were physically robust and far more conscious of the demands of system than the Brazil of 1970 had been.

The Brazil of 1974 were unrecognisable from that of 1970, something for which Zagallo was widely blamed, although he was not helped by withdrawals. Pelé had retired, while Tostão, Gérson and Clodoaldo were all injured. Still, there was a cynicism to them that had been absent four years earlier, which manifested itself most obviously against Holland in the second group phase. Marinho Peres knocked Johan Neeskens out cold, and Luís Pereira was eventually sent off for a horrible hack on the same player. Holland, who had always had a chip of ice in their hearts, gave as good as they got and won comfortably, 2-0. Brazil finished fourth, but it was widely perceived that that flattered them.

By 1978, Brazil were in the hands of Coutinho, the army captain who had worked with Zagallo in 1970. He insisted his goal was 'polyvalence' – which appears to have been another term for Total Football – and as he recalled Francisco Marinho, the adventurous left-back, for the qualifying series, there seemed a measure of truth to that. Come the training camp ahead of the finals, though, and he had fallen back on what he knew best – physical preparation. His side were no more fluent and no less brutal than Zagallo's team of four years earlier: Coutinho's relationship with Zico was fractious, Rivellino was unfit and they ended up playing Toninho, a right-back, on the right-wing. Somehow they blundered on to finish third.

Not until 1982 did Brazil really cut loose again, perhaps significantly amid the atrocious heat of Spain. Falcão only started Brazil's opening game, against the USSR, because Cerezo was suspended, but he played so well he had to be retained, leaving their coach Telê Santana to follow Zagallo's policy from 1970 and just let his players get on with it. With Zico and Socrates also in the side, Brazil had four vastly talented creative midfielders, but no wide players whatsoever apart from Eder. So again a deficiency was made a virtue as Cerezo and Falcão – both *registas*, deep-lying playmakers – sat behind Zico and Socrates – the *trequartistas* – while Eder was deployed as an auxiliary centre-forward, playing off the lumbering Serginho, who would surely never have been anywhere near the side had either Reinaldo or Careca been fit.

The formation was thus a 4-2-2-2, with a strong central column flanked by two marauding full-backs in Leandro and Júnior. In a European context, it would have been perceived as lacking width, but this was a team of such fluency and poise in possession that they created it with their movement. It was a system that never spread – the Brazilian coach Vanderlei Luxembourgo's attempts to institute what he called 'the magic quadrilateral' at Real Madrid in 2005 failed amid general bewilderment – but it seemed to suit the Brazilian mentality, the two deep-lying midfielders (by 1994, when Dunga and Mauro Silva occupied the positions, they would be *bona fide* holding players) providing a platform for four out-and-out attacking players – two centre-forwards and two *trequartistas* – while still allowing the full-backs to tear up and down the flanks as they had been doing in Brazil since the days of Nílton Santos.

The Brazil of 1982 produced the most exhilarating football the World Cup had known since 1970. They beat the USSR 2-1, swatted aside Scotland 4-1 and New Zealand 4-0, playing an effortless, fluid game full of deliciously angled passes and fearsome long-range shooting. In the second group phase, they comfortably beat the reigning world champions Argentina, leaving them needing just a draw against Italy to reach the semi-finals. It was considered a formality.

Italy were in the phase of *il gioco all' Italiana* rather than out-and-out *catenaccio*, but they were still notably defensive. Just as much as the game in the Azteca in 1970, their meeting with Brazil in the Estadi de Sarrià was seen as an allegory. To try to alleviate the shortfall in midfield caused by Herrera's version of *catenaccio*, Italian football had followed the route of Dutch and German football, by making the *libero* a far more rounded player – a converted inside-forward such as Pierluigi Cera or Gaetano Scirea rather than a converted full-back like Ivano Blason or Armando Picchi – capable of stepping out from the back and making an extra midfielder when his side had possession.

Italy had begun the tournament slowly, progressing through the first group – in which they drew all three of their games – only by virtue of having scored a goal more than Cameroon, who also drew all three of their matches. Paolo Rossi, returning after a ban for his involvement in a match-fixing scandal, looked far from his best, but a 2-1 win over Argentina gave them belief, and raised doubts among the Brazilians. Waldir Peres, the latest in a long line of hapless Brazilian goalkeepers, admitted before the game that his great fear was that Rossi would suddenly spring into life. He proved a far better mystic than he was goalkeeper.

Was it the greatest World Cup game ever? Probably, although Hungary's 1954 victory over Uruguay will always have its devotees. Certainly it had an epic feel, something enhanced by overcrowding as far more than the official 44,000 squeezed in. Had Brazil scored an early goal, Italy could easily have wilted, their system and their mentality not equipped for chasing a game, but it was the Italians who took a fifth-minute lead, as Bruno Conti, having been allowed to advance almost forty yards down the right, cut infield and released the attacking left-back Antonio Cabrini, who crossed for Rossi to repay the faith of his manager Enzo Bearzot with a fine header.

And so was set in motion the pattern for the game: Brazilian attacking, and Italian resistance. Within seven minutes, it was level, as Socrates played a one-two with Zico, and advanced to drive the ball in at Dino Zoff's near post. Then surely, it seemed, Brazil would kick on to win. Perhaps they would have done, had it not been for a dreadful error from Cerezo after twenty-five minutes, casually knocking a square pass in the vague direction of Júnior. Rossi, suddenly a poacher again, stole in, and beat Waldir. This time the lead lasted, and Brazil became increasingly edgy. Rossi, with the chance to make it 3-1 midway through the second half, sidefooted badly wide, and when, two minutes later, Brazil equalised through Falcão's ferocious drive, it looked once again as though they would prevail.

Perhaps, needing only a draw to progress, they should have tightened up and held what they had, but that was not the Brazilian way. They kept attacking, and paid the price. A Conti corner was half-cleared, Marco Tardelli half-hit his shot from the edge of the box and Rossi, played onside by a dozing Júnior, hooked the ball past Waldir. It was, as Glanville said, 'the game in which Brazil's glorious midfield, put finally to the test, could not make up for the deficiencies behind and in front of it.'

It was a game, moreover, that lay on a fault-line of history and,

Italy 3 Brazil 2, World Cup second group phase, Sarrià, Barcelona, 5 July 1982

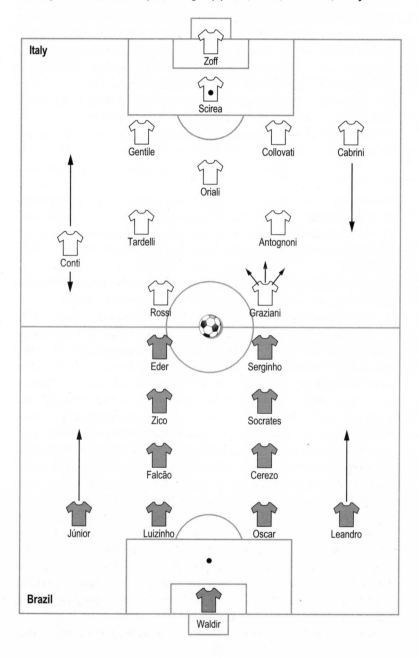

unlike 1970, football followed the victors, in style if not in formation. Zico called it 'the day that football died', but that is to percolate everything through the consciousness of a particularly romantic Brazilian. Rather it was the day that a certain naivety in football died; it was the day after which it was no longer possible simply to pick the best players and allow them to get on with it; it was the day that system won. There was still a place for great individual attacking talents, but they had to be incorporated into something knowing, had to be protected and covered for.

The irony is that '*il gioco all' Italiana*' was itself dying. 'It was effective for a while,' Ludovico Maradei explained, 'and, by the late 1970s and early 1980s everybody in Italy was playing it. But that became its undoing. Everybody had the same system and it was rigidly reflected in the numbers players wore. The No. 9 was the centre-forward, 11 was the second striker who always attacked from the left, 7 the *tornante* on the right, 4 the deep-lying central midfielder, 10 the more attacking central midfielder and 8 the link-man, usually on the centre left, leaving space for 3, the left-back, to push on. Everyone marked man to man so it was all very predictable: 2 on 11, 3 on 7, 4 on 10, 5 on 9, 6 was the sweeper, 7 on 3, 8 on 8, 10 on 4, 9 on 5 and 11 on 2.'

The match in which the shortcomings of *il gioco all' Italiana* were exposed came less than a year after it had beaten the Brazilian game, as Juventus lost the 1983 European Cup final to SV Hamburg. Three of Juventus's back-four had played for Italy in Barcelona, with Claudio Gentile and Cabrini as the full-backs and Scirea as the sweeper, the only difference being the presence of Sergio Brio as the stopper central defender. Hamburg played with two forwards: a figurehead in Horst Hrubesch, with the Dane Lars Bastrup usually playing off him to the left. That suited Juventus, because it meant he could be marked by Gentile, while Cabrini would be left free from defensive concerns to attack down the left.

Realising that, the Hamburg coach Ernst Happel switched Bastrup to the right, putting him up against Cabrini. That was something almost unheard of in Italian football. Their asymmetric system worked because everybody was equally asymmetric: the marking roles were just as specific as they had been in the W-M. Giovanni Trapattoni decided to stick with the man-to-man system, and moved Gentile across to the left to mark Bastrup. That, of course, left a hole on the right, which Marco Tardelli was supposed

Hamburg 1 Juventus 0, European Cup final, Olympiako, Athens, 25 May, 1983

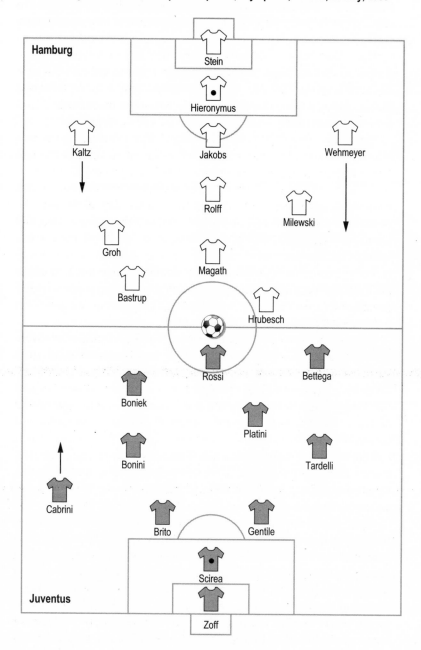

to drop back and fill. In practice, though, Tardelli was both neutered as an attacking force and failed adequately to cover the gap, through which Felix Magath ran to score the only goal of the game.

How then, were playmakers to be fitted into a system? France, under Michel Hidalgo, and blessed with a side almost as talented as Brazil's, shifted shape according to the opposition, with Michel Platini playing sometimes as a centre-forward, sometimes in the hole and sometimes more as a *regista*. He was an exceptional player and Hidalgo's use of him was probably unique, but what is significant is that he asked the playmaker to adjust to the demands of the system, rather than building the side around him. In that it should be said, he was helped by the quality of the players around him: Alain Giresse and Jean Tigana were world-class playmakers in their own right and Hidalgo's task was simply to find the right balance between creativity and structure; he could reasonably expect chances to arrive.

With Argentina in 1986, Carlos Bilardo had no such luxuries and, hardly surprisingly given he had grown up under Osvaldo Zubeldía, he adopted a more pragmatic approach. In any team, he said, seven outfield players were needed to defend, three to attack. It helps, of course, when one of those three is Diego Maradona. Presenting one of the most system-driven managers of all time with arguably the greatest individual player of all time could have been one of football's great jokes; as it turned out, it simply inspired Bilardo to the last great formational change, although he claims to have experimented with it for the first time at Estudiantes in 1982.

The trend through history had been to add defenders, from the two of the pyramid to the three of the W-M to the four of pretty much everything post-1958. Bilardo took one away. Or at least, he claims he did. If there were no wingers any more, he reasoned, why bother with full-backs? Since Nílton Santos, full-backs had been becoming more attacking, so why not re-designate them as midfielders and play them higher up the pitch? And so was born the 3-5-2. Played with midfielders in the wide positions, that was what it was; played with attacking full-backs – as for instance West Germany did in 1990 with Stefan Reuter and Andreas Brehme or Croatia in 1998 with Mario Stanić and Robert Jarni – it was a little more defensive; played with orthodox full-backs, it was, although managers habitually denied it, a 5-3-2. The pyramid had been inverted.

Bilardo retired from playing in 1970, and succeeded Zubeldía as manager of Estudiantes the following year. While coaching, he also helped run his father's furniture business and practised as a gynae-cologist, only retiring from medicine in 1976, when he moved to Deportivo Cali in Columbia. He then had spells with San Lorenzo, the Colombia national team and Estudiantes, before being appointed to replace César Luis Menotti after the 1982 World Cup. At that stage, although the two clearly represented fundamentally opposed philosophies of the game, their relationship was relatively cordial.

At least initially, Bilardo spoke glowingly of Argentina's performance in winning the World Cup in 1978. After he had succeeded Menotti, they met in the Arena Hotel in Seville in March 1983. Menotti told him there that Estudiantes had set back the development of Argentinian football by ten years, but they parted on good terms. Bilardo, though, then ignored his predecessor's advice and omitted Alberto Tarantini and Hugo Gatti from his squad for his first game, a friendly against Chile, to which Menotti reacted by writing a highly critical piece in *Clarín*. The détente over, they became implacable enemies.

While Menotti spun his visions of *la nuestra* revisited, Bilardo simply got on with the business of winning. 'I like being first,' he said. 'You have to think about being first. Because second is no good, being second is a failure... For me it's good that if you lose you should feel bad; if you want you can express it crying, shutting yourself away, feeling bad ... because you can't let people down, the fans, everyone, the person who signed you. I'd feel very bad if we lost a match and that night I'm seen out eating calmly in some place. I can't allow it. Football is played to win... Shows are for the cinema, for the theatre... Football is something else. Some people are very confused.'

In the early part of his reign, Bilardo himself was widely perceived as being confused. His start was disastrous, as Argentina won just three of his first fifteen games, a run that included a humbling exit from the Copa América and a defeat to China in a mini-tournament in India. By the time Argentina embarked on a tour of Europe in September 1984, Bilardo's position was under severe threat. 'We were at the airport about to leave, when José

María Muñoz, the commentator for Radio Rivadia, came up to me,'
Bilardo remembers. '"Don't worry," he said. "If we win these three
games, everything will be calm again."'

That, though, seemed far from likely, and when Bilardo read out
his team to face Switzerland in the first game of the tour, his
reputation had sunk so low that it was widely assumed he had
made a mistake. 'They told me I was wrong, that I'd named three
central defenders,' he said. 'But I told them I was not confused,
that they should not panic, that everything was well. We were
going to use three defenders, five midfielders and two forwards.
We had practised it for two years, and now I was going to put it into
practice in tough games.'

Switzerland were beaten 2-0, as were Belgium, and then West
Germany were beaten 3-1. 'The system worked out, and afterwards
we used it in the 1986 World Cup, where the entire world saw it,'
said Bilardo. 'When we went out to play like that, it took the world
by surprise because they didn't know the details of the system.'

Perhaps, like Alf Ramsey in 1966, Bilardo deliberately decided to
shield his new formation from spying eyes; perhaps the truth is
that his achievement was rooted less in any grand plan than in
strategic tinkering as and when necessary (as, to an extent, was
Ramsey's). Either way, Argentina did not go to Mexico on any great
cloud of optimism. They won their last warm-up game 7-2 against
Israel, but that was their first victory in seven games. As Maradona
put it in his autobiography, fans watched their opening game
against South Korea 'with their eyes half-closed', fearing the sort of
humiliation that was eventually inflicted upon them by Cameroon
four years later. 'They didn't even know who was playing,' he went
on. '[Daniel] Passarella had left; [Jorge Luis] Brown, [José Luis]
Cuciuffo and [Héctor] Enrique had come into the squad. We
trusted, we trusted, but we had not yet a single positive result to
build on... All Bilardo's meticulous plans, all his tactics, his
obsession with positions, suddenly it all fell into place.'

Cuciuffo and Enrique, though, did not play in that opening
game. Rather Argentina began with a 4-4-2, with Brown playing as
a *libero* behind Néstor Clausen, Oscar Ruggeri and Oscar Garré, and
Pedro Pasculli alongside Jorge Valdano up front. Argentina won
that comfortably enough, but against Italy, Bilardo decided
Cuciuffo would be better equipped to deal with the darting Italy
forward Giuseppe Galderisi. Ruggeri took care of Alessandro

Altobelli and so, as in *il gioco all' Italiana*, the left-back, Garré, was left free to push on and join the midfield. The same system was retained for the third group game against Bulgaria and the second-round victory over Uruguay.

It was only against England in the quarter-final that Bilardo settled upon the eleven that would go on to beat Belgium in the semi-final and West Germany in the final (Ramsey, of course, had only settled on his final eleven in a quarter-final against Argentina). In Brown he had a *libero* who seemed a throwback to the days of uncomplicated sweepers like Picchi. In front of him were the two markers, Ruggeri and Cuciuffo, who picked up the opposing centre-forwards. Sergio Batista operated in front of them as a ball-playing ball-winner, with Julio Olarticoechea – preferred to the more defensively minded Garré – and Ricardo Giusti wide. Jorge Burrachaga, as a link between midfield and attack, was a certainty, as, obviously, were Valdano and Maradona, which left just one position left to fill. Pasculli had scored the winner against Uruguay in the previous round, but Bilardo decided to drop him, deciding instead to pick Enrique 'You can't play against the English with a pure centre-forward,' he explained. 'They'd devour him, and the extra man in midfield will give Maradona more room.'

So Maradona played as a nominal second striker, but given the freedom to roam wherever he saw fit by the defensive platform behind him. His first goal, after fifty-one minutes, was an example of *viveza* at its worst; his second, four minutes later, quite breath-taking. Called upon to attack by the two-goal deficit, the England manager Bobby Robson threw on two wingers in John Barnes and Chris Waddle, and the defensive weaknesses of Bilardo's system were immediately exposed. Gary Lineker converted a Barnes cross to pull one back, and was a hair's breadth away from a repeat in the final seconds.

Would a side with wingers have overrun Argentina? Possibly. It could be argued that their central midfield three of Batista, Enrique and Burruchaga would have dominated possession, but they failed to cut out the supply to Barnes and Waddle even against a central midfield duo as lacking in ferocity as Glenn Hoddle and Steve Hodge. Carlos Tápia replaced the more attacking Burruchaga with fifteen minutes to go, but Barnes still ran riot.

Still, it hardly mattered. Belgium had no wide players of any note – who is to say they would have had the courage to play them even if they had? – and restricted their semi-final to a midfield battle, only to be beaten by more Maradona brilliance. In the final, Argentina met a West Germany side going through their own uneasy transition to a wing-back system. The acknowledgement of the possibilities of 3-5-2 seems to have happened all but simultaneously in Europe and South America, and although the outcome was similar, as with the move to 4-2-4, the processes of evolution were different.

After defeat in the 1966 World Cup final West German football had moved slowly towards the *libero* as practised by the Dutch, with Franz Beckenbauer, by 1974, established as an attacking sweeper in a 1-3-3-3. He had played in the role for Bayern Munich from the late sixties, encouraged by Zlatko Cajkovski, their Yugoslav coach, who had grown up in an environment that saw the value in having ball-playing central defenders. It is no coincidence that the first great Ajax *libero*, Velibor Vasović was produced by the same culture. Beckenbauer himself always insisted his attacking style resulted from him playing in midfield for West Germany, where Willi Schulz remained the *libero*, which meant he was less prone to the discomfort defenders commonly felt when advancing with the ball.

Whatever the origins, a 1-3-3-3 with man-marking and the libero as a true free man became the default in German football, and, with the minor modification of one of the forwards being withdrawn into a playmaking role, it was still essentially that system that Beckenbauer, by then their coach, had West Germany use in Mexico in 1986. In the quarter-final, for instance, when they beat the hosts on penalties, Ditmar Jakobs played as the sweeper with, from right to left, Andreas Brehme, Karl-Heinz Förster and Hans-Peter Briegel in front of him. Thomas Berthold, Lothar Matthäus and Norbert Eder made up the midfield, with Felix Magath as the playmaker behind Karl-Heinz Rummenigge and Klaus Allofs.

For the semi-final against France, though, which was won 2-0, West Germany also went with three central defenders, as Eder dropped in alongside Förster and Wolfgang Rolff came into midfield to perform a man-to-man marking job on Michel Platini. Beckenbauer instructed Förster to remain deep, and so, as the defender said, 'we ended up playing zonal marking almost by default'. It would be another decade before the debate was properly addressed in German football.

With Rolff standing down for the return of Berthold from suspension, the job of man-marking Maradona was given to Matthäus in the final. West Germany stuck with the 3-5-2 and Maradona was kept relatively quiet, but he also neutralised Matthäus, dragging him so deep that it was though West Germany had four central defenders. With two holders in front of the back line, that left them shorn of creativity and left Magath isolated, with the result that he was barely involved.

West Germany's narrowness – and their system didn't even allow the full-backs to push on – played into Argentina's hands. Brown headed them in front after Schumacher had flapped at a corner, and when Valdano calmly added a second eleven minutes into the second half, the game seemed won. Only then was Matthäus released from his marking duties, and only then did West Germany begin to play, exposing a weakness that had tormented Bilardo. Set-plays were supposed to be his speciality, but he was so anxious about his side's ability to defend them that, at 4 a.m. on the morning of the final, he burst into Ruggeri's room, pounced on him, and, with the defender disoriented and half-asleep, asked who he was marking at corners. 'Rummenigge,' came the instant reply, which Bilardo took as evidence that Ruggeri was sufficiently focused.

With sixteen minutes to go, though, and with Brown nursing a fractured shoulder, Rudi Völler glanced on a corner for Rummenigge to score. Eight minutes later, Berthold headed another corner back across goal and Völler levelled. Perhaps having done so, West Germany should have gone back into the negativity their system seemed to demand, but they did not. The momentum was with them and, at last, they left space in behind their defence. It took Maradona just three minutes to exploit it, laying a pass beyond Briegel for Burruchaga to run on and score the winner.

Looking back, their success seems almost freakish and, while the jibes they were a one-man team were unfair, the dangers of being quite so reliant on Maradona were seen as Argentina won only six of the thirty-one games they played between the end of that World Cup and the start of the next one. They went on, somehow, to reach the final. Bilardo did not win many games as

Argentina 3 West Germany 2, World Cup final, Azteca, Mexico City, 29 June 1986

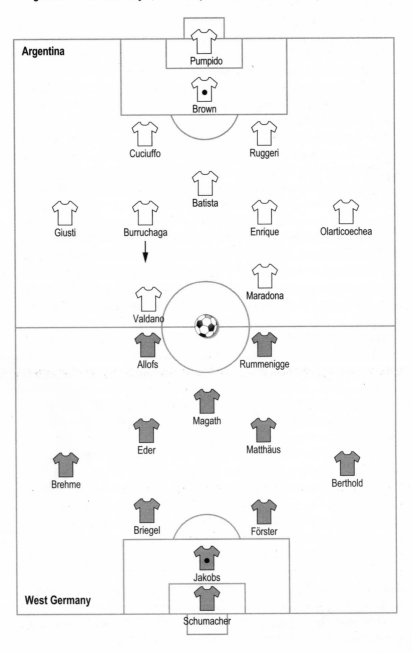

national coach, but he did have a habit of winning the ones that mattered. Moreover, his thinking came to seem axiomatic. By Italia '90, three at the back was a common sight.

The champions, West Germany, employed the formation, with Klaus Augenthaler, Guido Buchwald and either Berthold or Jürgen Kohler providing the foundations for a midfield trio of Matthäus plus two of Buchwald, Thomas Hässler, Uwe Bein, Pierre Littbarski and Olaf Thon, depending on circumstance. That was the beauty of the system – it allowed changes of tone to be made simply, without great wrenches of shape. Against Holland in the second round, for instance, Buchwald, usually a central defender, was used a midfielder to help break up the Dutch passing game.

For Brazil, it required only minor modification, one of the two holding players in their 4-2-2-2 becoming a third centre-back, although they never seemed to have much confidence in the formation and were generally uninspired, losing 1-0 to Argentina in the second round. More surprisingly, even England adopted the *libero*, almost as a last resort after they began the competition with a 1-1 draw against the Republic of Ireland so bad that the *Gazzetta della Sport* reported it under the headline 'No football, please, we're British.'

With Mark Wright as a sweeper, flanked by Terry Butcher and Des Walker, England felt able to deploy the attacking talents of Chris Waddle, David Platt and Paul Gascoigne in the same midfield. They may have been fortuitous at times, but the outcome was that, in a paradox that seemed to blind England fans to the wider truths of that tournament, they played with greater adventure than for years and reached a semi-final for the first time since 1966. There, they were good enough to match West Germany before losing on penalties.

Still, that was not a good World Cup. Goals were down to a record low of 2.21 per game; red cards up to a record high of sixteen. Even West Germany, clearly the best side there, managed just three goals in their final three games: two penalties and a deflected free-kick. Theirs was a team built predominantly on muscle, something the 3-5-2 seemed to encourage. Johan Cruyff despaired of it, later speaking of the replacement of the winger with the wing-back as the 'death of football'.

This was the result of the other facet of Bilardo's thinking coming into play: that the best place for a playmaker was perhaps not in the midfield, but as a second forward. His insistence on three players and seven runners may have been extreme, but the balance certainly tipped in that direction. Even Holland in 1988 ended up deploying Ruud Gullit, who would surely once have been a deeper-lying player, as a second striker behind Marco van Basten in a 4-4-1-1.

As players became fitter and systems more organised, defences became tighter. The idealism of the Brazilians faded, and the playmaking second striker morphed into a fifth midfielder. After the sterility of the 1990 World Cup, the low point came in the European Championship of 1992, a festival of dullness that yielded an average of just 2.13 goals per game. Even as Fifa desperately changed the rules to outlaw the backpass and the challenge from behind, football seemed to have embarked on an endless march away from the aesthetic. With the game so well analysed and understood, and defensive strategies so resolute, by the early nineties the great question facing football was whether beauty could be accommodated at all.

△▽△▽△▽△▽△▽

Chapter Fifteen

The English Pragmatism (2)

△▽As so often, progress began with defeat. Chris Lawler's goal in a 2-1 loss in the first leg in the Marakana had given Liverpool hope of overcoming Red Star Belgrade in the second leg and reaching the quarter-final of the 1973–74 European Cup, but at Anfield, Red Star, under the guidance of Miljan Miljanić, played a brilliant counter-attacking game and struck twice on the break through Vojin Lazarević and Slobodan Janković to complete a 4-2 aggregate win.

The following day, 5 November 1973, in a cramped, windowless room just off the corridor leading to the Anfield dressing room, six men set in motion the stylistic shift that led English clubs to dominate Europe in the late seventies and early eighties. The boot-room, as history would know it, was not an obvious place to plot a revolution. It was small and shabbily carpeted, hung on one side with hooks for players' boots and decorated with team photographs and topless calendars. Joe Fagan, the first-team coach under Bill Shankly, had begun the tradition of post-game discussions there, stocking the room with crates of beer supplied by the chairman of Guinness Exports, whose works team he had once run in nearby Runcorn. Initially he met only with Bob Paisley, in those days the team's physiotherapist, but gradually other members of the club's backroom staff began to drop in. 'You got a more wide-ranging discussion in the boot-room than the boardroom,' Paisley said. 'What went on was kept within those four walls. There was a certain mystique about the place.' Managers of opposing teams willing to offer information and opinions about players were invited, and even Elton John visited during his time as Watford chairman. When offered a drink,

Anfield legend has it, he asked for a pink gin; he was given a beer.

Gradually the boot-room grew in importance, becoming effectively a library where coaches could refer to books in which were logged details of training, tactics and matches. In *Winners and Losers: The Business Strategy of Football*, the economist Stefan Szymanski and the business consultant Tim Kuypers claimed Liverpool's success in the seventies and eighties was a result of their organisational structure, of which the boot-room was a key part. 'The boot-room,' they wrote, 'appears to have been some kind of database for the club, not merely of facts and figures, but a record of the club's spirit, its attitudes and its philosophy.'

On Bonfire Night 1973, though, the greater part of that success was still to come, and Liverpool seemed to have reached an impasse. Red Star, European Cup semi-finalists in 1970, were a useful side, of that there was no question, but the manner of their victory seemed to point to a more essential deficiency than the vagaries of form. So a meeting was convened, Shankly, Fagan and Paisley being joined in the boot-room by Ronnie Moran, the reserve team coach, by Tom Saunders, the head of youth development, and by the chief coach Reuben Bennett, a dour Scottish disciplinarian famed for his habit of telling injured players to rub away the pain with a wire-brush or a kipper.

They weren't crisis talks exactly, but the issues they discussed were fundamental: just why did Liverpool, imperious domestically, look so vulnerable in Europe? Despite the background of English underachievement, it is a mark of Shankly's perfectionism that a flaw was perceived at all. After all, Liverpool had won the Uefa Cup the previous season, beating Borussia Mönchengladbach 3-2 on aggregate in the final. In the years before that success, though, Liverpool had gone out of European competition to the likes of Ferencváros, Athletic Bilbao and Vitória Setúbal, none of them complete minnows, but none of them the cream of Europe, either. If the Uefa Cup triumph suggested Liverpool had found a solution, the defeat to Red Star emphatically disabused them.

'They are a good side,' Shankly said, 'even though our fans would not pay to watch the football the play.' The way they were prepared to hold possession and frustrate their opponents, though, taught Liverpool an important lesson. 'We realised it was no use winning the ball if you finished up on your backside,' said Paisley. 'The top Europeans showed us how to break out of defence effectively. The pace of their movement was dictated by their first pass. We had to learn how to be patient like that and think about the next two or three moves when we had the ball.'

The days of the old-fashioned stopper centre-half, the boot-room decided, were over: it was necessary to have defenders who could play. Larry Lloyd, exactly the kind of central defender they had declared extinct (although he would later enjoy an unlikely renaissance at Nottingham Forest), then ruptured a hamstring, and Phil Thompson, originally a midfielder, was pushed back to partner Emlyn Hughes at the heart of the defence. 'The Europeans showed that building from the back is the only way to play,' Shankly explained. 'It started in Europe and we adapted it into our game at Liverpool where our system had always been a collective one. But when Phil Thompson came in to partner Hughes it became more fluid and perhaps not as easy to identify. This set the pattern which was followed by Thompson and [Alan] Hansen in later years.

'We realised at Liverpool that you can't score a goal every time you get the ball. And we learned this from Europe, from the Latin people. When they play the ball from the back they play in little groups. The pattern of the opposition changes as they change. This leaves room for players like Ray Kennedy and Terry McDermott, who both played for Liverpool after I left, to sneak in for the final pass. So it's cat and mouse for a while waiting for the opening to appear before the final ball is let loose. It's simple and it's effective... It's also taken the spectators time to adjust to it.'

Shankly was no great tactician – he tended to leave that side of the game to Paisley, and was so bored when he did attend a week-long coaching course at Lilleshall that he left on the Tuesday – but from the moment of his arrival at Liverpool, he had a clear sense of the general style his wished to play. 'Shankly,' said a piece in the *Liverpool Echo* from December 1959, 'is a disciple of the game as it is played by the continentals. The man out of possession, he believes, is just as important as the man with the ball at his feet. Continental football is not the lazy man's way of playing soccer. Shankly will aim at incisive forward moves by which continentals streak through a defence when it is "closed up" by British standards. He will make his players learn to kill a ball and move it all in the same action... he will make them practise complete mastery of the ball.'

That might have been overstating it, but Shankly certainly had a belief in the value of control almost as profound as Jimmy Hogan's. At the Melwood training ground, he set up four boards to form a square. A player would stand in the middle, and would be called upon either to strike first time or to trap balls flung at him from the four corners.

'Above all,' Shankly said, 'the main aim is that everyone can control a ball and do the basic things in football. It's control and pass ... control and pass ... all the time. At the back you're looking for someone who can control the ball instantly and give a forward pass. It gives them more space and time to breathe. If you delay, the opposition have all run back behind the ball. It's a very simplified affair and, of course, very economical.

'At Liverpool we don't have anyone running into no man's land, running from their own half with the ball into the opposition half. That's not encouraged at all. That's nonsense. If you get a ball in the Liverpool team you want options, you want choices ... you want at least two people to pass to, maybe three, maybe more... Get the ball, give an early pass, then it goes from me to someone else and it switches around again. You might not be getting very far, but the pattern of the opposition is changing. Finally, somebody will sneak in.'

The side that won the championship in 1964 played an orthodox W-M, but Shankly was prepared to make changes. The following season, Liverpool faced Anderlecht in the second round of the European Cup, shortly after England had played a friendly against a Belgium side featuring seven Anderlecht players. Shankly was at Wembley to see the game, and recognised the attacking threat posed by the likes of Paul van Himst and Jef Jurion. It was his decision to switch to red shorts for the game – the first time Liverpool had worn all red – that caught most of the attention, but just as significant was his ploy of withdrawing an inside-forward to use Tommy Smith as an auxiliary central defender; an early example of an English club side using four at the back.

That suggested a flexibility, an awareness that the English way wasn't the only way, but Paisley admitted, 'Our approach was a bit frantic. We treated every match like a war. The strength of British football lay in our challenge for the ball, but the continentals took that away from us by learning how to intercept.' It was that fault that the Bonfire Night revolution of 1973 corrected, and after Paisley had replaced Shankly in 1974, Liverpool would come to be

Liverpool 3 Borussia Mönchengladbach 1, Olimpico, Roma, 25 May, 1977

defined by their patient passing approach. It took them to four European Cups between 1977 and 1984, and it was with a similar approach that Nottingham Forest under Brian Clough lifted their two European Cups.

While they espoused a possession-based passing game, there was at the same time a strand of English football that went in the opposite direction, and favoured a high-octane style readily dismissed as kick-and-rush. It was the basis to the rise of Watford and Wimbledon, small clubs who learned to punch above their weight, but, damagingly, it became orthodoxy at the Football Association. When Charles Hughes became technical director of the FA, English football was placed into the hands of a fundamentalist, a man who, Brian Glanville claims, 'poisoned the wells of English football'.

Hughes still has plenty of apologists, but even if Glanville's assessment is correct, the achievements of Watford and Wimbledon should not be decried – or at least, not on the grounds of directness alone. In English football, the seventies is remembered as the age of the mavericks, of the likes of Alan Hudson, Frank Worthington and Stan Bowles, individuals who did not fit into the increasingly systematised schema that had become the vogue since Ramsey's success in the World Cup. The historically more significant feature of the decade, though, was the introduction of pressing.

It came from a surprising source: a young manager who began his career with Lincoln City, and then brought, given the resources available to him, staggering success to Watford: Graham Taylor. England's failure to qualify for the World Cup in 1994 and the vilification that followed has rather sullied his reputation, but in the late seventies he was the most radical coach in the country. There were those who dismissed him as a long-ball merchant, but as he, Stan Cullis and a host of managers stretching back to Herbert Chapman have pointed out, it is simply impossible for a team to be successful if all they are doing is aimlessly booting the ball forwards. 'When,' as Taylor asked, 'does a long pass become a long ball?'

Many coaches have prospered after less than stellar playing careers – indeed, for the truly revolutionary, it appears almost a prerequisite – but Taylor seems to have known almost from the start that his future lay in the coaching rather than the playing side of the game. 'The intention had been to stay on at school, do A-levels and become a teacher,' he said. 'I left after a year of sixth-form to become a footballer, but I was still interested enough in my education to do a coaching badge, so I was qualified by the time I was twenty-one. I was always reading and looking for ideas.' One of the ideas he seized upon was pressing, the possibilities of which became clear to him after he had read a series of articles about Viktor Maslov in the Football Association's in-house coaching magazine.

Taylor spent four years at Grimsby Town, before moving on to Lincoln City. He became a fully-qualified FA coach at twenty-seven – the youngest man to do so – and, after a hip injury had curtailed his playing career, was twenty-eight when he took over as manager in 1972. Four years later, Taylor led Lincoln to the Fourth Division title, setting new records for most points, most wins and fewest defeats as he did so.

It was after Elton John appointed him as manager of Watford in 1977, though, that the real breakthrough came. Taylor was offered a five-year contract, but before agreeing to it, he asked his chairman what he was expected to achieve in that time. 'Watford were in the Fourth Division,' Taylor said, 'and they'd only spent three years in their history in the second flight, so I thought he'd say maybe he wanted Second Division football. He said he wanted us playing in Europe. Here was a singer at the top of his career offering me a five-year contract and asking me to get Watford into Europe – and five years later we were.'

Even by the volatile standards of the seventies, Watford's rise was extraordinary. They were promoted in 1978, again in 1979 and then again in 1982. The following season they finished second in the First Division, and the year after that, lost in the FA Cup final. Taylor admits the way his side played had its limitations, but makes no apology for it. 'Our style was based on pressing the ball wherever it was,' he explained. 'So even if the opposition right-back had the ball deep in his own half, we still pressed him. We played high-tempo football, which meant we had to be extremely fit. When the score's 0-0 and there are three or four minutes to go, what do players do? They get the ball forwards. My view is that players then are going looking for the ball. But if they can do that in the last few minutes, why can't they do that from the start? With the very fit side we had, that's what we tried to do. We were always attacking; I knew we couldn't defend our way into Europe.'

High-scoring games became the norm: in successive seasons Watford drew 4-4 at home to Everton and beat them 5-4. They twice won 5-3 against Notts County, and beat Sunderland 8-0. In that 1982–83 season they lost 6-1 at Norwich and went down 7-3 in the League Cup to Nottingham Forest. In the last three games of 1984–85, they beat Tottenham and Manchester United 5-1, then lost 4-3 at Liverpool. It was mad, harum-scarum stuff but, broadly speaking, it worked. Between 1982–83 and 1986–87, after which Taylor left for Aston Villa, Watford never finished lower than twelfth, a remarkable achievement for a club of their stature.

The shape mattered less than the method. Although 4-4-2 was the default, with full-backs such as Wilf Rostron and David Bardsley pushing on, and with *bone fide* wingers like Nigel Callaghan and John Barnes playing high up the pitch, the formation could come to resemble the 4-2-4 of the 1958 Brazilians, and there were times in the 1982–83 season when they played a 3-4-3. 'Because we kept going forwards, the opposition kept going back,' Taylor said. 'The wide midfielders either had to follow them and get pinned back, or leave them. We kept on posing questions. As you go higher, you keep expecting teams to work out how to cope, but often they didn't.'

Aesthetes were appalled, but Taylor insists much of the outrage was down to ignorance and snobbery. 'A lot of people who complained about long balls just looked at the club and the player,' he said. 'If Glenn Hoddle played one it was a long pass, but if Ian Bolton did it, it was a long ball because he played for Watford and was a centre-back who sometimes played in midfield who nobody had heard of. Hoddle was a much better player, but for accuracy in his long passing I'd take Bolton every time.'

For the purist, things got even worse. Wimbledon's apologists speak of their rise as a fairytale, but it was one noticeably lacking in magic. Their story, Stephen Crabtree wrote in *The Dons – The Amazing Journey* 'would seem far-fetched if it appeared in the pages of *Roy of the Rovers*... achieved despite little financial backing, pathetic support, a non-league standard ground and unknown players...' Perhaps at first it was, as they were elected to the league in 1977, and then, under Dario Gradi, who would become renowned for the passing football of his Crewe sides, won promotion to the Third Division. They were promptly relegated,

Everton 2 Watford 0, FA Cup final, Wembley, London, 19 May 1984

Gradi left for Crystal Palace in February 1981, and then, under their new manager Dave Bassett, they were promoted again. And immediately relegated. That next season in the Fourth Division, though, proved a watershed. They started promisingly, but as results fell away in the November, Bassett changed his approach. 'We began the season using a sweeper at the back which worked well,' Bassett said that February, 'but now we've changed to get the ball up to the front very fast. It suits the team.'

Of claims that it was awful to watch, Bassett was dismissive. 'It depends on what you mean by attractive,' he said. 'There is more goalmouth incident for our supporters to enjoy in our games than lots of other teams I've seen this season. Call it what you like. We're here to win games and win promotion.'

'Goalmouth incident', it turns out, is the last resort of coaches seeking to excuse mechanically unappealing football. If it had just been about uncomplicated forward passing, Wimbledon would have been forgiven, but right from the start, there was an ugly element to their play. The week after a 3-1 away win at Stockport County, the Stockport programme was moved to ask 'why they had to resort to some untidy tackling and time-wasting tactics... There seems to be little chance that anyone will stop them from achieving their objective, which appears to be promotion at all costs.'

Successful as they were, though, the crowds stayed away. 'We have tried everything by serving up good football, but the apathy of Wimbledon and the surrounding area is incredible,' said Bassett. But of course they hadn't served up good football; they'd served up winning football, and the two are not necessarily the same thing. Perhaps his despair was self-justificatory: if fans weren't going to turn up anyway, then why not play grim, flairless anti-football? There may have been goals, but this was emotionally empty football stripped of beauty.

It was awful to watch, but Wimbledon soared through the divisions, brushing aside bemused opponents as they did so. 'It's like schoolboys all chasing after the ball all at the same time,' said the Grimsby Town goalkeeper Nigel Batch after a 1-1 draw at Plough Lane in 1984. It was just like Watford all over again, only worse, as John Vinicombe of the *Brighton Evening Argus* made clear, describing them 'a poor man's Watford when four front men adopt a cavalry charge formation in pursuit of high passes slung from behind.'

They finished sixth in the First Division in 1987, and then, after Bobby Gould had replaced Dave Bassett, won the FA Cup the following year. 'Wimbledon don't play,' moaned the Coventry City manager George Curtis. 'As soon as they get it they just hit it.' That is perhaps a touch unfair, for they were at least hitting balls towards John Fashanu, a brash and ungainly but effective target man, while Dennis Wise, for all his faults, had talent, but they won few admirers. They revelled in their unfashionability, making much of their initiation rites – which consisted largely of destroying suits – and delighting in the brute physicality of their play. A key element in the victory over Liverpool at Wembley in 1988, most of their players claimed, was Vinnie Jones's crunching foul on Steve McMahon in the first minute: after that, Liverpool were intimidated.

Like all bristling outsiders, Wimbledon's apologists put their unpopularity down to the 'snootiness' – Crabtree uses the word repeatedly – of the establishment, but the attendance figures told their own story. This was football nobody wanted to watch. Budget perhaps dictated their style, but did not excuse the thuggery that lay just below the surface. This wasn't just pragmatic; it was nihilistic.

Taylor, by contrast, was simply being practical. He accepted his system had its limitations, and admits that at every stage he expected his side to be found out. When he got to Aston Villa, and had a viable budget, although his style remained direct, there was a refinement to it. Tony Daley may have got into the Wimbledon side of the time, but it is hard to imagine a player as cultured as Gordon Cowans would have done.

It wasn't until his first season of European competition with Watford that Taylor began to find opponents coming up with the sort of solutions to his direct style that he had expected to encounter far earlier. 'We were playing sides who were prepared to sit deep, play short passes, hold the ball and pick us off, who had fans who weren't demanding they thump the ball forward,' he explained. They overturned a 3-1 first-leg deficit with a 3-0 second-leg victory over Kaiserslautern at Vicarage Road in the first round of the Uefa Cup, and edged by Levski Sofia in the second round, but were comprehensively outplayed by Sparta Prague in the third round, losing 7-2 on aggregate. 'It was men against boys,' Taylor said. 'When you gave the ball away, they didn't give it back to you.'

And there, precisely, is the problem with a direct style based on pressing. It's all very well until you come up against a team good enough technically to be able to keep possession even when under pressure. And, as Taylor points out, when climatic conditions make it impossible to maintain a high tempo and render constant pressing impossible, its deficiencies become even more evident. That, of course, goes some way to explaining England's persistent underachievement in major tournaments, which are almost invariably staged in conditions far hotter than English players are used to at home.

Taylor, in his quest to broaden his knowledge, had spoken at length to both Stan Cullis and his captain in the Wolves side of the fifties, Billy Wright. Their influence on his thinking is clear and undisputed, but Taylor also came – inaccurately – to be associated with Charles Hughes. He rejects any notion that he was influenced by Hughes, and suggests that if anything the influence, stemming from his brief time as England Under-18 coach while Hughes was director of youth coaching, was the other way round. And this is where the interconnections between Taylor, Hughes and Charles Reep get complicated.

Hughes's first two books, *Football: Tactics and Teamwork*, published 1973, and *Soccer Tactics and Skills*, published 1980, are both practical manuals, giving guidance, for instance, on how to deal with near-post corners or how close a player should get to an opponent he is closing down. They are general works with similar content, although the second is slightly more targeted at the individual. Neither evangelises a particular philosophy of play: they are perhaps a touch over-pragmatic, but they are largely unobjectionable.

And then, in 1981 – or possibly 1982 – Taylor set up a meeting between Hughes and Reep at his house because, if a letter Reep wrote to the Norwegian coach Egil Olsen in 1993 is to be believed, Hughes wanted his secretary Mandy Primus trained in his shorthand techniques. Reep was initially happy to help, but he became suspicious when Hughes published an article in which he hinted that he and Reep worked together. Worse, Reep claimed in that letter – although it is hard to be sure of the veracity of this claim – that Hughes also set out some of the secrets of Watford's style of play, which neither Reep nor Watford wanted making public.

There does appear to be evidence of Reep's influence in a series of lectures Hughes gave in 1984. In one of them, Hughes stated that, 'Over the past two years, the Football Association has been striving to bring the Coaching Scheme into better, more objective and hopefully, more successful lines. To achieve these aims and objectives, the FA has been quite heavily involved in a study of match performance analysis.'

That last phrase – 'match performance analysis' – was a term Reep had used since the fifties, and one that does not appear in either of Hughes's first two books. It is an oddly fussy term – characteristic of Reep – using three words where two would have done, and it seems unlikely Hughes would have happened upon it without having heard of or read Reep. Reep was certainly angered; Hughes turned to the more obvious phrase he could have adopted in the first place, and dropped the word 'performance'.

Reep's feathers were ruffled further when Richard Bate, chief coach at Notts County, presented what was essentially a review of Reep's theories at the Science and Football forum in Liverpool in 1987, but credited Hughes for his help.

In his introduction to *The Winning Formula*, Hughes is keen to stress that he has come to his conclusions independently. 'My experience of match analysis,' he wrote, 'began in January 1964 when I joined the staff of the Football Association... At the FA headquarters at Lancaster Gate was a library of 16mm films of FA Cup finals and international matches. Between 1964 and 1967 I watched all these matches and extracted all the goals. These goals were then analysed more closely to establish what were the key factors in scoring goals and winning matches.

'The results of this analysis were used in the playing method of all the international teams I managed between 1964 and 1974 – seventy-seven matches in all. The essence of this work was published in 1973 in a book entitled *Tactics and Teamwork* and a series of eleven films under the same title.'

Well, maybe the results were, but the work is light on statistics and preaches no unified philosophy. It is hard to be sure either way, but it is easy to see why Reep was suspicious. As the Norwegian academic Øyvind Larson points out, 'The style of play recommended immediately changed from being general in nature to being penetration-based in particular.' Hughes had been an ordinary pragmatic coach; he became, to use the term applied by

Howard Wilkinson, his successor as FA technical director, 'a zealot'. There were differences in terminology and weighting (Hughes specified five passes or fewer rather than three), but Reep claimed in his letter to Olsen that that was because Hughes was unaware of some of the calculations he was performing.

'The work of analysing football matches has continued ever since,' Hughes went on. 'In the early part of 1982 [Reep says 1981; Taylor can't remember] I had the pleasure of meeting a wonderful man named Charles Reep, who had been analysing football matches for thirty years, successfully advising a number of Football League clubs.'

Hughes claims that he then got Primus to begin analysing games, using her shorthand skills. 'The method of analysis itself, which I devised around twenty-five years ago, is actually different from Charles Reep's... Although Charles Reep and I had come by our strategic philosophy by different routes, there was no disagreement on the major conclusion.'

There was significant disagreement between the three personalities involved though: Taylor denied Hughes, who denied Reep, who blamed Hughes. To both Reep and Taylor, Hughes is somebody who exploited their ideas for his own ends, gaining in reputation and selling his books and videos. Perhaps that is a familiar tale of committee-room back-biting, and of the impossibility of copywriting ideas, but it meant that by the time Taylor was appointed England manager in 1990, his relationship with Hughes was unworkable. It hardly helped either that Hughes was furious at having lost out to Graham Kelly in the battle to succeed Ted Croker as chief executive of the FA in 1989.

Reep had written to Taylor on 4 August 1980 – by which time he was seventy-five – explaining his theory that 'all goals come at random within a framework of probability'. They met in Exeter later that month for two hours, after which, Reep wrote in a piece in the Scottish football magazine *The Punter*, 'any time Graham Taylor wanted to ring me to get further details regarding aspects of the style of play, I would be willing to talk for as long as he wished. We did in fact have several very long indoctrination talks, during which a lot of ground was covered without the need to meet each other again.'

Reep did not see Watford play that season, but, he says, he met Taylor again on 11 March 1981 at Reep's house in Plymouth.

Receiving reports from Richard Pollard, a Watford fan who had co-authored an early article with him, Reep concluded that, for Watford, 'only one goal in five comes from passing moves containing more than three received passes.' In other words, Watford's goals fitted the pattern Reep had been demonstrating for thirty years – 80 percent of goals come from moves of three passes of fewer (which, of course, is still less than the 91.5 percent of moves that, he showed, consist of three passes or fewer).

One of Reep's other constants also remained true: that it took roughly nine shots to produce a goal. Convinced of this, he maintained records of how many goals Watford and their (combined) opponents were 'in credit' or 'overdrawn' (so if a team had had ninety shots he would expect them to have scored ten goals; if they only managed eight, they were two in credit; if they had had scored twelve, they were two overdrawn). In the first leg of a second round League Cup tie at Southampton, Watford lost 4-0. Reep, noticing ahead of the return leg that Watford were 2.5 goals 'in credit' while combined opponents were 4 goals 'overdrawn', wrote to Taylor, advising him that this could be evened out in one game, and that Watford should therefore pursue an attacking approach.

This, of course, is absurd. Taylor, presumably, would have worked out for himself that to overhaul a four-goal deficit, his side needed to attack. They did, led 5-1 after ninety minutes, and added two more in extra-time. 'I was enchanted to think,' Reep wrote, 'that the first time one of my teams had attempted to exploit the calculated situation regarding "goals in credit" and "overdrawn", it had succeeded brilliantly well – always with the admission, of course, that random chance had done us a huge favour. And as might be expected, random chance penalised Watford by awarding us a 1-2 defeat in the next game.'

And so the lack of mathematical basis to Reep's research is betrayed. 'Random Chance' is not a deity handing out or denying goals to level up some cosmic balance. It is just random. Toss a coin a hundred times and if the first ninety-nine land heads, the odds of the hundredth landing tails are still one in two. If there really is – and there isn't – a one in nine chance of scoring with any shot regardless of circumstance, it is still one in nine whether a forward has scored with his last ten or missed with his last hundred. That assumes the coin is unbiased, of course. If a coin keeps on landing heads, it is probably because it is weighted; if a striker keeps on missing chances, it's probably because he's not very good.

Nonetheless, ahead of the 1981–82 season, Taylor decided to employ one of Reep's trainees – an archaeology graduate from the University of Lancaster called Simon Hartley, who had become intrigued by Reep's ideas after seeing him taking notes one day at Plymouth. Reep did not speak to Taylor by telephone that season, but he did write him three letters, one of which dealt with the lack of goals Watford were scoring from the right wing (John Barnes scored thirteen from the left) and hinted at, but did not fully reveal, his plan for how wingers should play. As Watford were promoted that season, 93.4 percent of their goals came from moves of three passes or fewer. Reep notes this was 'superb', although if the number of moves consisting of three or fewer passes remained constant at 91.5 percent, of course, it is only just higher than would be expected if the number of passes in a move made no difference. Given Watford were a self-consciously direct side, it is probable that for them a greater proportion of moves consisted of three passes or fewer: even there, in other words, there is still little evidence for the greater efficacy of direct football.

Reep claims he and Hartley were both paid a £6,000 bonus, but that he then fell out with Taylor over his fee for the following season. Taylor's memory is that they fell out over an obscure statistical point. Reep was obsessed by 'reachers' – that is, balls that landed in the final third. Watford averaged 156 a game, although against Chelsea on 6 February 1982, a game they won 1-0, they achieved a record of 202 (this was later taken by John Beck's Cambridge United, with 219). Stan Cullis's Wolves side had managed around 180 a game, and Reep urged Taylor to try to raise Watford's level to match that. Taylor pointed out that his side's main strength was that they regularly won the ball back in the final third, something that did not count as a reacher under Reep's system, and suggested the figures should reflect that. Reep refused to change and, although Hartley stayed on for another season, his personal association with Watford came to an end. 'With Reep,' said Taylor, 'it was all or nothing. There was no room for compromise.'

Reep may not have liked him, but it was Hughes, as director of education and coaching at the FA between 1983 and 1994, who ensured his principles – or at least Hughes's version of them he set out in *The Winning Formula* – became enshrined at the highest level.

That book, in a link-up beyond the dreams of satirists, was sponsored by British Aerospace. 'The strategy of direct play,' Hughes asserts in his introduction, 'is far preferable to that of possession football. The facts are irrefutable and the evidence overwhelming.' Some might suggest that the record of an England team largely shaped by that philosophy is in itself a refutation, but then footballers are fallible: statistics are not.

Noting that the average number of goals per game in World Cup matches fell from 5.4 per game in 1954 to 2.5 per game in 1986, Hughes passes almost immediately to the conclusion that 'football is not as good as it was'. That a man whose authority came from the supposed application of reason and logic should be allowed to get away with such a leap is staggering. Discerning the quality of football is necessarily subjective and, anyway, there are bad 4-3 thrillers (excitement and quality are not synonyms) just as there are superb goalless draws. If goals alone were a mark of excellence, there would be thousands queuing to watch primary-school football.

The reason for the decline in goals scored, Hughes goes on, 'lies not in new efficient defensive strategies so much as a misguided attacking strategy, that of possession football.' Now, certainly, as Chapman argued and as a glance at the statistics for any given weekend of Premiership football will show, there is no necessary correlation between domination of possession and winning games, but neither does that mean that possession is a bad thing. Yet Hughes, deploying that word 'overwhelming' again, argues that 'the fact is that the longer a team takes to build an attack when it has possession of the ball ... the more time the defending team has to recover, regroup and reorganise.'

In *The Winning Formula*, Hughes uses the evidence of 109 matches between 1966 and 1986 in which 202 goals were scored. That, it might be noted, is not a huge sample, particularly not for somebody basing on it the claim that 'world soccer has been moving in the wrong strategic direction for the better part of thirty years'. It is also tempting to ponder the significance of the fact that while Hughes rails against a World Cup that produced 2.5 goals per game, the matches in his sample produced only 1.85. But still, the results are intriguing, and they have, presumably to head off those – like Taylor – who argue that direct football is ineffective at the very highest level, been filtered to include only successful sides: Liverpool, the England Under-16 and Under-21 teams, and World Cup or European Championship matches involving Argentina, Brazil, England, Holland, Italy and West Germany.

Of those 202 goals, fifty-three came from moves of no received passes, twenty-nine from one pass, thirty-five from two passes and twenty-six from three passes. In total, 87 percent of the goals came from moves of five passes or fewer, while fewer than 3 percent came from moves of ten or more passes (if Reep's statistic that 91.5 percent of all moves consist of three passes or fewer is correct, of course, that is still no endorsement of direct football). Then there is the issue of how many of those goals scored from three passes or fewer are the result of breakdowns brought about by longer moves. Hughes anticipates the question and presents his figures with a misplaced sense of triumph. Of nineteen no-pass goals (that is, penalties, free-kicks struck directly into the net, or shots fired in from a rebound off the goalkeeper or after a tackle or misplaced pass by the defending team) analysed by Hughes from sixteen England international matches, only twelve resulted from moves of three passes or fewer – 63 percent: far fewer than Reep's benchmark of 91.5. The question then becomes not whether Hughes is right or wrong, but how he got away with it for so long.

Perhaps not surprisingly, Brazil were the side most likely to score after a long string of passes, 32 percent of their goals coming from moves of six passes or more, with West Germany next on 25 percent (given, at the time, they had won between them six of the thirteen World Cups to have been played, that might be taken as an argument in favour of possession football). Almost unbelievably, none of the ten Dutch goals under consideration came from moves of six passes or more. And that's when the alarm bells really start to ring: why are there only ten Dutch goals under consideration? They scored fifteen in the 1974 World Cup finals alone. This is not only a small sample, but it is a selective one ('we have extracted 109 games from all those analysed'), and nowhere in *The Winning Formula* is that selection process explained.

Even assuming there is nothing sinister in that, Hughes is, at the very least, guilty of identifying a symptom and not a cause. 'The first objective,' he states in his conclusion, 'is to get into the attacking third of the field more often than the opponents do, and the final objective is to achieve a minimum of ten shots on target every game... If the strategies we have proposed are adopted and the tactical objectives are achieved, the chances of winning are extremely good – over 85 percent. The chances of not losing are even better. We have *never* recorded a match in which a team achieved ten shots on target and lost.' Yes, but are the shots really the reason for that? Or are they simply a natural result of one team dominating? Do teams win games because they're having shots, or do they have shots because they're winning games?

Where Hughes does have a point is in his advocation of pressing. Chapman and Helenio Herrera had great success by getting their teams to sit deep, but in modern football pressing is almost universal. 'If a team can increase the number of times they regain possession in the attacking third,' Hughes says, 'they will score more goals.' His statistics show that 52 percent of goals were scored when possession was gained in the attacking third, as opposed to 18 percent in the defensive third, and that moves begun when possession is regained in the attacking third are seven times more likely to produce goals than when possession is regained in the defensive third. Now those figures are skewed, clearly, by occasions when moves break down in the attacking third and the loose ball breaks for the attacking side, but they are a striking vindication of pressing nonetheless. Pressing, of course, has the added advantage of smothering an opposing attack almost before it has begun. This is the basis of Taylor's disagreement with Reep. Pressing is an action that can help a team win a game; getting the ball into dangerous areas is something that happens as a result of those actions.

Hughes goes on to argue that a team should shoot whenever it gets the opportunity, noting that 'even at the highest level, more than half of all shots miss the target, so players should never shy away from shooting for fear of missing the target'. Should a player really shoot even if a team-mate is in a markedly better position? Should he always shoot from 20 yards? From 30? From 40? Hughes argues that even mishit shots can create scoring opportunities, which is true, but why turn the situation into a lottery if a well-placed pass would significantly increase the chances of the initial shot, when taken, being a telling one? It is as though there is a distrust of technique, a fear that by adding an extra element into the move, the chances of it going wrong are increased to a level that makes relying on a lucky bounce or deflection preferable. Allen Wade, the technical director of the FA from 1963 to 1983, was no aesthete, but he was horrified by his successor's dogma. 'This slam-bang-wallop stuff will be the death of football,' he said. 'Football in which players are controlled by off-pitch Svengalis, backed up by batteries of statisticians and analysts, will never hold the magical appeal of what Pelé called the beautiful game.'

There is, perhaps, a nod here back to the days of the head-down charging of the Victorians: where Italian paranoia led to *catenaccio* and a faith in strategy over ability, English insecurity led to a style that similarly distrusted ability, favouring instead a thoughtless physicality – keep battling, keep running, keep trying. As the German journalist Raphael Honigstein put it sardonically in the title of his work on English football, '*Harder, Better, Faster, Stronger*'. But not more skilful.

Although Hughes advocates increasing shooting practice to improve accuracy – and, supposedly, demonstrates his success in that area with England Under-16s, although his sample includes only four matches – this surely is just the kind of argument that had so appalled Jimmy Hogan almost a century earlier at Fulham: buy enough tickets and you'll win the raffle eventually.

Quite aside from that there is a baffling lack of subtlety to Hughes's work. He claims that by applying his 'formula' – which arguably just comes down to being better than the opposition anyway – a side has a greater than 85 percent chance of winning. The question then is whether there is a pattern to the other 15 percent. What Hughes's statistics do not show is the possibility Taylor accepts, the possibility that feels intuitively true, that direct football can take a team only so far, that there comes a certain level of opposition capable of keeping the ball, capable of controlling possession, against which it is rendered ineffective. Brian Clough was typically unequivocal. 'I want to establish without any shadow of a doubt that Charles Hughes is totally wrong in his approach to football,' he said. 'He believes that footballs should come down with icicles on them.'

That is an exaggeration, but the flaws were obvious enough. Chapman's direct approach worked because he lured teams out and encouraged them to leave space behind them that his team then exploited. Taylor's Watford, with their high-tempo pressing game, were vulnerable to just that kind of attack. Hughes's formula makes no distinction as to the style played against. Given Taylor's direct approach foundered against a Sparta Prague side adept at retaining possessing and launching astute counter-attacks, wouldn't Hughes's have too? Organisation and energy, Taylor found, will carry a team so far, but only so far.

The irony is that while Taylor was well aware of the defects of the method, it was he who was left to reap the pitiful harvest after Hughes had implemented Reep's principles as FA policy. Yes, there were players missing through injury, but still, have England ever sent out a weaker team in a major championship than that which lost 2-1 to Sweden in the final group game of Euro '92: Woods; Batty, Keown, Walker, Pearce; Daley, Webb, Palmer, Sinton; Platt; Lineker? To rub salt into the wound, when England then failed to qualify for the 1994 World Cup, they were knocked out by Norway, a side practising the Reepian model taken to its extreme.

△▽

The links between Britain and the Scandinavian game had always been strong. Football was introduced to Sweden through the usual route of British sailors, with a little help from Anglophile Danes. When the Swedish Football Federation (SvFF) decided to appoint their first professional coach after the Second World War, they sought advice from the FA, and appointed George Raynor, who had been reserve team coach at Aldershot. Under his guidance, and advantaged by their wartime neutrality, Sweden won gold at the 1948 London Olympics, finished third at the 1950 World Cup and then reached the final against in 1958. There, they played a typical W-M with man-marking, something that, largely because of the amateur ethos of the SvFF, did not change until the late sixties.

Professionalism was finally sanctioned in 1967, and, in the aftermath of Sweden's failure to qualify for the 1970 World Cup, Lars Arnesson, a leading coaching instructor, was appointed to work alongside the national manager, Georg Åby-Ericson. Arnesson envisaged a unified playing style across Swedish football, and decided it should feature a German-style *libero*. That seemed to be vindicated at the 1974 World Cup, as Sweden finished third in their second-phase group, effectively fifth in the tournament. Although there had not been sufficient time for his idea of uniformity across all levels of coaching to have taken effect, that success did prove that Sweden could be internationally competitive with the system.

Almost immediately, though, a counter-movement sprang up as

Eric Persson, an ageing autocrat who had been chairman-coach of Malmö FF, decided to stand down to allow greater specialisation of management roles at the club. A high-profile banker, Hans Cavalli-Björkman, was appointed as chairman, while for a manager, feeling local coaches were overly conservative, the club turned to a twenty-seven-year-old Englishman called Bobby Houghton.

Houghton had played at Brighton and Fulham, but decided early to become a coach. He came through Wade's training course at the FA with top marks, and, in 1971–72, was appointed player-manager at Maidstone United. There he signed as player-coach a former school-mate, Roy Hodgson, who had also shown promise on Wade's coaching courses.

Wade was a modernising force, who argued repeatedly against coaching drills that were not directly related to match-situations. His main concern was less individual skills than shape and the distribution of players on the pitch. It was those ideas Houghton instituted at Malmö. When, two years later, he installed Hodgson at Halmstads BK, a division was created between their modern English school and those who favoured the *libero*. Houghton and Hodgson employed a zonal defence, pressed hard and maintained a high offside line. They counter-attacked, not in the way of the Dutch or Dynamo Kyiv, but with long passes played in behind the opposition defence. According to the Swedish academic Tomas Peterson, 'they threaded together a number of principles, which could be used in a series of combinations and compositions, and moulded them into an organic totality – an indivisible project about how to play football. Every moment of the match was theorised, and placed as an object-lesson for training-teaching, and was looked at in a totality.'

That, according to Arnesson, 'stifles initiative, and turns players into robots', and, as critics dismissed the English style as 'dehumanising', the debate about the relative merits of beauty and success came to Sweden. Peterson compares it to listening to Charlie Parker after Glenn Miller or viewing Picasso after classical landscapes: 'the change does not just lie in the aesthetic assimi-lation,' he wrote. 'The actual organisation of art and music happens on a more advanced level.' Naivety is gone, and there is a second order of complexity.

Success Houghton and Hodgson certainly had. They won five out of six league titles between them, while Houghton took Malmö to the 1979 European Cup final, where they were narrowly beaten by Clough's Nottingham Forest. At the 1978 World Cup, though, Sweden finished bottom of a first-phase group that included Austria, Brazil and Spain, a poor showing that was blamed on the corrosive influence of the English style (England themselves, of course, had failed to qualify).

When Sweden then failed to reach the finals of the 1980 European Championship, the SvFF was moved to act and, on 11 December 1980, formally declared that the English-style would not be played by the national team, nor taught at any national institution. As Houghton and Hodgson left to take up positions at Bristol City, it seemed that the *libero* may prevail, but their influence was carried on by Sven-Göran Eriksson, who as part of his coaching education had observed Bobby Robson at Ipswich Town and Bob Paisley at Liverpool.

Eriksson had worked as a PE teacher in Orebro, playing at right-back for BK Karlskoga, a local second division side. There, his thinking on the game was heavily influenced by his player-manager, Tord Grip, who had himself become convinced of the merits of the English style. After his retirement as a player, Grip became manager of Orebro before moving on to Degerfors IF. When, at the age of twenty-eight, Eriksson was badly injured, Grip asked him to join him as assistant coach. Grip was soon appointed as assistant to Georg Ericsson with the national side, leaving Eriksson, in 1976, to take over at Degerfors.

He twice led them to the playoffs, finally winning promotion to the second division in 1979, at which, to widespread surprise, he was appointed manager of IFK Gothenburg. 'Here was this really shy man, who had been the manager of a little team called Degerfors,' said the defender Glenn Hysen, 'and now he was suddenly in charge of the biggest club in the country. We had never heard of him, as a player or as a coach, and it took us a while to get used to him and respect him.'

Gothenburg lost their first three games under Eriksson, at which he offered to quit. The players, though, encouraged him to stay, their form improved and Gothenburg finished runners-up in the league, winning the cup. That did not, though, make him popular. 'Eriksson has been at variance with the ideals of the fans since, like most managers, he wants results before anything,' the journalist Frank Sjoman wrote. 'Before long, he had introduced more tactical awareness, work-rate and had tightened the old cavalier style. The result has been that while Gothenburg are harder to beat, they are harder to watch.' Their average gate fell by 3,000 to 13,320.

Eriksson, like Wade, was obsessed by shape. 'Svennis would place us like chess pieces on the training pitch,' the midfielder Glenn Schiller said. '"You stand here, you go there," and so on... The biggest problem was fitting all the pieces together and getting them to move in harmony. The defensive part was the key to it all. When we were attacking, there was a fair amount of freedom to express ourselves, but we had to defend from strict, zonal starting positions.'

Gothenburg finished second again in 1981, but they settled the debate decisively the following year, winning the league and cup double and, improbably, lifting the Uefa Cup. Although Eriksson soon left for Benfica, the English 4-4-2 was firmly established.

In Norway, the debate was less ferocious, and more decisively won by the pragmatists. Wade and Hughes had visited repeatedly in the sixties and seventies, and Wade's *The FA Guide to Training and Coaching* became central to Norwegian coaching and thinking, as is evident from *Understanding of Football*, the manual written by Andreas Morisbak, the technical director of the Norwegian football federation, in 1978.

The Norwegian University of Sport and Physical Education was established in 1968 and, in 1981, a lecturer there, Egil Olsen, who had won sixteen caps for Norway, dissected Wade's model and presented a revised version. He argued that Wade had made possession too much of a priority, almost an end in itself, whereas he believed attaining it should be the aim of defensive play and the application of it to produce goals the aim of attacking play. That may seem obvious, but the slight semantic clarification was to have radical effects, as Olsen extended the thought. He felt that in Wade's model too little attention was paid to penetration, that it was more important to pass the opposition longitudinally than to retain possession.

His work came just as the Swedish debate between system and beauty spread to Norway, stimulated largely by Vålerenga IF's title success in 1983 under Gunder Bengtsson, a Swede who had become convinced by Houghton and Hodgson's methods. He was followed at Vålerenga and FK Lyn by another Swede, Olle Nordin –

'Marching Olle' as he was mocked after the 1990 World Cup, at which his highly-regarded Sweden lost all three games by the same scoreline: 1-2, 1-2, 1-2 – and Grip then became national manager.

Olsen and his colleagues at NUSPE had begun statistically analysing games, the results of which led Olsen to a series of conclusions outlined in his Masters thesis, the most eye-catching of which is that the probability of scoring before the ball goes dead again is higher when it is with the opposing goalkeeper than with your own. This in turn led him to postulate that position of the ball is more important than possession.

In 1987 Olsen presented a paper at the Science and Football conference in Liverpool. While there, he met George Wilkinson, who was a match analyst for Howard Wilkinson, then the manager of Leeds. Through them he came upon the work of Reep, which to his mind confirmed his own theories about the role of chance in football and the inutility of possession. Olsen met Reep in 1993, and the two maintained a friendship so close that when Olsen was appointed manager of Wimbledon in 1999, Reep, then ninety-five, offered to act as his analyst.

Olsen became Norway national coach in 1990. He implemented a 4-5-1 formation, often playing a target man – Jostein Flo – wide to attack the back post where he would habitually enjoy a height advantage over the full-back who was supposed to be marking him. Taylor, interestingly, did something similar with Ian Ormondroyd at Aston Villa, and the theory was at least partially behind the use of Emile Heskey wide on the left under Gérard Houllier at Liverpool and for Eriksson's England. Olsen, nicknamed 'Drillo' because of his dribbling skills as a player, demanded balls be pumped into the '*bakrom*' – 'the backroom' – that is, the area behind the opponent's defensive line, as his own side followed up with attacking runs. The phrase '*å være best uten ball*' – 'to be the best at off-the-ball running' – initially attached to the midfielder Øyvind Leonhardsen, became a signature. Olsen was stunningly successful. Norway had not been to a World Cup since 1938, but he led them to qualification in both 1994 and 1998 and, briefly, to second in Fifa's world rankings.

Presumably because of their historical lack of success, Olsen's philosophy seems to have been more widely accepted in Norway than the long-ball game was elsewhere. As Larson notes, under him Norwegian fans became used to dealing in 'goal-chances':

England 1 Norway 1, Wembley, World Cup Qualifier, 14 October 1992

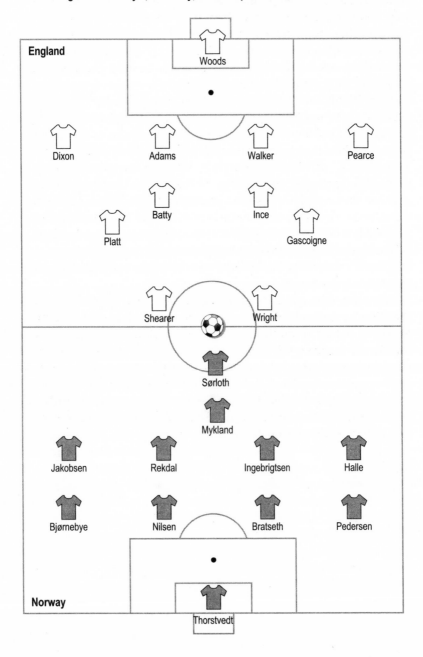

a 1-1 draw in a World Cup qualifier at home to Finland in 1997, for instance, did not prompt anguish because it was recognised that they had won 9-2 on chances; they then beat the same opponents away, having won just 7-5 on chances. The issue, though, as it should have been for Reep and Hughes, is the quality of the chances. An open goal from six yards is not the same as a bicycle kick from thirty: not all chances are equal.

More significant was the qualifying campaign for the 1994 World Cup. When Norway beat England 2-1 in qualifying for the 1982 World Cup, it was such a shock it sent the radio commentator Børge Lillelien into barely coherent delirium: 'Lord Nelson, Lord Beaverbrook, Sir Winston Churchill, Sir Anthony Eden, Clement Attlee, Henry Cooper, Lady Diana, *vi har slått dem alle sammen, vi har slått dem alle sammen* [we have beaten them all, we have beaten them all]. Maggie Thatcher, can you hear me? Maggie Thatcher [...] your boys took a hell of a beating! Your boys took a hell of a beating!' When Norway beat England 2-0 in Oslo in 1993, a game that also produced a notorious catchphrase – Taylor's 'do I not like that' – it was entirely predictable.

The more damaging result, though, had been the 1-1 draw at Wembley, a game England had dominated and led until Kjetil Rekdal, a defensive midfielder, thrashed a 30-yard drive into the top corner fourteen minutes from time. This, for the dice-rollers, was vindication. Did Rekdal really think he would score? Did he send screamers like that flying in on a regular basis? Or was he simply, as Hughes would have urged him to do, buying another ticket for the raffle? Either way, random chance, as Reep no doubt saw it, had its revenge on Taylor.

△▽△▽△▽△▽△▽

Chapter Sixteen

The Coach Who Wasn't a Horse

△▽ It was AC Milan's success in Europe in the sixties that introduced the *libero* as the Italian default and, a quarter of a century later, it was AC Milan's success in Europe that killed it off. Hamburg's victory over Juventus in the 1983 European Cup final may have alerted coaches and pundits to the flaws in *il giocco all'Italiano*, but Juventus's 1-0 victory over Liverpool amid the horror of Heysel two years later confirmed its predominance.

There were efforts to move away from the *libero* and man-marking, but they were isolated. Luis Vincio introduced zonal defence at Napoli in 1974, but the experiment fizzled out, and then the former Milan forward Nils Liedholm employed a form of zonal marking with Roma, a tactic that got his side to the European Cup final in 1984. He moved on to Milan, but it was only after Arrigo Sacchi had succeeded him in 1987 that Italian football was awakened to the possibilities of abandoning man-marking altogether and adopting an integrated system of pressing. 'Liedholm's zone wasn't a real zone,' Sacchi said. 'My zone was different. Marking was passed on from player to player as the attacking player moved through different zones. In Liedholm's system, you started in a zone, but it was really a mixed zone, you still man-marked within your zone.' It is probable no side has ever played the zonal system so well as Sacchi's Milan. Within three years, he had led them to two European Cups and yet, when he took charge, he was a virtual unknown and the club appeared to be stagnating.

Born in Fusignano, a community of 7,000 inhabitants in the province of Ravenna, Sacchi loved football, but he couldn't play it. He worked as a salesman for his father's shoe factory and, as it became apparent he wasn't even good enough for Baracco Luco, his local club, he began coaching them. Not for the last time, he faced a crisis of credibility. 'I was twenty-six, my goalkeeper was thirty-nine and my centre-forward was thirty-two,' he said. 'I had to win them over.'

Even at that stage, though, for all the doubts he faced, Sacchi had very clear ideas about how the game should be played. 'As a child I loved the great sides,' he said. 'As a small boy, I was in love with Honvéd, then Real Madrid, then Brazil, all the great sides. But it was Holland in the 1970s that really took my breath away. It was a mystery to me. The television was too small; I felt like I need to see the whole pitch fully to understand what they were doing and fully to appreciate it.'

Those four sides were all great passing sides, teams based around the movement and interaction of their players. Honvéd, Real Madrid and Brazil – with varying degrees of self-consciousness – led the evolution towards system; the Holland of Rinus Michels were one of the two great early exponents of its possibilities. Tellingly, when watching them, the young Sacchi wanted to see not merely the man on the ball, not merely what most would consider the centre of the action, but also the rest of the team; he approached the conclusion Valeriy Lobanovskyi had come to, that the man out of possession is just as important as the man in possession, that football is not about eleven individuals but about the dynamic system made up by those individuals.

Most simply, though, Sacchi warmed to attacking sides, and that alone was enough to set him apart from the mainstream of a football culture conditioned by the legacy of Gipo Viani, Nereo Rocco and Helenio Herrera. 'When I started, most of the attention was on the defensive phase,' Sacchi said. 'We had a sweeper and man-markers. The attacking phase came down to the intelligence and common sense of the individual and the creativity of the number ten. Italy has a defensive culture, not just in football. For centuries, everybody invaded us.'

It was that that led Gianni Brera to speak of Italian 'weakness', to argue that defensive canniness was the only way they could prosper, an idea reinforced by the crushing defeat of the Second World War, which seemed to expose the unreliability of the militarism that had underlain Vittorio Pozzo's success in the Mussolini era. Sacchi, though, came to question such defeatism as he joined his father on business trips to Germany, France, Switzerland and the Netherlands. 'It opened my mind,' Sacchi said. 'Brera used to say that Italian clubs had to focus on defending because of our diets. But I could see that in other sports we would excel and that our success proved that we were not inferior physically. And so I became convinced that the real problem was our mentality, which was lazy and defensive.

'Even when foreign managers came to Italy, they simply adapted to the Italian way of doing things; maybe it was the language, maybe it was opportunism. Even Herrera. When he first arrived, he played attacking football. And then it changed. I remember a game against Rocco's Padova. Inter dominated. Padova crossed the halfway line three times, scored twice and hit the post. And Herrera was crucified in the media. So what did he do? He started playing with a *libero*, told [Luis] Suárez to sit deep and hit long balls and started playing counterattacking football. For me, *La Grande Inter* had great players, but it was a team that had just one objective: winning. But if you want to go down in history you don't just need to win, you have to entertain.'

That became an abiding principle, and Sacchi seems very early to have had an eye on posterity, or at least to have had a notion of greatness measured by something more than medals and trophies. 'Great clubs have had one thing in common throughout history, regardless of era and tactics,' he said. 'They owned the pitch and they owned the ball. That means when you have the ball, you dictate play and when you are defending, you control the space.

'Marco van Basten used to ask me why we had to win and also be convincing. A few years ago, *France Football* made their list of the ten greatest teams in history. My Milan was right up there. *World Soccer* did the same: my Milan was fourth, but the first three were national teams – Hungary '54, Brazil '70 and Holland '74. And then us. So I took those magazines and told Marco, "This is why you need to win and you need to be convincing." I didn't do it because I wanted to write history. I did it because I wanted to give ninety minutes of joy to people. And I wanted that joy to come not from winning, but from being entertained, from witnessing something special. I did this out of passion, not because I wanted to manage Milan or win the European Cup. I was just a guy with ideas and I loved to teach. A good manager is both screenwriter and director. The team has to reflect him.'

The sentiment is one with which Jorge Valdano, these days the eloquent philosopher prince of aesthetic football, is in full agreement. 'Coaches,' he said, 'have come to view games as a succession of threats and thus fear has contaminated their ideas. Every imaginary threat they try to nullify leads them to a repressive decision which corrodes aspects of football such as happiness, freedom and creativity. At the heart of football's great power of seduction is that there are certain sensations that are eternal. What a fan feels today thinking about the game is at the heart of what fans felt fifty or eighty years ago. Similarly, what Ronaldo thinks when he receives the ball is the same as what Pelé thought which in turn is the same as what Di Stefano thought. In that sense, not much has changed, the attraction is the same.'

As Gabriele Marcotti pointed out in an article in *The Times*, for Valdano that attraction is rooted in emotion. 'People often say results are paramount, that, ten years down the line, the only thing which will be remembered is the score, but that's not true,' Valdano said. 'What remains in people's memories is the search for greatness and the feelings that engenders. We remember Arrigo Sacchi's AC Milan side more than we remember Fabio Capello's AC Milan side, even though Capello's Milan was more successful and more recent. Equally, the Dutch Total Football teams of the 1970s are legendary, far more than West Germany, who beat them in the World Cup final in 1974, or Argentina, who defeated them in the 1978 final. It's about the search for perfection. We know it doesn't exist, but it's our obligation towards football and, maybe, towards humanity to strive towards it. That's what we remember. That's what's special.'

Even as Sacchi entered his thirties, though, his quest for perfection was in its infancy. From Baracco Luco, he moved on to Bellaria before, in 1979, joining Cesena, then in Serie B, where he worked with the youth team. That was a Rubicon. 'I was still working for my father's business, so that was a real lifestyle choice,' Sacchi said. 'I was paid £5,000 a year, which is roughly what I made in a month working as a director for my father's company. But in a way that freed me. I never did the job for money because thankfully I never had to think about it.' It was a gamble that was to bring an almost unthinkably rapid return.

After Cesena, Sacchi took over at Rimini in Serie C1, almost leading them to the title. Then he got his great breakthrough as he was taken on by Fiorentina, a Serie A club at last, where Italo Allodi, once the shadowy club secretary of Inter and Juventus, gave him the role of youth coach. His achievements there got him the manager's job at Parma, then in Serie C1. He won promotion in a first season in which they conceded just fourteen goals in thirty-four matches – his attacking principles were always predicated on a sound defence – and the following year took them to within three points of promotion to Serie A. More importantly for Sacchi, though, Parma beat Milan 1-0 in the group phase of the Coppa Italia, and then beat them again, 1-0 on aggregate, when they were paired in the first knockout round. They may have gone out to Atalanta in the quarter-final, and they may not have won a single game away from home in the league that season, but Silvio Berlusconi, who had bought Milan earlier in the year, was impressed by what he had seen. He, too, had dreams of greatness and seems to have bought into Sacchi's idealism. 'A manager,' Sacchi said, 'can only make a difference if he has a club that backs him, that is patient, that gives confidence to the players and that is willing to commit long-term. And, in my case, that doesn't just want to win, but wants to win convincingly. And then you need the players with that mentality. Early on at Milan I was helped greatly by Ruud Gullit, because he had that mentality.'

Still, the problem of credibility remained. Sacchi admitted he could barely believe he was there, but responded tartly to those who suggested somebody who had never been a professional footballer – Berlusconi, who had played amateur football to a reasonable level, was probably a better player – could never succeed as a coach. 'A jockey,' he said, 'doesn't have to have been born a horse.'

Sacchi addressed the issue straightaway, reputedly saying to his squad at their first training session, 'I may come from Fusignano, but what have you won?' The side may have been expensively assembled, but the answer was not a lot. Milan had lifted the *scudetto* just once in the previous twenty years, and were still struggling to re-establish themselves after their relegation to Serie B in 1980 as part of the Totonero match-fixing scandal. The previous season they had finished fifth, pipping Sampdoria to the last qualification slot for the Uefa Cup only in a play-off.

Sacchi's resources were bolstered by the arrival of Gullit from PSV Eindhoven and Marco van Basten from Ajax for a combined fee of around £7million, but still there was no great expectation, particularly as Van Basten suffered a series of injuries, required surgery and ended up playing just eleven league games, most of them towards the end of the season. They lost their second game of the campaign, 2-0 at home to Fiorentina, but that was one of only two defeats they suffered that season as they won the *scudetto* by three points.

That summer, Frank Rijkaard became the third Dutchman at the club. He had walked out on Ajax the previous season, having fallen out with their head coach Johan Cruyff, and had joined Sporting in Lisbon. Signed too late to be eligible for them, though, he ended up being loaned out to Real Zaragoza; when Sacchi insisted on signing him, there was a distinct element of risk, particularly as Berlusconi was convinced that the best option was to attempt to resurrect the career of the Argentina striker Claudio Borghi, who was already on the club's books, but had been loaned out to Como. Sacchi was vindicated, emphatically so, as Rijkaard's intelligence and physical robustness helped Milan to their first European Cup in twenty years.

'The key to everything was the short team,' Sacchi explained, by which he meant that he had his team squeeze the space between defensive line and forward line. Their use of an aggressive offside trap meant it was hard for teams to play the ball behind them, while teams looking to play through them had to break down three barriers in quick succession. 'This allowed us to not expend too much energy, to get to the ball first, to not get tired. I used to tell my players that, if we played with twenty-five metres from the last defender to the centre-forward, given our ability, nobody could beat us. And thus, the team had to move as a unit up and down the pitch, and also from left to right.'

They were not, though, defensive, although as with so many innovations, those who sought to copy the system frequently became so. 'I always demanded, when we had possession, five players ahead of the ball,' Sacchi said. 'And that there would always be a man wide right and a man wide left. But it could be anybody. It wasn't always the same people.'

Sacchi's first experience of European competition had ended with an embarrassing Uefa Cup second-round defeat to Espanyol, but it was Europe that would prove his greatest stage. By the time of the European Cup final in 1989, Milan seemed unstoppable but, as Sacchi's detractors always point out, they had a huge stroke of luck in the second round. Vitosha of Bulgaria (the club that is now Levski) were beaten 7-2 on aggregate, but Red Star Belgrade were far tougher opponents and held Milan to a 1-1 draw at the San Siro. Red Star led the second leg at the Marakana 1-0 through a Dejan Savićević goal and, with Milan down to nine men after the dismissals of Pietro Paolo Virdis and Carlo Ancelotti, they seemed sure to go through. Fog, though, has a tendency to gather where the Danube meets the Sava, and as it thickened in the second half, the game was abandoned after fifty-seven minutes.

The sides returned the following day. Van Basten and Dragan Stojković exchanged goals, but the game was overshadowed by the horrific injury suffered by Roberto Donadoni as he was fouled by Goran Vasilijević. As Donadoni lay unconscious on the pitch, his life was saved only by the quick-thinking of the Red Star physio, who broke his jaw to create a passage for oxygen to reach his lungs. Gullit, still far from fit following a knee operation but on the bench, insisted on being allowed to take his place. Milan should have won it when Vasilijević deflected the ball over his own line, but neither referee nor linesman gave the goal, and they ended up progressing only by means of a penalty shoot-out.

There was controversy too in their quarter final against Werder Bremen. In the first leg in Germany, Werder had a goal ruled out for a far from obvious foul on the goalkeeper Giovanni Galli, while Milan were again left pointing to a shot that seemed to cross the line without being given as a goal, and felt they should have had two penalties. In the second, it was a debatable penalty converted by Marco van Basten after Donadoni – back in action after the winter break – had gone down under challenge from Gunnar Sauer that gave Milan a 1-0 aggregate victory. At that stage Milan seemed merely fortuitous, but what happened in the semi-final confirmed their brilliance.

Poor Real Madrid: twenty-three years on from their last European triumph, it had come to feel that they existed merely for other teams to prove their excellence against. Benfica had seized the mantle from them in the 1962 final; Ajax had confirmed they were the best side in Europe by hammering them in the semi-final in 1973; and Sacchi's Milan similarly gave notice of their ascension into the pantheon with a superlative performance and a 5-0 win. Perhaps it is simply their reputation that inspires pretenders

AC Milan 5 Real Madrid 0, European Cup Semi-Final, San Siro, Milan, 19 April 1989

against them; but perhaps it is also the case that their historical insistence upon the individual renders them prone to destruction by well-drilled teams. Potent as their strike force of Emilio Butragueño and Hugo Sánchez were, there was an imbalance in their midfield, with the arrival of Bernd Schüster from Barcelona forcing the incisive Michel into a deeper role.

Milan had the better of the first leg in the Bernebéu but conceded a late equaliser and were held to a 1-1 draw. Madrid's coach, the Dutchman Leo Beenhakker, opted to start the second leg with Paco Llorente, a rapid right-winger who was usually used as a substitute. The idea was presumably that his pace could undo Milan on the break, but the effect was rather to weaken the midfield. Schüster was not quick enough to make any impression on Milan's central midfield pairing of Rijkaard and Ancelotti, and Butragueno ended up being dragged right to shore up the right flank, disabling his partnership with Sánchez.

Perhaps Beenhakker got it wrong, but that is not to detract from the excellence of Saachi's side. 'Milan's performance,' Brian Glanville wrote, 'was a compound of technical excellence, dynamic pace and inspired movement. Gullit, playing up front with Van Basten, can seldom have been better, seldom have shown such an irresistible combination of power, skill and opportunism.'

Ancelotti got the first after eighteen minutes, working space for himself with a couple of neat sidesteps before smacking a thirty-yard drive into the top corner. Even his presence in the side, never mind the goal, was a vindication of Sacchi's methods. When he had arrived in 1987 from Roma, he was twenty-eight, and he took time to adapt to the new coach's approach. 'He struggled at first,' Sacchi said. 'Berlusconi said we had an orchestra director who couldn't read sheet music. I told him I would teach him to sing in tune in our orchestra. Every day, I would make him come an hour before training with some kids from the youth team and we would go through everything. Eventually he sang in perfect tune.' And never better than in that semi-final.

Rijkaard converted a right-wing cross from Mauro Tassotti to make it two, and Gullit added a third before half-time with a characteristic header from Donadoni's clip from the left. The three Dutchmen combined for the fourth, four minutes after half-time, Gullit heading down Rijkaard's pass for Van Basten to crash into the top corner. Donadoni rounded off Madrid's humiliation with a fifth, scudded in at the near post from the edge of the box. 'It is hard to play like that,' said Franco Baresi, 'but when we do we are unbeatable.'

Steaua Bucharest offered little resistance in the final and were beaten 4-0, Gullit and Van Basten getting two goals each. 'I was exhausted by the end,' said the Steaua goalkeeper Silviu Lung. 'In all my life I'd never had so many shots to deal with.'

That, Sacchi said, was as near as he got to the perfection he sought, the nearest he came to fulfilment. 'The morning after we beat Steaua Bucharest I woke up with a feeling I had never experienced before,' he said. 'It was one which I have never experienced since. I had this unusual, sweet taste in my mouth. I realised it was the apotheosis of my life's work.'

A decade after leaving the shoe factory, in two great performances, Sacchi saw his vision made flesh. 'Many believe that football is about the players expressing themselves,' he said. 'But that's not the case. Or, rather, it's not the case in and of itself. The player needs to express himself within the parameters laid out by the manager. And that's why the manager has to fill his head with as many scenarios, tools, movements, with as much information as possible. Then the player makes decisions based on that. And it's about being a player. Not just being skilful or being athletic. I didn't want robots or individualists. I wanted people with the intelligence to understand me, and the spirit to put that intelligence to the service of the team. In short, I wanted people who knew how to play football.'

In that, he differs from Valdano, whose romanticism is of a less pragmatic bent. 'There is room for all theories, but individual expression on the pitch is something I don't think we can give up,' Valdano said. 'The brain of one manager can't compete with the infinite possibilities of eleven thinking brains on the pitch. Ultimately, while the concept of team is very important, you need individuals to go to the next level.'

For Sacchi, though, the system was the most important thing. 'Football has a script,' he said. 'The actors, if they're great actors, can interpret the script and their lines according to their creativity, but they still have to follow the script.' There is no doubt that in his conception the scriptwriter was the manager, and the script itself was to be interpreted, not improvised upon. 'I was the only one who could guide them and get them to develop a collective game which would maximize their potential as a unit,' he said. 'My philosophy was teaching players as much as I could, so they would know as much as possible. This would then enable them to make the right decision – and to do so quickly – based on every possible scenario on the pitch.'

There is a sense in which his greatest triumph was persuading the great players and the great egos in his Milan squad of that. 'I convinced Gullit and Van Basten by telling them that five organised players would beat ten disorganised ones,' Saachi explained. 'And I proved it to them. I took five players: Giovanni Galli in goal, Tassotti, Maldini, Costacurta and Baresi. They had ten players: Gullit, Van Basten, Rijkaard, Virdis, Evani, Ancelotti, Colombo, Donadoni, Lantignotti and Mannari. They had fifteen minutes to score against my five players, the only rule was that if we won possession or they lost the ball, they had to start over from ten metres inside their own half. I did this all the time and they never scored. Not once.'

Pressing was the key, but there was no sense of hounding the man in possession as Dynamo Kyiv or Ajax had done. 'Many things influenced me,' Saachi said. 'Dutch football for one. But I think they were different from us, they were based more on athleticism; we were more about tactics. Every player had to be in the right place. In the defensive phase, all of our players always had four reference points: the ball, the space, the opponent and his team-mates. Every movement had to be a function of those four reference points. Each player had to decide which of the four reference points should determine his movement.

'Pressing is not about running and it's not about working hard. It's about controlling space. I wanted my players to feel strong and the opponents to feel weak. If we let our opponents play in a way they were accustomed to, they would grow in confidence. But if we stopped them, it would hurt their confidence. That was the key: our pressing was psychological as much as physical. Our pressing was always collective. I wanted all eleven players to be in an "active" position, effecting and influencing the opposition when we did not have the ball. Every movement had to be synergistic and had to fit into the collective goal.

'Everybody moved in unison. If a full-back went up, the entire eleven adjusted. People think we had these big, strong players, but we had guys like [Alberigo] Evani and Donadoni, who are slight. No, they became big, strong players because of their positioning and movement. That's what made them seem big.

'And we had several types of pressing, that we would vary throughout the game. There was partial pressing, where it was more about jockeying; there was total pressing which was more about winning the ball; there was fake pressing, when we pretended to press, but, in fact, used the time to recuperate.'

It was based around a back four who played, radically for Italy, not with a *libero*, but in a line – a sliding arc that was only flat when the ball was in the centre of the field – and it was practised relentlessly, as it needed to be. 'Before he came to Milan, the clash between two opposing players was always the key, but with him it was all about movement off the ball, and that's where we won our matches,' said Paolo Maldini. 'Each player was as important defensively as he was in attack. It was a side in which players and not positions were the key.'

So crucial was mutual understanding between players that when Sacchi, as Italy national manager, gave his squad a day off during the 1994 World Cup, Baresi asked for a training session so the process of integration would not be checked.

A key part of that was shadow play, something that had been common in England from the sixties, but that was revolutionary in continental Europe. 'On match-days, in the morning,' Sacchi said, 'we had a special training session. Butragueno told me that, before the semi-final against Real Madrid, they sent a scout to watch our session. The scout reported back: "They played a game with a full eleven on a full-sized pitch against nobody and without the ball!" We would line up in our formation, I would tell players where the imaginary ball was and the players had to move accordingly, passing the imaginary ball and moving like clockwork around the pitch, based upon the players' reactions.'

As Gullit suffered a series of knee injuries and underwent a string of operations, Milan never achieved quite the same heights again under Saachi, although they did retain the European Cup the following season. Again they beat Real Madrid, this time in the second round, when the efficacy of their offside trap, marshalled by Baresi, was particularly obvious.

Mechelen of Belgium were unconvincingly overcome in the quarter-final, beaten 2-0 in extra-time in the second leg after Donadoni had been sent off for retaliation, and they needed extra-time in the semi-final as well, as they beat Bayern Munich on the away goals rule. That set up a final against Benfica, who had surprisingly – and undeservedly – eliminated Marseille in their semi, thanks in no small degree to a goal handled over the line by Vata García. There was no repeat of the exhibition of a year earlier, and the game was won by a single goal, elegantly shaped home with the outside of his right foot by Rijkaard.

Milan had retained the European Cup, an increasingly rare feat, but they had been less convincing than the previous year, and Sacchi ran into further difficulties the following season. He fell out with Van Basten and, with the Italian Federation making little secret of their desire to make him national coach, Fabio Capello was appointed to work alongside him. Milan finished the season second in Serie A, but the more lasting impression was made by their disgraceful exit from the European Cup. Having drawn the home leg of their quarter-final against Marseille 1-1, Milan were 1-0 down when the floodlights failed with two minutes of the second leg remaining. The players went off, the lights came back on, and Milan refused to return to the field. The game was awarded 3-0 against them, and they were banned from European competition for a season.

Sacchi, as expected, left to take charge of the national side, but his career, after an astonishing rise, had already reached its peak. Like Lobanovskyi, he found the rhythm of coaching a national team difficult, for he could not spend every minute of every day schooling his players, working on their understanding. 'It's impossible,' he said. Added to which, his insistence that good footballers did not necessarily make good players meant an uneasy relationship with some of Italy's more vaunted players, most notably Roberto Baggio.

The two issues came together in Italy's second game in the 1994 World Cup. After losing their opener 1-0 to the Republic of Ireland, Sacchi made three changes to the side, the most significant of which turned out to be the replacement of Tassotti with Antonio Benarrivo. 'Baresi and Costacurta attacked the Norwegian centre-forward,' Sacchi explained. 'Benarrivo, who was not used to playing with us, did not follow them. So he played an opponent onside, [the goalkeeper Gianluca] Pagliuca had to come out and commit a foul outside the box, getting himself sent off.'

Sacchi had to sacrifice a player to bring on his substitute

goalkeeper, Luca Marchegiani, and, to general amazement, chose to take off Baggio. Baggio himself was shown on television looking aghast as Sacchi signalled him off, clearly asking, 'Has he gone mad?' A scrappy 1-0 win did little to resolve the argument either way, but it make clear Sacchi's attitude to marque players, something that remained constant through his career. 'When I was director of football at Real Madrid I had to evaluate the players coming through the youth ranks,' he said. 'We had some who were very good footballers. They had technique, they had athleticism, they had drive, they were hungry. But they lacked what I call knowing-how-to-play-football. They lacked decision-making. They lacked positioning. They didn't have that subtle sensitivity of football: how a player should move within the collective. And, for many, I wasn't sure they were going to learn. You see, strength, passion, technique, athleticism, all of these are very important. But they are a means to an end, not an end in itself. They help you reach your goal, which is putting your talent at the service of the team, and, by doing this, making both you and the team greater. So, in situations like that, I just have to say, he's a great footballer, but perhaps not a great player.'

Italy reached the final of that tournament, losing on penalties to Brazil, but that was not enough to stem the criticism, and when they were bundled out of Euro 96 in the group stage, Sacchi's fate was sealed. He returned to Milan, but could not replicate his earlier success and lasted only a season. He had a similarly brief spell with Atlético Madrid, where he struggled against inter-ference from the club's president, the notorious Jesús Gil. A subse-quent spell with Parma lasted only twenty-three days encompassing three games before he quit citing stress. 'The difference between Milan and elsewhere was that at Milan I had quality players, at other clubs they obviously weren't as good,' he said. 'And you can only do it of you have a great club behind you. If Berlusconi hadn't backed me, not just in public, but with the players as well, I don't think I could have succeeded. I don't know that the players would have listened to me. When you try to do something new, when you try to do things differently, you need a tremendous amount of support.'

It is just as easy to believe, though, that having achieved his apotheosis so quickly, Sacchi, like Viktor Maslov, found it impos-sible to summon the emotional energy to impose his vision again.

AC Milan 4 Barcelona 0, Champions League Final, Spiros Louis Stadium, Athens 18 May 1994

Perhaps too, towards the end of his first spell at Milan, there was an element of Béla Guttmann's three-year rule kicking in: the exhausting, repetitive training session could be endured only for so long.

Certainly Milan soon proved not as moribund as Sacchi had believed them to be when he left. 'I thought they were a great side near to their sunset boulevard, reaching the end of an unrepeatable cycle of success,' he said. 'Obviously, I was wrong. Managed by Capello, Milan won the Champions League and four league championships in five years, one of which passed without any defeats.'

Sacchi, of course, must take some of the credit for laying the groundwork, but Milan were substantially different under Capello. Although the 4-4-2 principle remained the same and although they continued to press, Capello's Milan were far less fluid, far more defensive, often featuring an out-and-out holder like Marcel Desailly at the back of the midfield, something that was anathema to Sacchi's doctrine of universality. That trend reached its peak when Milan completed a hat-trick of *scudetti* in 1994, despite scoring only thirty-six goals in thirty-four games; the strength was that same back four of Tassotti, Baresi, Costacurta and Maldini, which conceded just fifteen.

Yet that season they also produced one of the indelible European performances, arguably the greatest in a final since Real Madrid's 7-3 victory over Eintracht Frankfurt in 1960, as they hammered Johan Cruyff's Barcelona 4-0 in Athens. It was a game wholly incongruous with the rest of the season. For one thing, Dejan Savićević, whose individualistic brilliance was out of keeping both with Saachi's team-centred ideals and with Capello's pragmatism, played; and for another, Baresi and Costacurta, both suspended, did not.

The game was billed as another allegory: the attacking of Johan Cruyff's Barcelona, with their total footballing heritage and their maverick strike force of Romario and Hristo Stoichkov, against the defence of Milan. Barcelona had won a fourth straight Spanish title that year, but they were hopelessly outclassed. Milan were already well on top when they took a twenty-second-minute lead, Savićević gliding by Miguel Ángel Nadal before hooking the ball across goal for Daniele Massaro to knock in. Their second was a sumptuous team goal, Savićević, Boban and Cristian Panucci working the ball to Donadoni, whose cut-back from the byline was whipped into the far corner by Massaro. Savićević then added a wonderful lob, and hit the post in the move that led to Desailly curling a glorious fourth. 'They were just perfect,' said the Barcelona goalkeeper, Andoni Zubizarreta.

'The press, especially the foreign media, had given us no hope,' said Maldini. 'Barcelona were certainly a good side, but we knew they had weaknesses and how to exploit them and we went for it, ruthlessly. We played an almost perfect game. We completely stifled difficult opponents and gave them almost nothing.'

Sacchi, though, was never convinced, and Maldini acknowledged that the 1989 side was the best he ever played for. 'Football is born in the brain, not in the body,' Sacchi said. 'Michelangelo said he painted with his mind, not with his hands. So, obviously, I need intelligent players. That was our philosophy at Milan. I didn't want solo artists; I wanted an orchestra. The greatest compliment I received was when people said my football was like music.'

Chapter Seventeen

△▽△▽△▽△▽△▽

The Turning World

△▽The classical winger was all but dead, butchered in the sixties by Viktor Maslov, Alf Ramsey and Osvaldo Zulbeldía. By the mid-nineties, it seemed that all *fantasistas* might go the same way, sacrificed before that great bugbear of Willy Meisl, the fetishisation of speed. Arrigo Sacchi may have found a beauty in system, but more generally the effect of pressing was to stifle creativity. As had happened throughout history, after Herbert Chapman, after Helenio Herrera, after Alf Ramsey, the defensive elements of the innovation took root far more readily than the attacking. Blanket five-man midfields became commonplace, muscularity seemed to matter more than finesse; the aesthetic fell before the pragmatic. West Germany's less than inspiring success in the 1990 World Cup was followed by victory for an overwhelmingly functional Denmark in Euro 92. Brazil won the 1994 World Cup by that least Brazilian of methods – a penalty shoot-out following a goalless draw – and with a team that featured two midfield destroyers in Dunga and Mauro Silva. The future seemed negative. And yet, come the turn of the millennium, football was as attacking as it had been for two decades.

Euro 2000 was arguably the best tournament of the modern era. Germany, torpid, physical and outdated, went home without winning a game; England, despite squeezing Steve McManaman, Paul Scholes and David Beckham into their midfield, were made to look almost as sluggish and failed to progress from the group stage; and, although Italy proved defensive soundness will never go out of fashion, battling with their modified 3-4-1-2 to reach the final almost despite themselves, there was much that was joyous.

France, the champions, fielded not merely Thierry Henry as a graceful and unorthodox centre-forward, but also Youri Djorkaeff, Zinédine Zidane and Christophe Dugarry. The two losing semi-finalists were almost as blessed. Holland fitted Boudewijn Zenden, Dennis Bergkamp and Marc Overmars behind Patrick Kluivert, while Portugal found room for three of Luís Figo, Manuel Rui Costa, Sergio Conceicão and João Pinto behind Nuño Gomes. There were even swansongs for two of the great creative players of the previous decade, Gheorghe Hagi and Dragan Stojković, although both were slower and played deeper than they had in their heyday. Compare that to the Germany side that won the tournament in 1996 with a back five protected by Dieter Eilts, and the contrast is astonishing. It wasn't just that playmakers had been preserved; over the span of four years, wingers had been resurrected as well.

In a sense, the very defensiveness of the football led to the call for players capable of unpicking opposing defences, who were often themselves given very little defensive responsibility. This was particularly true in Italy – hence their 3-4-1-2 formation in the Euro 2000 finals – where what was known as the 'broken team' developed. There would be an attacking three (occasionally joined by a wing-back or a midfielder) and a defensive seven. Alberto Zaccheroni's *scudetto*-winning AC Milan of 1997–98, for instance, played a 3-4-3 that featured a front two of George Weah and Oliver Bierhoff, with Leonardo just behind. Occasionally Thomas Helveg or Christian Ziege would get forward from wing-back to support, but the two central midfielders, Demetrio Albertini and Massimo Ambrosini, were largely defensive. Fabio Capello's Roma had Francecso Totti playing behind Paulo Sergio and Marco Delvecchio, with a midfield that included three holders in Luigi Di Biagio, Damiano Tommasi and Eusebio Di Francesco; at Juventus, Zinédine Zidane, Alessandro Del Piero and Filippo Inzaghi were backed up by the industry of Edgar Davids, Didier Deschamps, Angelo Di Livio and Antonio Conte. The role of the playmaker became increasingly necessary, increasingly exalted and increasingly impossible; and by 2000 Italian football was heading down a cul-de-sac from which they arguably didn't escape until Carlo Ancelotti, at Milan, deployed Andrea Pirlo, a modern *regista*, deep in midfield.

Other countries, though, reacted to the negativity with greater adventure, fielding as many as three *fantasistas*. Fifa, rightly, accepted the credit for the rule changes that followed the 1990

Germany 1996 (2-1 (AET – Golden Goal) v Czech Republic, Euro 96 final, Wembley, London)

France 2000 (2-1 (AET – Golden Goal) v Italy, Euro 2000 final, De Kuip, Rotterdam)

World Cup – abolishing the backpass and outlawing the tackle from behind – but it wasn't quite as simple as that, for these artists were not the same as the artists of old. As Adolfo Pedernera had pointed out at the beginning of the era of pressing and of the dominance of system, in such an age there can be no place for bohemians. Yet there is, clearly, a place for artistry; it can't all be about physical effort and defensive positioning. 'There's a right-wing football and a left-wing football,' said César Luis Menotti. 'Right-wing football wants to suggest that life is struggle. It demands sacrifices. We have to become of steel and win by any method ... obey and function, that's what those with power want from the players. That's how they create retards, useful idiots that go with the system.'

Menotti has a particular ideological drum to beat, and his sides were always rather more systematised than he cared to admit, but here, surely, there is a truth (although the left-wing/right-wing dichotomy is unhelpful: for one thing, the Soviets played highly systematised football – 'right-wing' by Menotti's definition; and for another, if political terms are to be ascribed to footballing styles, is there not a reflection of social democracy in the egalitarian 4-4-2s of Scandinavia?). Gianni Brera, in his quest for perfect goalless draws, may have appreciated the idea of a team without such fallible flamboyances as artistry, but few others would: even Zubeldía had Juan Ramón Verón, even Helenio Herrera had Sandro Mazzola, even Carlos Bilardo had Diego Maradona. A compromise between the two is necessary. As Marcelo Bielsa, Argentina's coach from 1998 to 2004 and an inveterate romantic, put it, 'Totally mechanised teams are useless, because they get lost when they lose their script. But I don't like either ones that live only on the inspiration of their soloists, because when God doesn't turn them on, they are left totally at the mercy of their opponents.'

The question then becomes how that artistry is to be incorporated into a system, without becoming systematised to the point of predictability. It is in Argentina, presumably because the eternal conflict between the *Bilardistas* and the *Menottistas* brings the issues to the surface, that the debate has been most fierce. There, the playmaker, the number ten, is revered as it is nowhere outside the Balkans. Italians divide playmakers into *trequartistas* (three-quarters), who play in the hole behind the attack (Totti, for instance), and *registas*, who are deeper lying (Pirlo). In Argentina, though, the playmaker is the *enganche* – literally 'the hook' – who always operates between midfield and attack.

Juan Carlos Lorenzo popularised the position in the 4-3-1-2 he instituted with the national team at the 1966 World Cup, with Ermindo Onega in the role. There is a certain irony in that, given his reputation as a pragmatist, which is indicative of how signif-icant the changes that followed the switch to four at the back were. Lorenzo saw artistry had a place, incorporated it within his system and was seen as opposing romance; today romantics in Argentina demand his formation be preserved.

Others followed Lorenzo's lead and, even two decades on from Bilardo's success with a 3-5-2, 4-3-1-2 remained the most common formation in domestic Argentinian football. Miguel Russo was part of Bilardo's Estudiantes side of the seventies and is temperamen-tally inclined to his way of doing things, but in his time as coach of Boca, which ended in December 2007, he felt unable to do away with the *enganche*. 'Boca has a tradition of its own, its own structure, and you don't change things when they've won so much,' he said. 'Even if I want to change it I have to do it slowly.'

Onega may have been the first to be deployed in the hole behind two strikers – a development, essentially, on the *ponta da lança* position, itself a development of the inside-forward – but he was certainly not the first playmaker, not even in Argentina. Arguably River Plate in the days of *la Máquina* had five, despite selling Alfredo di Stéfano. Independiente became famous for them. There were Miguel Giachello, Norberto Outes and José Percudani, the heart of the side that won the Intercontinental in 1984; before them there was Ricardo Bochini, described by the journalist Hugo Asch as 'a midget, ungainly, imperturbable, without a powerful shot, nor header, nor charisma', and yet still a wonderfully imagi-native player; elsewhere, most spectacularly, there was Diego Maradona, and after him, a host of new Maradonas: Ariel Ortega, Pablo Aimar, Javier Saviola, Andres d'Alessandro, Juan Roman Riquelme, Carlos Tevez and Leo Messi.

Are such players relevant to the modern game? Of course they are. Or rather, of course Tevez and Messi are. But then neither are really playmakers in the traditional sense. Tevez is a support forward – and even he found himself briefly consigned to the wing at West Ham – while Messi tends to be used on the flank at Barcelona, cutting inside in a 4-3-3. It is Riquelme, mournful of demeanour, graceful of movement and deft of touch, who best embodies the old-style *enganche*. When Eduardo Galeano drew the comparison between footballing artists and the devotees of *milonga* clubs, it was to players like Riquelme he was referring, and it is upon him that the debate about the future of such players has focused. Riquelme has become less a player than a cipher for an ideology.

'In the pause,' the columnist Ezequiel Fernández Moores wrote in *La Nacion*, quoting a phrase common in the blues tradition of Argentina, 'there is no music, but the pause helps to make the music.' He went on to recount an anecdote about Charles Mingus walking into a bar to see an impetuous young drummer attempting a frenetic solo. 'No,' the great jazz musician said, 'it's not like that. You have to go slowly. You have to say hello to people, introduce yourself. You never enter a room shouting. The same is true of music.'

But is it true of football? Nostalgists and romantics would like to believe so but, Moores argued that Riquelme would have to change, that he would have to learn, like Messi, a directness. Can the game today cope with a player who does not charge and hustle and chase, but exists apart from the hurly-burly; the still point of an ever-turning world, guiding and coaxing through imagination rather than physique? 'Riquelme's brains,' Jorge Valdano said, 'save the memory of football for all time... he is a player of the time when life was slow and we took the chairs out on the streets to play with the neighbours.' Perhaps his melancholic demeanour reflects his knowledge that he was born out of his time. Then again, perhaps his lack of pace would have found him out whichever era he played in: he is, after all, not a paradigm for theoretical debate but an individual with many very great gifts and one very obvious weakness.

In Argentina, Riquelme is adored and despised in equal measure, the depth of feeling he provokes indicative of how central the playmaker is to Argentinian notions of football. The *enganche*, Asch wrote in a column in *Perfil* in 2007, is 'a very Argentinian invention, almost a necessity'. The playmaker, he went on 'is an artist, almost by definition a difficult, misunderstood soul. It would, after all, hardly seem right if our geniuses were level-headed'; it is as though they must pay a price for their gifts, must wrestle constantly to control and to channel them.

Certainly there is that sense with Riquelme, who eventually frustrated the Villarreal coach Manuel Pellegrino to the extent that he exiled him from the club.

'We are not,' Asch wrote, 'talking necessarily about a leader. Leaders were Rattín, Ruggeri, Passarella or Perfumo, intimidating people. No. Our man is a romantic hero, a poet, a misunderstood genius with the destiny of a myth... Riquelme, the last specimen of the breed, shares with Bochini the melancholy and the certainty that he only works under shelter, with a court in his thrall and an environment that protects him from the evils of this world.' Perhaps, Asch said, he should never have left Boca.

Well, perhaps, but it is not that Riquelme cannot prosper away from the club he clearly adores. He struggled with Barcelona, but he was the major reason Villarreal reached a Champions League semi-final 2005–06, and his intelligence was central to Argentina's sublime progress to the quarter-final of the World Cup later that summer. And yet he took blame for his sides' exits from both competitions. He missed a penalty against Arsenal in the Champions League, and was withdrawn after seventy-two anonymous minutes against Germany. Some cited Riquelme's supposed tendency to go missing in big games; but what is striking is that the coach, José Pekerman, replaced him not with a similar *fantasista*, despite having Messi and Saviola available, but with the far more defensive Estaban Cambiasso, as he switched to a straight 4-4-2. He either decided that Torsten Frings, the more defensive of the two German central midfielders in their 4-4-2, would get the better of any playmaker he put on, or, as many argued, he lost his nerve completely and lost faith in the formation because of Riquelme's ineffectiveness. Little wonder that Riqelme has commented – as a matter of fact, rather than from bitterness – that when his side loses, it is always his responsibility.

And this, really, is the problem with a designated playmaker: he becomes too central. If a side has only one creative outlet, it is very easy to stifle – particularly when modern systems allow two holding midfielders without significant loss of attacking threat. That is true of the 4-3-1-2, its close cousin the diamond, and the 3-4-1-2. All three can also be vulnerable to a lack of width. Significantly, under Bielsa, not that Riquelme got much of a look in, Argentina played at times with a radically attacking 3-3-1-3, a formation almost unique at that level. Bielsa had already experimented with a 3-3-2-2, using Juan Sebastian Verón and Ariel Ortega behind Gabriel Batistuta and Claudio López, with Javier Zanetti and Juan Pablo Sorín as wing-backs and Diego Simeone as the holding midfielder in front of three central defenders. That was essentially a variant of the 3-4-1-2, with one of the central midfielders becoming an additional *trequartista*, but it was just as prone to the lack of width as the more orthodox version. Shifting one of the centre-forwards and one of the *trequartistas* wide and converting them into wingers, though, alleviated that. The playmaker was provided with a wealth of passing options and the formation was so unusual it was difficult to counter.

'In the defensive phase,' the Argentinian coach Cristian Lovrincevich wrote in *Efdeportes*, 'the collective pressing method was adopted, with all lines pushing forwards to recover the ball as close as possible to the opposition goal. In essence it was very similar to the Total Football of the Dutch. In the offensive phase, once the ball had been recovered, the team tried to play with depth, avoiding unnecessary delays and the lateralisation of the game. In attack, five or six players were involved; only four positions were mainly defensive – the three defenders and the central midfielder.'

The problem with both variants, though, is that once possession is lost, regaining it can be difficult and the team is necessarily vulnerable to the counter. Argentina employed the 3-3-2-2 at the 2002 World Cup and, after the group stage, they had had more possession, created more chances and won more corners than any other side. Unfortunately they were also on their way home, having managed just two goals and four points from their three games, raising questions both about defensive weaknesses and about the quality of the chances created. When attacks are funnelled down the centre, the defending side can simply sit deep, watch the opponents pass the ball around in deep areas, and restrict them to long-range efforts. In the 4-3-1-2 or the 3-4-1-2, width can be provided by good movement from the forwards, or by the *carrileros*, the shuttling midfielders, pulling wide, or by attacking full-backs, but when the system goes wrong, the problem tends to be either lack of attacking width, or the holes left defensively by trying to provide it.

That is not to say that both formations are necessarily doomed,

Yugoslavia 2 Finland 0, Euro 2004 qualifier, Marakana, Belgrade, 16 October, 2002

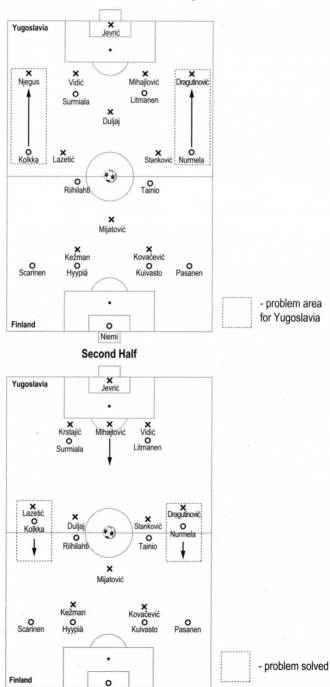

Second Half

Shakhtar Donetsk 2007-08

merely that they are restricted in their application. In October 2002, for instance, in a Euro 2004 qualifier in Naples, Yugoslavia fielded a flattened diamond to try to frustrate Italy. Goran Trobok sat in front of the back four, with Siniša Mihajlović to his left, Nikola Lazetić to his right, and Dejan Stanković as a deepish *trequartista*, with Predrag Mijatović dropping off Mateja Kežman. Playing defensively, the plan worked as Alessandro Del Piero found his space restricted, and Yugoslavia arguably had the better of a 1-1 draw. At home in Belgrade against Finland four days later, though, Yugoslavia adopted a similar system and struggled. With the onus on them to create, rather than relying on breaks, they lacked attacking width, while they struggled defensively as their full-backs were repeatedly isolated against Mika Nurmela and Joonas Kolkka, the two wide players in Finland's 4-4-2. At half-time it was 0-0, at which Yugoslavia switched to a 3-4-1-2, with Mihajlović stepping out from the back three to become an additional midfielder. Nurmela and Kolkka suddenly found themselves having to deal with wing-backs, which both gave them a defensive responsibility and diminished the space in which they had to accelerate before meeting a defender; Yugoslavia, with a spare man both in the middle at the back and in the middle of midfield, began to dominate possession, and ended up winning by a comfortable 2-0.

That, perhaps, is the major reason the diamond is slipping out of fashion. Of the thirty-two sides who reached the Champions League group stage in 2007–08, only Mircea Lucescu's Shakhtar Donetsk deployed it in its classic form, and they ran into the classic problems. Particularly in their opening game, at home to Celtic, but also in their second, away to Benfica, they were superb, Razvan Rat and Darijo Šrna flying forward from full-back with the holding midfielder Mariusz Lewandowski dropping back to protect them (the diamond becoming effectively a 3-4-1-2), and the slight Brazilian Jádson operating as a playmaker behind a front two. In their next two games against AC Milan, though, their weakness high up the pitch in wide areas was exposed. They were well beaten in both and, as confidence waned, ended up failing to qualify even for the Uefa Cup.

Shifting to a 3-4-1-2 worked for Yugoslavia against Finland largely because it negated the impact of the opposing wingers, but it is just as liable to render a side one-dimensional, as Croatia found at the 2006 World Cup as they persisted with three at the back long after the rest of Europe had abandoned it. When they finished third at the World Cup in 1998, Ciro Blazević managed at times to squeeze three playmakers into their line-up. Fielding Zvonimir Boban, Robert Prosinečki and Aljosa Asanović together in central midfield defied logic – it was, as Slaven Bilić said, 'the most creative midfield ever' – and yet somehow it worked. That, though, was a one-off, aided by the fact that their back three included, in Bilić and Igor Štimac, two stoppers who were also comfortable on the ball plus either Dario Šimić or Zvonimir Soldo, both of them equally capable of playing in midfield, who would step out to become a midfielder when necessary. It is notable too that the 3-0 quarter-final victory over Germany, their best performance of the tournament, came when Prosinečki was absent, leaving Soldo to operate as a holding midfielder in what was effectively a 3-3-2-2 – another of those simple shifts of balance the 3-5-2 permits.

By the time of the 2006 World Cup, their coach Zlatko Kranjčar had gone down the route of Italy in the late nineties and decided that to play with an out-and-out playmaker in his son, Niko Kranjčar, it was necessary to bolster the midfield with two holding players – a formation not dissimilar to that adopted by West Germany in the latter stages of the 1986 tournament. However aggressive Šrna and Marko Babić were as wing-backs, it couldn't disguise the fact that with Igor Tudor, often a centre-back with Juventus, and Niko Kovač, a more complete midfielder, but somebody who has become decreasingly creative as his career has gone on, at the back of the midfield, they were effectively playing with seven defenders.

That was enough to earn a battling 1-0 defeat to Brazil, but when Croatia had to take the initiative, as they did against Japan and Australia in their other two group games, they were tiresomely predictable, reliant for creativity either on the forward surges of the wing-backs, or on an out-of-sorts Kranjčar. They played stodgy, tedious football, and as their frustration got the better of them, they became over-physical and boorish. The only silver lining for Croatia was that Serbia-Montenegro had an even worse tournament, but their impressive qualifying performances, having switched away from the traditional Balkan three at the back, did not go unnoticed. In ten qualifying games they conceded only one goal, with their quartet of defenders – Goran Gavrančić, Mladen Krstajić, Nemanja Vidić and Ivica Dragutinović – attracting the nickname 'the Fantastic Four'. Serbia-Montenegro could blame injuries and disintegrating team morale for their embarrassment in Germany; Croatia's problems seemed to be rooted rather in the very way they played the game: Serbia had at least begun their process of evolution.

The debate about the merits of 3-5-2, or 3-4-1-2, had dogged Croatian football for years. Bilić ended it at a stroke when he replaced Zlatko Kranjčar as coach after the tournament. His side, he announced, would play four at the back, preferably, but not necessarily, in a Dutch-style 4-3-3. The fear among traditionalists was that that would mean the end of the playmaker, but Bilić found a way of accommodating not just one, but two. It might not have been quite the heady days of Blazević's 3-3-2-2, but it was far better than anyone had hoped, far better than it had been during Kranjčar's reign.

Bilić supplemented his back four with Niko Kovač as a deep-lying

1998 (3-0 v Germany, World Cup quarter-final, Stade Gerland, Lyon, 4 July 1998)

2006 (2-2 v Australia, World Cup Group Phase, Gottlieb-Daimler Stadium, Stuttgart, 22 June, 2006)

2007 (2-0 v Estonia, Euro 2008 qualifier, Maksimir, Zagreb, 8 September 2007)

midfielder, and found room for not merely two forwards, but also Kranjčar on the left, with Luka Modrić in the middle, and Šrna on the right. With his slight, almost fragile build, Modrić resembles the traditional playmaker, but there is more to his game than that. 'My role in the national team is very different to the one I perform with Dinamo,' he said. 'Here I have a freer role, but I also have more defensive responsibilities.' Significantly, Zlatko Kranjčar had praised his 'organisational' qualities when he first called him into the national squad ahead of the World Cup.

Modrić and Niko Kranjčar represent the new style of playmakers – *fantasistas* with a certain robustness, and also a sense of tactical discipline. 'Nobody wants playmakers, nobody buys them,' Asch wrote. 'Why? Do they hate poetry, do they hate colour?' It comes back, it would seem, to Tomas Peterson's point about a second order of complexity. Once the systems are understood, once football has lost its naivety, it is no longer enough simply to be beautiful; it must be beautiful within the system. 'It happens that nobody in the world plays with a playmaker anymore,' Asch went on. 'Midfielders are multi-function and forwards are a blend of tanks and Formula One cars.' Maybe so, and the playmaker will be missed, but just as the traditional winger was superseded and phased out by evolution, so too will be the traditional playmaker. Riquelme is a wonderful player. He may prosper at Boca, to whom he returned at the beginning of 2008. He may even prosper for Argentina, for international defences are not so well drilled as those at club level, but he is the last of a dying breed, a glorious anachronism.

The Nigerian cult of Kanu, which slightly mystifyingly sees him not as a second striker, as he has been used throughout his career in Europe, but as a *trequartista*, regularly forces him into the playmaking role for his country, but that has served only to highlight its redundancy. At Portsmouth, Kanu worked because he had in Benjani Mwaruwari a partner who charged about with an intensity that rather cloaked the intelligence of his movement. Benjani did the running while Kanu strolled around in the space between midfield and attack: one was energy, one was imagination, an almost absolute division of attributes that, at Portsmouth's level at least, worked.

At the African Cup of Nations in 2006, Kanu was used to great effect as a substitute. Once the pace of the game had dropped, he would come on, find space and shape the game. Eventually, the pressure from the Nigerian press grew until their coach, Augustin Eguavoen, felt compelled to start him against Côte d'Ivoire in the semi-final. Kanu barely got a kick, shut out by the pace, power and nous of Côte d'Ivoire's two holding midfielders, Yaya Touré and Didier Zokora. Two years later, in Nigeria's opening game in Sekondi, their new coach, Berti Vogts, threw him into exactly the same trap. Against one anchor-man, perhaps Kanu could have imposed his will and thrived; against two, it was impossible. To say it is to do with his age is to miss the point. The playmaker belongs to an era of individual battles: if he could overcome his marker, he could make the play. Against a system that allows two men to be deployed against him, he can't. Yes, by deploying two men against the playmaker the defensive side is potentially creating space for another, but zonal marking is designed to counter precisely that sort of imbalance. There exactly is the deficiency of the 4-3-1-2: stop the designated playmaker and the flow of creativity is almost entirely staunched.

So how then can a playmaker be used in the modern game? Early versions of Bilić's system – such as that played by Croatia when they beat England 2-0 in Zagreb in October 2006 – included Milan Rapaić, a forward-cum-winger on the right; Šrna, as a wing-back who is also a fine crosser of the ball, gives them rather more balance. Still, Bilić's Croatia employ five attacking players, something almost unique in the modern game, which may explain why they conceded three away to Israel and two at Wembley in qualifying for Euro 2008.

Using a single creator raises the danger of becoming one-dimensional, but there are other reasons why three at the back is declining in popularity in every major football country apart from Brazil. José Alberto Cortes, head of the coaching course at the University of São Paulo, believes the issue is physical. 'With the pace of the modern game,' he said, 'it is impossible for wing-backs to function in the same way because they have to be quicker and fitter than the rest of the players on the pitch.'

Most others, though, seem to see the turn against three at the back as being the result of the effort to incorporate skilful players by bolstering the midfield. There is, of course, an enormous irony here, in that Bilardo's formation in 1986 both popularised three at the back and included a playmaker as a second striker, the very innovation that has led ultimately to the decline of three at the back. Bilardo's scheme had two markers picking up the opposing centre-forwards, with a spare man sweeping behind. If there is only one centre-forward to mark, though, that leaves two spare men – one provides cover; a second is redundant – which in turn means a shortfall elsewhere on the pitch. 'There's no point having three defenders covering one centre-forward,' explained Miroslav Djukić, the former Valencia defender who became Partizan Belgrade coach in 2007.

Nelsinho Baptista, the experienced Brazilian coach who took charge of Corinthians in 2007, has developed software to explore the weaknesses of one system when matched against another. 'Imagine Team A is playing 3-5-2 against Team B with a 4-5-1 that becomes 4-3-3,' he said. 'So Team A has to commit the wing-backs to deal with Team B's wingers. That means Team A is using five men to deal with three forwards. In midfield Team A has three central midfielders against three, so the usual advantage of 3-5-2 against 4-4-2 is lost. Then at the front it is two forwards against four defenders, but the spare defenders are full-backs. One can push into midfield to create an extra man there, while still leaving three v two at the back. So Team B can dominate possession, and also has greater width.'

One of Team A's central defenders could, of course, himself step up into midfield, but the problem then is that Team A has four central midfielders, and still lacks width. And anyway, if a defender is going to step into midfield, why not simply play a defensive midfielder in that role anyway?

Egypt won the African Cup of Nations with a 3-4-1-2 in both 2006 and 2008, but that was probably largely because straight 4-4-2 still tends to dominate the thinking in Africa. In fact, aside from Egypt – and at times Cameroon – only Guinea and Morocco, both of whom used a 4-2-3-1, did not set up in some form of 4-4-2. Significantly, the majority of the genuine contenders had strong spines and deficiencies wide and, in a generally excellent tournament, the one consistent disappointment was the standard of crossing. That could be a generational freak, or it could be related to the fact that when European clubs are looking to sign African talent, they tend to have what Manchester United's Africa scout Tom Vernon calls 'the Papa Bouba Diop template' in mind. The African players who have succeeded in Europe in the past have

Decline of 3-5-2

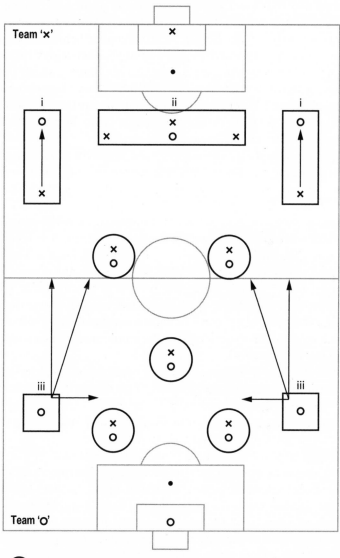

Team 'x'

Team 'O'

◯ - simple cancellation

| i | - x wing-backs forced back to deal with O wingers

| ii | - 3x defenders dealing with one O forward

| iii | - O full-backs spare - can provide extra man at back;
drive down flank or help out in midfield

Egypt 4 Cameroon 2, African Cup of Nations group, Baba Yara Stadium, Kumasi, 22 January 2008

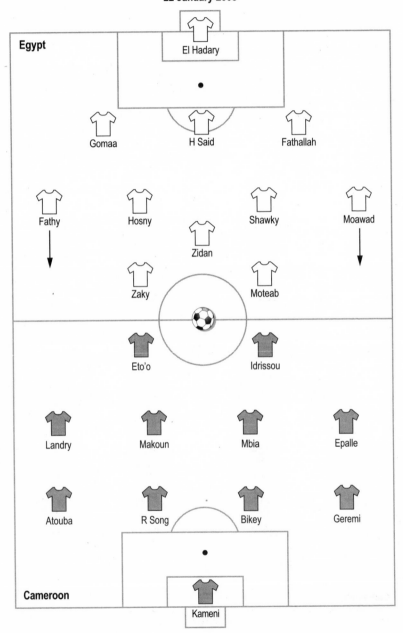

Egypt 1 Cameroon 0, African Cup of Nations final, Ohene Djan Stadium, Accra, 10 February 2008

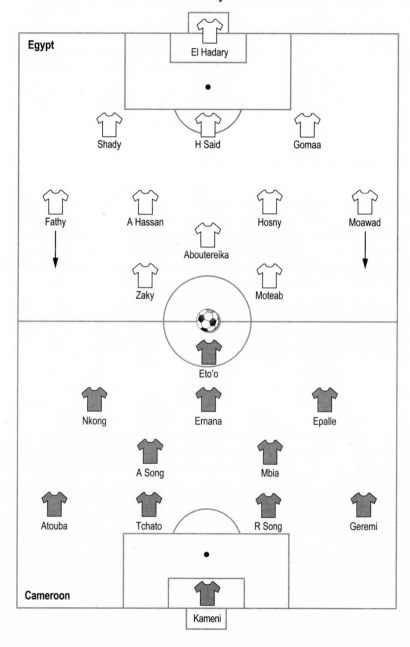

usually been big and robust, and so clubs look only for something similar. Players called up by European clubs at a young age develop faster and have a higher profile, and so it is they who make it into the national team.

Vernon, who runs an academy in the hills above Accra, also believes the way the game is first experienced by children – at least in Ghana – has a tendency to shape them as central midfielders. 'Look at how kids play,' he said. 'They have a pitch maybe twenty or thirty yards long, and set up two stones a couple of feet apart at either end, often with gutters or ditches marking the boundaries at the sides. So it's a tiny area. The game becomes all about receiving the ball, turning and driving through the middle.' The result is that most West African teams – and this was particularly true of Côte d'Ivoire – have at least two good central strikers, so tend to play them, with little width that could have unsettled Egypt's two excellent wing-backs, Ahmed Fathy and Sayed Moewad.

In their first game in the 2008 Cup of Nations, Egypt hammered Cameroon 4-2. They went on to add a further ten goals in disposing of Sudan, Zambia, Angola and Côte d'Ivoire before meeting Cameroon again in the final. In that first game, Cameroon's coach Otto Pfister had his players a 4-4-2; in the final, he opted for a 4-2-3-1 and for the first time in the tournament, Egypt struggled for fluency. The defender Wael Gomaa looked like a spare part, anxiously and uncertainly wandering into midfield, and, although Egypt bossed possession, they ended up beating a limited side only because of a terrible individual error from Rigobert Song.

Even Steve McClaren acknowledged that three at the back is only effective if the opposition play with two out-and-out centre-forwards. Given Bilić's Croatia are one of the few sides left who do still play with two strikers – Eduardo da Silva drifting and sniffing, with either Mladen Petrić or Ivica Olić providing a more physical foil – McClaren's decision to adopt a 3-5-2 for England's Euro 2008 qualifier away in Zagreb actually, for all the scorn subsequently directed at him, at least made theoretical sense. The problem was that England are so unused to playing with anything other than a back four that they played it badly – and, moreover, against a team whose players were just as adept at picking apart an inadequate 3-5-2 as England's would have been against an inadequate 4-4-2.

There is a theory that England had been holding Croatia before Eduardo gave them a sixty-second-minute lead, but that neglects the half-dozen decent chances they had had before then and, besides, the way Eduardo was left unmarked to head in Niko Kovač's cross was evidence of how the discipline of their marking had disintegrated in the unfamiliar system. Gary Neville's subsequent own-goal, as a divot confounded Paul Robinson, added a misleading element of farce to what had been a comprehensive defeat. 'I really wanted them [England] to play with three at the back because then at each side we have one player more,' Bilić said. 'If we are playing slow, they have no problem because they can close you down. But sometimes we play really fast. We were very direct, very brave, and we caused them problems.'

Bilardo suggested teams should be split with three attackers and seven defenders; Bilić opted for five and five, but the general move in the nineties was towards a middle ground, with four attacking players and six defensive. When the 4-5-1 first became popular in western Europe in the late eighties and early nineties, it was widely seen as a defensive system: 'the right of the weak', like early *catenaccio*, to be employed against stronger sides to try to frustrate them. Even today, it is not unusual to read or hear pundits complaining of sides who refuse to use 'two up', yet 4-5-1 was always as implicit in 4-4-2 as 4-4-2 was in 4-2-4.

At least in a British context, strike partnerships in a 4-4-2 tend to fall into two categories: the big man-quick man (John Toshack and Kevin Keegan; Mark Hateley and Ally McCoist; Niall Quinn and Kevin Phillips) or the creator-goalscorer (Kenny Dalglish and Ian Rush; Peter Beardsley and Gary Lineker; Teddy Sheringham and Alan Shearer). In the former, there genuinely were two strikers, but in the latter, did the creator not drift deeper, linking the space between midfield and attack? The remarkable impact on English football of Eric Cantona and Gianfranco Zola was largely the result of their ability to drop off and play between the lines, confusing English centre-backs just as surely as had Matthias Sindelar and Nándor Hidegkuti. The issue, then, seems one of notation: nobody would have thought of describing, for instance, Sunderland's promotion side of 1989–90 as playing 4-4-1-1, but with Eric Gates tucked behind Marco Gabbiadini, that is assuredly what it was. And once the instinctive recoil against 4-5-1 has been got over, it becomes apparent that it is just as flexible, just as easily recalibrated according to circumstance as the 3-5-2.

It is arguable, in fact, that the first team to deploy a 4-5-1 to international success was the great Flamengo side of Paulo César Carpegiani, which beat Liverpool 3-0 to win the Intercontinental Cup in 1981, and could not be described as being even remotely negative. Faced with the problem of choosing between four *fantasistas* – Lico, Zico, Adília and Tita – Carpegiani did exactly what Brazil would do at the 1982 World Cup: he played them all. Rather than laying them out behind two strikers, though, Carpegiani opted to play with Nunes as a lone front man, with Andrade operating as a holding midfielder behind them in what would now be called a 4-1-4-1.

Of course, five in midfield can be a defensive system. Numerous sides in the eighties used it, particularly away in Europe. Everton were particularly adept. In the first leg of the quarter-final of the Cup-Winners' Cup away to Bayern Munich in 1985, for instance, Howard Kendall left out Andy Gray, bringing Alan Harper into midfield in his place and leaving Graeme Sharp as a lone striker. After a 0-0 draw away, Everton restored Gray in a 4-4-2 and won the home leg 3-1. Gray admits that there was nothing particularly subtle about their play that night: they realised the Bayern defence was uncomfortable against the aerial threat they posed and so set out to exploit it.

Generally speaking, the more direct a side, the more defensive they will be in a 4-5-1. The aim for them is simply to plant nine men between the opposition and the goal, then look for the centre-forward to battle for possession, hold the ball up and either lay it off to breaking midfielders or win a dead-ball. Ian Wright performed the role to perfection for George Graham's Arsenal in a number of European ties in the early nineties. Once the game becomes about possession and short-passing, though, a five-man midfield becomes a far more subtle tool.

Just who invented the 4-2-3-1 that so invigorated Europe in the late nineties, it is impossible to say. It may seem logical to place its development as happening at some time between the European Championships of 1996 and 2000, and certainly that was when it became popular, but in a sense any side whose 4-4-2 included a withdrawn centre-forward and two advanced wide players was employing it. Nobody described it as such at the time, but the Manchester United side of 1993–94, with Paul Ince and Roy Keane sitting deep in the midfield, Ryan Giggs and Andriy Kancheslskis pushing forward wide and Eric Cantona dropping off Mark Hughes

Flamengo 3 Liverpool 0, Intercontinental Cup, National Stadium, Tokyo, 13 December 1981

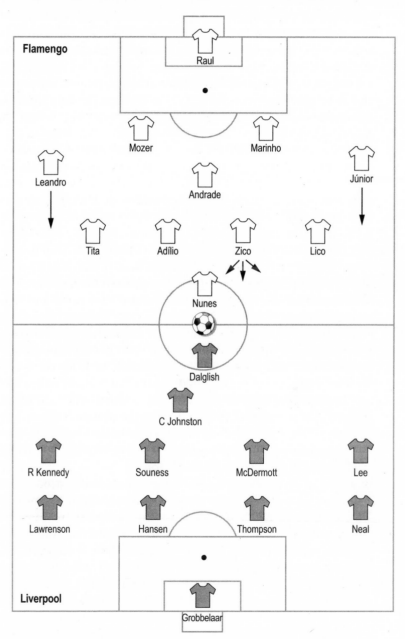

used something very close to a 4-2-3-1. Arsenal did similarly in
Arsène Wenger's first full season in England, with Emmanuel Petit
and Patrick Vieira deep, Marc Overmars and Ray Parlour wide and
Dennis Bergkamp behind Nicolas Anelka, although Parlour could
tuck in and Overmars push on to produce something more akin to
an old-style 4-3-3.

There is a sense too that 4-2-3-1 is an inevitable development
once sides start withdrawing one of the centre-forwards. Initially a
holding midfielder would be deployed to pick him up – hence the
late-nineties boom in players capable of playing 'the Makélélé role'
– at which the *trequartista* would start drifting wide to find space.
If the holding player followed him, that created space in the
middle, so an additional player would be dropped deeper as cover,
with concomitant effects for the more attacking midfielders.

In Spain, the credit for the 4-2-3-1 tends to be given to John
Toshack on his return to Real Madrid in 1999, when he used
Géremi and Fernando Redondo as his holding midfielders, with
Steve McManaman, Raúl and Elvir Baljić in front of them and
either Anelka or Fernando Morientes as the lone striker. That said,
Spanish sides have long played with split forwards – with a *media
punta* behind the central striker – so, as in England, any team using
that system with particularly advanced wingers could have been
said to have been playing 4-2-3-1. Javier Irureta had been using it
with Deportivo la Coruña for a couple of seasons before they won
the league title in 2000, while Juan Manuel Lillo has strong claims
– supported by the Spanish magazine *Training Fútbol* – to have
invented the system while coach of the Segunda División side
Cultural Leonesa in 1991–92. He had Sami and Teófilo Abajo as his
two pivots, with Carlos Núñez, Ortiz and Moreno in front of them
and Latapia as the lone forward. Seeing the success of the system
Lillo took it to Salamanca. There, according to an editorial in
Training Fútbol, the players reacted with 'faces of incredulity
because they thought it was a strange way to play; they responded
to the positions they were told to adopt and the distribution of
each line of the team with the same sense of strangeness and
surprise as someone who had just come face to face with a
dinosaur.' Nonetheless, it took them to promotion.

The formation's transfer to England – at least in terms of a
recognition of the formation as something distinct from 4-4-2 –
came with Manchester United as an emphatic 3-2 home defeat by

Real Madrid in the Champions League in 1999–2000 convinced Sir Alex Ferguson that the more orthodox 4-4-2 he had employed to win the treble the previous season had had its day in European competition (although he maintains, with some justification, that he has never played 4-4-2, but has always used split forwards).

The 4-2-3-1, though, is just one variant of the five-man midfield. One of the attacking midfielders can be sacrificed for an additional holder, producing either a 4-3-2-1 – the Christmas tree – or the modern 4-3-3. Co Adriaanse seems to have been the first exponent of the 4-3-2-1 at Den Haag in the late eighties, and Terry Venables experimented with it with England ahead of Euro 96, but it was at the 1998 World Cup that a side using it achieved its first notable success, and it entered the mainstream.

Aimé Jacquet's problem was accommodating Zidane, one of the greatest playmakers the world has known, but a player of limited pace and almost no defensive instinct. His solution was to give him effectively a free role, but to do that without destabilising his team defensively, he followed the Italian convention and fielded three midfielders whose function was primarily defensive – Didier Deschamps, Emmanuel Petit and Christian Karembeu. Youri Djorkaeff was included as a further creative presence, with Stéphane Guivarc'h as the lone centre-forward. He was much derided – and it may well be that, from a technical point of view, he is the worst centre-forward ever to win a World Cup – but he performed his function, which was, broadly speaking, to provide a focal point and hold the ball up for the creators behind (once that has been accepted, the possibility opens up that Serginho's role in Brazil's 1982 World Cup side could be open to reinterpretation). By 2000, Jacquet had more confidence – and in Patrick Vieira a superb and mobile defensive midfielder – and felt able to align the three creators behind Henry in a 4-2-3-1.

AC Milan are the best modern exponents of the 4-3-2-1, although theirs is rather more attacking than France's had been. When they won the Champions League in 2006, Kaká and Clarence Seedorf were the advanced midfield presences, with Andrea Pirlo operating as a *regista* behind them, flanked by the snapping and snarling of Gennaro Gattuso and the unfussy efficiency of Massimo Ambrosini. Again, though, the key is fluidity, for both Pirlo and Ambrosini are comfortable advancing and Seedorf, equally, can play in a more defensive role.

More common is the 4-3-3, which bears little resemblance to the 4-3-3 as practised by the Brazil of 1962. Theirs was a lopsided 4-2-4, with Mario Zagallo dropping deep from the wing to become an extra midfielder. With occasional exceptions, it remained asymmetric through to the eighties when, for instance, Newcastle would set out a 4-3-2, then deploy Chris Waddle on one or other flank according to which of the opposing full-backs looked weaker. The modern 4-3-3, as practised by José Mourinho's Chelsea and many others, though, is really a modified 4-5-1.

Here, perhaps, becomes clear the most significant recent shift in the understanding of tactics: the notion that there are only three bands – defence, midfield and attack – is gone. There is a general recognition now that each of those categories can be subdivided into smaller bands, although as that process goes on, it may be that the bands are so narrow as to cease to be meaningful. 'It's about the movement of your players, up and down, left and right,' Bilić said. 'There are no lines any more.' Mourinho didn't go quite so far, acknowledging that lines still exist, while maintaining that his players' job, at least when going forward, was to break them.

Under his management, Chelsea's back four was relatively orthodox. Claude Makélélé then sat immediately in front of them, with Frank Lampard and Tiago – or, later, Michael Essien – operating effectively as *carrileros* ahead of him. Didier Drogba was the single centre-forward, with two wide men – some combination of Damien Duff, Joe Cole and Arjen Robben – operating both as wingers and auxiliary midfielders; not quite forwards, but not midfielders either. Sometimes it was 4-1-2-3, sometimes it was 4-1-4-1, but it became more easily understood as 4-3-3.

It remains debatable just how new the breaking of the lines is. There have, after all, always been defensive midfielders and attacking midfielders, while the notion of the pitch being divided into four bands was there in the W-M. Perhaps rather, as with Flavio Costa's *diagonal*, what has changed is the notation. As that becomes increasingly sophisticated and more adept at representing the reality, so those realities become easier to grasp. Certainly today the term '4-5-1' is so vague as to be almost useless to describe how a team lines up on the field. It is rather a generic term, describing a family of formations.

Arrigo Sacchi is adamant that there have been no innovations since his Milan and, while there is self-interest in his claims, there

Mourinho's Chelsea

is also a large degree of truth to them. Perhaps more significant, though, is his attitude to the likes of Makélélé. Sacchi is sceptical about the 4-2-3-1 and the modern 4-3-3 with its designated holder because, to him, they are too restrictive. 'Today's football is about managing the characteristics of individuals,' he said. 'And that's why you see the proliferation of specialists. The individual has trumped the collective. But it's a sign of weakness. It's reactive, not pro-active.'

That, he believes, was the fundamental flaw in the *galacticos* policy at Real Madrid, where he served as director of football between December 2004 and December 2005 as the club signed a host of stars and tried to balance them with hard runners from the youth set-up. 'There was no project,' he explained. 'It was about exploiting qualities. So, for example, we knew that Zidane, Raúl and Figo didn't track back, so we had to put a guy in front of the back four who would defend. But that's reactionary football. It doesn't multiply the players' qualities exponentially. Which actually is the point of tactics: to achieve this multiplying effect on the players' abilities.

'In my football, the *regista* – the playmaker – is whoever had the ball. But if you have Makélélé, he can't do that. He doesn't have the ideas to do it, although, of course, he's great at winning the ball. It's become all about specialists. Is football a collective and harmonious game? Or is it a question of putting x amount of talented players in and balancing them out with y amount of specialists?'

△▽

When he returned to AC Milan in 1996 after his stint in charge of the national team, Sacchi ensured that Marcel Desailly, who had been used in midfield by Fabio Capello, was returned to the defensive line. Like Valeriy Lobanovskyi, for whom he professes a great admiration, Sacchi believes in the benefits of universality, in players who are not tied by their limitations to certain roles, but who can roam, taking as a reference for their positioning their team-mates, their opponents and the available space as much as the pitch. When that is achieved the system is truly fluid.

That, of course, is precisely what the new breed of wingers and playmakers offer. They are not merely creators, but also runners and, to a degree, defenders. As *fantasistas* have evolved, so other positions have changed. It is very rare, for instance, to find a top side that plays with two stopper centre-backs. There is a need always for at least one who can pass the ball, or advance with it into midfield. More strikingly, the sniffer centre-forward has all but vanished. 'Those half-chances that poachers used to seize on don't exist any more,' explained Zoran Filipović, once a striker with Red Star, later their coach, and then the first manager of an independent Montenegro. 'Defences are organised better, players are fitter. You have to create chances; you can't rely on mistakes.'

Filippo Inzaghi is among the last of a dying breed, but at least obsolescence crept up on him toward the end of his career; Michael Owen was in his mid-twenties when it became apparent that, however good he is at sitting on the shoulder of the last defender or darting across the near post, it is not enough in modern football. 'I've definitely developed my game, coming off and holding the ball up better and trying to link a bit more, but I've got to keep the main thing which is scoring goals and trying to get in behind people,' he said. 'The main aim at the end of the day is to put the ball in the back of the net.'

The attitude is typically English and one that is a great source of frustration to managers. 'I can't believe that in England they don't teach young players to be multi-functional,' Mourinho said. 'To them it's just about knowing one position and playing that position. To them a striker is a striker and that's it. For me, a striker is not just a striker. He's somebody who has to move, who has to cross, and who has to do this in a 4-4-2 or in a 4-3-3 or in a 3-5-2.'

Owen was highly critical of the then-England coach Kevin Keegan's efforts to expand his repertoire in the build-up to Euro 2000, but the reality may be that putting the ball in the back of the net is no longer sufficient – or, at least, not at the very highest level. Owen could be one of those players who wins teams the occasional game, but prevents them playing good football (which means that he may prove extremely useful to mediocre sides, or even to a good side playing badly, but rarely if at all to a good side playing well). Even allowing for his history of injuries, it is surely significant that when he left Real Madrid in 2005, no Champions League qualifier was prepared to take him on and he ended up at Newcastle. He appears a player left behind by the tactical evolution of the game.

The modern forward, rather, is far more than a goalscorer, and it may even be that a modern forward can be successful without scoring goals. The example of Guivarc'h has already been mentioned, but at Euro 92, Denmark's two centre-forwards, Fleming Povlsen and Kim Vilfort, were both widely perceived as having had excellent tournaments but scored between them only one goal – and that not until the final. Their job was rather to challenge for long balls, retain possession if they won it, and lay it off for Henrik Larsen and Brian Laudrup, the two more attack-minded midfielders. That seemed at the time an aberration, but it was a sign of things to come.

Goals are obviously part of it – a particularly valuable one – and the non-scoring forward a particular case, but the truly great modern forwards appear rather as a hybrid of the old strike partnerships. The likes of Didier Drogba and Emmanuel Adebayor are both target-man and quick-man, battering-rams and goalscorers, imposing physically and yet also capable of finesse. A Thierry Henry or a David Villa mixes the best qualities of the

Roma 2006-07, Manchester United 2007-08

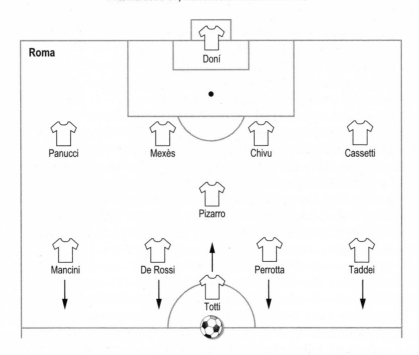

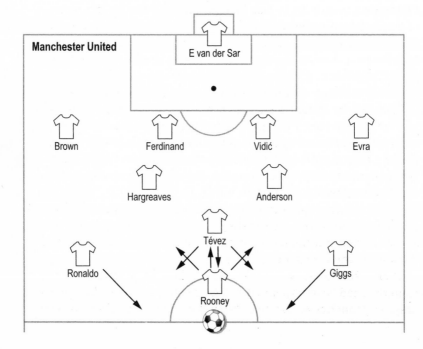

creator and goalscorer, capable of dropping deep or pulling wide, as adept at playing the final ball as taking chances himself. Somewhere in between the two extremes are ranged Andriy Shevchenko (in his Dynamo Kyiv and Milan days), Zlatan Ibrahimović, Samuel Eto'o and Fernando Torres.

Maslov spoke of football being like an aeroplane, becoming increasingly streamlined, but perhaps the gradual adoption of a front-line of one is not quite the end of evolution. Carlos Alberto Parreira, who led Brazil to victory in the 1994 Word Cup and was in charge of them again in 2006, after all, has spoken of the possibilities of a 4-6-0. 'You'd have four defenders at the back although even they'd be allowed to run forward,' Andy Roxburgh, the former Uefa technical director, explained. 'The six players in midfield, all of whom could rotate, attack and defend. But you'd need to have six Decos in midfield – he doesn't just attack, he runs, tackles covers all over the pitch. You find him playing at right-back sometimes.'

Yet what is Deco but the classic example of Lobanovskyi and Sacchi's notion of universality? It is notable that in 2005–06, although Frank Rijkaard often deployed the combative Mark van Bommel or the converted central defender Edmílson in the Champions League, in La Liga he regularly played a midfield three of Deco, Xavi and Andrés Iniesta, all of whom are under 5'9" and none of whom are exactly terrifying physical presences. Industrious players properly organised don't need to intimidate by size.

Slowly, it seems, Parreira's vision is beginning to become reality. In 2006–07, for instance, Luciano Spalletti's Roma played a 4-1-4-1, but with Francesco Totti, the archetypal *trequartista*, as the lone striker. David Pizarro operated as the holding player, with Taddei, Simone Perrotta, Daniele De Rossi and Mancini in front of him. What regularly happened, though, was that Totti dropped deep into the *trequartista* position in which he'd spent so much of his career, creating a space into which one or more of the attacking midfielders advanced. As the distinction between centre-forward and attacking midfielder dissolved, Roma's formation became, if not a 4-6-0, then certainly a 4-1-5-0.

Their experiment was taken on, slightly surprisingly, by the team that had beaten them 7-1 in the previous season's Champions League: Manchester United. With Cristiano Ronaldo, Wayne

Rooney, Carlos Tevez and Ryan Giggs or Nani slung in front of a holding pair of two from Owen Hargreaves, Michael Carrick, Anderson and Paul Scholes, United regularly have no obvious front-man, with the front four taking it in turns to become the *de facto* striker, which helps explain Ronaldo's remarkable goals return. It is a system that requires much work to develop a mutual understanding – as was shown by United's lack of goals in the early games of the season, and by the desperate use of the defender John O'Shea as a makeshift target-man as they struggled to find fluency in drawing 0-0 against Reading on the opening day of the 2007–08 season – but when it does click it can produce exhilarating football.

Fluidity is all. Gianni Brera's insight in his report on the first World Cup final remains just as true today as it was then. Assuming a rough parity of ability, the team that wins will almost certainly be the one that best balances attacking fluency with defensive solidity, and in the pursuit of that the centre-forward may be the next casualty. Even Makélélé, whose uncomplicated discipline at the back of midfield was so key to Chelsea's success under Mourinho, and the loss of whom did so much to undermine Real Madrid, has seen himself usurped at Chelsea by Mikel Jon Obi, a far more complete midfielder. As system has replaced individuality, the winger has gone and been reincarnated in a different, more complex form; so too has the playmaker; and so, now, might the striker be refined out of existence. The future, it seems, is universality.

△▽△▽△▽△▽△▽

Epilogue

△▽ It would be easy to survey modern football and insist there can be nothing new. Roberto Mancini, in fact, did just that at a lecture he gave in Belgrade in 2007, arguing that future advances in football would come not in tactics but in the physical preparation of players. To an extent he is probably right. Football is a mature game that has been examined and analysed relentlessly for almost a century and a half, and, assuming the number of players remains constant at eleven, there probably is no revolution waiting to astonish the world. Even if there is, even if some coach in some unlikely corner happens upon some radical departure, it will not have the stunning impact that, say, Hungary's withdrawn centre-forward had in the early fifties. Even that was, as I hope this book has demonstrated, part of a continuum, drawing directly from Matthias Sindelar's interpretation of the centre-forward's role in the Austrian *Wunderteam*, and having a parallel in Martim Francisco's work with Vila Nova.

England could not deal in 1931 with Sindelar dropping off, British sides struggled to cope with Vsevolod Bobrov doing the same when Dinamo Moscow toured in 1945, and they were humiliated by Nándor Hidegkuti 1953. Lessons, evidently, should have been learned, but that they were not is explicable by the fact that those three examples were isolated, and spread over twenty-two years. These days Hungary's *Aranycsapat* would not have come to London as a mystery: their successes would have been seen on television, videos would have been picked over, the movement of their players would have been analysed by computer. A tactical innovation will never again spring up as a surprise.

Besides which, a talented Hungarian coach such as Gusztav

Sebes would almost certainly not be working in Hungary, but would have followed the money to western Europe. As cross-pollination between different football cultures increases, so national styles become less distinct. We are not yet homogenised, and probably never will be, but the trend is in that direction.

And yet there are always imaginations ready to defy expectation. A promoted side, particularly one with limited resources, usually adopts a defensive style. Spoil the game, the logic goes, restrict the influence of skill, reduce the number of goals likely to be scored, and a weaker team increases its chances of stealing a draw or a 1-0 win. Yet in 2006–07, Pasquale Marino, having led Catania to promotion to Serie A the previous season, had his side play a 4-3-3 with attacking full-backs and no holding midfielder. They were encouraged not to play the percentages, but to try the outrageous and the difficult. Occasionally they came unstuck – they were hammered 7-0 by Roma, for instance – but exuberance proved just as hard to play against as niggardliness. Following the murder of a policeman during rioting at the derby against Palermo in the February, Catania were banned from playing games at their home stadium, but they still finished as high as thirteenth. It wasn't a new system, but it was a revolution of style, a rebellion against convention.

Old styles can be successfully reintroduced in new contexts, particularly in the shortened form of major tournaments. Greece, for instance, at Euro 2004, were the only team who played without a zonal-marking back four. Their coach, Otto Rehhagel, employed a *libero* with three man-markers and then added further solidity with a five-man midfield and a lone striker. 'Rehhagel won because he posed a problem people had forgotten how to solve,' said Andy Roxburgh. 'It wasn't fashionable but it was effective. They controlled matches without having control of the ball. Otto's view was: why should he try a watered-down version of somebody else's system? Whatever you say about his system, you have to admit that Greece got the ball into attack very quickly every time they had possession.'

France, in particular, seemed to struggle against Greece, losing 1-0 to them in the quarter-final. 'They needed to get the ball to Thierry Henry faster,' Roxburgh said. 'Henry is at his most dangerous running into the centre from the left or running just left of centre. Against Greece, he drifted too wide because he wasn't getting any space. That's one of the things you want to do: push a threat to the touchline. Greece's opponents weren't used to being marked so tightly. The old method turned out to be a novelty.'

The move away from out-and-out forwards, perhaps, is something new, although – at least towards the end of the 2007–08 season – it remains tentative. Perhaps the 4-6-0 will, in time, become just as much the orthodoxy as 4-4-2 was in England until the mid-nineties, or the *libero* was in Italy until the late-eighties; perhaps it will prove merely a passing fad.

Certainly its emergence hints at the death of the old-fashioned striker in favour of something more versatile, and the move to universality, it can be said with some confidence, is an on-going trend. Then again, perhaps that simply proves Mancini's point, and all that is actually happening is that the technicians of old are, thanks to improved nutrition and better training methods, becoming physically more imposing; if everybody is fit and powerful, then there is necessarily less demand for those players who offer little beyond their physique or their engine. If strikers are heading the way of old-school wingers and playmakers, though, then the question is who next? Centre-backs, maybe? After all, if there is no centre-forward to mark, the second centre-back in a 4-4-2 would seem as redundant as the third in a 3-5-2 playing against a lone forward.

It is hard to believe, equally, that the increasingly detailed analysis afforded by technology will not also make a difference. Computers and a knowledge of cybernetics helped Valeriy Lobanovskyi devise his system, and it stands to reason that the more sophisticated technology becomes, the more sophisticated systems will become. The biggest obstacle to that, in fact, is the egos of players. Puffed up by years of immense wages and celebrity status, are they willing, as Lobanovskyi and Arrigo Sacchi demanded, to sacrifice themselves utterly to the collective? The experience of Real Madrid in the *galacticos* era suggests not.

That, perhaps, is the other side of the paradox at which Jorge Valdano hinted when he spoke of television's influence on the modern game: that it is the very popularity of modern football that prevents its advancement. Fans, arguably, are complicit in that. Terraces tend to conservatism, and the example of Sweden in the seventies indicates that there is a love of individualism – of football of first-order complexity, to use Tomas Petterson's term – that exceeds the demand for victory. Argentina's experiences as the period of *la nuestra* came to an end show just how damaging that decadence – of thought if nothing else – can be. That said, globalisation is an in-built defence; if nobody is progressing, then nobody is being left behind, so a wake-up like Argentina's 6-1 defeat to Czechoslovakia in 1958 is unlikely, unless a country outside the footballing mainstream is suddenly blessed with a hugely gifted generation of players who can resist the lures of western European materialism long enough to submit themselves to the system of a tactically astute coach. South Korea's success in reaching the semi-final of the 2002 World Cup is evidence of what can be achieved with rigorous organisation, even with essentially average players.

Sacchi, certainly, finds it 'remarkable, worrying' there has been no significant tactical development since the radical systematised approach of his AC Milan, but remains convinced evolution will continue. 'As long as humanity exists,' he said, 'something new will come along. Otherwise football dies.'

Many before have hailed the end of history; none have ever been right.

△▽△▽△▽△▽△▽

Bibliography

BOOKS AND JOURNALS

Alabarces, Pablo, Ramiro Coelho and Juan Sanguinetti, 'Treacheries and Traditions in Argentinian Football Styles: the Story of Estudiantes de la Plata' in Armstrong and Giulanotti (eds), *Fear and Loathing in World Football*

Alcock, Charles W, *Football. The Association Game* (George Bell & Sons, 1902)

Aleinikov, Sergei and DI Belenky, *I Zhizn, I Slyozy, I Futbol [And Life, and Tears, and Football]* (Polymya, 1992)

Allison, Malcolm, *Soccer for Thinkers* (Pelham, 1967)

Archer, Ian and Trevor Royle (eds), *We'll Support you Evermore: The Impertinent Saga of Scottish Fitba'* (Souvenir Press, 1976)

Archetti, Eduardo P, *Masculinities: Football, Polo and the Tango in Argentina* (Global Issues, 1999)
  'Masculinity and Football: The Formation of National Identity in Argentina' in Giulianotti and Williams (eds), *Game Without Frontiers*

Armstrong, Gary and Richard Giulanotti (eds), *Entering the Field: New Perspectives on World Football* (Berg, 1997)
  Fear and Loathing in World Football (Berg, 2001)

Assaf, Roberto and Clóvis Martins, *Almanaque do Flamengo [The Flamengo Almanac]* (Abril, 2001)
  Campeonato Carioca: 96 Anos de História, 1902–1997 [The Carioca Championship, 96 Years of History 1902–97] (Irradiação Cultural, 1997)

Bakema, JB, *Thoughts about Architecture* (St Martin's Press, 1981, ed. Marianne Gray)

Ballard, John and Paul Suff, *The Dictionary of Football: The Complete A–Z of International Football from Ajax to Zinedine Zidane* (Boxtree, 1999)

Bangsbo, Jens and Birger Pietersen, *Soccer Systems and Strategies* (Human Kinetics, 2000)

Barend, Frits and Henk van Dorp, *Ajax, Barcelona, Cruyff: The ABC of an Obstinate Maestro*, translated David Winner and Lex den Dam (Bloomsbury, 1997)

Barnade, Oscar and Waldemar Iglesias, *Mitos y creencias del fútbol argentino [Myths and Beliefs of Argentinian Football]* (Al Arco, 2006)

Barthes, Roland, *Mythologies* (Éditions de Seuil, 1957, trans. Vintage 2000)

Bate, Richard, 'Football Chance: tactics and strategy' in Reilly *et al* (eds), *Science and Football* (Spon, 1988)

Bayer, Osvaldo, *Fútbol argentino [Argentinian Football]* (Editorial Sudamericana, 1990)

Ben-Ghiat, Ruth, *Fascist Modernities: Italy 1922–45* (University of California Press, 2001)

Blokhin, Oleh, *Futbol na vsyu zhyzn [Full-life Football]* (Veselka, 1988)

Booth, Keith, *The Father of Modern Sport: The Life and Times of Charles W. Alcock* (Parrs Wood, 2002)

Borges, Jorge Luis and Adolfo Bioy Casares, '*Esse est Percipi*' in Kuper and Mora y Araujo (eds), *Perfect Pitch: Dirt*

Bottenburg, Maarten van and Beverley Jackson, *Global Games* (University of Illinois Press, 2001)

Bowler, Dave, *Winning isn't Everything: A Biography of Sir Alf Ramsey* (Victor Gollancz, 1998)

Bray, Ken, *How to Score: Science and the Beautiful Game* (Granta, 2006)

Brera, Gianni, *Herrera e Moratti* (Limina, 1997)
　　Storia critica del calico Italiano [A Critical History of Italian Football] (Tascaballi Bompiani, 1978)

Buchan, Charles, *A Lifetime in Football* (Phoenix House, 1955)

Burn, Gordon, *Best and Edwards: Football, Fame and Oblivion* (Faber and Faber, 2006)

Burns, Jimmy, *Barça: A People's Passion* (Bloomsbury, 1999)
　　Hand of God: the Life of Diego Maradona (Bloomsbury, 1996)

Buxton, Peter, *Stoke City Football Club: A Centenary* (Pyramid, 1963)

Caldas, Waldenyr, *O Pontapé Inicial: Memória do Futebol Brasileiro (1894–1933) [The First Kick: Memories of Brazilian Football]*, (IBRASA, 1990)

Camus, Albert, *La Chute [The Fall]*, trans. Justin O'Brien (Penguin, 1990, first published 1956)

Castillo, Juan José, *Ladislao Kubala* (Barcanova, 1998)

Castro, Ruy, *Garrincha: The Triumph and Tragedy of Brazil's Forgotten Footballing Hero*, translated by Andrew Downie (Yellow Jersey, 2004)

Chapman, Herbert, *Herbert Chapman on Football* (Garrick, 1934)

Connolly, Kevin and Rab MacWilliam, *Fields of Glory, Paths of Gold: The History of European Football* (Mainstream, 2005)

Connor, Jeff, *The Lost Babes* (HarperSport, 2006)

Cox, Richard, *The Encyclopaedia of British Football* (Routledge, 2002)

Crabtree, Stephen, *The Dons – The Amazing Journey 1982–87* (Baron, 1987)

Craig, Jim, *A Lion Looks Back* (John Donald, 1998)

Crampsey, RA, *The History of Queen's Park, 1867–1967* (Nisbet, 1967)

Crerand, Paddy, *Never Turn the Other Cheek* (HarperSport, 2007)

Crick, Michael, *The Boss: The Many Sides of Alex Ferguson* (Simon & Schuster, 2002)

Csaknády, Jenő, *Die Béla Guttmann Story: Hinter den Kulissen des Weltfussballs [The Béla Guttmann Story: Behind the Scenes of World Football]* (Verlag Blintz-Dohány, 1964)

Csanádi, Árpád, *Soccer* (Corvina Kiadó, third edition, 1978, trans. István Butykai and Gyula Gulyás, trans. rev. Charles Coutts)

Cullis, Stan, *All for the Wolves* (Rupert Hart Davis, 1960)

DaMatta, Roberto, *O que faz o brasil, Brasil? [What makes Brazil, Brazil?]* (Rocco, 1984)

DaMatta, Roberto et al., *Universo do Futebol: Esporte e Sociedade Brasiliera [The Universe of Football: Sport and Brazilian Society]* (Edições Pinakotheke, 1982)

De Galan, Menno, *De Trots van de Wereld [The Pride of the World]* (Prometheus BV Vassallucci, 2006)

Di Giano, Roberto, *Fútbol y cultura política en la Argentina, identidades en crisis*

[*Football and Political Culture in Argentina, Identities in Crisis*] (Leviatán, 2005)

Diéguez, Luis and Ariel Scher, *El libro de oro del mundial* [*The Golden Book of the World Cup*] (Clarín, 1998)

Downing, David, *The Best of Enemies: England v Germany, a Century of Football Rivalry* (Bloomsbury, 2000)
 England v Argentina: World Cups and Other Small Wars (Portrait, 2003)
 Passovotchka (Bloomsbury, 1999)

Edwards, Leigh and Andy Watson, *Mission Impossible: The Story of Wimbledon Football Club's Historic Rise from Non-league to the First Division* (Dons Outlook, 1986)

Filatov, Lev, *Obo vsyom poporyadku* [*About Everything in an Orderly Manner*] (Fizkultura I Sport, 1990)

Filho, Mário, *O Negro no Futebol Brasileiro* [*The Black in Brazilian Football*] (second edition) (Civilizaçao Brasiliera, 1964)

Finn, Ralph, *A History of Chelsea FC* (Pelham, 1969)

Foot, John, *Calcio: A History of Italian Football* (Fourth Estate, 2006)

Fox, Norman, *Prophet or Traitor: the Jimmy Hogan Story* (Parrs Wood, 2003)

Freddi, Cris, *Complete Book of the World Cup 2002* (CollinsWillow, 2002)

Freyre, Gilberto, *The Gilberto Freyre Reader* (Knopf, 2002)

Galeano, Eduardo, *Football in Sun and Shadow* (trans Mark Fried, Fourth Estate, 1997)

Galinsky, Arkady, *Nye sotvori syebye kumira* [*Don't Create Idols for Yourself*] (Molodaya Gvardiya, 1971)

Galinsky, Vitaly, *Valeriy Lobanovskyi. Chetyre zhyzni v futbolye* [*Valeriy Lobanovskyi: Four Lives in Football*] (ID Computerpress 2003)

Gardner, Paul, *The Simplest Game: The Intelligent Fans' Guide to the World of Soccer* (Collier Books 1976, rev ed. 1994)

Garland, Ian, *History of the Welsh Cup 1877–1993* (Bridge, 1993)

Giulianotti, Richard, *Football: A Sociology of the Global Game* (Polity, 1999)

Giulianotti, Richard and John Williams (eds), *Game Without Frontiers: Football, Identity and Modernity* (Arena, 1994)

Glanville, Brian, *Champions of Europe: The History, Romance and Intrigue of the European Cup* (Guinness, 1991)
 Cliff Bastin Remembers (Ettrick, 1950)
 Soccer Nemesis (Secker and Warburg, 1955)
 The Story of the World Cup (Faber and Faber, 2001)

Goldblatt David, *The Ball is Round: A Global History of Football* (Viking, 2006)

Golesworthy, Maurice, *The Encyclopaedia of Modern Football* (Sportsman's Book Club, 1957)

Gorbunov, Alexander, *Trenerskoe Naslediye. Boris Arkadiev* [*Coaching Heritage. Boris Arkadiev*] (Fizkultura i Sport, 1990)

Górski, Kazimierz, *Piłka jest okràgła* [*The Ball is Round*] (Kazimierz Górski, 2004)

Gould, Stephen Jay, *Triumph and Tragedy in Mudville* (Cape, 2004)

Gray, Andy with Jim Drewett, *Flat Back Four: The Tactical Game* (Boxtree, 1998)

Green, Geoffrey, *The Official History of the FA Cup* (Naldrett, 1949, rev. ed. Heinemann, 1960)
 Soccer: the World Game – a Popular History (Phoenix House, 1953, rev. ed. Pan 1956)
 There's Only One United (Hodder and Stourton, 1978)

Hamilton, Aidan, *An Entirely Different Game: The British Influence on Brazilian*

Football (Mainstream, 1998)

Handler, Andrew, *From Goals to Guns: The Golden Age of Football in Hungary 1950–56* (Columbia University Press, 1994)

Heizer, Teixeira *O Jogo Bruto das Copas do Mundo [The Brutal Game of the World Cup]* (Mauad, 1997)

Herrera, Fiora Gandolfi, *Tacalabala, Esercizi di magia di Helenio Herrera [Attack the Ball, The Magical Exercises of Helenio Herrera]* (Tapiro, 2002)

Herrera, Helenio, *La Mia Vita [My Life]* (Mondo Sport, 1964)

Hesse-Lichtenberger, Ulrich, *Tor! The Story of German Football* (WSC, 2002)

Hey, Stan, *The Golden Sky* (Mainstream, 1997)

Hidegkuti, Nándor, *Óbudától Firenzéig [From Óbuda to Florence]* (Sport, 1965)

Holden, Jim, *Stan Cullis: The Iron Manager* (Breedon, 2000)

Holt Richard, JA Mangan and Pierre Lanfranchi (eds), *European Heroes: Myth, Identity, Sport* (Frank Cass, 1996)

Honigstein, Raphael, *Harder, Better, Faster, Stronger: Die geheime Geschichte den englischen Fussballs [Harder, Better, Faster, Stronger: the Secret History of English Football* (Kiepenheuer & Witsch, 2006)

Hopkins, Stephen, 'Passing Rhythms: The Modern Origins and Development of "The Liverpool Way"' in Williams, Hopkins and Long (eds) *Passing Rhythms*

Horak, Roman and Wolfgang Maderthaner, 'A Culture of Urban Cosmopolitanism: Uridil and Sindelar as Viennese Coffee-House Heroes' in Holt, Mangan and Lanfranchi, *European Heroes*

Hughes, Charles, *Football: Tactics and Teamwork* (EP, 1973)
Soccer Tactics and Skills (BBC and Queen Press, 1980)
The Winning Formula (Collins, 1990)

Hunt, David, *The History of Preston North End Football Club: the Power the Politics and the People* (Carnegie, 1992)

Inglis, Simon, *Football Grounds of Britain*, (Collins Willow, 1996)

Iwanczuk, Jorge, *Historia del fútbol amateur en la Argentina [A History of Amateur Football in Argentina]* (Autores Editores,1995)

Jackson, NL, *Association Football* (Newnes, 1900)

Johnston, Harry, *The Rocky Road to Wembley* (Sportsman's Book Club, 1954)

Johnston, William, *The Austrian Mind: An Intellectual and Social History* (University of California Press, 1983)

Jones, Ken, *Jules Rimet Still Gleaming: England at the World Cup* (Virgin, 2003)

Jones, Peter, *Wrexham: A Complete Record 1972–1992* (Breedon, 1992)

Joy, Bernard, *Forward Arsenal!* (Phoenix, 1952)
Soccer Tactics: A New Appraisal (Phoenix, 1957, rev ed, 1963)

Kassil, Lev, *Vratar Respubliki [The Keeper of the Republic]* (reprinted Detgiz 1959; first published 1938)

Keith, John, *Bob Paisley: Manager of the Millennium* (Robson, 1999)
The Essential Shankly (Robson, 2001)

Kelly, Stephen, *The Boot Room Boys: Inside the Anfield Boot Room* (CollinsWillow, 1999)

Kovacs, Ştefan, *Football Total* (Calman-Levy, 1975)

Kucherenko, Oleg, *Sto let rossiyskomu futbolu [One Hundred Years of Russian Football]* (Russian Football Union, 1997)

Kuper, Simon, *Ajax, the Dutch, the War: Football in Europe during the Second World War* (Orion, 2003)
Football against the Enemy (Orion, 1994)

Kuper, Simon and Marcela Mora y Araujo (eds), *Perfect Pitch: Dirt* (Headline, 1999)
Lacey, Josh, *God is Brazilian: Charles Miller, the Man who Brought Football to Brazil* (NPI, 2005)
Larson, Øyvind, 'Charles Reep: A Major Influence on British and Norwegian Football' in *Soccer and Society*, 2, 3, Autumn 2001, 58–78
Lawson, John, *Forest 1865–78* (Wensum, 1978)
Lawton, James, *On Football* (Dewi Lewis Media, 2007)
Lawton, Tommy, *Football is my Business* (Sporting Handbooks, 1946)
   My Twenty Years of Soccer (Heirloom, 1955)
Le Corbusier, *Vers une architecture [Towards a New Architecture]* (first published 1923, trans. F Etchells, Architectural Press, 1970)
Lebedev, Lev, *Rossyiskiy futbol za sto let [Russian Football for 100 Years]* (Russian Football Union, 1997)
Leite Lopes, José Sergio, 'Successes and contradictions in "Multiracial" Brazilian Football' in Armstrong and Giulianotti (eds), *Entering the Field*
Lidbury, Michael, *Wimbledon Football Club: The First Hundred Years* (Ward and Woolverton, 1989)
Lobanovskyi, Valeriy, *Beskonyechnyy match [Endless Match]* (IN Yura, 2003)
Lovejoy, Joe, *Sven-Göran Eriksson* (Collins Willow, 2002)
Mangan, JA, *Athleticism in the Victorian and Edwardian School: The Emergence and Consolidation of an Educational Ideology* (Cambridge University Press, 1981)
Maradona, Diego, with Daniel Arcucci and Ernesto Cherquis Bialo, *El Diego* (Yellow Jersey, 2005, trans Marcela Mora y Araujo)
Marples, Morris, *A History of Football* (Secker and Warburg, 1954)
Martin, Simon, *Football and Fascism: The National Game under Mussolini* (Berg, 2004)
Mason, Tony, *Passion of the People? Football in South America* (Verso, 1995)
Matthews, Sir Stanley, *Feet First* (Ewen & Dale, 1948)
Mazzola, Ferruccio and Fabrizio Calzia, *Il terzo incomodo – Le pesanti verità di Ferruccio Mazzola [The Third Inconvenience: The Difficult Truth of Ferruccio Mazzola]*, (Bradipolibri 2004)
Mazzoni, Tomás, *O Brasil na Taça do Mundo 1930–50 [Brazil in the World Cup, 1930–50]*, (Leia, 1950)
História do Futebol no Brasil 1894–1950 [A History of Football in Brazil, 1894–1950] (Leia, 1950)
McCarra, Kevin, *Scottish Football: A Pictorial History from 1867 to the Present Day* (Third Eye Centre and Polygon, 1984)
McCarra, Kevin and Pat Woods, *One Afternoon in Lisbon* (Mainstream, 1988)
McIlvanney, Hugh, *McIlvanney on Football* (Mainstream, 1994) *World Cup '66* (Eyre & Spottiswoode, 1970)
McKinstry, Leo, *Sir Alf* (HarperSport, 2006)
Meisl, Willy, *Soccer Revolution* (Sportsman's Book Club, 1956)
Melegari, Fabrizio, Luigi La Rocca and Enrico Tosi, *Almanacco Ilustrato del Milan [The Illustrated History of Milan]* (Panini, 2005)
Menotti, César Luis, *Como Ganamos la Copa del Mundo [How we won the World Cup]* (El Gráfico, 1978)
Menotti, César Luis and Ángel Cappa, *Fútbol sin trampa [Football without Tricks]* (Muchnik, 1986)
Merrick, Gil, *I See it All* (Museum Press, 1954)
Midwinter, Eric, *Parish to Planet: How Football Came to Rule the World* (Know the Score, 2007)

Mikes, George and Nicholas Bentley, *How to be an Alien: A Handbook for Beginners and Advanced Pupils* (Penguin, 1970)

Milan, Betty, *Brasil o Pais da Bola* [*Brazil: Football Country*] (Berst, 1989)

Miller, David, *Cup Magic* (Sidwick and Jackson, 1981)

Morales, Víctor Hugo and Roberto Perfumo, *Hablemos de fútbol* [*Let's talk about Football*] (Booket, Planeta, 2007)

Morisbak, Andreas, *Fotballforståelse* [*Understanding of Football*] (Norges Fotballforbund of Folkets Brevskole, 1978)

Motson, John and John Rowlinson, *The European Cup 1955–1980* (Queen Anne, 1980)

Mourant, Andrew, *Don Revie: Portrait of a Footballing Enigma* (Mainstream, 1990)

Müller, Salo, *Mijn Ajax: Openhartige Memoires van den Talisman van Ajax in den gouden Jaren '60 en '70* [*My Ajax: The Frank Memoirs of the Talisman of Ajax in the Golden Years of the 60s and 70s*] (Houtekiet, 2006)

Murray, Bill, *The World's Game: A History of Soccer* (University of Illinois Press, 1996)

Oliveira, Cândido de, *A Evolução da táctica no futebol* [*The Evolution of the Tactics of Football*], (Capa de Pagarna, 1949)
Sistema W-M [*The W-M System*] (Capa de Pagarna, 1950)

Olsen, Egil, 'Scoringer i Fotball' ['Scoring in Football'], Masters thesis, NUSPE, Oslo, 1973

Panzeri, Dante, *Burgueses y gangsters en el deporte* [*Bourgeois and Gangsters in Sport*] (Libera, 1974)
Fútbol, dinámica de lo impensado [*Football, Dynamics of the Unthought*] (Paidós, 1967)

Papa, Antonio and Guido Panico, *Storia sociale del calcio in Italia* [*A Social History of Football in Italy*], (Il Mulino, 2002)

Paulo Emílio, *Futebol: Dos Alicerces ao Telhado* [*Football: From Grass-roots to the Summit*], (Oficna do Livro, 2004)

Pawson, Tony, *100 Years of the FA Cup* (Heinemann, 1972)

Pelé, with Orlando Duarte and Alex Bellos, *Pelé: the Autobiography*, trans. Daniel Hahn (Pocket Books, 2006)

Perdigão, Paulo, *Anatomia de una Derrota* [*The Anatomy of a Defeat*] (L&PM, 1986)

Persson, Gunnar, *Stjärnor På Flykt: Historien om Hakoah Wien* [*Stars on the Run: A History of Hakoah Vienna*] (Norstedts, 2004)

Peterson, Tomas, 'Split Visions: The Introduction of the Svenglish Model in Swedish Football, *Soccer and Society*, 1, 2 (Summer 2000), 1–18

Pinto, Edson, *Flávio Costa: O Futebol no Jogo da Verdade* [*Football in the Game of Truth*] (Cape, 1996)

Powell, Jeff, *Bobby Moore: The Life and Times of a Sporting Hero* (Robson, 1993)

Pozzo, Vittorio, *Campioni del Mondi: Quarant'anni do Storia del Calcio italiano* [*Champions of the world: Forty years of the history of Italian Football*] (Centro Editoriale Nazionale, 1960)
'Il fallimento del calcio italiano' ['The Failure of Italian Football'], *Successo*, 2, 1959, pp107–08

Puskás, Ferenc, *Captain of Hungary* (Cassell, 1955)

Radnedge, Keir, *50 Years of the European Cup and Champions League* (Carlton, 2005)

Rafferty, John, *One Hundred Years of Scottish Football* (Pan, 1973)

Ramsey, Alf, *Talking Football* (Stanley Paul, 1952)

Reep, Charles and Bernard Benjamin, 'Skill and Chance in Association football', *Journal of the Royal Statistical Society*, Series A, 131, 581–585, 1968

Reilly T, A Lees, K Davids, and WJ Murphy (eds) *Science and Football* (Spon, 1988)

Revie, Don, *Soccer's Happy Wanderer* (Museum, 1955)

Riordan, James, *Sport in Soviet Society: Development of Sport and Physical Education in Russia and the USSR* (Cambridge University Press, 1977)

Sábato, Ernesto, *Sobre Héroes y Tumbas* [*On Heroes and Tombs*] (Súdamericana, 1961)

Sabaldyr, Volodymyr, *Vid matchu smerti do matchu zhyttya* [*From the Match of Death to the Match of Life*] (Lesya, 2005)

Saldanha, João, *Futebol & Outras Histórias* [*Football and Other Histories*] (Record, 1988)

Histórias do Futebol [*Histories of Football*] (Revan, 1994)

Sarychev, Vasily, *Mig i Sudba* [*The Moment and the Destiny*] (Pressball, 2004)

Sebes, Gusztáv, *Örömök és csalódások* [*Joys and Disappointments*] (Gondolat, 1981)

Smith, Stratton (ed), *The Brazil Book of Football* (Souvenir, 1963)

Smith, Stratton and Eric Batty, *International Coaching Book* (Souvenir, 1966)

Soar, Phil, *And the Spurs Go Marching On* (Hamlyn, 1982)

Soar, Phil and Martin Tyler, *Arsenal: The Official History* (Hamlyn 1998)

Soter, Ivan, *Enciclopédia da Seleção 1914–2002* [*An Encyclopaedia of the National Team 1914–2002*] (Folha Seca, 2002)

Souness, Graeme with Bob Harris, *No Half Measures* (Collins Willow, 1985)

Starostin, Nikolai, *Futbol skvoz' gody* [*Football through the Years*] (Sovetskaya Rossiya, 1989)

Zvyozdy Bol'shogo Futbola [*Beginnings of Top-level Football*] (Sovetskaya Rossiya, 1969)

Steen, Rob, *The Mavericks* (Mainstream, 1994)

Stiles, Nobby, *Soccer My Battlefield* (Stanley Paul, 1968)

Studd, Stephen, *Herbert Chapman: Football Emperor* (Souvenir, 1981)

Syzmanski, Stefan and Tim Kuypers, *Winners and Losers: The Business Strategy of Football* (Penguin, 2000)

Taylor, Chris, *The Beautiful Game: A Journey Through Latin American Football* (Victor Gollancz, 1998, rev ed. Phoenix, 1999)

Taylor, Rogan and Klara Jamrich (eds), *Puskas on Puskas: The Life and Times of a Footballing Legend* (Robson, 1998)

Todrić, Mihailo, *110 Years of Football in Serbia* (Football Association of Serbia, 2006, trans. Borislav Bazić and Marijan Franjia)

Torberg, Friedrich, *Die Erben der Tante Jolesch* [*The Heirs of Aunt Jolesch*] (DTV, 1978)

Kaffeehaus war überall [*Coffee-house was Everywhere*] (DTV, 1982)

Trapattoni, Giovanni, *Coaching High Performance Soccer* (Reedswain, 1999)

Valentim, Max, *O Futebol e sua Técnica* [*Football and its Technique*] (ALBA, 1941)

Vargas, Walter, *Fútbol Delivery* [*Football Delivery*] (Al Arco, 2007)

Végh, Antal, *Gyógyíthatatlan?* [*Incurable?*] (Lapkiadó-Vállalat-Ország-Világ, 1986)

Miért beteg a magyar futball? [*Why is Hungarian Football Sick?*] (MagvetŒ, 1974)

Vialli, Gianluca and Gabriele Marcotti, *The Italian Job: A Journey to the Heart of Two Great Footballing Cultures* (Transworld, 2006)

Vignes, Spencer, *Lost in France: The Remarkable Life and Death of Leigh Richmond Roose, Football's First Playboy* (Stadia, 2007)

Wade, Allen, *The FA Guide to Training and Coaching* (Football Association, 1967)

Wagg, Stephen, *The Football World* (Harvester, 1984)

Wall, Sir Frederick, *50 Years of Football, 1884–1934* (Soccer Books, 2005)

Ward, Andrew, 'Bill Shankly and Liverpool' in Williams, Hopkins and Long (eds) *Passing Rhythms*

Whittaker, Tom, *Tom Whittaker's Arsenal Story* (Sportsman's Book Club, 1958)

Williams John, Stephen Hopkins and Cathy Long (eds) *Passing Rhythms: Liverpool FC and the Transformation of Football* (Berg, 2001)

Williams, Richard, *The Perfect 10: Football's Dreamers, Schemers, Playmakers and Playboys* (Faber and Faber, 2006)

Williams, William Carlos, *Selected Essays* (Random House, 1954)

Wilson, Jonathan, *Behind the Curtain: Travels in Eastern European Football* (Orion, 2006)

Winner, David, *Brilliant Orange: The Neurotic Genius of Dutch Football* (Bloomsbury, 2000)

Those Feet: A Sensual History of English Football (Bloomsbury, 2005)

Young, Percy M, *Football in Sheffield* (Sportsman's Book Club, 1964)

A History of British Football (Stanley Paul, 1968)

Zauli, Alessandro, *Soccer: Modern Tactics* (Reedswain, 2002)

Zelentsov, Anatoliy and Valeriy Lobanovskyi, *Metodologicheskiye osnovy razrabotki modelyey trenirovochnykh zanyatiy* [*The Methodological Basis of the Development of Training Models*] (Zdorouya, 1985)

Zubeldía, Osvaldo and Geronazzo, Argentino, *Táctica y estrategia del fútbol* [*Tactics and Strategy of Football*] (Jorge Álvarez, 1965)

WEBSITES

Russell Gerrard's searchable archive of international fixtures at:
    http://www.staff.city.ac.uk/r.j.gerrard/football/aifrform.html

Milos Radulović's searchable archive of European club fixtures at:
http://galeb.etf.bg.ac.yu/~mirad/

www.dfb.de

www.icyb.kiev.ua

www.playerhistory.com

www.rsssf.com

www.soccerassociation.com

www.soccerbase.com

www.thefa.com

www.uefa.com

MAGAZINES AND NEWSPAPERS (UK unless stated)

Aftonbladet (Sweden)

Arbeiter-Zeitung (Austria)

Brighton Evening Argus

The Boys' Champion Story Paper

Buenos Aires Herald (Argentina)

Champions

Clarín (Argentina)

Corriere della Sera (Italy)

Daily Mail

Daily Record

East Anglian Daily Times

Efdeportes (Argentina)

L'Équipe (France)

Evening Standard

FourFourTwo

Futbol (Russia)

Futbolnyy kuryer (Ukraine)

A Gazeta (Brazil)

El Grafi (Argentina)

El Gráfico (Argentina)

The Guardian

The Herald

Hol (Ukraine)

The Huddersfield Examiner

The Independent

Kievskiye vedomosti (Ukraine)

Konsomolskaya Pravda (Russia)

Kronen Zeitung (Austria)

Lance (Brazil)

Literaturnaya Rossiya (Russia)

Liverpool Echo
Manchete Esportiva (Brazil)
Manchester Evening News
O Mundo (Brazil)
La Nacion (Argentina)
News of the World
Neues Wiener Journal (Austria)
Pariser Tageszeitung (France)
The Punter
The Scottish Athletic Journal
Scottish Referee
Scottish Umpire
The Sheffield Independent
Sovetsky Sport (Russia)

Sport (Serbia)
Sport Express (Russia)
Lo Sport Fascista (Italy)
Sport den za dnyom (Ukraine)
Sporting Chronicle
Sports (Brazil)
Sportyvna Hazeta (Ukraine)
Lo Stadia (Italy)
The Standard (Argentina)
Sunday Times
Tempo (Serbia)
Ukrayinskyy futbol (Ukraine)
Welt am Montag (Austria)
World Soccer

△▽△▽△▽△▽△▽

Index